Mulroney

The Making of the Prime Minister

L. Ian MacDonald

McClelland and Stewart

McClelland and Stewart Limited
The Canadian Publishers
25 Hollinger Road
Toronto, Ontario
M4B 3G2

Canadian Cataloguing in Publication Data

MacDonald, L. Ian
    Mulroney: the making of the prime minister

Includes index.
ISBN 0-7710-5469-6

1. Mulroney, Brian, 1939 –   2. Prime ministers –
Canada – Biography.   3. Progressive Conservative
Party of Canada – Biography.   I. Title.

FC631.M85M22 1984   971.064′092′4   C84-099373-0
F1034.3.M85M22 1984

Printed and bound in Canada

Contents

By the same author:
From Bourassa to Bourassa
(1984)

For the memory of
my father,
Arthur Lamond MacDonald

"It is a great country where the son of an electrician can seek the highest office in the land."— Brian Mulroney, Baie Comeau, December 16, 1975

1

JUNE 11, 1983

Brian Mulroney looked like someone who was witnessing a bank holdup or a shooting in the street. His face was frozen in helpless fascination. He was unable to stop it, unable to cry for help, unable to look but unable to look away.

"My God," Mila Mulroney said to her husband. "Michael's going somewhere else."

For weeks, Mulroney had been saying that the Progressive Conservative leadership convention wasn't about the vote on June 11, but all the Tory tomorrows that would follow it. But when the day finally came, June 11 was about itself and all of Mulroney's tomorrows.

Now came the moment in this day when he thought his tomorrows might be slipping away from him. It was the moment after the first ballot when Michael Wilson left his box, adjacent to Mulroney's, to join Peter Pocklington on the floor of the Ottawa Civic Centre. Until then, Brian Mulroney had been sure that Pocklington and Wilson were both coming to him. But then they both kept moving, through the crush of handlers and delegates and reporters and onlookers, moving beyond the Mulroney box in the direction of John Crosbie's area, the only section left at that end of the convention floor.

Mulroney had come so far this time, in his second try for the leadership. He had bent himself to the hard discipline of an eighty-day campaign, driving himself to the brink of exhaustion and beyond, living for three months on a diet of cigarettes, coffee, and chocolate bars. And always his mind had been preoccupied with the numbers and spreads needed to win. How many times, in his broad hand, had he written them down on an airline napkin or anything that happened to be handy?

And he had played by the hard rules of the game. For he was a peculiar Irish and Québécois blend of politician, one part poet and one part pol. He had done everything he could, and as he said, left nothing out. And now in this moment of slow motion, it was out of his hands. He was more than a witness. He might yet become the next victim.

"There was no doubt in my mind where they were going except at this moment," Mulroney later conceded. He would recall that Wilson had gone down his steps "without looking at me. He didn't wave and say 'I'll be seeing you in a minute.'" At this moment, Mulroney would acknowledge: "I didn't know what the hell was going on."

Neither did millions of Canadians watching or thousands of Tories participating in the proceedings of the 1983 Conservative leadership convention. After the first ballot, Mulroney was confident that his numbers were good, that his spreads were sufficient, that his deals would stick. He was sitting a comfortable second. Mulroney had room to grow ahead of him and room to breathe behind him. It had broken pretty much as he had predicted in a meeting the night before in Pocklington's sixteenth-floor suite at the Inn of the Provinces. It was the last of several get-togethers. And there was no mystery as to what it was all about. Pocklington wanted to be a kingmaker. Mulroney wanted to be king.

"I'll be second, a strong second," Mulroney told Pocklington. "And Crosbie will be third, substantially behind, and that's where you'll have to make your move. That's where it all is. And you won't have much time. I've been around these conventions long enough to know that you'll only have about ten minutes to make up your mind."

Pocklington replied that his mind was already made up, that he knew what he had to do.

Pocklington had already rendered a considerable service to the other challengers by virtue of being a western candidate who challenged Clark for favourite-son votes in Alberta. Pocklington had done a particular favour to Mulroney simply by coming into the race. As the second candidate who did not hold elective office, Pocklington took some of the sting and stigma out of Mulroney's not being a member of the Conservative caucus, which had hindered his previous bid for the leadership in 1976. In the long runup to Ottawa, Pocklington had demonstrated one personal quality that Mulroney saw in himself and acknowledged in others, namely a capacity for growth. From the simplistic, sloganeering gunslinger of the right who began the 1983 campaign, Pocklington soon demonstrated that he was capable of assimilating his polling data and gradually tried to position him-

8

self closer to the centre of the Conservative spectrum. If he wasn't bilingual, he would make himself bilingual. If he wanted to sell off Crown corporations, he was not against social services provided by the state to the elderly, the sick, and the needy.

Pocklington wanted to be treated with some respect, not just as some eccentric westerner whose celebrity rested solely upon his ownership of the Edmonton Oilers hockey team and his flying around the country in his private jet. Pocklington hadn't just spent his way into the leadership campaign, he had earned his way. In terms of where he would go after the first ballot, he not only wanted to do the right thing, he wanted to do it right.

For Mulroney, "it was pretty clear to me when I left there that he was going to go with the guy who had the best chance, either Crosbie or me, whomever was strong enough to win." In Pocklington's view, it was "strictly a numbers game." If there was a 200-vote spread between Mulroney and Crosbie, he would jump to the man from Baie Comeau.

For Mulroney to be strong enough to win, strong enough to bring over Pocklington and Wilson and perhaps David Crombie, everything depended on the spreads. And where his spreads were concerned, everything depended on his numbers out of Quebec.

It was the last thing, the only thing Mulroney was still worried about that bright Saturday morning. On the short drive from the Château Laurier over to a provincial caucus at the Skyline Hotel, Mulroney asked a long-time friend and adviser, Michel Cogger, to check the Quebec numbers one more time.

Mulroney had painful memories of another leadership race when he had been second after the first ballot, but with less than 100 votes between himself and the third man, an Alberta MP named Joe Clark. Then as now, the party had been determined to head off the frontrunner. Then it was Claude Wagner. Now it was Joe Clark. On both occasions, the man in the middle was Brian Mulroney. The first-ballot shake-out on the afternoon of February 22, 1976, had been as significant in another sense as today's would be. The 1976 numbers were engraved on Mulroney's memory: Wagner, 531; Mulroney, 357; Clark, 277. The reason for Wagner's relatively long lead over Mulroney and Mulroney's relatively short lead over Clark was Quebec. Of the 550-odd Quebec delegates to the 1976 convention, one favourite son, Mulroney, had no more than 150 and probably did well to get 100, while the other, Wagner, had most of the rest stashed away in hotels and motels across the river in Hull.

It was an experience and a lesson Mulroney never forgot, and now, on the last morning of his second run for the gold, he

9

needed to know the true situation in Quebec.

And he had to know from Cogger, his law school classmate from Laval University in Quebec and the campaign director who knew where it had gone wrong in 1976. Cogger left Mulroney at the Skyline and made his way down to the Mulroney staging area in a tent across Bank Street from the Civic Centre. With Rodrigue Pageau, who had fought the scorched-earth campaign against Clark for Quebec delegates, Cogger went over the final "pointage," or canvass. By their count, they had 431 votes out of 726 registered delegates from Quebec. Clark had most of the rest, with an insignificant sprinkling for Wilson and Crosbie. When Cogger called in his numbers to Mulroney, by this time back in his suite at the Château, the candidate could breathe a sigh of relief. It had been a tough battle, but he had the basic 60-40 split of Quebec he needed to win the convention.

Afterwards, there would be much discussion and disagreement as to how the Quebec delegation voted in Ottawa. Clark's chief Quebec organizer, Marcel Danis, was not alone in maintaining that they had achieved a 50-50 split of Quebec. If that had been the case, insisted Mulroney's chief number cruncher, Charley McMillan, Clark would have won the convention. "The point is," said McMillan, "that if we hadn't had our numbers in Quebec, Clark would have had his, and he would have been leader."

McMillan's analysis appears to be correct. If Clark had fought Mulroney to a draw in Quebec, with a 350-350 split of the delegation, then the man from High River would have been about 75 to 100 votes higher on the first ballot, closer to 1,200, and within bandwagon distance of the 1,450-odd votes needed to win. And Mulroney would have been at least 75 votes further back, around 800, and definitely within striking distance for Crosbie at 639.

Interestingly, there were disagreements even within the Mulroney camp as to how the Quebec vote split at the convention. Former Newfoundland Premier Frank Moores, who had been a key operative for Mulroney, suggested in a post-convention memo that "Clark did better here than we thought." Moores went along with the Clark camp's assessment, suggesting that Mulroney had received only 325 first-ballot votes from his home province. Moores' view was in line with all the pre-convention polling, which gave Clark a slight edge in Quebec, as well as with convention day exit polling conducted for the CBC by Queen's University Professor George Perlin. For once, Charley McMillan disagreed with Moores. McMillan later figured the Quebec numbers around 400-300 in Mulroney's favour.

But the point is that on the morning of June 11, Mulroney

believed what he was getting back from Cogger, that he had more than 425 Quebec votes. And Mulroney was satisfied with that. "I knew that I had 850 votes for sure then," he said later. And if he had those first-ballot numbers, then he would have the minimum spread he was looking for between himself and Crosbie. "Back to Crosbie?" he asked rhetorically, "Two hundred votes, that's all I needed."

If Mulroney's feeling had been one of nervous expectation, he now reverted to the buoyant optimism that generally was a mark of his moods when things got tense. "The undecideds are deciding," he told one caller about half an hour before he was to leave his fifth-floor suite at the Château to go down to the convention. "And they're going Mulroney."

The Quebec numbers were the last of the building blocks that Mulroney was worried about. He could see that he had the numbers with his other major voting bloc, the campus and youth delegates. "The youth saved our bacon," Moores would say later. Particularly in Ontario, where Mulroney's strength had fallen considerably short of expectations among senior delegates.

The youth had been put together by Peter White, another of Mulroney's Laval group. White, a businessman from London, Ontario, had played a low-profile but critical campaign role as a "connector" to the Wilson and Pocklington camps. White later estimated that Mulroney grabbed 60 per cent of the Ontario youth vote. As Moores later figured it in his post-convention memo to Mulroney, this pushed them close to 250 votes in Ontario, "thanks to the youth and Peter White."

Mulroney had seen his youth delegates for himself twice within the previous twelve hours. Before going over to see Pocklington on Friday night, he stopped briefly at a youth rally. "It was just a riot," he said. "The most incredible meeting I've ever been to in my life." The youth regrouped on Saturday morning in the Esplanade room of the Château. "There must have been 300 of them," White said later. "It was seven o'clock in the morning. The joint was jumping by the time Brian got there at eight."

By then, Mulroney had nearly lost his voice, and he still had to appear at a few provincial caucuses. But by this time, the general design of the convention was clear. For weeks Mulroney had been saying that "this party has made up its mind to dump Joe Clark. What it hasn't decided yet is who to replace him with."

For weeks, he had also been saying that "one of the two names on the last ballot will be Martin Brian Mulroney of Baie Comeau, Quebec, I can tell you that much."

For the rest, it would depend on who was on the last ballot

11

with him. If it was the incumbent, then the ABC factor, Anyone But Clark, would carry Mulroney to victory. If it was Crosbie, the ABM factor, Anyone But Mulroney, would come into play. The ABM sentiment was stronger than the Mulroney camp had acknowledged, deeper than they had feared. It was measured at 20 per cent of the sample in a privately commissioned Gallup Poll that Mulroney had received only the previous weekend. The ABC factor was only slightly stronger at 23 per cent of the sample of 250 delegates who would never, under any circumstances, support Joe Clark. So Mulroney had to have Clark on the last ballot. The other leading camps had final-ballot scenarios of their own. Crosbie needed Mulroney to become the beneficiary of the ABM sentiment. And Clark needed Crosbie so that Mulroney's Quebec delegates and the incumbent's bilingualism would push Clark over the top.

Now Mulroney was sure. If the spreads were right back to Crosbie, the other serious candidates would be coming to him, and Crosbie would eventually go off the ballot. And the two names on the last ballot would be Martin Brian Mulroney of Baie Comeau, Quebec, and Charles Joseph Clark of High River, Alberta.

The only imponderable troubling Mulroney's advisers was the distance between themselves and Crosbie. "Could we make it on a spread of 200 to 250?" Charley McMillan asked later. "We thought so. But it was important to get Crosbie off the ballot." In a taxi on the way over to the convention, McMillan and Moores went over their final projections. Both had played crucial roles in the Mulroney campaign. McMillan, a thirty-seven-year-old economist at York University in Toronto, was Mulroney's top adviser on polling and policy. "Charley was the only guy whom I allowed to see all our polls," Mulroney would say later.

More than that, McMillan's analysis of a survey three weeks before the convention, and his recommendations in an eyes-only memo to Mulroney and Cogger, constituted an important piece of fine-tuning for Mulroney's campaign. A Gallup sample for Mulroney in mid-May indicated that Crosbie was coming up fast in all regions of the country and among all groups of delegates outside Quebec. At that point, McMillan advised Mulroney in a May 25 memo, he stood to be overtaken by Crosbie's second-ballot support. McMillan's recommendations: "Drop the boony strategy and go on the offensive in a positive way, emphasizing your economic themes and winnability."

The boonies were where Mulroney had been through most of the "frugal campaign," in his "rusty station wagon," living down the slick and sleazy reputation that was left over from his high-flying, media-oriented 1976 campaign. McMillan's advice was sound and succinct. He was Mulroney's kind of intellectual, the kind who did not shrink from the hardball of electoral politics, the kind of egghead who was not shocked by Mulroney's profanities.

When it came to political hardball, there were few more formidable operatives in the Conservative Party than Frank Moores. Here he was riding to the convention with Mulroney's chief policy and polling adviser. And when he got there, he would sit in John Crosbie's box. Moores may have been something of a double agent. But he did not consider himself a double-dealer. "I genuinely didn't want to do Crosbie any harm," he said of his fellow Newfoundlander. "And I genuinely wanted Brian to win it."

Nobody was sure what the previous evening's speeches might be worth except that they weren't worth much, maybe one, maybe two per cent. But in terms of the Mulroney-Crosbie spread, it could be the best one or two per cent. Crosbie had wowed the English-speaking delegates with a strong conclusion to his speech in which he pledged to learn French within two years. Crosbie's lieutenants figured the speech had swung as many as forty Wilson and Mulroney votes, and Charley McMillan did not disagree. "We were lower than we thought in Ontario" he said, "a good thirty-forty votes lower from the Crosbie speech." All night, the Crosbie workers had tried to create a bandwagon effect from the speech, and the feeling carried over onto the floor the next morning.

Now came the shake-out. Clark, 1,091, or 36 per cent. Crombie 116, or 4 per cent. Crosbie 639, or 21 per cent. For Michael Mc-Sweeney, an Ottawa city councillor who had travelled for three months with Mulroney, this was the lowest moment of the campaign. "When the Crosbie numbers went up I thought the world had ended," McSweeney remembered. It went through his mind, as it did others in the Mulroney camp, that the first three names in the alphabetical order had gobbled up more than 1,800 votes, with Pocklington and Wilson still to come after Mulroney. McSweeney was not alone in worrying about how many votes Mulroney had and about the spread back to Crosbie. But, after another long half minute, after Neil Fraser's five votes and John Gamble's seventeen, there came Mulroney's bundle of 874, for 29 per cent.

Pocklington, at 102, and Wilson, though stunned by his low score of 144 delegates, knew at once what they must do. But in the Pocklington box, some of his advisers made one last attempt

13

to move him over to Crosbie. As Bob Howard, president of the London West riding association later told Peter White, Pocklington campaign aide Skip Willis brought Crosbie emissary Jean Piggott into the box to enter a last-minute plea for her candidate. According to White's notation in his pocket agenda, Pocklington's Edmonton business associate, Harry Knudsen, pollster Peter Regenstreif, and another aide all pressed their candidate to go to Crosbie. Howard and Ralph Lean told Pocklington he couldn't do it, that the Alberta delegates would never follow him, and that it would be going back on his word.

It was Pocklington, the political novice, who acted with the aplomb of a political pro. He got on the phone to Wilson and said they had to "go to Brian." And he got his people on the phone to pass the word that he was coming down. "Pocklington," said Michel Cogger, a boardroom lawyer by profession, "was like a client at a closing." At this point, Cogger was standing outside the adjacent box, waiting for a signal from Chris Speyer, Crombie's campaign director and Cogger's "connector" in the Crombie campaign. But no signal was forthcoming. Not only was Crombie not going anywhere, he was staying in for a second ballot, even though he was certain to be eliminated as the low man.

Pocklington had waited long enough. The call went over from his campaign manager, Ralph Lean, to the Mulroney box, and McSweeney was dispatched to walk them over. "He's coming," Regenstreif told McMillan on the phone. "The deal's on."

For his part, Wilson was soon getting back to Pocklington. "You come over here," Wilson suggested. "I'll meet you in front of Brian's box and we'll go up together." Wilson and Pocklington might bring just slightly more than half of their delegates with them. But they brought something else, a laying on of hands, an air of legitimacy, a bandwagon effect of going with a winner.

Pocklington and Lean made their way past Paul Godfrey, then chairman of Metro Toronto. While nominally neutral in the leadership race – he had been chairman of the April 30 all-candidates' meeting in Toronto – Godfrey was actually an important Mulroney connector into the Pocklington camp, through Ralph Lean. Both Godfrey and Lean had been present the previous evening when Mulroney called on Pocklington after the speeches.

Pocklington made his way across centre ice and into a throng of reporters and workers crowding around the Mulroney box. Wilson met him there on the floor.

"It didn't dawn on me that both of them were going to come at the same time," said Mulroney, "until I saw them right in front of my box down on the floor." But then they kept right on going. Mike McSweeney, to his horror, looked up and saw "they had walked me right past Brian. Ralph Lean had missed the stairs."

It was the one moment of Brian Mulroney's doubts about his tomorrows, a moment, he said, that was "engraved on my memory." It was the moment, he said, while looking at it on his home video-cassette machine, when "I didn't know where Wilson was going. As you see he doesn't look my way. So I didn't know what the hell was going on."

Neither did Pocklington. At least, he didn't know where the hell he was going.

"You're going the wrong way," Wilson told him.

"No, it's this way," Pocklington insisted.

"No, it's over here," Wilson said.

The moment passed. Wilson and Pocklington got pointed in the right direction and tried to make their way through the throng of photographers to find the stairs into Mulroney's box. On the floor, Tom McPhail was the first to signal Mulroney's box that Wilson and Pocklington were coming to them. McPhail, a University of Calgary communications professor, had been doing some work on the polling data with Charley McMillan. A bearded, burly figure, McPhail was difficult to miss even in a crowd. He waved his right fist in the air and forced an opening in the crowd. Wilson and Pocklington slipped through it and into Mulroney's waiting arms.

The three of them stood there, arms linked and raised. As Mulroney later recalled it, Pocklington said something about coming to the winner, and Wilson said it had been a big decision for him and he hoped Mulroney would always be supportive of the people who had been kind enough to support him.

For eighty days, Mila Mulroney had maintained her poise and never put a foot wrong in the campaign. But the tension of the moment proved to be too much for her. "I had visions of '76," she later said of the moment when she thought Wilson was going somewhere else. "I just thought it was all over, that all the work we had done was down the drain." She had turned from the scene on the floor and wept, and by the time Wilson and Pocklington were standing beside her husband, she was brushing away her tears with a pocket tissue. Hardly anyone noticed except Jean Bazin, another of the Laval gang, and Roger Nantel, Mulroney's communications adviser, who put an arm around her and asked if she was all right. Before long, she regained her composure and joined the celebration in the row below.

"At this point," Mulroney later recalled, "I figured we're going to pull substantially ahead on the second ballot, and that's going to be it for Crosbie, that we've got this thing nailed, and the party can make up its mind between Clark and me."

But there was one thing that hadn't been in the cards, and that was Crombie staying in for a second ballot.

"The only worry we had was did we have the right script when Crombie stayed," McMillan would observe later. "And then what really bothered us was the time it took to count the first ballot." It was enough time to make some deals and undo some others.

Mulroney, for his part, began to relax. He went back to his dressing room to grab a quick shower. He had a word with Fernand Roberge, the general manager of the Ritz-Carlton Hotel in Montreal, who was in charge of Mulroney's hospitality suites and the switchover operation with Clark's Quebec delegates. "Fern," Mulroney told him, "c'est dans le sac."

It's in the bag. But it wasn't. Not yet. David Crombie was the joker in the deck. By staying in, Crombie prolonged the process by another ballot. He gave John Crosbie a life, time to grow, time to deal. In this context, it would be Mulroney's good fortune not to overtake Clark on the second ballot. As it was, Clark came under enough pressure to jump off and go to Crosbie in an attempt to stop Mulroney.

Clark, though he slipped six votes to 1,085, held his position in first place. Mulroney, at 1,021, closed to within striking distance, and maintained his gap over Crosbie, at 781. Clark, as the front-runner, was able to reject the preposterous suggestion that he take his name off the ballot in favour of the third man, Crosbie.

In the history of North American-style leadership conventions, no one had ever heard of such a ridiculous proposition. Even had he been so inclined, there were two factors that weighed against him jumping to Crosbie, whatever his feelings about Mulroney. First, as a former prime minister, he could hardly be a party to such an obvious settling of accounts. And then there was Crosbie's total lack of French. Most of Clark's English-speaking delegates would have gone to Crosbie, all right, and his Quebec delegates would have gone to Mulroney, producing a bitter English-French split that might have torn the party to pieces. Had Crosbie won such a confrontation, it would have set back the party's efforts in Quebec by another generation. And if there was one thing Joe Clark cared about, other than the unity of the Tory party, it was the efforts he had made, the respect he had won, the yards he had gained in Quebec.

Even so, the Mulroney forces could count themselves fortunate that Clark's vote held on the second ballot. "Without Clark's support we would have been screwed but good," Michel Cogger would say several months later. "Thank God he had that much support, and thank God it was loyal."

Crosbie's problem was that his potential for growth was more apparent than real. He might be the clear second choice of one-third of the delegates, but for that to happen, either Clark or Mulroney had to be off the ballot. It wasn't enough that David Crombie, under cover of his distinctive yellow umbrellas, walked over to Crosbie after going out on the second ballot. "There, for what's it worth," said Cogger, as the Crombie parade made its way past the Mulroney box, "go 40 votes and 400 umbrellas."

Cogger was one Mulroney operative, Moores was another, who could have sworn they had a deal with Crombie, a deal that clearly wasn't on after the first ballot, a deal that may have come unstuck after Mulroney's ill-advised visit to Crombie's tent two days earlier. Even if Crombie didn't come to them now, he had already given them enough of a scare by staying in for another ballot.

"That surprised me," Mulroney said later, "because I couldn't for the life of me understand the rationale in it for him. I just couldn't see how that would be in any way beneficial."

Nor had it escaped Mulroney's notice that Crombie had made a speech three weeks before the convention in which he said the party needed a leader who was bilingual. In the same speech, as reported by *The Toronto Star*, Crombie had scored Crosbie's free-trade policy with the United States as potentially harmful to Ontario industry. None of that, when the time came, prevented David and Shirley Crombie from making the walk over to Crosbie. "When I saw David go over to John," Mulroney said, "I just felt it hadn't been in the cards, he and I hadn't been able to establish a good enough relationship that he felt he could support me."

But Mulroney was not in a mood for self-recriminations that day. Until the first-ballot results were announced, he was nervous as a cat. In his dressing room between ballots, he could finally unwind, and to Charley McMillan he looked relaxed. "I know in my heart I've done everything I could," Mulroney said, "and I haven't left anything out." At another moment in his dressing room, he looked over to Mila and Manitoba campaign director

Janis Johnson, who had their feet up on a sofa. "Everything's going to be okay, gang," he said.

It was still too close a thing for Frank Moores' liking. "I was there to shift bodies from one camp to the next," Moores said later. "Gosh, towards the end there, I wasn't sure which bodies were to be shifted." Worried about erosion of Clark's vote, and rumours that he would be moving to Crosbie, Moores impulsively started working the floor. "Crosbie is going to Clark, spread the rumour," he later remembered himself saying. More seriously, he said later, "we couldn't have won in my opinion against Crosbie, we had to have Clark on the last ballot." It had to be an ABC proposition rather than ABM.

Michel Cogger had much the same concern. Some of Clark's Quebec delegates, particularly the youth, had apparently been prepared to move over to Mulroney after the second ballot. Nothing doing, Cogger instructed his floor people. "We told them," he said, "to stay with your chicken until it's fried."

At this point, there was only one way for Mulroney to lose and only one way for Clark to win. It was a long shot, but it was not impossible for Clark to sandbag his own support on the third ballot, to instruct some of his delegates to vote for Crosbie in the hope of knocking off Mulroney and forcing a run-off with Crosbie. "There was no concern in my mind about that," Mulroney said. "It couldn't be done." For two reasons. First, the fanatical loyalty of Clark's delegates. And second, Clark didn't have enough of a cushion to play that kind of game without running a serious risk of being eliminated himself. Nevertheless, as Mulroney later acknowledged, it was the only way he could have lost. "That's right," he said. "If they had sent out a signal then, if they had sent enough of their people to support Crosbie. But it was too risky for them, they knew they weren't growing. They had no strength coming from anywhere else. I could have passed him."

Now Crosbie had run out of room to grow. He went out on the third ballot at 858 votes, exactly 200 behind Clark, who had slipped further to 1,058; Mulroney, meanwhile, had grown only fifteen votes to 1,036. When Clark's numbers were announced by co-chairperson Pat Carney, Mulroney knew the incumbent had held up, knew Crosbie was out, knew he had the showdown he needed to win.

Mulroney later allowed as how he thought "the whole thing was over, right there." At this point, the one-two position of Clark and Mulroney became meaningless. "This was the shakedown," Mulroney said. "The polarization was then complete. At that point in time, when I heard Crosbie's numbers, I knew that left me just about where I was. There were two things – Clark hadn't moved, and just a trickle upward for us. But I knew that 67 per cent of those 850 Crosbie votes were coming to us."

In dressing room 65, down the hall from Mulroney's room 60, John Crosbie must have known this, too. Premier Brian Peckford of Newfoundland wanted him to go to Clark. But caucus representative Bob Wenman made it quite clear that most of his twenty-one MPs would go to Mulroney. And so they sawed it off and kept their own counsel. And Frank Moores was finally able to deliver the bodies to the right place.

By his reckoning, as he wrote Mulroney in a memo, Peckford was unable to deliver a majority of his own provincial caucus to Clark. And the Clark people were unable to get near the Crosbie section with their signs. A Mulroney youth claque had that end of the floor blocked off. "They organized a phalanx," said Peter White, "to prevent the Clark people from getting at the Crosbie box." It was no coincidence that the Mulroney box was adjacent to the Crosbie section. In the draw for places before the convention, the Mulroney organizers had a choice between being next to Crosbie or down in Clark's end of the arena. "It was important," said Mulroney's box manager, Brian Gallery, "that we be close to Crosbie and far away from Clark. Crosbie was to be our friend and Clark our enemy."

For Mulroney, there was nothing much left to do but go to vote one final time and then try to collect his thoughts in his dressing room. In the voting area under the centre-ice exit, his legal representative, Bernard Roy, had been able to catch his eye and walk out with him after Mulroney had cast his ballot. Like so many of the Mulroney people, Roy went back a long way with the candidate. They had been at Laval together and studied for their third-year law exams together. As bachelors, they had shared an apartment in Montreal. Roy had been best man at Mulroney's wedding. In the tough going of the 1983 Quebec campaign, it had been Roy who had stood in many church doorways and checked the bona fides of Clark delegates. He was a former collegiate hockey star, and he wasn't the sort you messed with. As Mulroney later said of him, "don't get between Bernard and the net." Now Bernard Roy was able to pass Mulroney a simple signal. If he was wearing his glasses when they walked up on stage after the vote, Mulroney had lost. If he wasn't, he had won.

In room 60, the spacious home dressing room that Cogger had had the good fortune to draw first, Brian Mulroney had another quick shower. He wrapped a towel around his waist, sat down on a bench, and began writing his acceptance speech. After a couple of minutes, out of the corner of his eye, he noticed something odd occurring on a television screen.

"All of a sudden, holy Jesus," Mulroney said later, "on the TV, a commentator is saying Joe Clark is heading over to see Brian Mulroney. And I'm just as naked as bonkers."

Clark was making what his opponent later called "an elegant gesture." But his people had forgotten to phone ahead to inform Mulroney he was coming down. When Clark got down in front of Mulroney's box, Charley McMillan and Jean Bazin rushed over with apologies. Someone phoned Mulroney's dressing room to check on his whereabouts. "Brian's not ready," replied Sonny Mass, another of his Laval Mafia, who was manning the switchboard in Mulroney's dressing room. That was understating the case. "It would have created a considerable scandal," Mulroney said later that evening, "if I had gone out there dressed as I was." At that point, Mila Mulroney walked into the room and, as her husband said, "we got her turned around" to go out there and meet Clark and Maureen McTeer.

After a few minutes, they got it organized for Mulroney to meet Clark halfway at centre ice.

"I'm sorry I wasn't there," Mulroney said.

"I'll see you in a few minutes, up on stage," Clark replied.

And then there unfolded in the Mulroney box a wild celebration by anticipation, and in those moments the packaged part of the man finally fell away and the country saw him for the first time as his friends knew him, as a kindred spirit who loved nothing better than to sing, dance, and have a good time. Before going out to meet Clark, he had put out one request: for the announcement of the last ballot, he wanted his friends with him in the box. And so they were. There were Jean Bazin and Michel Cogger from the Laval days; Sam Wakim and Fred Doucet from the St. Francis Xavier gang; Roger Nantel and Rodrigue Pageau from the Quebec wars. Mulroney's mother and his brother, Gary, were a couple of rows behind him. Irene Mulroney, though seventy-one years old, later said she wasn't bothered by the heat that day. "I felt twenty-five years old that afternoon," she said. Her feeling was one of pride, she continued, tempered by sympathy for Joe Clark's mother, for she knew how Grace Clark felt, having watched her son lose on another day when Clark had been the winner.

And those who weren't in the box weren't far away. Peter White deliberately stayed down on the floor so he could see the scene rather than be part of it.

Somewhere in the crowd near the exit was Guy Charbonneau, the man Mulroney had insisted Joe Clark put in the Senate during the Tory interlude of 1979. Charbonneau had been castigated as being an ingrate, but he had always known he owed his Senate seat at least as much to Mulroney as to Clark. An insurance executive in Montreal, Charbonneau had been an influential Mulroney adviser through both leadership reviews in 1981 and 1983. It was Charbonneau who hosted a meeting of the inner circle of Mulroney advisers the previous December 5, the day Mulroney announced he was "getting out of the traffic" of the leadership review, the day before his highly publicized endorsement of Clark. Charbonneau had warned him against making such a big production of it, and Mulroney had indeed been criticized as a hypocrite, but it had worked out all right in the end.

As the convention managers walked up on stage with the final result, Mulroney saw that Bernard Roy was with them, and that he was not wearing his glasses. Now, Mulroney had only one problem: he had forgotten his speech back in his dressing room and had to send Mike McSweeney scurrying off to get it.

When the words of the occasion were over, when the decencies and niceties had been observed, when a final television interview had been given, Mulroney climbed into a car for the ride back to the Château. Fred Doucet, who was with him, later recalled that he said almost nothing, "that he was already thinking ahead" to his meetings the next morning with the defeated candidates.

In suite 581, Pat MacAdam was waiting for him along with Ginette Pilotte. He was another of the St. F.X. crowd, and she had been his private secretary for nearly ten years. Mulroney and MacAdam embraced. "Not bad," Mulroney said, "for a couple of raggedy-ass kids from eastern Nova Scotia."

MacAdam had filled the bathtub with Dom Perignon, but neither he nor Mulroney was having any. MacAdam had stopped drinking five years before and Mulroney had given it up in 1980. They settled for soda water and coffee. Mulroney changed into a polo shirt and a pair of slacks and began to take calls and receive friends. One call was from Ronald Reagan. "Nice to see another Irishman in there," said the President of the United States, inviting Mulroney to come down and see him some time. Finally, around 2:30 the next morning, Mila Mulroney began shooing

21

people away. "You're all going to hate me," she said, "but he has to be up in four hours."

Mulroney saw one old friend to the door, with the comment that Michael Wilson would never know how grateful he was.

"And if he wants a domed stadium for Toronto?" he was asked.

"How many does he want?" Mulroney said with a laugh.

And so the day of his tomorrows ended. It had taken ten hours, four ballots, and about five shirts. But he had done it. Or as he had been telling people on the phone for weeks: "There she be, my friend, there she be."

2

THE BOY FROM
BAIE COMEAU

Jean Bazin was soaking in a hot tub, trying to do something about his aching back, when the phone rang in his room down the hall from Mulroney's fifth-floor suite at the Château Laurier. It was Gérard Guy and a whole bunch of people calling for Bazin's candidate, who had been leader of the Conservative Party for little more than an hour. It was the boys from Baie Comeau on the line, looking for the Boy from Baie Comeau.

Bazin had the call transferred down to room 581.

"Allo," said the voice familiar to those people crowding around the telephone on the bar of the recreation centre in Mulroney's home town. He could hardly hear them for all the shouting, as they could hardly hear him, for after all the hours of shouting and smoking, there wasn't much voice left in him.

"Gérard," he said. "I've nearly lost my voice."

It didn't matter. He had taken a minute to say hello. For them, it was enough, the evidence for their argument that while he may have left them long ago, he hadn't forgotten where he came from, and wouldn't now.

In the days after the June convention, as reporters descended on Baie Comeau, they were hard put to find anyone who knew him *when* who had a bad word to say about him *now*. There was something "almost uncannily unreal" about this, observed Glen Allen in a *Montreal Gazette* profile of the town and its people, "as if when he was born here 44 years ago, he was a young Superman, rocket-borne and dropping from the sky on a bewildered but eternally grateful Smallville."

Here was a case of metaphor as hyperbole, and even the townspeople who had known Mulroney all his life didn't think of him as someone who changed in a phone booth. But they would be the first to acknowledge what he had told columnist Lysiane Gagnon of *La Presse* on the day after the big win: "One thing for sure. Baie Comeau is now on the map."

The town was built before he was born there on March 20, 1939, but not by much.

The North Shore of the Lower St. Lawrence is a 700-mile strip that runs from the Saguenay River to the Labrador boundary. When Jacques Cartier first saw this coast in 1534, he dismissed it as the land God gave Cain. It was to remain a wilderness for the next 400 years.

But then in the 1930's, a man named Robert McCormick, everywhere known as the Colonel, needed to expand his pioneer newsprint operations for his prospering American papers, the *Chicago Tribune* and the *New York Daily News*. McCormick, whose military rank was attained as a regiment commander in the First World War, had previously dispatched his wartime adjutant, Arthur Schmon, to establish a timbering and pulp operation at a place known as Shelter Bay, later called Port Cartier, a few miles west of the future boom town of Sept-Iles.

By the mid-1930's, McCormick was ready to build another town out of the wilderness at the mouth of the Manicouagan and Outardes rivers, where Hydro-Québec would build its huge dams in the 1960's. But in 1936, when Schmon's engineers came ashore at Baie Comeau, there was nothing except a disused wharf, five weatherbeaten lean-tos, and a partially completed power house on the Outardes. The story is told by one of Schmon's Princeton University contemporaries, Harvey Smith, in his book on the North Shore, *Shelter Bay*, published by McClelland and Stewart in 1964. At the end of his life, an electrician named Ben Mulroney had it among his books at home on Champlain Street in Baie Comeau. And he knew the story from his own life's experience, for he had gone out to Baie Comeau from Quebec in 1936. He was thirty-two, and he was one of the pioneering generation of men and women who built the town out of a wilderness.

"It was Colonel McCormick's dream of a town," Irene Mulroney said nearly half a century after she had gone down there with her husband. Quite deliberately, McCormick had set out not to build a boom town but a family town. To all appearances, and according to the recollection of Olive Elliott, the eldest of the six Mulroney children, "it worked."

Since McCormick would go fishing there, and his executives from Chicago would be put up there, he built a hotel called Le Manoir that in later years still maintained comforts and culinary standards second to none. In the town, the pioneer generation built community and recreation centres, a hospital, and a town library and brought in nuns to run the Catholic primary and

24

secondary schools. It was a model town, in an idyllic setting, and would always remain so. Where Sept-Iles would have the image of a modern boom town, with Corvettes racing up and down its streets, Baie Comeau would always retain the reputation as a good place to make money and bring up a family at the same time. "It was a planned company town," observed Dick Elliott, an engineer who first came there in 1956 and ended up marrying the oldest of the six Mulroney children.

Their parents had married in 1934, at the height of the depression. Mary Irene O'Shea was twenty-one, from the Irish community of Shannon, east of Quebec City. Her forebears, Irish tenant farmers, had come to Canada from County Kilkenny in the 1820's, fully a generation before the wave of immigration in the era of the Irish potato famine.

The first of the Mulroneys on this side of the water was named Pierce, son of Thomas Mulroney and Dora Dozaney from the parish of Anghalan Bridge in County Cavan, near the Ulster border, and he first turned up in the parish records at Ste. Catherine in 1834, when as a young émigré he took a bride named Ellen Buckley from Offaly County in Ireland. Over the next twenty-two years, she bore a dozen children, of whom eleven survived childbirth.

The eighth child, Jeremiah, married Margaret Ann Donovan in 1881, and they had thirteen children of their own. The youngest son, and the twelfth of the thirteen children of this union, was born in 1903. Ironically enough, there was an older brother named John A., but it was Benedict Martin Mulroney who would be the father of a future Conservative leader.

As for the founding father of the clan, Pierce Mulroney lived to a ripe old age, dying in 1894 at Ste. Catherine, where he is buried in the church cemetery along with his grandson, Ben Mulroney, and more Mulroneys and O'Sheas than are accounted for by the tombstones. The church records do not record the politics of any of them, though it is safe to venture that most were Liberals. Nor do the records spell the family name in any way other than Mulroney, though many members of the fourth generation thought it must have been O'Mulrooney or Mulrooney in the beginning. Brian Mulroney used to joke that his great-grandfather must have lost the other "o" on the way over.

For a young couple starting off in life, there wasn't much doing in Ste. Catherine-de-Portneuf in the middle of the depression, nor was there much economic opportunity in Quebec City. But there was a new town being started on the North Shore. Ben Mulroney was among those who built it from a tent city. By the time the

Quebec North Shore paper company opened its first mill for business in 1938, he was one of its first employees and had moved his family to the new town.

Their two daughters, Olive and Peggy, had been born in 1936 and 1937. The first of their four children to be born in Baie Comeau, and their older son, was born on March 20, 1939. They called him Martin Brian Mulroney. Three more children would follow – Doreen in 1942, Gary in 1943, and Barbara in 1948. Like many homes in which there were a lot of kids, everyone later said it was like having two families.

The "first family" consisted of Olive, Peggy, and Brian. The "second family" would be composed of the younger ones. "The other three almost seemed to be of a younger generation," Irene O'Shea Mulroney remarked one Sunday afternoon about six months after her older son had become leader of the Conservative Party. And a week before Christmas, he would be having them all around to Stornoway for a family dinner.

"Everybody in our family is completely different, in a completely different space," said the younger brother, Gary, a fine arts teacher at a secondary school in the big Montreal bedroom community of Laval. The oldest girl, Olive, had married Dick Elliott, and they had lived and raised their four children wherever the big jobs were, from Trinidad to Iran. The second sister, Peggy, entered the convent and then left it, eventually to become Mrs. Joe Fitzpatrick of New York. Brian's younger sister, Doreen, became a nurse in Montreal, where she married and later divorced. Gary, still a bachelor in his early forties, had inherited his father's talent to do things with his hands. "By the time the three eldest were in boarding school," he explained, "my father had a second job and needed someone to hold the tool box." While his older brother was never known for puttering around his house on the hill in Westmount, Gary stripped a lower Westmount duplex down to the brick and renovated and refurnished it from top to bottom. "By the time I was in my teens," he would recall, "my father was probably less severe with us. We were Irene's kids. The older ones got the best and the worst of the old man. They were taught that if you worked hard you would succeed. You were expected to produce. We had the same kind of drive but channelled it differently."

Gary freely acknowledged that their mother had a bit of a soft spot for her sons, even when they were grown up and living in Montreal. "Her two boys," said the younger son, "could do damn near anything and get away with it."

And the definitive appraisal on the older son's childhood would come from his mother. "Brian wasn't a goody two-shoes," she said. "He had a lot of fun."

Irene Mulroney, who had lost her first-born son after a premature birth in 1935, had no problems delivering the first of her two surviving sons in the morning of March 20, 1939. He was the first of the four children who would be born in the hospital at Baie Comeau. In those early years, the Mulroneys lived in a little house at 132 Champlain Street, quickly outgrew it, and moved to the neat white house just above Le Manoir, where Brian would do most of his growing up. The last of their three homes was at 79 Champlain, a smaller house that Ben Mulroney bought a year before his death in 1965.

Brian Mulroney's first boyhood friend, who would remain a life-long friend, was his next-door neighbour, Peter Dawson, who became a noted Montreal opthamologist. Even when he moved to Houston in the late 1970's, Dr. Dawson tried to stay in touch and learned from his sister in Toronto of Mulroney's victory in the evening of June 11, 1983. Dawson was later reminded by his father, Hedley, by this time retired to British Columbia, that his dad used to play Santa Claus on Christmas Eve, and that his arrival was not unremarked by the little boy with his face in the window next door. "I saw Santa Claus go in your house but I didn't see him go out," the preschool-aged Brian told his next-door neighbour.

Champlain Street was on the English or management side of town, even if Ben Mulroney was hardly a management employee. "I was a little more associated with the English-Protestant camp," Dr. Dawson recalled in 1984. "Brian acted for me as a bridge. He moved back and forth even then."

Mulroney's boyhood friends were a mix of English and French, and some of them, in that mongrel Quebec way, were francophones with English names, like Jimmy Green, the first of their generation to die, in the mid-1970's. The others were called Gilles Lachance, Wilbur and Blair Touchie, Jacques Provencher and Gérard Guy, Jackie Malloy and Danny Scott. Jackie Malloy would become a Montreal cabbie. Scott would become an engineer with Hydro-Québec International. Some would leave home, and some would not. Pierre Rocque was one of those who stayed at home, where he was a beer distributor. Lachance would become a draughtsman for the town of Baie Comeau.

It was Lachance who was waiting for Mulroney on the tarmac when he came on home for the first time as Conservative leader, on June 1, 1984, nearly a year after the convention. Lachance and the other boyhood chums had spent months organizing a homecoming with one purpose, to persuade the Boy from Baie Comeau to become the candidate from Manicouagan, the sprawling North Shore riding that includes his home town.

For most of the week, it had been drizzly and damp along the North Shore, but the weather lifted and gave way to sunshine about an hour before Mulroney flew in from Quebec on a small charter. The town's employees rolled out a seldom-used red carpet for him as they had a few minutes earlier when Mila and the three children arrived on another plane from Ottawa. They had the obligatory airport welcome and motorcade on the half-hour drive into town, where they had scheduled a "friends of Brian" meeting at Le Manoir and a stretch of main-streeting in the town, followed by a $35-a-plate supper attended by 500 towns-people in the hilltop Recreation Centre, concluding with an arena rally where the organization of the day kind of trailed off into the night. In all of this, there were plenty of "photo opportunities" and colour sidebars, including a stop at the Taverne aux Amis, Mulroney's first watering hole where, as he explained it as he stood on a tavern chair, he had learned about culture and pickled eggs.

But it was an unscheduled event, a walk down Champlain Street, up from the Manoir, that would make it a memorable homecoming. Reporters and cameramen who often observed that he seemed tight and tense had never seen him more relaxed as he set off from the Manoir with his family and a surprisingly well-behaved media circus.

"Is this where the Boy from Baie Comeau lived?" asked *La Presse* reporter Pierre Vennat as Mulroney walked out of the guest house on the Manoir grounds.

"Are you kidding?" he replied. "We used to throw rocks at this place when it was the mill manager's house."

In bright sunshine made to order for photo opportunities, this moving scrum set off down Champlain Street, where every space between houses afforded a breathtaking view of the boundless St. Lawrence below. Mulroney first came upon number 79 Champlain, the last of the three houses he lived in and the only one his father ever owned. "All the family got together every nickel we could get," he said, and "the Old Man" went down and bought the place. Number 99 Champlain was just across the street from "Old Man Bodker's," site of the fire that Mulroney and Jimmy Green had tried to set against a concrete foundation. "You can see," he said some thirty-five years later, "why we didn't succeed."

And at 132 Champlain, the only one of the three houses on the river side of the street, Mulroney went out and stood in the back yard, admired the view, and mentioned to someone that "we're missing someone, we're missing Jimmy," who had died in 1976.

"We were very close, very tight," said Lachance, who had lived across the street from 132 Champlain.

It was from Lachance that Brian Mulroney started to pick up a good smattering of street French, as Gilles learned his first English from Mulroney. In later years, they would still switch back and forth from one language to the other. Lachance was one of the Baie Comeau boys who chartered two aircraft to fly into Central Nova for another victory scene as Mulroney won his by-election on August 29, and he stood off to the back of the steamy hall, waiting for his old friend to catch his eye and say a few private words of greeting.

The Mulroneys were different from most of the English kids in town in that they were Irish, and thus Catholic. And the Sisters of the Holy Cross, who ran the Ste. Amélie elementary school, made room for the English-speaking Catholic kids. "The French and the Irish were apart but together, if you know what I mean," Irene Mulroney said. And one of the ways they were together was in school. "It wasn't a French school or an English school. It was both."

Then a bit smaller than most boys his age, Mulroney struck most people as rather diffident and shy. For himself, he had enduring memories of the nuns. "I remember the art teacher," he said in 1984. "She happened to teach art apart from everything else. Her name was Soeur St. Jean. And I remember another one, Sister Rosarita. And so on. I can see them in my mind's eye right now. And that was nearly forty years ago. They were excellent."

Apart from the classroom and the schoolyard, Mulroney spent a good deal of time during his primary school years in the public library, which his sister Olive recalled as being surprisingly good for a town of that size. "That's where we got our books," he said. "My routine was books and sports," and later on, he added, working in the summer. "That's what I did."

As he grew older and went to college, the books he couldn't get out of the library he would write away for or get someone to buy for him. "If someone was going to Montreal," Mulroney said, "I'd give him a list of books to buy for me, because I wouldn't get there all summer. So I'd give them lists. I knew everybody who was going to Montreal, and I'd give them lists and say, 'When you get to Montreal, you go and buy these for me.' They'd go all over Montreal looking for these things for me. I had half the town busy." The books they would bring back, or that would arrive in the mail, in the summers of his college years, would be histories and biographies.

"I can remember being very taken with the biography of David Ben-Gurion by Adele Rogers St. John," he said. "And I can remember I read C.P. Snow's work on China and Mao, and so I was a great reader of political biographies and Canadian history. But I was very taken with the lives of people. You know, for example, I can still remember being intrigued by the fact that Ben-Gurion used to work and then he'd fall asleep, and then he'd wake up at four in the morning and work some more. I remember being fascinated as to how that formed his personality, living in that little house in Tel Aviv, and things like that."

When it came to organized hockey in the peewee years, "He may not have been the fastest player on the team," recalled Peter Dawson, but he didn't lack for determination as a centre.

"We had skating rinks everywhere," Mulroney said. "We were always playing hockey and baseball. It was a great town for recreation. I mean the company, like a lot of those company towns, it was extremely well done. We had access to the ice any time we wanted it. There was a swimming pool that I remember, right from the very beginning, and there were tennis courts, which is where I learned to play tennis, played well, too."

Dawson remembers that one summer Mulroney simply decided he was going to "take up this game" of tennis, and all summer long "he went at it," and by summer's end "he won the tournament."

But it was in singing and public speaking that young Brian began to come into his own. Peter Dawson later surmised that "This ability to speak and this ability to sing was perhaps his way of compensating for being a little bit small." In any event, Dawson recalled "He always had a flair for speaking, and he always loved to sing, and turned out to be the leader in the singing. We all loved to sing, too, but he would be the leader."

Mulroney's first memories were of music, of songs being sung in the kitchen. In his parents' house, there was always a piano, and usually someone plunking away at it. In those pre-television days, family and community singalongs were one of the principal forms of entertainment.

In this way, Mulroney learned all the old Irish songs and French-Canadian ballads, as well as just about anything that had come down from Tin Pan Alley. And he was a member in good

30

standing of the Mary Schmon Singers. A former nightclub singer in Chicago, she was the wife of the mill manager, Bob Schmon. In Baie Comeau, she put together a group of kids and other towns-people, and they were known as the Mary Schmon Singers. And this was how Brian Mulroney, seven or eight years old, got to sing solo for Colonel McCormick. There was a knock at the Mulroney door one day. It was Johnny Pope, the company's public relations man.

"The Colonel's in town," he explained, and they were looking for someone to sing for him over at the guest house. And he explained to Irene Mulroney that he had heard her son sing at Mary Schmon's.

"Well, Mother said fine," Mulroney recalled, "so I remember being driven out there, quite a long drive, by Johnny Pope. And I got up on the piano and they asked him what his favourite song was. And he said that his favourite song was 'Dearie,' but that I wouldn't know it, because how could a kid from Baie Comeau be expected to know that.

"But I knew it and I sang it," he continued, "and others as well. And they gave me $50, U.S., and put me in the car and drove me home. And I gave it to my mother and she just about had a cardiac arrest. Any time he came to Baie Comeau, he asked for me, and I'd go sing. I'd perform any song that he'd want. He'd just name them and I knew them."

As for his speaking career, ten-year-old Brian Mulroney made his debut in the Rotary Club public-speaking contest in 1949. There were two members of the family entered that year. His sister Olive, three years older than himself, won the girls' competition with her speech entitled "Welcome, Newfoundland," on the province's entry into Confederation. "I was the leader for a very few years," Olive Elliott would recall. Her kid brother would win the boys' contest with his speech on "Comics." The audience was suitably impressed. One man sitting behind Mulroney's parents leaned forward and told his father, "Ben, that boy's going to make a damn good bishop someday."

Over the years, the oldest daughter and the older son would become "very close," as Brian put it, "because Peggy was away, and Olive and I were together." And later on, when his father died, they had to share the familial and financial responsibilities. "I think Olive and I were probably closer for those reasons than the rest of the kids, who were younger, and had different lifestyles, and different youths."

It was at a public event, on the stage of the Arcade Theatre, that Brian Mulroney gave an early indication of his career plan.

31

Both the Ste. Amélie children and the Protestant kids were taken to see a show where the emcee was John Fisher, later known as Mr. Canada for his role as the greeter of centennial year. "Brian got up on the stage and he sang 'McNamara's Band' or something," recalled Wilbur Touchie, another of his oldest friends. Then Fisher leaned down to him with the microphone and asked what he wanted to be when he grew up.

"Prime Minister of Canada," he replied.

As he finished his elementary schooling with the nuns of Ste. Amélie and his first two years of high school with the brothers of the Clercs St. Viateur, he got the idea to go away to school at St. Thomas in Chatham, New Brunswick, an announcement which in due course he made to his parents.

"Brian, we didn't expect him to go away," Irene Mulroney said. "The two sisters had already gone away. Brian always knew where he wanted to go, and I think it was because the two sisters were gone."

His recollection was more along the lines that "our facilities in Baie Comeau were quite inadequate in high school, and we used to listen to the radio from New Brunswick all the time. I can't tell you just how the decision was arrived at, but I certainly was influenced by New Brunswick and educational opportunities there and so on. And I knew people who had been down there, and I knew that was a better opportunity."

However it was decided that he would go away, go away he did, in September of 1953. With his two older sisters, who were on their way to the convent, he crossed the St. Lawrence on a decommissioned naval vessel called the *Jean Brillant*, named for a lieutenant in the Royal 22nd Regiment who had won the Victoria Cross in the First World War.

His sister Olive would always remember that as the boat pulled out of Baie Comeau, a group of nuns sang a song of which the refrain was "Partons, la mer est belle." At that point, the St. Lawrence might as well have been an ocean for a boy to cross. It was some thirty miles across to the South Shore, and eventually to the trains that would take them their separate ways, the girls to Montreal and to the Iona Academy in eastern Ontario, and the lad to wait for his train going in the other direction. Many years later, Olive Elliott could still "remember Brian standing at the train," quite alone, in the pitch dark, in a strange town called Rimouski.

"My train went later," he would explain. "My train was the

Ocean Limited, going into Halifax. It was an overnighter that you got on late. And I can still remember that, putting the girls on the train, and they'd get on the train, and I'd bring their luggage for them, get them all together, and then I'd have to wait for, not too long, maybe an hour, an hour and a half. Then my train would come, and I'd get on the coach, and I'd get off sometime the next day down in Newcastle."

From there he would make his way to Chatham, where a group of diocesan priests and lay teachers ran a high school on the campus of St. Thomas College. When he first arrived there, he said, "I was taken up by the newness of it all," and it wasn't until about ten days later that he realized how homesick he was. There was a phone on a wall panel, and walking by one day, he noticed another Baie Comeau boy, Andy Morrow, talking to his parents and bawling his eyes out. Until then, it had never occurred to Mulroney to be homesick. "But then I phoned, because I saw him on the phone, I phoned home, collect, and when I heard my mother and father, then I started to bawl as well. Probably worse than Andy. Yeah, I felt lonely at the time, but I got over it."

The curriculum at St. Thomas High was pretty much the usual fare of a Catholic classical college, with the emphasis on Latin, Greek, history, and literature. "All that stuff," Mulroney said. "It was not a wealthy place, but it was a well-run place. There was a small college on the campus, which is now a part of UNB, so you also had the university influence, in a modest way, in the same area. And so we had our small group, maybe 100 of us, and while we were going to high school, we had the university symbols in front of us, which was a great benefit, because you could see the activities they were engaged in."

For Christmas and summer holidays, Mulroney would get back on the train, and then the boat, and go home. "The build-up to Christmas at home was just extraordinary," Gary Mulroney remembered. "It wasn't just Christmas, but our elder brother and sisters were coming home."

But Christmas was not particularly different from other times of the year, in that there were always lots of people in the house. "Six kids, a mother, a father, and a boarder in a small house, there was lots going on," Brian Mulroney would say many years later. "But it was a great family atmosphere, you know, kids playing piano in the living room, or playing baseball on the back lawn, always something."

With all those mouths to feed and boarding schools to be paid for, the Mulroneys were hardly rich, though they were not exactly

33

impoverished. "We paid the bills," Irene Mulroney said evenly. "And one of the joys of rearing a family was that for our children there was something better."

"We weren't poor," Olive Elliott maintained, "though Brian jokes about it." Her younger brother agreed. "This stuff about being poor, it's all relative," Gary Mulroney said. "Compared to city kids, we had everything. I don't remember hearing the word poor, when we were kids."

The older brother, who often referred to his humble beginnings, acknowledged that one shouldn't overdo it. "Hell, this was a mill town," Brian Mulroney explained. "You don't bring people that far away to make them poor. There's a difference between being poor and not having any money. That means that you're always able to look after the necessities of life. I can remember, lots of times, my parents not having enough money to make ends meet, and being very troubled by it. The kinds of problems that most people have. But I can never remember not having enough to eat. We always had all we needed to eat and a house to live in."

To help with the bills, and like most other teen-agers, Brian Mulroney worked summers. His first job was as a security guard at the entrance to the forestry ministry's reserve on the English River Road outside of town. His friend Wilbur Touchie, who graduated that summer from Baie Comeau High School, would sometimes go out and see him "with a couple of girls and a radio." On summer nights, in all the Baie Comeau years, there would be bonfires and singsongs down at the beautiful, unspoiled beach. During his summers home from college and law school, Mulroney's jobs were usually a little more backbreaking, though there was one year when he worked as a driver for a boss on one of the big construction sites.

"One of those summers," he recalled, "I was a labourer in the grain elevator for Cargill, carrying these hundred-pound bags of grain that had come off the grain elevator. You know, the elevator in Baie Comeau would block, it used to feed all the ships down in the harbour, and the grain would overturn on the floors. So our job was to keep that elevator clean, and make sure that they didn't lose this grain. So when it blocked we would go around with our masks and shovel the grain into hundred-pound bags, bind them, secure them, then when the work was done, carry them down to a loading area where they could then be put on the ship. That's what we did."

The sons of the men who worked in the town never had any trouble finding summer jobs. By this time, Ben Mulroney was a foreman in the mill and had a little electrical repair business on the side. In those days, Quebec paper mills were shut down by law on Sunday, and every Sunday, all Sunday, Ben Mulroney would work on the maintenance and then the start-up for the new week's work that would begin at midnight.

"In those days, in the summer, I was there, too," his older son said. "I'd work every Sunday on the mill repair, and so when I finished at midnight, then I'd wait for my father, who'd sometimes finish at five after twelve, sometimes at two o'clock in the morning, depending on when the paper would come off the machine.

"And then we'd go home and have a beer." Mulroney could still see his father clearly, sitting in a La-Z-Boy chair the kids had given him, and which his older son still had somewhere in his house. He would clasp his hands behind his head and say something like, "Well, son, one more year and we're over the hump. One more year."

"And that meant that everything was going to be fine," Brian Mulroney said as he sat in the Opposition Leader's fourth-floor Centre Block office one bright afternoon in March of 1984. "There'd be no more worries and no more burdens. He knew and I knew that that wasn't right. But that's the way he was, an optimist. He was an optimist because he could see progress. He saw my sisters doing well and he saw me doing well. A modest progress, but he knew that this was a long-term thing, and he was very much a believer in education. He was very much committed to the proposition that we should have an equal opportunity. He knew from his experience that the educated fellows had a better chance. And that's what he was like."

There was never any doubt, then or later, that Ben Mulroney was the most important figure in his son's life. "He had a great influence," Mulroney said, "probably the greatest of anyone on me, and I learned from him a great sense of dedication to whatever you're doing. He was very loyal to his family and friends and quite selfless in his attitudes. He was a very impressive person.

"He was very selfless in his outlook and he was a strong believer in the importance of the family unit. And he was like a lion, defending his family, protecting his family."

By the time a young engineering graduate named Dick Elliott came calling on his older sister in the summer of 1956, Brian Mulroney was between his freshman and sophomore years in college. The two became fast friends, and many years later Elliott would recall one night when the two of them lay awake one night as they roomed together on a visit to one of Mulroney's

35

uncles from the O'Shea side of the family down in Shannon. "Brian told me, 'I'm going to be Prime Minister of this country someday,'" Elliott said.

It was Elliott who went down to the Hudson's Bay store with Ben Mulroney to buy his son a steamer suitcase to replace the cardboard suitcase that Brian Mulroney had first packed his belongings in when he went away to college. "It was like a suitcase, but it was cardboard, painted to look like a suitcase," Mulroney would recall. "And quite frankly, I didn't have very much to put in it anyway. But I can remember my father getting me a big blue trunk, a steamer trunk, because he said that I shouldn't be travelling around with an old cardboard suitcase with nothing in it."

However he left Baie Comeau, then as later, it would always be with a suitcase full of memories. As Dick Elliott put it: "He had his goals, and Brian set those goals living in Baie Comeau."

3

"BONES"

Pat MacAdam always remembered the first time he saw Brian Mulroney, a skinny runt of a sixteen-year-old, out in front of MacPherson House, wearing his high school athletic jacket. It was September, 1955, and Mulroney had arrived as a freshman on the campus of St. Francis Xavier University in Antigonish, Nova Scotia.

He did not look like a college man; he looked like a scrawny, scared, baby-faced kid with a brushcut.

Nearly thirty years later, on the first Friday of December in 1983, one of the university's more famous graduates came back to Antigonish to speak to a student and faculty assembly on the eve of the feast of St. Francis Xavier. By now, forty-four-year-old Brian Mulroney was the MP from the neighbouring riding of Central Nova and the leader of the Progressive Conservative Party of Canada. On the university as well as the country's protocol list, he still ranked behind another St. F.X. graduate, Allan J. MacEachen, Deputy Prime Minister and Secretary of State for External Affairs in the Trudeau government. The university was located in MacEachen's riding, and the St. F.X. faculty, as well as the nuns across the way at Mount St. Bernard women's college, had long supported MacEachen and the Liberal Party.

Mulroney was no stranger to this. It had been this way since his student days on the campus. When he was elected leader of the campus PCs in 1957, the student paper, the *Xaverian Weekly*, reported that in his victory speech he noted "the Achilles heel of the Progressive Conservative party this year has been Mount St. Bernard, where we didn't draw too well. Next year, we will try to do better there."

"Look, they were all Liberals," Mulroney explained on a flight out of the jet strip that MacEachen had put next to the Cape Breton Causeway. "All the nuns were Liberals, a bunch of goddamn Grits. Don't forget the most famous son of St. F.X., its most revered graduate, was Angus L. MacDonald, and his daughter was at Mount St. Bernard. He was the greatest Premier in Nova Scotia history."

Mulroney's choice of university determined his choice of party. It was an accident of history, or perhaps of geography, that he became a Tory. Had Brian Mulroney gone to school in his home province, if he had gone to Loyola High School in Montreal rather than St. Thomas High in Chatham, New Brunswick, had he attended Loyola College or McGill University in his undergraduate days, it is almost certain that he would have become a Liberal like nearly everyone else of his generation in Quebec. In those days, most of the Irish Catholic kids from Quebec City went to Loyola for their bachelor's degree, as some of them had attended high school on the same Jesuit-run campus. But Quebec City and Montreal were out of the orbit of the North Shore boys. "The guys from Baie Comeau who went away to school went to the Maritimes," Mulroney explained. In his high school years at St. Thomas, it was just a matter of "taking the ferry across the river and the train down to Newcastle."

And it was because of his St. Thomas years that Mulroney decided to go to college in Antigonish. "St. F.X. was well known in the Atlantic Provinces," Mulroney would say a quarter of a century after he had left the place. "You just heard a lot about it. I was very much oriented towards the Atlantic Provinces in those days."

Mulroney's choice of school was also determined by his Catholic background and modest family means. In a way, it was kids like him that the founders of St. F.X. had in mind when they started the place up in Arichat on Cape Breton Island in 1853 before moving to Antigonish two years later. It was never intended to be an elitist operation. From the beginning it was administered by diocesan priests, rather than by a teaching order like the Jesuits or Dominicans, and the school came under the aegis of the Bishop of Antigonish, a sprawling diocese that took in the eastern shore of Nova Scotia and Cape Breton, and the parishioners were by and large farmers, fishermen, miners, and steelworkers.

Fred Doucet, who would become Opposition Leader Mulroney's chief of staff, was one of six kids from a Cape Breton hamlet called Grand Etang, where they didn't even have running water. Somehow, Doucet made it through college, became a geologist, obtained a Ph.D. in philosophy from the University of Ottawa, and eventually returned to St. F.X. as its development officer. His brother Gerry went through St. F.X. as well and later became Education Minister in Robert Stanfield's provincial cabinet in Nova Scotia.

"One of the reasons you came here was because you weren't rich," Mulroney explained at a small reception for student Tories after his speech in December of 1983. "Anyone here with another pair of shoes, he, in our minds, was known as a rich kid. This was a place where the sons of farmers and fishermen came, and one of the reasons they came here was because they couldn't afford to go anywhere else."

For Mulroney, the electrician's son from the North Shore of Quebec, there was never any question of going anywhere else. As he said many times, in many places, "nobody from Harvard was knocking at my door." And he would always maintain that without the opportunity to go to a place like St. F.X., "I'd be back home in Baie Comeau, driving a truck," as he did during summers. This may be a bit of romantic nonsense on his part. It is likely his father, with his dreams of a better life for his children, would have driven his son out of the house rather than see him become a workingman. And Mulroney, who worshipped his father, would not have been likely to disappoint him. With his curiosity, ambition, and born leadership talents, he would have graduated from some college, somehow. It turned out to be St. F.X., a place where, as Mulroney recalled, "nobody pressed you to pay your bills because we couldn't afford to pay them. Most students worked all summer to pay last year's bill. Very few of us left here with our accounts in order; it was only the year after we left here that we managed to catch up."

It may not have been the Ivy League, or even Dalhousie, but when Mulroney and his contemporaries left Antigonish they had a piece of paper that said they had a university degree. They had formed the ambitious, upwardly mobile outlook that was to shape their lives. And they had something else: friends for life.

The Mulroney Mafia in the Conservative Party started at St. F.X. Besides the Doucet brothers, there were Sam Wakim, Pat MacAdam, and Paul Creaghan. Their friends in student politics included Bobby Higgins, later leader of the New Brunswick Liberals before going to the provincial bench, and Rick Cashin, who would become a Liberal MP from Newfoundland during the Pearson years and who later, as head of a Newfoundland fishermen's union, served as a Trudeau appointee on the Task Force on Canadian Unity.

At the time Mulroney came on the campus in the fall of 1955, MacAdam was rooming with Lowell Murray, who would become chief brain truster for Joe Clark. Murray was just about the only one of the St. F.X. crowd who did not fall in behind Mulroney's first run at the leadership in 1976, and Mulroney never really forgave him for it.

MacAdam, then entering his senior year as managing editor of the student paper, gave Mulroney his first job as a sportswriter for the *Xaverian Weekly*. It was like any other campus paper. As MacAdam said: "If you showed up they gave you something to do."

For someone who was a year or two younger than most other freshmen, Mulroney fit in rather quickly. "His good humour and desire to be accepted were infectious," MacAdam would recall. Also the fact that he was from Upper Canada, Upper Canada being anywhere west of New Brunswick, even the North Shore of Quebec. "We looked in awe at Upper Canadians and Bostonians. I was always a little extra respectful of them," said MacAdam, who was out of the Cape Breton mining town of Glace Bay, one of those places where when your mother hung out the wash, the white sheets would come back black with coal dust.

When Mulroney arrived on the campus, there were less than 1,000 students, though they came from dozens of countries. There were, for starters, a good number of students from northern New England, not just because of the familial and trade affinities with the Maritimes but because of the GI plan, which enabled American students to get a college education on the cheap at lower Canadian rates and have a few dollars left over.

From the other countries, they came mostly because of a man named Moses Coady and an idea known as the Antigonish Movement. Moses Coady was a radical priest with a salty tongue, who in the years of the Great Depression started a bootstraps operation among the woefully disadvantaged farmers and fishermen of eastern Nova Scotia and Cape Breton. A strapping man of 6'4", he bore a striking resemblance to Jack Dempsey, and he spread a message of self-help through adult education and the founding of community co-operatives. His motto was simple but profound: "Social reform through economic activity."

Even in those pre-ecumenical times, he recognized no denominational boundaries. Legend had it that when he was once upbraided by his superior for embracing too many Protestants in his flock, Coady replied: "Bishop, there is no Catholic or Protestant way of catching fish." Half a century later, an institute that bore his name at St. F.X. could boast that it had trained more than 2,500 leaders from more than 100 countries during their stay at Antigonish. But even in the mid-1950's, the movement's fame had spread abroad, attracting students from more than three dozen Third World countries.

There were also a few students down from Quebec, English-speaking kids like Mulroney and French-speaking students like Bertrand Lavoie, who would go on to become a wealthy car dealer who tried to keep the Conservative flame alive in the town of Ste. Eustache, in Francis Fox's riding northwest of Montreal. "Brother Bert," as he called himself, delivered Opposition Leader Mulroney's first limo, a Buick, to his office. The keys were for the man Lavoie called "Brother Bones."

The "Brother" part came from Lavoie; the "Bones" part came from Sam Wakim, who would become Mulroney's roommate, closest friend, and faithful foot soldier in the long march to June, 1983. "It was because he was skinny," Wakim recalled, "and then he grew. He was just a big bag of bones. So we called him 'Bones.'"

As freshmen in 1955, Wakim and Mulroney ate together in Morrison Hall at St. F.X. "He just sort of strode in and sat down," said Wakim, a future Toronto lawyer. Wakim was of Lebanese immigrant stock, from the East End of Saint John, New Brunswick. His tablemates, Mike Jennings, Brian McGoughty, Gordie Weeks, and Gene Neury, were all New Brunswickers as well. "Mulroney had been to high school in New Brunswick," Wakim said, "and with the rest of us from there, it became a kind of New Brunswick table." They were, Wakim recalled, all from the same modest origins. "You didn't need your dinner jacket to sit at our table," he said. "I wore my high school football jacket for four years." Or as Mulroney put it many years later: "We all sort of came from common stock, but that was what it was all about."

Mulroney did his freshman year in Arts, then moved over to Commerce in his sophomore year to pick up some credits in economics and the like before switching back to honours political science in the Arts faculty. He had no such inclination to change his politics. As a freshman, he became whip of the campus Tories. As a seventeen-year-old sophomore, he worked off-campus for the election of Conservative Bill MacKinnon in the provincial election of October 30, 1956, that heralded the accession of Robert Stanfield as Premier of Nova Scotia. "I think Brian, more than anyone else of that crowd, dared to test himself outside the safety of the campus," Fred Doucet observed late in 1983. "He took on the rough and tumble of politics on the outside."

As for Mulroney's becoming a Tory, he once explained that

"the Grits were no fun, they took themselves too seriously," for in those days they had been in power for years both federally and provincially. Bob Stanfield had something to do with it, too, in that he took over a moribund provincial party and, after eight years of hard work at the grassroots, was elected Premier of the province.

That still did not explain what Mulroney, an Irish Catholic from the most Catholic and Liberal province in Christendom, was doing in the party of WASPs and Orangemen. "Way back then," said Finlay MacDonald, who was Stanfield's chief organizer, "Catholicism and Liberalism were almost synonymous in Nova Scotia, and the Tory party was a WASP party."

But then after a twenty-year reign, Angus L. MacDonald died in office in 1954. Since MacDonald had been a Catholic, there was a strong feeling that his successor as Liberal leader should be Protestant, and it was agreed that Harold Connolly, a Catholic, would be interim leader and Premier. "Then Harold, who liked being Premier, changed his mind and ran against Henry Hicks for the leadership and lost," Mulroney explained on a bumpy charter flight out of Port Hawkesbury after his appearance at his alma mater. "And all the Catholics got mad and went to Stanfield, and that's the only reason Stanfield won."

Working in Bill MacKinnon's campaign in Antigonish, Mulroney wrote speeches, did radio spots, and knocked on doors. It was the making of a Tory and a campus leader. "He quickly became known on campus. He was never one to hang back," recalled Bill MacKinnon's brother Greg, then campus chaplain and later president of the university. "Even in those days, Brian was thinking big. He went to the president of the school, to make a suggestion for an honorary degree. Even then he had a flair for public relations and that sort of thing." The name Mulroney suggested to Father Hugh Somers was that of Ed Sullivan, then at the peak of his fame as the host of his weekly variety show. "I had visions of us all on television," Mulroney recalled at a small university reception attended by the elderly but still acute Dr. Somers, whom Mulroney kidded as "one of Nova Scotia's most distinguished former Liberals. He never recovered from the best advice I ever gave him."

Six weeks after the election of Stanfield in 1956, Mulroney and Paul Creaghan were named as campus delegates to the national Conservative leadership convention held in Ottawa in December of that year. The two of them sat up in the coach for the thirty-six-hour journey. Mulroney was going as national vice-chairman of Youth for Dief.

42

But even in those days, even in the youth section of the party, Mulroney discovered that the Toronto crowd gave the orders. John Diefenbaker's national youth chairman was young Ted Rogers, later a cable television magnate. His chief henchman was Hal Jackman, later head of a big insurance company and a prominent Tory of the Rosedale persuasion. In 1984, at the Albany Club's annual Sir John A. Macdonald Day dinner, Mulroney would remind these two members of the audience of his humble beginnings in their service. "I arrived and announced that I was the national vice-chairman," Mulroney told the black-tie audience of rock-ribbed Tories, "and they said, fine, we need someone to go out and put up some posters." Mulroney went out, organized his own kids, stayed up all night, and papered the town with Dief posters. "He came back the next day," Jackman would tell people many years later, "and said, 'What do you want me to do now?'"

Diefenbaker would win handily on the first ballot, with 774 votes to Donald Fleming's 393 and 117 delegates for Davie Fulton.

It was as one of Dief's youth organizers that Mulroney got his picture taken with the Chief. Some twenty years later, at the beginning of 1976, Mulroney included the autographed souvenir in a campaign brochure for his own leadership campaign. There was Dief, arm in arm with this skinny kid who had a brushcut that couldn't quite discipline the cowlicks on his forehead. "Wait till the old guy sees that," Mulroney said mischievously on a flight a month before the 1976 convention. "He'll just about croak."

Back at St. Francis Xavier in the winter and spring of 1957, Mulroney moved into a leadership role in campus politics. "Mulroney elected Tory leader," the *Xaverian Weekly* announced on its front page on March 22, 1957: "Thursday night's meeting was well attended and saw another candidate, Sam Wakim of Saint John N.B., contest the leadership."

"Is that right? I had forgotten all about that," Mulroney said more than twenty-five years later when reminded he had run against his best friend. "Was it close?"

"It says here," he was told, that 'Mulroney carried the vote by a slim margin.'"

"Sam must have tried to pack the meeting," Mulroney said with a laugh. "Those Saint John guys, you never saw one of them but you saw twenty."

Student politics were not Mulroney's only campus activity. During his sophomore year he organized a $1,100 relief fund for refugees from the Hungarian uprising of the previous October. It

43

was his first of many attempts at raising money for a charitable or political cause, many of them obscure, not a few of them hopeless, and some of them close to his heart.

When Greg MacKinnon became president of St. F.X. in 1978 he set his sights on having Mulroney to head up a $7-million capital campaign to get the school some sorely needed facilities, such as swimming pool and a library extension. "He didn't agree immediately," MacKinnon said, "because he doesn't like to lose in anything. The point is, he plans carefully and doesn't undertake anything lightly." Once Mulroney took the thing on, he gave it a scope and scale it might not otherwise have attained. In three years, and with a target of $7 million, Mulroney's team raised over $11 million. He put together a national campaign committee that started with Denison Mines chairman Steve Roman as honorary chairman. In Atlantic Canada, he brought on Rick Cashin from Newfoundland and his old debating partner, Charles Keating, from Halifax. In the United States, Mulroney got Canadian Consul General Ken Taylor in New York to join the committee, along with retired hockey idol Bobby Orr and Theodore Hesburgh, the president of the University of Notre Dame in Indiana. And Mulroney gave the university, a university for kids who weren't rich, as he said, gave it entrée in rarefied places, collecting one year at the annual supper of Hollinger Mines in Toronto, an event that establishment chronicler Peter C. Newman has described as the annual meeting of the Canadian corporate elite. Mulroney even managed to lower the boom on his friend Jim Coutts, the former aide to Pierre Trudeau. "The boys love it," he would always say.

Twenty-seven years to the day before his campus appearance on December 2, 1983, sophomore Commerce student Brian Mulroney and sophomore Engineering student Charles Keating defended the affirmative of a proposition that "Compulsory military training should be inaugurated in Canada." Conscription was one of the issues that passed for campus controversy in those days. Ironically, Mulroney would deal with the peace and security issue, disarmament, and Pierre Trudeau's peace initiative in his St. F.X. speech of 1983:

> The search for peace must be pursued. I can only remind you of the folly of unilateral disarmament, of the need for honest brokerage, East and West. The peacemaker must be patient and persevering, the search for peace demands all the courage

and wisdom we can muster: To contemplate the alternative, nuclear annihilation, or the gross euphemisms, "nuclear accident," or "limited nuclear war," is to contemplate the ultimate tragedy: the destruction of our planet, the destruction of all the works and arts man has so ingeniously devised, and finally the destruction of man himself.

Mulroney began his sophomore year as the unanimous winner, in a field of eight contestants, in the university's oratorical contest. "Mulroney lambasted Quebec's corrupt politics," the student paper reported, "and stated that the politics in that province needed a thorough cleaning up."

He won the oratorical contest again in his junior year, and again spoke to the politics of his home province, to a theme that pointed to his future career path as a labour lawyer. "Mulroney spoke on the Quebec unions," the *Xaverian Weekly* noted on November 15, 1957. "He pointed out the 'dictatorial dealings of Premier Duplessis with regard to the Murdochville and Arvida strikes,' and said that 'the Quebec workers were under the domination of the Union Nationale party.'"

In his senior year, Mulroney retired as the undefeated three-time champion. But it was in campus and intercollegiate debating that he was tested not only on his oratorical talents, but in his ability to think on his feet and in his capacity for team leadership. Of the campus debaters in those days, it was pretty clear that Mulroney was emerging as the most gifted member of a talented group. His only serious rival for the rhetorical limelight appeared to be Rick Cashin.

In the winter of 1958, the St. F.X. students organized a model parliament of Maritime universities. It was one of those events – the Laval Congress of Canadian Affairs in 1961 was another – that would leave a mark on Mulroney's generation of Canadian students. Not only did they draw student politicians to Antigonish over the first weekend of February, they managed to attract three prominent national politicians in the middle of a winter campaign, the March 31 election that would give John Diefenbaker the most resounding majority in Canadian history. Diefenbaker's Trade Minister, Gordon Churchill, was there for the Tories. Paul Martin represented the national Liberals. And Doug Fisher, later an Ottawa columnist but then an MP, was there for the CCF, forerunner of the NDP. The Prime Minister of the model parliament was eighteen-year-old Brian Mulroney.

By the end of his junior year, Mulroney was beginning to push his horizons beyond Tory campus politics. He appeared on a panel at which the participants were to discuss "the West's Stand against Communism." The chairman was his rival from campus party politics, Rick Cashin. The student paper announced the event by running both their pictures, under the humorous caption "United At Last."

"Cashin was here four years and led four different parties," Mulroney said with only slight exaggeration during his 1983 meeting with campus Tories at St F.X. "One year there was no party to lead so he invented his own. And Rick was pretty heavy, pretty husky, and the party he invented and led with some distinction was called the Order of Obese Occidentals, and he ran on the slogan, 'If men who are thin, make you chagrined, why not try putting Cashin in.' And he almost won, he was a very good parliamentarian."

By the beginning of Mulroney's senior year he was pushing his interests off-campus as vice-president of the National P.C. Student Conservatives. In October, he was involved in a United Nations Day symposium on the theme "To Live Together in peace as Good Neighbours." And in mid-November he travelled up to Montreal as one of two St. F.X. representatives to McGill University's portentously titled "Conference on World Affairs." It was an ambitious undertaking, with students from across the country as well as from fourteen schools in the United States.

Mulroney's major activity of his senior year was the presidency of the student co-op, consisting principally of the student cafeteria and student bookstore. It was his first experience at managing, as distinct from raising, a significant amount of money. "The Co-Op society has had a gross revenue of close to one hundred thousand dollars for the fiscal year, just ended," he reported before the annual meeting in April of 1959. "This is an all-time high and the year has been one of the most successful in the history of the society."

Such was student life in the mid and late 1950's, the age of Dwight Eisenhower in the United States, the twilight of Louis St. Laurent and the beginning of the Diefenbaker years in Canada. It was not a time when students were given to wholesale rejection of societal values and standards, as they would only a few years later in the mid-1960's. "I came to Antigonish in the mid-fifties, when life was somewhat more tranquil than it is today," Mulroney told the St F.X. community in December of 1983. "The turmoil of the sixties, the war in Vietnam, the energy crisis, the escalating nuclear buildup, and here at home, the debate on the constitution and the spectre of separatism, all lay in the future."

The yearbook pictures tell the story of any campus in the

1950's: short hair, shirts and ties, and girls in chiffon dresses. "I went to the senior prom with Rosann Earl," Mulroney remembered. "She was the most beautiful girl on campus. She's now married to Rick Cashin and she's still a knockout." Mulroney had no recollection of the rock-and-roll craze hitting the campus, perhaps because he has no memory for that sort of thing. If you asked him if Elvis Presley's music was big on campus, he would look at you in a curious way as if to say that Presley was an idol in the 1960's.

But if campus life at St. F.X. was tranquil and free of controversy, it was not dull. The Mulroney gang was noted for pulling some memorable student stunts. Nearly twenty-five years before Rosie Ruiz got the idea of cheating in the Boston Marathon, Mulroney and his MacPherson House roommates stole the laurels of the first long-distance running event on the St. F.X. campus. "I was the spiritual director of our team," Mulroney recalled with considerable mirth on that December night's bumpy flight. It had been a sentimental day for him, "a moving experience," and he was in a mood for reminiscing on the flight to Montreal.

As Mulroney told the story, MacPherson House entered Bert Lavoie, who even then gave promise of being a corpulent gentleman who would run no further than the corner store. "What they didn't know," said Mulroney, "was that Sam Wakim had got hold of a car. We picked him up downtown at Wong's restaurant, then we let Bert out of the back of the car and he collapses across the finish line, to the astonishment and surprise of everyone. We pick up the prize, run like hell for MacPherson House, and lock the door."

Lavoie, the future GM dealer and supplier of the Opposition Leader's Buick, also had the beer concession in MacPherson House. Students were not permitted to have booze in their rooms (when Mulroney returned to the campus in 1983, the boys in one dorm used forty-ounce windowstoppers of gin to let fresh air in their rooms). But in those days, Lavoie would go downtown on a bicycle with a rack, throw his coat over a case of beer, and pedal back to MacPherson House, all under the watchful and perhaps knowing eye of the prefect of discipline.

Perhaps the all-time campus stunt of the Mulroney years, and the one for which they might have been expelled, was the time Mulroney and the MacPherson House boys flushed a rival clan of students out of their residence with firehoses. Amazingly, they never got caught. Perhaps behind the curtains, the diocesan priests knew what was going on, had a good laugh, and looked the other way. "We were always in trouble," Mulroney said, "but nothing serious. We were too innocent, really."

They were not entirely innocent when it came to girls. Mount St. Bernard College was nearby, and the students collaborated on the usual sorts of projects between colleges for young Catholic men and women. Mulroney once appeared in a student production of *Everyman* alongside Marty Robertson, who would become Sam Wakim's wife.

There was also the hospital, "up the hill," as they said, where student nurses trained under the watchful Sisters of St. Martha. Brian Mulroney was known to have spent a good deal of his time "up the hill." It was a legend about St. F.X., as at many schools, that the university authorities put saltpeter in the food to diminish the male interest in the opposite sex. If so, it evidently failed to have the desired effect on Mulroney.

In 1983, when he returned to give a speech, all that had changed, too. By this time, women were living on the campus, and a few of them were hanging out a second-storey window of a residence as he walked over to deliver his speech. "Hey, Brian," one of them called out, "we've been waiting for you all afternoon."

"I'll be over after the speech," he yelled back.

Walking along a few yards behind him was Walter Kontak, the only Brooklyn-born Jewish navy veteran with an Oxford degree, at least on this faculty. Kontak, long-time head of the university's political science department, was the professor who had supervised the senior essay that was required for an honour's degree. Mulroney's senior paper was nothing if not ambitious. It ran to 100 pages and dealt with "The Politics of Quebec, 1933-58."

In the summer of 1983, Walter Kontak rummaged it out of the university archives to see how it stood up. "It seems to me," Kontak said, "that it's a very good piece of work of its kind." The difficulty in researching it, Mulroney remembered a quarter of a century later, was in finding books on contemporary Quebec history in the St. F.X. library, which was not then a great repository of books. Or, for that matter, in practically any other university library. "Since 1960," Mulroney said, "nearly everyone and his cousin has written a book about Quebec. But back then, Duplessis was still alive, [so] no one did, [because] he would have thrown them in jail."

So what Mulroney did, in the summer between his junior and senior years, was go around and interview people. In Quebec City, he met Josie Quart, a future Tory senator who would support his 1976 leadership bid from her wheelchair. Her grandson, Gary Ouellet, would become a Grande Allée attorney and one of Mulroney's Mafia in both leadership campaigns.

48

At the McGill library in Montreal, Mulroney discovered a treasure trove of articles in back issues of *Saturday Night* and *Maclean's*, and he came on one jewel in Professor Herbert Quinn's 1946 master's thesis analysing the 1944 election that restored Duplessis to office after the five-year Liberal reign of Adélard Godbout.

Interestingly, the authors Mulroney cited on French Canada would become acknowledged French-Canadian scholars in the next generation, fixtures in virtually any learned paper or article dealing with Quebec. It was not just that he relied heavily on Mason Wade's epic history, *The French Canadians*. He also quoted the likes of Gérard Bergeron, from an article on Quebec political parties published in the *University of Toronto Quarterly*. In the next two decades, Bergeron would become a noted constitutional authority. But back in the summer of 1958, hardly anyone, certainly hardly anyone in English-speaking Canada, had ever heard of him. It was the same with Duplessis scholar Robert Rumilly, nationalist historian Michel Brunet, and *Le Devoir* editorialist Jean-Marc Léger, who would become René Lévesque's delegate-general in Brussels. The scholarly and journalistic sources that he quoted then would become acknowledged authorities only much later on. It was interesting for someone of his tender years – Mulroney was then only nineteen years old – that he took the trouble to inform himself not only of the heroic perspective of the English-Canadian historians, but of the francophone survivalist stream of historical scholarship.

"To the French," he wrote, "[Confederation] is a pact between French and English, which guarantees each group an equal right to its own faith, language, laws and customs." A committee of constitutional scholars could edit that for a week, but they could not improve on it as a succinct statement of the Canadian duality. And the young Mulroney found a quote from Pierre Chauveau, Quebec's first Premier after Confederation, making an analogy between Canada and the double staircase of the Château de Chambord:

English and French, we climb by a double flight of stairs towards the destinies reserved for us on this continent, without knowing one another, without meeting each other, and without even seeing each other except on the landing of politics.

Quebec politics was, indeed, as Mulroney wrote in his introduction, "a unique and intricate puzzle." He had set out to chronicle the age of Maurice Duplessis, and he ended up on a personal voyage of discovery of French-Canadian history, from the Quebec Act of 1774 and the Constitution Act of 1791, to the Act of Union in 1840 and Confederation in 1867, down to the series of misunderstandings and the unfortunate occurrences in English Canada – notably the Manitoba Act of 1890 and Regulation 17 in Ontario – that effectively limited the scope of the French-Canadian community to Quebec.

Mulroney demonstrated more than a sense of history and considerable flair for writing in his senior paper, he was also clearly someone his fellow Quebecers would describe as "un gars sympathique," someone who understood them, cared for their concerns, and felt as they did.

"Well, I'll be damned," Mulroney said when shown his senior paper on a charter from Ottawa to Nova Scotia. "Where the hell did you get that? I haven't seen that in twenty-five years." In the 1960's, he had given his only copy to one of his law partners, Tommy Montgomery, for his wife to read.

"It's pretty well-written stuff, if I do say so myself," he said as he thumbed through it the next day on the flight back from Port Hawkesbury. "Except for the overwritten parts, of course. In those days, in college, a sense of economy never intrudes. You use a big word or an adjective wherever you can."

And so W.A.C. Bennett, the Social Credit ruler of British Columbia, was referred to as a "suave Conservative apostate." Saskatchewan received a mention as "Canada's most fecund wheat province," while Ontario had been governed by the Tories for "nigh on two decades."

When Mulroney was asked where a kid from a North Shore town had got himself such a fancy vocabulary he said that when he would go home for the summer from college, "I would read all summer, read everything I could find, and when I would come across a word whose meaning I didn't understand, I would research it." He was particularly taken by Winston Churchill's epic *History of the English-Speaking Peoples*, as well as his *History of the Second World War*. And in later years, Mulroney's mother still remembered him "going to bed with his list of words to look up."

For Irene and Ben Mulroney, it was a day of their dreams when their son graduated from college in the spring of 1959. Now grown out to his full height of 6'1", Brian Mulroney stood between his parents to have his picture taken in cap and gown and holding a sheepskin rolled up in a tube. It is a picture like any other, with his mother in her best dress with a fur collar, with a smile as wide as the St. Lawrence River at Baie Comeau, and his father, in a self-effacing, almost downcast way, standing off to the other side. By now, his twenty-year-old son stood half a head taller. But in Brian Mulroney's mind, his father would always be ten feet tall.

The friends Brian Mulroney had made at St. F.X. for the most part would remain his friends and stand behind him when he later reached for the brass ring. It was the beginning of a pattern. Once people turned up in Mulroney's life, they had a way of reappearing. The Antigonish years marked the start of his network. And among his contemporaries, he was already marked as a man to watch.

4

THE LAVAL
GANG

"Of all the times in my life, Laval was the golden years," Brian Mulroney said some twenty years after he had graduated from the law faculty of Canada's oldest university. "I don't remember it in any way other than a very pleasurable experience, of being young and living in exciting times and a great learning experience, learning every day."

If Mulroney could have picked his time to come of age in the twentieth century, he would have found no time to compare with the excitement and exhilaration of Quebec City during the years he lived there, from 1960 to 1964. First of all, at Laval, the university authorities abdicated their campus in the old Quartier-Latin, leaving behind only the law and social science faculties, who literally took over the walled city while their contemporaries staged a forced retreat to the new campus in suburban Ste. Foy, a spectacularly modern place that looked like the Brasilia of higher learning. And then, Mulroney's years at law school coincided with Quebec's Quiet Revolution and the creation of a modern state just up the street in the legislature, and after hours in the convivial atmosphere of the lobby bar of the Château Frontenac, then the only big hotel in town, and the place where politicians, lobbyists, contractors, and journalists met and mingled after hours and long into the night.

It was here that a young law student named Mulroney struck up more than a passing friendship with Daniel Johnson, then Leader of the Opposition. Johnson's charm was legendary, but in those euphoric days of the Liberal reign, hardly anyone would waste his time talking to the leader of the discredited Union Nationale, whose regime was cursed as a darkness and whose activities in government were even then being investigated by the Salvas Commission, the first in a long line of spectacular Quebec inquiries.

"He was a pariah in the Château Frontenac," Mulroney would recall many years later. "Nobody would talk to him. I mean nobody." But Mulroney did. And Johnson, on his way down to the Château, would stop in at Mulroney's boarding house on the Rue St-Louis and ask a certain Miss Angeline Fortin, who ran it, if she wouldn't mind telling *l'irlandais*, the Irish kid, that the Leader of the Opposition was waiting for him. "Many a night, many, many a night," Mulroney recalled, "I'd walk down with him, sit around the bar and chat, shoot the breeze."

With this time and place went the people of Mulroney's era, one of the most remarkable groups, as measured by their station in later life, that ever went through Laval or any other Canadian university. In his class, as well as in the years just ahead and behind, they turned out a generation of political activists who manned the ramparts of the Quiet Revolution or implemented the designs of French Power in Ottawa. Some of them chose political options that would take them down divergent paths, and though they might become mortal political foes, they would always remain friends.

In Mulroney's faculty, in his year alone, there were two future cabinet ministers, Pierre de Bané in Ottawa and Clément Richard in Quebec, several senior public servants, such as Associate Deputy Justice Minister Paul-Arthur Gendreau, and outstanding attorneys, such as Raynold Langlois, who would be a principal author of the Trudeau government's patriation package. And Lucien Bouchard, who fit into no category except that he saw the romance of life and the fun of politics, until some of the fun went out of it for him in the early 1980's when, as the Lévesque government's chief negotiator, he spent six exhausting months outmanoeuvring Quebec's public service unions. It was a masterful performance to behold, like watching a chess master going around a room playing novices one move at a time.

Even then, in the first flush of the age of Jean Lesage, there was one whom some classmates sized up as a man who would be prime minister. At least, Pierre de Bané remembered thinking as much. He was also struck by Mulroney's maturity. "If you look at his behaviour, he hasn't changed in twenty years," said the future federal Fisheries Minister. "At the time, he had the maturity of a man of forty-five or fifty. On the other hand, Brian missed his youth."

He nearly missed out on the Laval experience and was a year late in getting there. In his senior yearbook picture at St. F.X., it was noted that his "future plans point to Laval University and a career in law." But somewhere along the way, Mulroney got sidetracked and spent a year in Halifax at the Dalhousie law faculty. "It was tough to choose between Nova Scotia and Laval," he said later. "I got an entrance scholarship to Dal. I found out you could transfer, and then I was ill for part of the year. By Christmas, it was pretty clear I wanted to transfer. I enjoyed it, but I wanted to get back to Quebec. So at Christmas I went home and decided to transfer to Laval, with a series of accepted credits." While Mulroney went through the motions of finishing up his first year of common law studies at Dalhousie, he immersed himself also in Robert Stanfield's campaign for re-election in the spring of 1960.

"He was with us for the duration," recalled Finlay MacDonald, who was involved in all the Stanfield campaigns from 1953. In Halifax, where MacDonald was running the show with Dalton Camp, Mulroney became the voice on their radio spots. And then, MacDonald said, "Brian took off and visited every Catholic parish from Yarmouth to Cape Breton."

In the summer of 1960, Mulroney went home to Quebec. If there was any doubt about his decision, it evaporated in the election of Jean Lesage on June 22. It was clear that, with the change of government after sixteen years of Unioniste rule, Quebec City would be an interesting place for the next four years. Of his decision to transfer to Laval, he said nearly a quarter of a century later: "I'm glad now that I did. It turned out to be much more interesting."

Other than the way they hung together, there was another distinguishing characteristic about Mulroney's class. "It was the year of the invasion of the English," said Lucien Bouchard, just out of classical college in Jonquière in the Kingdom of the Saguenay. "It was the year Westmount invaded Laval."

There was Michael Meighen, later president of the Conservative Party, and Peter White, later a key backroom operative for Mulroney in both his runs for the Tory leadership. Others included Peter Kilburn, Brian Buchanan, and Paul Amos, as well as a couple of local Jewish kids named Sonny Mass and Michael Kastner. And there was a boy from Baie Comeau named Brian Mulroney. They were the object of considerable curiosity and attention along the Grande Allée where, as Bouchard noted, "they were well received" because they were considered prize catches for the daughters of the bourgeois of Sillery.

"For me anyway, with my simplistic outlook," Bouchard said, "because they were all English and well dressed, they had to be rich, and since Brian was as well dressed as any of them, he had to be rich."

In fact, Mulroney was a stranger to them, as he was to money.

54

Many years later Mike Meighen recalled how Mulroney introduced himself. "On the first day I arrived," Meighen said, "Brian came up to me and said, 'You speak English, too, eh?'"

From this rather arresting group of non-francophones, fully 10 per cent of their law class, Mulroney was as difficult to miss as his chin. "Rather quickly," Lucien Bouchard observed, "he distinguished himself from the others." For even then, he had a way of making friends, if not influencing people.

"Brian was the only guy in the class everybody liked," Pierre de Bané said in 1984. "He was very popular with all the guys, left-right, federalist-indépendantiste, English or French. He crossed all those lines." But while he was crossing lines, he was also creating a second Mulroney Mafia, gathering to himself the people Bouchard called "les inconditionnels de Mulroney."

Because most professors had their own law practices, their students' classes would be split from eight to ten in the morning and two to four in the afternoon. In the four-hour interval, the professors went out and made some money while their students went out and had some fun.

The Mulroney gang could usually be found at one of three hangouts: in the basement bar of the old Clarendon Hotel, a rather dingy place they called La Chapelle; at La Page Blanche on the Rue St. Jean; or at the Café de la Paix on the Rue Desjardins. "That's where we hung out, all the time," Mulroney would say. "You could always find us in one of those three places. Either that or we were up in the National Assembly."

They spent their hours between classes doing a good deal of drinking and womanizing and talking things over. In short, as Mulroney said many years later, "We lived bohemian lives in the Quartier-Latin. I mean, hell, we were having the time of our lives."

Quebec City in those days, as he said, "was in constant ferment." And the students from the big universities, Laval and Montréal, were very much a part of it. "There were only three or four universities in Quebec at the time," he said, "so we all knew each other by and large, the leaders of the various associations. So it was quite a generation. And our class was very much a part of it." Mulroney would become president of his class. In other faculties and other years at Laval, were Jean Garon and Denis de Belleval, future members of the Lévesque government. André Ouellet was in the law faculty for a year or so. At Montréal, there were future Lévesque ministers Pierre Marois and Bernard Landry, and prominent federalists such as Francis Fox. "I didn't know Brian at the time," said Fox, who would become a good friend.

"But I was very much aware of who he was."

As for the life in the provincial capital, Mulroney remembered that the politicians could always be found in one of two places, the legislature or the Château. "We weren't far behind," he said. "And so there was always a great deal of activity and fun going on. And it became a mixture of study, political involvement, social activism, journalism – it became a constant fabric of our lives, which kept us involved, and which was mostly social activism, as opposed to partisan activity. We were always involved with conferences and debates, it was very exciting."

One such conference, above all, made headlines across the country in English and in French for nearly a week, and it pulled the Mulroney gang together for the next generation. It was the Congrès des Affaires Canadiennes at Laval on November 15-18, 1961. It started out as an idea from Peter White, and it ended up being a seminal event of the Quiet Revolution. The conference theme was "Le Canada, experience ratée ou réussie," failure or success. With speakers ranging from Justice Minister Davie Fulton to Premier Jean Lesage, who opened and closed the conference, it was bound to attract some attention. And with some of the participants in the workshops, from journalists André Laurendeau and Gérard Pelletier to academics Maurice Lamontagne and Mason Wade, to René Lévesque and Marcel Chaput, well, there were bound to be some fireworks.

For four days, it seemed nothing else of consequence was going on in Quebec or anywhere else. Fulton opened with a dramatic pledge to patriate the constitution with an amending formula satisfactory to the provinces by the time of the country's centennial celebrations in five years' time. Lesage closed out with a warning that unless the power-sharing arrangements of the constitution were rearranged in a manner pleasing to the provinces, it would mean the end of Confederation. In between, there were a few gestures and quite a bit of gesticulating, and a lot of big, bold headlines.

"Everything seemed to stop during the week of that Congrès," Mulroney said many years later. "Everything in Quebec. It was just a fluke. Nothing major seemed to have happened in the rest of the country that week, or around the world, as a result of which the Congrès certainly got more publicity than we anticipated. I think it was just a major, major event, eight-column headlines on a regular basis.

"It was a very exciting and positive kind of thing," he continued. "When you look back on it, we were twenty, I guess, twenty-one and twenty-two years of age, and this was a pretty positive and constructive thing for young students to be doing, to be engaged in, to be organizing a national congress and to be anticipating the kinds of problems that are still with us today, and trying to find some solutions. It was unduly ambitious as it turned out. But I look at some of those names, and they're all very much still with us, and it was a very exciting time."

Fulton and Lesage were the bookends of the conference in the ballroom of the Château Frontenac, and for the remaining three days, the plenaries and workshops were held in the amphitheatre of the medical faculty out on the new suburban campus in Ste. Foy. The Justice Minister and the Premier made headlines with packaged performances. But the remaining three days were live and in colour, extemporized performances that produced something resembling guerilla theatre. The way the workshops were set up, one interlocutor was a francophone and the other was an anglophone. And the themes were guaranteed to throw off some sparks. Gérard Pelletier and Murray Ballantyne, who had the appearance of a progressively-minded young WASP from central casting, debated the question "What French Canadians have against us," a new and intriguing twist of an old question that francophones used to ask themselves about the English. In the second session, *Le Devoir* editor André Laurendeau and constitutional scholar Eugene Forsey went at it on the infernal question of "Canada: One Nation or Two."

René Lévesque and James Mallory argued "The Proper Role of the State in Canada, federally and provincially." Separatist pioneer Marcel Chaput and McGill political science professor Michael Oliver debated "The Future, Separation, Integration, or . . . ." With these people, and these topics, in that setup, there was certain to be a good deal of lively controversy. The participants disappointed neither the students nor the news media who flocked to the new campus.

"You need us more than we need you," Lévesque was quoted by Bob McKenzie, then in the Quebec press gallery for the *Montreal Gazette*. "I may be wrong but I think we don't need you as a group, and I think it is a growing feeling." Confederation, Lévesque continued, had to be "re-thought, re-organized or re-interpreted," to give Quebec "sovereignty in its education, in social security and in the economy." And in a statement that could have framed his referendum question nearly twenty years later, Lévesque said, "Sovereignty is essential, perhaps not complete sovereignty – there will always be things like monetary policy which will escape us – but French Canadians must be given their economic emancipation."

57

Amidst all this constitutional turmoil, there was a daily soap opera as to whether Marcel Chaput would even attend the conference. The president of the Rassemblement pour l'indépendance nationale, Dr. Chaput was also an employee of the federal government with the Defence Research Board. He had been warned that if he attended the conference he would be fired by Defence Minister Douglas Harkness. Even Chaput's journey became part of the story. While changing trains at Montreal West, he was interviewed by a young *Montreal Star* reporter named Peter Desbarats, to whom he insisted that civil servants were entitled to their opinions on their own time, and he was on legitimate leave from his work. Chaput made a triumphal entry into Quebec, where a group of RIN militants cheered his arrival at the old Gare du Palais railway station. "Only the Governor-General can fire me," Chaput declared confidently when asked about his future employment prospects in the federal capital. Chaput went on to create headlines across the province with his declaration at the conference that Quebec was a colony of Ottawa, and the only solution was separation and independence.

When he finished his speech, Peter White came forward to inform him that the organizers had just received a telegram from Harkness, notifying Chaput that he had been suspended and, in effect, fired. The person sitting beside Chaput as he received the news was the moderator of the panel, a second-year law student named Brian Mulroney.

It was one of those moments that could be frozen in time as a turning point in Quebec and Canadian affairs. The federal government had given the separatist movement its first martyr, and one who had not yet expired. "They have taken the separatist cause to the people," Chaput proclaimed as he left the hall. "Separatism has so far been a matter of doctrine, a thing discussed by intellectuals. Now I think they have personalized it. They have brought it out into the realm of fact."

The Chaput affair was by no means the last sensational story to come out of the conference. At the closing plenary session the following day, socialist MP Doug Fisher shook up the joint with a deliberately provocative reply to Lévesque's appearance of forty-eight hours earlier. "René Lévesque said in his speech, 'We don't need you,'" Fisher began. "Well, I'm tempted to say, 'That goes double.'" Fisher continued that if he was speaking to his constituents in the Lakehead city of Port Arthur, "their reaction would be 'What have the French to offer us?'" For most of his voters, Fisher went on, the French culture meant "Maurice Richard and

Lilli St. Cyr." It was many years before Douglas Fisher would live down that remark, or before it was evident that he was speaking for the average voter in his riding, not for himself. But in his own way, he succeeded in being as outlandish as Lévesque.

Altogether, it was quite a show. When André Laurendeau arrived back in Montreal, he was moved to write an editorial entitled "An exciting experience" that ran November 18 under *Le Devoir's* banner at the top of page one.

"The atmosphere was one of the warmest, one of the most vibrant I've seen in many years, at least in a group as mixed as that," wrote the future co-chairman of the landmark Royal Commission on Bilingualism and Biculturalism. "At Laval," he noted, "even the conference was the result of anglo-franco collaboration." And he named the executive: Peter White, president; Michael Meighen, Brian Mulroney, and Michel Cogger, vice-presidents; and so on down the list of the organizing committee. These three, plus Jean Bazin and Bernard Roy, would form the heart of Mulroney's Laval Mafia in the long quest for the Conservative leadership.

Bazin, who was a year ahead of the Mulroney gang, was a student leader in his own right. At one point, Bazin lost a toss of a coin with an Albertan named Joe Clark as to who would become president of the national campus Conservative organization, the loser becoming vice-president. Bazin went on to become the president of the Canadian Union of Students. As for Roy, who would become Mulroney's best man at his wedding, law partner, and chief Quebec organizer, he was not a part of those student activities. He was a varsity hockey player with a reputation for being as tough as nails on the ice and a nattily dressed man about the Latin Quarter, where his colleagues dubbed him the French-Canadian Ivy Leaguer. Roy came from generations of Quebec City Liberal stock – he was a great-nephew of long-time Liberal Premier Alexandre Taschereau, who governed Quebec for fifteen years before Maurice Duplessis came on the scene in 1936. But Roy and Mulroney did a fair amount of studying and socializing together.

Mulroney's political gang clearly owed its formation to the Congress of Canadian Affairs. "The Congress was the thing that got us all together," Michel Cogger said more than twenty years later. "But had that Congress not been a success, had it not reflected glory on Laval, it is far from certain that we would have been allowed to finish school. There was the real possibility of, one, Laval being disgraced, and two, the thing running up a big deficit. Mulroney rolled up his sleeves and went to work, and personally, with help from White, got the donations to cover the deficit."

What had started as a modest $6,000 project funded by the student council had quickly become a $50,000 extravaganza. Mulroney sold ads for the program, and he pushed down the discretionary costs. "He would go around telling speakers that André Laurendeau had waived his fee," Cogger said, "and so shamed others into doing so."

If the Mulroney gang was formed out of the conference, it was Peter White who created the Congress, borrowing on an idea from the McGill Conference on World Affairs, which had been organized by two law students named Yves Fortier and Pierre Lamontagne, who would become two of Mulroney's Liberal friends in Montreal.

"Peter had a few dollars, and a great sense of freedom," Mulroney said, "which didn't necessarily involve coming to class. In fact, I remember that if White would show up for a law class, we would give him a standing ovation, because he'd make one about once every month. So he was very committed to this and unquestionably it would never have taken place without his dedication. Peter was the chairman, he was the boss, and I didn't really want any title, but then it became clear they were going to need money and organizational direction, and guest speakers, and I got guest speakers and things like that."

As for his student activities, they were by no means confined to Quebec City. Early in 1961, Mulroney was one of six young political activists invited to Ottawa to participate in a round-table discussion with the political editors of *Maclean's* for a special issue they were preparing called "The Young Canadians." Mulroney and Ted Rogers represented the Tories; David Greenspan and Jean David were there for the Liberals; John Brewin and Jean-Pierre Fournier were representatives of the old CCF. For an entire day, they sat around talking with Peter C. Newman and Peter Gzowski. Mulroney, at twenty-one, was the youngest member of the group. He was also the most talkative. By now executive vice-president of the Conservative Students' Federation, he explained that he became interested in politics because of "the opportunities that existed then. This was in 1955, and the Conservative party was down and out, if you will, and I became aware that students and the young people had quite a bit to say, and were given the leeway and opportunity to say it." He said he got into politics not as "some sort of holy crusade," but to "get my feet wet." As for getting things done, he claimed the fact that

60

students were now able to deduct their tuition fees on their income tax for the first time was the result of initiative by the student Conservative federation, presented to cabinet by Ted Rogers.

Newman tried to twig the young men in the neat suits by asking whether "tomorrow's politicians will do anything different from today's." Mulroney replied that "all young people who are interested in politics have one main aim, and that is to do the best they can to advance the welfare of every citizen in the country." While this sounded sophomoric and platitudinous, there was a hard edge of pragmatism in his subsequent observation that "there are different ways of doing that. The CCF party seems to have forgotten that you cannot do anything unless you are in office; you have to get into office before you can implement anything." Newman and Gzowski were not satisfied with what clearly were rather pat answers. They kept prodding and pushing. "Do you think the politician of the future will also change?" Newman asked. "What do you think will be his attitude towards patronage, for instance?"

Mulroney jumped right in. "I think his attitude is going to be drastically changed from the attitude of those who are in government today," he replied. "The young people of today are going to strengthen the nation at the cost of partisan politics, and they are going to take a much more idealistic view of things 20 years from now than we do today."

That was in 1961, before Mulroney discovered some of the harsh verities of politics, especially the hunger of an opposition party for the perks, privileges, and patronage of power. Fifteen years later, in his first leadership campaign, he would become fond of quoting Senator Allister Grosart, the former Diefenbaker aide: "What this party wants is its two feet right in the trough." And by the time he finally became Tory leader in 1983, Mulroney had achieved such a reputation as a "patroneux" that he was finally able to laugh about it. The prospect of Senate reform with an enlarged upper chamber, he joked privately one day, would hold the possibility "of more seats than even I can fill."

But in 1961, he saw things through the eyes of a twenty-one-year-old hanging around Ottawa for the first time, as one of Dief's student advisers. And then after finishing his second year of law school in the spring of 1962, he was taken on as summer help in the office of Agriculture Minister Alvin Hamilton, who was looking for a window on French-speaking Canada. Hamilton's long-time personal secretary, Muriel Hunt, who would still be with him in 1984, remembered that "of course, he just charmed all the women." Hamilton, though he said his memory sometimes played tricks on him, remembered him as a hard and willing worker who did everything from delivering semen to farmers for an experimental program with Charolais cattle to drafting position papers on how to open up the department to more francophones.

With an election that year, in which the June 18 vote saw Diefenbaker's mighty majority reduced to a tenuous minority, Mulroney had the opportunity to travel with his minister to his home riding of Qu'Appelle in Saskatchewan and throughout the West. This was also the spring of Mulroney's brief and unremunerated radio career as a stringer for CKRM in Regina, the station that beamed into Hamilton's riding. On a stop at the radio station, Mulroney mentioned to somebody that Alvin would be out of the riding for the duration of the campaign, stumping in the West, and would they be interested in "reasonably objective reports on how he was doing." With that deep voice, and a free holler, to cover the minister's riding in his absence, the station jumped at the chance. "So I'd call them twice a day," Mulroney would remember, "and I'd say, 'Brian Mulroney reporting from downtown Dauphin, Manitoba. Alvin Hamilton today received a standing ovation from 800 people.' Sure, I reported on all his campaign, throughout the West, and East. We were everywhere."

Alvin was covered for that campaign, but in the spring election of the following year, which finally saw Diefenbaker's defeat on April 8, Mulroney stayed home at Laval, though he did organize a claque of faithful supporters to serve as a rent-a-crowd for Diefenbaker's whistlestop tour through eastern Quebec. "We got on the train at Lévis," Michael Meighen said. "And we'd get off at every stop and we were Dief's crowd."

In his class back at Laval, Mulroney was not remembered as the most conscientious student. "He was always," Pierre de Bané maintained, "the last one to study." But if they didn't burn much midnight oil, the students in those days had the benefit of some pretty outstanding legal talent. Mulroney would remember "seeing Louis St. Laurent in my first year," not as one of his profs, because the former Prime Minister taught in third year. "But I can still see him in the corridor, on the third floor of the law faculty, teaching law in 1960."

The professors included Julien Chouinard, who would go on to an outstanding career as secretary to the Quebec cabinet, and later as chairman of the federal inquiry into bilingual air traffic control procedures, before he was promoted from the Quebec Court of Appeal to the Supreme Court of Canada in 1979. Yves

Pratte, another future Supreme Court Justice, taught corporate law. And Louis Marceau, who went on to the Federal Court of Canada, taught his students how to write up a bond issue.

But there was one professor, more than any other, who made a deep and lasting impression on Brian Mulroney. His name was Robert Cliche, whom Mulroney came to love like his own father. Cliche was a self-described bastard socialist. The first leader of the NDP's Quebec wing, Cliche always used to say that he was a socialist during working hours and a capitalist on his own time. In time, he would chair the Quebec inquiry into the construction industry that would thrust Mulroney into the news in the mid-1970's.

There were several distinguishing characteristics about Professor Cliche, even in those days. He loved his native Beauce region of Quebec, which he considered the centre of the universe. He loved to have a good time. And he hated injustice and intolerance. All these passions would come together in his two-hour afternoon lectures in trial procedure. "He was the only one who gave two-hour lectures," Mulroney said. "And he'd stop at the Château before and have a couple of gins. So he'd act out what you would do in a trial. So every point of law, of procedure, that he developed, he illustrated with one of his most recent cases. This thing was terrific, it was like going to a play every time. We'd just roll on the floor. I mean, we learned a lot, but he was the most entertaining speaker I've ever seen in my life. I've never seen anyone that good."

From the exposure to Cliche and the others in four hours of class a day, Mulroney and his classmates somehow muddled through on the academic side, in spite of their heavy load of student activities. "I don't think any of us, with a few exceptions, burnt up the academic track," he would say. "People tend to joke, including me, about the secondary position we put our studies into. But I think there's more wishful thinking than anything else. You know, this was a pretty rigorous schedule, four hours of class a day, and pretty demanding stuff."

Mulroney was working hard at something else in those years, improving and perfecting his French. "His French wasn't all that good in those days," said Lucien Bouchard. "He was, in effect, a French student. He learned fast, asked a lot of questions, and spoke French so much that today I can't recall ever having had a conversation with him in English."

Mulroney would pick up the idiom and the jargon quickly enough, but immersing himself in French law books was a daunting task. "Well, you see," he explained, "I had been out of

Quebec, and Baie Comeau, which is not the Lycée in any case, from the time I was twelve or something. And so while I certainly had a good vocabulary by Baie Comeau standards – I always had the accent from the time I was three or four – I now arrived at a pretty challenging university, and I obviously had a lot of work to do. All the lectures were in French, everything was in French." And there were people around, like Bouchard and Pierre de Bané, who had, as he observed, "a pretty substantial culture."

Nevertheless, it wasn't for their academic records that Mulroney's class would be remembered at Laval, but for the mark they made in later life, owing largely to their intense commitment to student activities.

As he had been at St. F.X., Mulroney was involved in another model parliament. But this one, held in the public accounts committee room of the legislature, had a different flavour and a different texture from the one in the Maritimes. In a very real sense, it was in another country.

"Different?" Mulroney repeated the question many years after the 1962 model parliament. "Sure. Everything was different. First of all, it was all in French. Secondly, the players were completely different. Thirdly, the problems were different." They were the problems of Confederation, the questions of country. Mulroney sat as leader of the opposition. And Jean Garon, who would become René Lévesque's agriculture minister, was the Prime Minister, "the first separatist Prime Minister in Quebec," as Mulroney always recalled with considerable mirth.

And then there was Mulroney's constant involvement in campus Conservative politics, which was somewhat less unusual then than it would be for the next generation of young Quebecers. "You've got to remember," said Lucien Bouchard, "that we had just buried Duplessis, and there was nothing but *bleus* around Quebec." And *les bleus* were in office, if not in power, in Ottawa in the government of John Diefenbaker.

Mulroney seemed to have his own lines of communication to the Chief, who was bewildered and confused by goings-on in Quebec and was always looking for advice or what he called "stuff" on Quebec. Mulroney, his one-time national youth co-chairman, could give him some stuff on the phone. None of his classmates, gathered in their various hangouts, ever believed he really talked to the Prime Minister.

"We all thought it was bullshit," Michael Meighen said much later. Pierre de Bané would recall that "Mulroney would say he had just been consulted by the Chief. I had a lot of difficulty believing that, until the day he brought Diefenbaker into class."

Mulroney had produced the Prime Minister on a dare from his pals. If he was such a great crony of Diefenbaker, why wouldn't he come down to the law school to talk to the students?

"I talked to the Chief about it, and he said, sure," Mulroney recalled. "So the Chief arrives. I produced him right in the law school for the boys, and he stayed, and he spoke, and he was hilarious. And then they had a big reception for him in the library. Dief loved it, and all the boys loved it. I got them all there, all the disbelievers and the cynics, I got all the boys there, just about stampeding themselves to get their picture taken with the Chief."

And in his normal routine, Mulroney would come into regular contact with Daniel Johnson, who introduced him to Scotch and water, and to a few home truths about the game of parliamentary politics. "I was never a partisan of the Union Nationale, I was a partisan of Daniel Johnson," Mulroney recalled. "Dan Johnson was funny, he had a great sense of humour, and he was a partisan. I remember him saying to me one day, he said, 'Listen Brian, I'm telling you the basic rule of the game, which never changes, and that's that we always shoot at the Grits, qu'on tire toujours sur les rouges.' And that's what he did."

But in those days when the law students used to hang out in the visitors' gallery during question period, the undisputed star of the legislature was Jean Lesage. "Lesage himself had attributes of genius in regard to his knowledge of the legislation that was before the House," Mulroney recalled. "Unquestionably. I remember the debate on the Quebec Pension Plan, and Lesage, his command of the details, which was really superb."

Mulroney managed to strike up something of a relationship with the Premier, a fairly remarkable fact when it is considered that Lesage, who had developed some pretensions of grandeur that would have been worthy of Charles De Gaulle, would not be considered likely to waste too much of his time on a young law student, and a *bleu* at that. But Mulroney talked him into buying the back page of the program for the Congrès des Affaires Canadiennes. And he then persuaded the Premier to come on the weekly public affairs show he was hosting on the local English-language television station. "Here he was, twenty-one or twenty-two years old," recalled journalist Bob McKenzie, who occasionally appeared on the program as a panelist, "and he gets them to give him his own show. And then he gets the Premier to come on it. And he was just a kid. It was pretty impressive."

Years later, Mulroney developed a personal and professional relationship with the former Premier, when they sat together on the board of an insurance company. Occasionally, they would find themselves in each other's company, as they did in Paris one day in the late 1970's, comparing the importance of the Quiet Revolution to the excitement around Quebec after the accession to power of the Parti Québécois in 1976.

For Lesage, as for Mulroney, there was no comparison at all. Lesage said that 1960 marked the beginning of a new Quebec and a new Canada, with all the good and bad things that went with it, whereas 1976 marked a turn in the road, an important turn but no more than that.

"I had to sort of smile somewhat in 1976," Mulroney said, "when some of these journalists suggested that things were just beginning. There was no comparison, no comparison whatsoever to the sense of excitement that swept Quebec in 1960, to that which we saw in 1976.

"In 1976," he continued, "you had a highly sophisticated, pluralistic society, which opted for a different kind of government which might or might not have heralded profound change. In 1960, what Quebec had was the beginning of the process of overturning 200 years of history. Everything was brought into question in that period. From the church, to education with the Parent Commission, to trade unionism, which began to blossom to the political system itself. What happened after 1976 will be remembered with good and bad emotions. You'll remember such things as the reform of party financing and Bill 101, and there will be positive and negative aspects to those things. The fundamental difference was that they were peripheral, not unimportant, but peripheral to the main thrust of society that was already well engaged and well in train. That happened in 1960, and there was just a world of difference between them."

And that's what Mulroney and Lesage agreed upon, one rainy afternoon in Paris, many years later. "The guy who built the road was the guy who was there in 1960," Mulroney said. "And that's the difference."

And there was Brian Mulroney, a hitchhiker at the side of that road, going along for the ride.

There was one other influence on Mulroney during those politically formative years, distant and indirect, but in many ways the most profound of all. It was John F. Kennedy, a man he never met but whom he knew from afar, from television and magazines and books. For anyone of Mulroney's generation, Kennedy was an heroic figure, and a role model. "He was unique, absolutely unique," Mulroney said in 1984. "I mean even today, there's that influence, and this is nearly twenty-five years later. In those days, it was pervasive."

In the years that Mulroney was a law student on the Laval campus, Kennedy was running for and being President of the United States, with the high-minded rhetoric and the high style that influenced young people far beyond the borders of the United States.

"I think it was his style," Mulroney agreed. "The human quality, the sense of romance and public service, and the Peace Corps and the trip to Berlin. We were all captivated by it. I don't think there's any way that anyone of my age could have gone through life interested in politics and public life, and not have been deeply affected and influenced by President Kennedy. I mean it just could not have happened, unless I suppose someone knew him personally, which none of us did, and took a strong aversion to him, and for those reasons decided, or for ideological ones, and was committed to the opposition. All we knew was what we saw and what we heard, and that, we liked."

One of the things Mulroney saw and heard was an Irish Catholic President of the United States. And he acknowledged that might have had something to do with it. "It probably did, in a subliminal sense," Mulroney said. "I think he did a great deal to dissipate the stereotype of Irish Catholics and I think there was a certain amount of vicarious pride that went into witnessing his elegant performances and his witty, literate addresses. I think there was probably some of that. I can't remember anyone spelling it out, but I suspect it was probably true."

What they saw was the elegant way Kennedy carried himself, the pointed forefinger and the flashing wit and the carefully crafted rhetoric of his speechwriter, Ted Sorensen. The Sorensen influence, with the balanced phrases and clarion calls, would become strikingly evident in Mulroney's later speeches. Mulroney might say, of maintaining the health system, for example, that "no trust is more sacred, no cause more compelling," and the traces of the Sorensen style would be quite apparent to anyone who bothered to look. Many years later, Mulroney said he saw some favourable comment Sorensen had made about his speechwriting style. "And maybe," he said, "it is because I have unconsciously imitated that style, without realizing it. I write the way I write."

Like everyone else who lived through those days, Mulroney always remembered where he was on the afternoon of November 22, 1963. "I was having lunch with my old Aunt Jennie in Quebec

City, and my cousin Elmer came down the back stairs of this restaurant and said President Kennedy has been shot."

In a daze, Mulroney left the table, went to a gymnasium for a two-hour workout, "and never talked to anybody. I went home, turned on the TV, and went to bed." And the next day, he went to a friend's place down the street and stayed up most of the night keeping a vigil on television.

By this time, Mulroney was doing his graduate year of law and articling. Most of his gang had gone on to Montreal to do their fourth year, but Mulroney stayed in Quebec, and during this year of 1963-64 he became particularly close to Lucien Bouchard. Of all the people Mulroney would meet in the many worlds he would inhabit, none understood him better than Bouchard, a dark-eyed romantic. Of all the people Mulroney had known, Bouchard was the one who could look into his soul. "He was an amazingly literate guy, even in those days," Mulroney said. "He had a deep sense of literature and history. And he was a lot of fun, always a lot of fun."

While Bouchard and Mulroney solved the problems of the world in their old Quebec haunts, Bernard Roy was working as an articling student in Montreal. When he heard the city's biggest firm, then called Howard, Cate, Ogilvy, had an opening for another young employee, Roy told Mulroney about it. At this point, Mulroney had an offer to go home and join a firm in Baie Comeau, where he could make some money and consolidate his political base. "I had no intention of going to Montreal," he said. "It was weird that I wound up there. It was just a total fluke that I wound up in Montreal. Chances were ninety-nine to one against my going there."

The odds shortened considerably after one of the senior partners, John Kirkpatrick, reached Mulroney in the law library and offered to pay his way to Montreal for an interview. And so he came down with Roy for a Friday interview to which, as his friend recalled, "he arrived wearing his only suit."

Twenty years later, he could vividly recall discussing it over dinner with his father, who happened to be in Quebec City. They sat in the Marie-Antoinette restaurant and talked. "You can always go home," Ben Mulroney said. "But you may never get this kind of opportunity to work for a big law firm. See if it's what you like. And if you don't like it, you can always come home."

He never did.

5

THE YOUNG
LAWYER

For Lucien Bouchard, his friend's arrival in Montreal was a page out of Honoré de Balzac's *Père Goriot* in which Eugene de Rastignac, a notable character from *The Human Comedy*, asserts his claims on Paris. "A nous deux, maintenant," he tells a companion as they look down on the city from the heights.

"Rastignac was a provincial," Bouchard explained, "who had been studying in Paris for about a year, whose poverty and youth had until then seen the doors of a better world closed to him." And Bouchard was often reminded of that, that when he came to Montreal with Mulroney, his friend was Rastignac, and the city was theirs.

Montreal was that kind of a town for a young man starting out in the mid-1960's. In those years Montreal was a booming city, growing by leaps and bounds during the day and gloriously alive after dark.

"My God," Mulroney remembered twenty summers after he first came to the city in 1964, "Montreal was excitement and it was glamour, and it was progress, prosperity, and it was promise. I remember the excitement of Expo as they were building it, building the islands in the St. Lawrence, and getting the Expos baseball, and new buildings going up. And it seemed as if the boom was gonna go on forever. And that's what it was about, excitement, glamour. I mean, for someone like me, this was all brand new."

It was a good place to work, as well as to live, especially for a young lawyer just trying to get himself established. There was so much work, and the big corporate firms were growing so quickly, that old-boy networks could still flourish while room was found for new talent from the law faculties. "For someone starting out in law in the mid-sixties," recalled Mulroney friend and contemporary Stanley Hartt, called to the bar in the same year of 1965, "Montreal was an equal-opportunity town. There would be guys right out of school with mandates you wouldn't dream of having. Brian had influence and clients beyond his dreams."

But first he had to pay some dues and take a couple of unexpected lumps.

"He came in literally off the street," recalled Yves Fortier, then a total stranger but soon a fast friend. "I'm sitting in this office next to Tommy Montgomery, and Tommy calls me in to meet this guy. He had that deep, baritone voice, and said, 'Bonjour, M'sieu Fortier.'

"Obviously he knew a few things about me," continued Fortier, a Rhodes Scholar who would one day become president of the Canadian Bar Association. "He knew I had studied at Oxford, and found a way of fitting it into the conversation."

Tommy Montgomery was then one of the senior partners of the firm. After the job interview with Mulroney on that Friday afternoon in the spring of 1964, another of the senior partners, John Kirkpatrick, turned to Montgomery after Mulroney had left the room. "Put that man in any situation," he said, "and he'll scramble out of it."

They put their new employee to work in the general litigation department, "where they put everybody," Mulroney recalled. "You start out as a gopher, you do all that, all the files."

"When I first got to know Brian," said another contemporary, Art Campeau, "he was pleading bumpers."

Pleading bumpers, doing title searches, and dropping off lawyers' letters were not things Mulroney was going to spend his life doing. But then in the winter and spring of 1965, he had some other problems. At home in Baie Comeau over Christmas of 1964, his father went into the hospital and found out he had cancer. He had only six weeks to live. On February 16, 1965, he was dead. Mulroney was shattered by his father's death. Nearly twenty years later, he still could not speak of it without excusing himself to go blow his nose in the private washroom of the Opposition Leader's office.

And then, he flunked civil procedure in his bar exams.

"The code is the kitchen work," as Fortier later explained it.

"I wrote the same bar exam in 1965," said Stanley Hartt, "and I think I came first in the province, but I couldn't tell you in advance whether I had passed. In those days, you memorized the Civil Code and the Code of Procedure. It was about as useful as the Los Angeles telephone directory and about as difficult to learn. It was true torture and totally irrelevant to the practice of law. Flunking it was no great disgrace."

Disgrace or not, flunk it Mulroney did, and though he later

offered no excuses, he suggested one explanation. "Quite frankly," he said, "there was illness in the family, and there were amendments. If you go back and look you will see there were amendments to the code, nothing complicated," that had passed in the Quebec legislature after his father's death, while Mulroney was otherwise occupied with family business, settling his father's interment and moving his mother, brother Gary, and sister Barbara to Montreal in the spring.

"Very straightforward amendments," Mulroney said. "Nothing complicated. I didn't have the amendments. Three or four questions out of ten were on the new amendments. Right on. Just a stroke of luck. Nothing complicated about it. Strange exams as I remember. My guess as best as I can reconstruct is that I was just preoccupied with other things, and just paid no attention to the fact that there had been these amendments, not complicated, not difficult at all, that had been snuck through the Legislative Assembly in sort of like a burst of final activity. Not major things, because the Code of Procedure is not major. A ten-day delay rather than thirty, that kind of stuff. I didn't have the damn amendments, and they happened to ask four questions right on them. So that was it."

Mulroney wasn't the only member of his crowd to have flunked the procedure exam. Jean Bazin, back from his year as CUS president, had also tapped out. They needed to get away for a month to study for the rewrite, so Mulroney arranged to borrow Yves Fortier's country house in St. Sauveur, where the Laurentians begin some forty miles north of Montreal.

"What else do you do with the Code of Procedure except memorize it?" Mulroney said many years later. "I mean it was just that silly, that's all we did."

But that wasn't all. For the first and only time in his life, Mulroney grew a beard. "A great spade beard," Tommy Montgomery remembered. "With the magnificent foundation it had to grow on, it was perfectly square, like a sailor's beard." He didn't keep it for very long after rewriting and passing his procedure in mid-1965. In those days, young lawyers in his firm weren't encouraged to grow beards. "He left it on long enough to let people see it, and then off it came," Montgomery said. "He was not one to tempt fate for any minor thing like having a beard. He was no crusader about anything as chickenshit as that."

The setback with the procedure exam may have confirmed to others what Mulroney already knew about himself, that his career would unfold somewhere else than a courtroom. "The courtroom was not his forte," Fortier said. "There were too many

71

details, and he did not have enough patience for it."

It was soon becoming apparent to his associates, however, that Mulroney was extremely adept at negotiating out-of-court settlements with opposite counsel. Montgomery suggested that Mulroney might want to have a crack at the firm's fledgling labour department, which then consisted of one of the senior partners, Paul Renault, and another lawyer, Marius Bergeron.

As the firm and the department grew, the labour group would spin off from the main office on the seventh floor of Place Ville Marie to its own corporate cubbyhole two floors above. Both the smallness of the labour department and its isolation from the rest of the firm would encourage Mulroney's growth and independence. He was neither working with nor under the nose of the sixty other lawyers in the firm, which then billed itself as not only the largest in Montreal, Quebec, and Canada, but the largest in the Commonwealth.

Then, in the fall of 1966, Mulroney began to make a name for himself on the waterfront in Montreal. For a year and more, he appeared as a junior counsel of The Shipping Federation of Canada before Laurent Picard's Inquiry Commission on the St. Lawrence Ports. There were more lawyers appearing before the Picard Commission than there were ships in the harbour, and Mulroney was soon keeping and holding his own in some pretty fast company that included two future justices of the Supreme Court – Louis-Philippe Pigeon, chief counsel of the commission, and Antonio Lamer, who appeared with Phil Cutler's armada of lawyers in behalf of the International Longshoremen's Association.

Montreal, and all the ports on the east coast, were in a terrible crisis. "There was a lot of featherbedding and a lot of unrest," recalled David Angus, later Mulroney's chairman of the PC Canada fund but then a young Montreal maritime lawyer representing the Interprovincial Association of Stevedoring Contractors. There was tension not only between the longshoremen and the checkers on the docks, but between Angus's client, the stevedoring contractors, and Mulroney's client, the shipping federation, which did the bargaining on behalf of the stevedores with Cutler's client, the ILA.

In retrospect, the eastern ports were going through nothing more than a painful period of automation. As Angus later pointed out, it was "the pre-container era of break bulk cargo." Picard, the future CBC president, noted in his report at the end of 1967 that he had to face "tremendous difficulties, both legal and technical."

The commission came into existence after the Pearson government sanctioned an inflationary wage settlement to end a month-long strike that had paralysed the ports of Quebec. The government and Picard were looking for longer-term solutions – to modernize the eastern ports, civilize labour relations, end feather-bedding and pilfering in the ports, and so improve their productivity and international reputation, then at an all-time low. Picard's solution was simple but expensive. The longshoremen would receive job security and improved safety on the job. In return, the employers could modernize their operations and institute tight inventory controls. As a model of felicitous simplicity, Picard could not have improved upon this in his later years as dean of McGill's management faculty. And Mulroney could not have gone to a better school of formal procedure as a cover for informal tradeoffs.

"I learned a great deal of the process of royal commissions," Mulroney said in mid-1984, "and of the process of investigation and using evidence and laying it out and synthesizing it, and writing. You know, that's where I developed a sense of economy in writing."

He learned more than the operations of a royal commission. He developed, as he said, "an unusual understanding of the whole shipping industry. It was really quite unique," he said, "for a young man to have at that age, to have intimate knowledge of one of the most important industries in Canada. I guess Stanley Hartt and I were the only ones in the country at that age. Plus an intimate knowledge of all the players on the union side, the management side, the government side." Then, as he also said, "it had the human element, because of the historic waterfront relations."

It was well into the 1970's before the eastern Canadian ports, and especially Montreal, came through their painful period of transition and technological change. In the port of Montreal in 1968, there were 6.6-million hours of work to move four-million tons of cargo in a season. By 1984, Montreal had an enviable productivity record with 1.3-million hours of work to move 5.5-million tons of cargo.

But it would be many years before that kind of peace and productivity came to the port of Montreal. The ILA and the employers went through another contract haggle in 1969, and there were another illegal strike in 1972, a financial crisis among the employers in 1974, and another strike ended by law in 1975. In each of these crises the interests of management were represented by Brian Mulroney, and with each settlement his reputation grew.

"One thing about Brian," said Arnie Masters, the long-time president of the Maritime Employers Association, "he's always been part of the solution, not part of the problem."

As the MEA's lawyer, Mulroney was called upon to deal with the ILA, and twenty-one union locals in seven ports from Halifax to Hamilton, in a period that saw the gradual stabilization of a volatile industry. With the founding of the MEA to represent all employers, there were more growing pains to be experienced. Adhering to the principle of job security as laid down by Picard, the employers decided to buy out any longshoreman who would accept a $12,000 settlement package. This did more than clear out the deadwood. It also left the employers' group broke, and more to the point, $15 million in debt.

The MEA's bankers, the Canadian Imperial Bank of Commerce, were not prepared to float that kind of loan to a client with no collateral. "Your problem is that you've got too many eggs in one basket," Mulroney told Masters one day as they tried to figure out what to do next. "You need another banker."

His law firm, by now called Ogilvy, Cope, had long been the lawyers for the Royal Bank of Canada. Mulroney got on the phone and got them both an appointment at nine o'clock the next morning with Jock Finlayson, then the senior vice-president of the Royal at their head office in Place Ville Marie. Finlayson was sympathetic to the problem, but the bank still wanted to know what the MEA had to offer for collateral.

"The port of Montreal, right out there," Mulroney said as he pointed out the window. "It's not going anywhere." They got the loan and the MEA got through one more financial crisis.

In those days, as Arnie Masters later observed, "Mulroney took us through a whole pile of fun." His noontime and after-hours hangout was the Carrefour bar off the PVM concourse. Here, with convivial spirits, he cut deals, hatched conspiracies, and kept the company of a steady stream of attractive women. From the Laval crowd, Michel Cogger, Jean Bazin, and Bernard Roy had all gravitated to Montreal by the time of Expo '67. Roy, who for a time was Mulroney's roommate, was also his associate at the Factory, as their firm was known around town. In those bachelor years, the members of the Laval gang rented a ski chalet "up north," as the Laurentians were called down in Montreal.

Mulroney owned a succession of big cars, from a Pontiac that Bazin dubbed "the USS Mulroney" to an Oldsmobile Toronado he bought from financier Peter Thomson and which, as Roy said, "was full of gadgets he didn't know how to work." Roy claimed that Mulroney, "a notoriously bad driver," was "the number-one cause of accidents in Quebec. Though he was never in any himself, he must have left 100 people in the ditch."

So on Friday evenings in winter, Mulroney and his Laval contemporaries would head up north to St. Sauveur and their rented house near the Rivière Simon, a picturesque stream between the village and the Mont Gabriel ski resort. "In skiing, he was a fast learner, quite fearless," Roy remembered. He also recalled that it was understood that Mulroney never did anything around the house. "He's completely helpless around the house," said Roy, who played Felix to Mulroney's Oscar.

In the office, they came under the protective custody of Tommy Montgomery. "When they were working for me," Montgomery would say many years later, "I used to say they were my good angel and my bad angel. Bernard disapproved of just everything Brian did. He enjoyed being shocked by Brian, and Brian enjoyed shocking him."

Montgomery was one of those people who always saw Mulroney clearly, but he regarded him with affection even when he was seeing through him. "There was always something he was promoting," Montgomery would recall with a smile nearly a decade after Mulroney had left the firm. "He would walk by my office without a flicker. Then five minutes later he would be back, walk part way past my office door, then pop in, lower his voice a couple of octaves, and take you into his confidence."

One of Mulroney's associates in the ninth-floor purgatory in which the labour department found itself was Don MacSween, who had joined the firm out of McGill in 1962, the year before the Factory moved uptown from its offices in the Royal Bank building on St. James Street. In a different sort of way, MacSween was another young attorney who wasn't shy about turning on his personality. He had been with Tim Porteous and the others who had written and performed McGill's celebrated "My Fur Lady" undergraduate review of 1957. MacSween and Mulroney were viewed, in the department as in the firm, as friendly rivals for advancement.

"I never saw it that way," MacSween mused many years later when he was director of the National Arts Centre in Ottawa. As someone who had been on tour with "Fur Lady," MacSween acknowledged that he was "a professional in a field where Brian prided himself on his amateur abilities." And he did see Mulroney as "a main-chance guy, but you can't become a national leader unless you are. But on the positive side, I don't know anyone who has as great a capacity for the art of negotiation."

Also, the NAC impresario observed, "People like being with

him. It's not just his affability, they like seeing him coming around a corner." Though MacSween noted that "Brian takes a lot of oxygen in any particular room," their former mentor, Montgomery, noted that "He had that quality that you'd know he was in the room before you turned around."

There was also a quality of audaciousness and daring to Mulroney in some of his courtroom antics, when he would dare incur the wrath of a judge, or a mediator or a commission. One instance of this occurred in the late 1960's when Stanley Hartt and Mulroney took a case involving checkers on the Montreal waterfront to the Canada Labour Relations Board in Ottawa.

The case involved the checkers being certified to join the ILA. As they were about to appear, Hartt got wind from one of his students who was clerking at the Supreme Court of a judgement requiring trade unions to respect the by-laws of locals being absorbed by expansion. Mulroney quickly thumbed through the checkers' constitution, which stipulated that in order to become a checker you had to pass a test.

With the leader of the checkers' union in the witness chair, Mulroney asked if he had passed his test.

"What test?" came the baffled reply.

The chairman of the tripartite tribunal leaned down from the bench and asked Mulroney what he was driving at.

"It's very simple," Mulroney replied. "If three checkers working six hours can steal eight cases of booze, how many cases can five workers steal in two hours of overtime?"

Or words to that effect, as Hartt later recalled. But one thing he had no difficulty remembering exactly was the pandemonium that reigned in the hearing room. "The dramatic effect was the maximum possible," Hartt said. "I'm not sure that wasn't what won the case."

There was another occasion in the port of Saint John, New Brunswick, where the longshoremen skirted the MEA's authority and signed a contract with the Irving family interests. Mulroney filed an unfair labour practices act against the longshoremen, something of a first between management and employees, and subpoenaed K.C. Irving's two sons to appear in court, which in New Brunswick was rather akin to issuing a summons to Her Majesty. When their counsel pointed out that the Messrs. Irving were very busy men and begged that they be excused, Mulroney refused and kept them sitting there throughout the hearing.

And one time in Montreal, appearing before Judge Alan Gold, who was investigating complaints of strong-arm tactics on the Montreal waterfront, Mulroney buzzed a witness who claimed he hadn't seen a beating with a baseball bat a few feet away from him. "You didn't see anything?" asked an incredulous Mulroney, as he put his arm around Gold, who would one day become Chief Justice of Quebec's Superior Court. "Do you see me? Do you see the judge? You do? But you didn't see him with the baseball bat?"

In the 1960's, Mulroney was not yet in the big money. At the beginning of 1967, he was still making less than $10,000 a year. But he was making a name for himself around town. "When I first met him," Stanley Hartt recalled, "he had a certain grace and a way with words, and that charm, and he didn't have to excuse himself in front of guys like me. He was a guy with tremendous magnetism. He was already having lunch with Peter Thomson." Thomson, who would often have Mulroney out to his country estate in Hudson for parties that tended to last all weekend, was then the principal owner of Power Corporation, which he subsequently sold to Paul Desmarais.

It was Desmarais who would become Mulroney's mentor in the business world. They first met at a party at Frank Common's, one of the senior partners of Mulroney's firm. Desmarais was already a client of the firm, and he often found himself in need of the services of the brash young labour lawyer, never more so than in two epic management-labour confrontations at *La Presse*, the newspaper flagship of the rapidly expanding Desmarais empire. The first strike in 1969 ended in bitter violence and inspired Jean Drapeau's Montreal administration to enact its notorious anti-demonstration by-law, which would later be found unconstitutional.

The second shutdown of *La Presse* started as a lockout in mid-1971 and lasted eight months. When Mulroney was finally called in, he settled the thing in a week. There was a fistful of union locals at *La Presse*, from the journalists to the pressmen, typesetters, and photoengravers. The issues were both technological and ideological.

"The question was the future of printing the paper, and how it would be done," said Jean Cournoyer, then Quebec's embattled Labour Minister. "For the craft unions, it was an ideological battle. The stalemate was such that Mr. Desmarais himself demanded a solution." And, as Cournoyer observed, Desmarais "brought in a young man, already well known, who turned out to be Brian Mulroney."

In the late 1960's, Mulroney had settled other labour problems in the transportation branch of the Power empire, with the Voyageur bus lines and Canada Steamship Lines. "Jack Porteous," Desmarais said of one of the senior Ogilvy partners, "sent him down here on a bus issue. I thought, here was a young guy, and was surprised to see a young guy involved in a labour dispute. I found him very articulate in French and in English. But the other thing that impressed me about him was how well he got along with people. He was amusing, had a good sense of humour, was tough, very tough, and objective. I was very impressed by him. I met him socially a few times before he was married. We would talk politics."

What they talked about at Desmarais's house at Christmas of 1971 was giving Mulroney a mandate to settle the work stoppage at the paper. By this time Mulroney had the clout, even with a client as important as Desmarais, to remind him that "I don't get involved in these things unless I get carte blanche." While they were having this conversation, Desmarais received a phone call with an update on the situation from his negotiating team. "You see, Paul," Mulroney recalled telling him, "this is exactly why I'm not going to get involved in this thing. It has to be clearly understood that I'm in charge, otherwise I don't get involved."

Mulroney had been on the periphery of the negotiations for months. When he finally got the mandate he wanted, he was able to call and deal directly with Louis Laberge, president of the Fédération des Travailleurs du Québec, and Marcel Pépin of the Confederation of National Trade Unions. This would become a hallmark of the Mulroney style – to define the problem in its simplest and most meaningful terms regarding both issues and personalities. Laberge and Pépin personified a common front of the big two Quebec unions and could speak for the confusing array of twelve union locals affiliated with them down at *La Presse*. Thus, Mulroney could finally deal directly with them, and they could finally deal with someone on the management side who had a mandate from the big boss.

With the players in place and both sides desirous of a settlement, it became a matter of negotiating logistics, of where and how to make a deal. Mulroney took a suite at the Queen Elizabeth, and they stayed there for seven days and nights. "No one went home," as Mulroney later recalled, until they had a deal. With the amount of wine and cognac that was consumed – "none of us was a slouch," as Mulroney could later confess – the room-service bill substantially contributed to the hotel's revenues for the entire year. But Desmarais could finally put out his paper again.

This was how Mulroney did most of his work: "In the labour side, you really made a lot of money when you were out of the office. It demands a physical presence. You don't make your money in labour law by writing learned legal briefs. I mean, you are out there with the boys, solving problems, treating cases, fighting injunctions, or whatever you are doing."

The fact Mulroney and his colleagues in the labour department were bringing in big fees may have shielded him from any animosity among his senior colleagues that he was better known around town than most of them and getting the firm's name in the paper more than any of them. There was also the fact that "being up on the ninth floor," two floors above the rest of the firm, "was like having your own shop but still being part of a larger one."

Moreover, Mulroney was single in those years and not really involved in the firm's stratified social life. "I was a bachelor," he said, "so I wasn't involved in the sort of husbandry of the firm. I was off on my own, and I would only touch base with the vast majority of them at sort of non-firm things because I would never come to a firm function."

Finally, the senior partners at the Factory were able to tolerate a certain amount of outside activity by a select few associates because, among other things, they reflected well on the firm even when they didn't bring in any money. Fortier was deeply involved in the activities of the Canadian Bar Association. Mulroney, as it soon became evident to them, was a political animal.

In September of 1965, Mulroney was standing on a Montreal street corner when he noticed Fred Kaufman on the other side of the street. Kaufman would later become a judge of Quebec's Court of Appeal, but in those days he was a Montreal Liberal lawyer and one of the party's faithful in Mount Royal riding, where they were about to do their duty, as ordained by the boys downtown, and nominate a candidate few of them had ever heard of, one Pierre Elliott Trudeau.

"Hey, Fred," Mulroney remembered shouting across at him, "I hear you guys are nominating a goddamn socialist."

Mulroney's involvement in the 1965 election was, he recalled, "strictly as a worker, raising money, trying to find new candidates. You know, not a high profile." Nor did he cut much of a profile at the 1966 PC meeting in Ottawa that decided to institute the proceedings of leadership review, whose immediate object was John Diefenbaker but which would eventually lead to the downfall of Joe Clark and the accession of Brian Mulroney.

Mulroney was not remembered as having been on either side of that debate, unlike Clark, who spoke in favour of review. As staunch a Diefenbaker loyalist as Bob Coates, who wrote a bitter polemic on the episode entitled *The Night of Knives*, could not remember that Mulroney was part of what he regarded as one of Dalton Camp's traitors. Years later, Mulroney himself could not recall for sure whether he had even been a delegate to the November, 1966, meeting, though he was certainly there in Ottawa. "But I'll tell you this," he said. "If I was a delegate, I would have voted for the idea that Dalton was trying to put forward... his position deserved a hearing." In other words, with most of the younger Tory activists, he was in favour of review and acknowledged having worked for it.

"The '66 review was in retrospect a painful thing for everyone who was involved," he said of that memorable shootout at the Château Laurier. "It turned out to be very unfair to Dalton. We didn't start out in any way with any malice. I wasn't involved at the beginning, but I remember full well reading about his initial steps. And they were totally free from malice."

Camp, as president of the party after the 1965 defeat, had publicly advocated a regular review of the leadership. At the 1966 meeting, on the heels of a highly charged appearance by the Chief, Camp was narrowly re-elected, by a margin of only sixty-two votes of more than 1,000 cast, against Diefenbaker's candidate, Arthur Maloney.

"The issue was joined in such a personal way," Mulroney recalled, "that the substance was never debated properly, as a result of which Dalton was very, very unfairly penalized. Dief was penalized, ultimately. And of course, the party was devastated. It was an idea," he continued, "that never got a proper hearing, that made its way into the consciousness of the party at great cost, and was accepted as a valid proposition only years later. And we were all involved in that."

Once Camp had withstood the Maloney challenge to his presidency of the party, a resolution to hold a leadership convention in 1967 passed with ease the next day, most of the Diefenbaker loyalists having walked out of the convention in disgust. In due course, with Diefenbaker himself calling for a convention, the time and place were set: September 5-9, at Toronto's Maple Leaf Gardens. It was the first real convention of the television age in Canada, and Mulroney found himself supporting the candidacy of the former Justice Minister, Davie Fulton. Some people later wondered why Mulroney, who understood the necessity of winning seats in Quebec, backed Fulton rather than the fluently bilingual Duff Roblin, the Premier of Manitoba.

"Well, because I knew Fulton better," replied Mulroney, who

among other activities had also put the bite on Paul Desmarais for a donation to the Fulton campaign. "He was very nice to me. I met him over the years. I thought he was an excellent Minister of Justice. He was very impressive on the Fulton formula, which reopened doors to Quebec. I was a law student when all this was going on. He cut an impressive figure."

Considering that he was running against Camp's candidate, Robert Stanfield, and that Roblin was a favourite son of western delegates, Fulton ran a very respectable third, with 343 first-ballot votes, only four votes behind Roblin at 347 votes, with the front-running Stanfield at 519. George Hees had 295 delegates. And Diefenbaker, who had decided to let his name stand at the convention, was a humiliating fifth with 271 votes. The second-ballot shake-out foretold the fifth-ballot showdown, with Stanfield at 613, Roblin at 430, and Fulton at only 346. Mulroney's candidate wasn't growing and most of Diefenbaker's western support would ultimately go to Roblin. As Martin Sullivan observed in his excellent book, *Mandate '68*, a source work to which Canadian journalists have been referring ever since: "Davie Fulton held the balance of power. Whoever he endorsed would be the next leader of the Progressive Conservative Party of Canada." When Fulton went to Stanfield, Mulroney was one of the young Tories who went with him.

The 1968 election marked the first time Mulroney had some organizational responsibilities in Quebec. On paper, he was the assistant to Jean Bruneau, one of Premier Daniel Johnson's top Union Nationale organizers, who was running the Conservative campaign. In a real sense, Mulroney was the connector between the Tories and Daniel Johnson.

"That's what this thing was all about," Mulroney recalled. "Johnson was the one who decided that Bruneau would run the campaign. And when Eddie Goodman, the national campaign chairman, went to see Johnson, I was the one who made the arrangements. He went down to the Château to see Johnson, and Johnson agreed to get involved.

"In Quebec," Mulroney continued, "we had zilch, and whatever we were going to get, Johnson was going to deliver, and he put out for us." In Quebec against Pierre Trudeau in that spring of 1968, they were not going to get much. But they did get four seats, more than they would in any of the next four Trudeau elections, and it was due in some measure to the assistance furnished by Johnson.

Mulroney's *bleu* friends may have been in power in Quebec from 1966 until they were ousted by Robert Bourassa's Liberals in 1970, but they knew hardly anyone in the predominantly English-speaking, overwhelmingly Liberal West End of Montreal. They offered him a seat on the Montreal Catholic School Commission, a highly remunerative part-time position he turned down "because I wasn't married, I didn't have any children, and I thought it was inappropriate."

Then Jean-Jacques Bertrand, who had succeeded to the premiership on Johnson's death in September of 1968, offered Mulroney some lottery winnings, or at least a substantial piece of the action. When the Quebec government started up Loto-Quebec in 1969, it was carving the province up into franchise territories. Mulroney, as he recalled, was offered "some or all, but a large chunk of the West Island of Montreal." First Mulroney turned down the Premier, and he turned it down again when the matter was raised by Mario Beaulieu, then provincial Finance Minister.

"I said no, because I felt it was improper for someone who had been involved in politics to gain from it. And I turned it down." Had he accepted, Mulroney would have been a millionaire by the early 1970's, such was the success of the lottery, such was the lucrative territory he had been offered. "In retrospect," he said, "everyone knew that they were going to make money. But to me, politics was something entirely different. I'm not blaming people who accepted them, but for me I knew that one day I would be actively involved, not in the back rooms, and I never wanted it said of me that I ever, ever, made a nickel in politics."

That may have been his real motive for turning down the offer of the lottery territory. But as he also said with a chuckle: "All politics ever did was cost me a fortune. If you were a Conservative from Quebec, let me tell you, you paid your own way."

By the time the 1972 election rolled around, Mulroney was paying his way to the extent that he was a co-chairman of the Conservatives' Quebec campaign with Claude Dupras and Claude Nolin. One of the things they were casting around for in a general sense was a Quebec lieutenant for Stanfield.

In a roundabout sort of way, it was Peter White who found Claude Wagner, who had been defeated for the provincial Liberal leadership by Bourassa in January, 1970, and subsequently appointed to the provincial bench by Bertrand as he was calling the election for April of that year. White was then running a small newspaper in Quebec's Eastern Townships along with his partner, Conrad Black.

"Conrad and I wrote him a letter out of the blue," White recalled. They would like to meet him, and the judge wrote back

82

saying he would be happy to do so. Wagner told White, who had been an assistant to Daniel Johnson, that he would not be a candidate for the UN. "Right on the spot," White recalled, "I said, 'If you're not interested in provincial, how about federal?'" When Wagner allowed as how that might be an interesting prospect, White said: "The first thing I want you to do is meet Brian Mulroney."

Meanwhile, Mulroney, Dupras, Nolin, and the others were kicking around an informal short list of prospective Quebec leaders for the party. "We would drop it," Mulroney said, "and keep working, and then somebody would come back and say that we need somebody to lead the team. So I can't tell you where the idea came from."

Certainly Wagner was not doing anything to discourage the notion of his availability. "You know, he might be interested," Mulroney suggested to Dupras after reading about another one of those Draft-Wagner stories in the newspapers, this time involving the Quebec Social Credit Party.

"So I can't remember," he said later, "whether I went alone, no, I must have talked to Stanfield about it. Stanfield would have told me to go ahead. Now I think that Dupras and I went to see him in his office, the two of us together. That was followed by a number of meetings in which it became clear that he was interested."

It also became clear that if they were going to get Wagner, they should find out what the voters thought of him. It was equally clear that they would have to provide for Wagner's security, since he would not be able to return to the bench in the event of his defeat.

The poll was the easy part. They had a survey done by Bob Teeter, the Detroit pollster who worked for the Republicans in the United States and occasionally for the Conservatives in Canada. Incredibly, the survey showed that Wagner was more popular in Quebec than Pierre Trudeau in early 1972. What respondents weren't asked was whether they would vote for him as a Conservative, a nuance that might have escaped a pollster from the U.S.

"They said, 'Grab him,'" recalled Dupras. Which is what, with the poll in their pocket, Dupras and Mulroney set out to do.

By then, they were aware of the matter of providing for Wagner's financial security. "He said to me, quite point blank, 'What happens to me if I lose?'" Mulroney would recall. "There is no mystery about it. What is more legitimate than asking that about a Conservative in Quebec?" Mulroney said he would scout around the big law firms about the prospect of taking Wagner on after the election as a counsel associated with one of them, a generally comfortable sinecure for a retired politician. Mulroney had no luck there and admitted as much to Wagner.

"He then said, 'Well, I still might do this, but I have to have some sort of assurance that my wife and family would be looked after, if anything happened to me,'" Mulroney recalled. "I didn't find anything outrageous in the proposition at all."

Mulroney then reported back to the campaign director, Finlay MacDonald. And that's where the famous $300,000 Wagner trust came about.

MacDonald decided to keep Stanfield in the dark about the details, "even though," as he said, "in those days there was nothing wrong with such an arrangement, it was not in violation of anything, [but] we felt that RLS shouldn't know about it. The logical person was the campaign chairman, me."

What did MacDonald know about the deal? "Oh," he said, without missing a beat, "I did it."

Having discussed it, as he said, "with my key people on the money side," he arranged to meet Wagner in Montreal "somewhere around June." The judge came to MacDonald's room at the Château Champlain. They cut the deal over a couple of lobster salads and a bottle of Pouilly-Fuissé. "Three hundred thousand dollars was mentioned at that particular lunch," MacDonald said. "And that he was prepared to do it. And that he was agreed upon the price."

As for setting up of the fund, said MacDonald, "that part, I walked away from." It was to be done, he remembered saying to Wagner "'by a lawyer we'll agree upon.' And it was Eddie Goodman."

Fast Eddie Goodman, the Toronto Conservative lawyer, flew into Montreal to close the deal. Mulroney was involved to the extent that he was the wheel man. "I picked up Eddie Goodman at the airport," he said, "and I drove Eddie to Wagner's house. Eddie went down to the basement and asked me to stay in the living room, because Eddie as a lawyer was acting in behalf of his client. I drove Eddie then to the airport, and he never told me, and I never asked him, and I never saw anything. But I knew full well that Eddie Goodman didn't go there for the good of his health. So I knew that there was something entirely proper, entirely legal, that Diefenbaker may have had, that Pearson had. So I had no quarrel with it. I knew that it was above board, it was legal, it was proper."

It was also a potential embarrassment that became a political time bomb when Wagner insisted on stating at his press conference where he announced his candidacy that he wasn't receiving any consideration for his services. Wagner and others went over his announcement before the press conference. "He said something like 'I have never received, I have never been offered, I have never asked for a penny to go into this,'" Dupras recalled. "I interrupted him, and I said, 'Claude, are you sure about that?'"

The recollection of Mulroney, who was also in the hotel room at the Queen Elizabeth prior to the announcement, corresponds with that of Dupras. "The problem arose when, on the night he announced his candidacy," Mulroney agreed, "he insisted on putting a phrase in here, in his opening statement, that he had never asked for and would never accept any financial security. He insisted on that. You can ask Claude Dupras.

"Dupras," he continued, "had a hell of an argument with him. I was agreeing with Dupras, saying 'You've got to take that out.' But you see, neither Claude nor I knew the details. We knew there had to be something. I didn't think there was any problem at all, until he insisted on putting that in the damn statement. Dupras and I, just the three of us in the hotel room, we fought like hell to get him to take it out. We didn't know why it wasn't true, because we didn't know what the details were. Whether it was a promissory note, or whether it was simply an undertaking by somebody to hire him. I didn't know what the hell it was. I had no idea."

As Peter White later put it, Wagner "lied through his teeth." Or as Finlay MacDonald put it, somewhat more euphemistically: "Wagner gave the clear impression that he had received no inducements, and by so doing caused those of us who knew about it to stonewall the whole thing."

It certainly appeared that Mulroney was stonewalling about his knowledge when the question arose in the 1976 leadership campaign, by which time he was running against Wagner. One of the reasons the story came up again was that Peter White was discussing his knowledge of the affair with a reporter from *The Toronto Star*.

This, Mulroney later insisted, "I genuinely did not know about," though he definitely sensed the backlash. "Peter, God love him, did that of his own accord," Mulroney said. "He didn't tell me, didn't tell anybody. The facts he revealed in that story I learned for the first time."

As Mulroney admitted, "the assumption was made" that the story had come from him. "The atmosphere at that convention was bad," he said, "but in any case, the assumption was made that I had something to do with it. There was a willingness to believe the worst of people. That was a negative convention. That was not a good convention for anybody."

Nor were any of the elections of the Trudeau era good for the Conservative Party in Quebec.

In those days, Mulroney was more concerned with building his law practice. In January of 1973, he was made the youngest partner in the firm. By then, he had established a name for himself in Montreal, and later he could look back upon those years as a formative period. "You could really make it big," he said. "I don't mean necessarily making a million dollars. You could make a reputation for yourself. You could build something solid, that would last a lifetime."

There were, he said, no barriers in Montreal in those days of boom and opportunity. And he seemed to have made a success of himself, as Lucien Bouchard observed, "because once again he had succeeded in imposing himself. He had to impose himself on Montreal and he did. And he succeeded not as a political man, but in the real world."

It was while he was at the Factory, Bouchard noted, "that he developed his professional links." He had also found what he was meant to do, and the way in which he was meant to do it. Or, as Bouchard also observed: "He was made to be a lawyer. If he hadn't been a lawyer, he wouldn't have succeeded."

Overleaf: Family portrait, circa 1949. Ben and Irene with daughters Peggy and Olive (rear), Barbara on her mother's lap, with Doreen, and sons Gary and Brian.

Overleaf inset: Irene and Ben Mulroney, at home on Champlain Street, Baie Comeau, 1948.

Above: Brian Mulroney as the eighteen-year-old Prime Minister of the Maritime universities model parliament in 1958, with three real-life parliamentarians. Left to right: Mulroney; Gordon Churchill, M.P.; Paul Martin, M.P.; Daniel Hurley, Student Opposition Leader; Douglas Fisher, M.P.; Leo Nimsick, Student CCF Leader.

Left: Brian Mulroney, at nineteen, in his senior year at St. F.X., retires undefeated as the three-time winner of the university's oratorical contest.

Below: At Laval's 1961 Congrès des Affaires Canadiennes, Mulroney chairs a workshop with McGill's Michael Oliver and separatist leader Marcel Chaput, who received word during the symposium that he had been fired by the federal government.

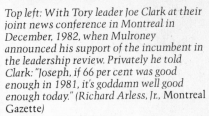

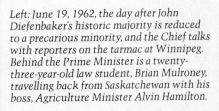

Top left: With Tory leader Joe Clark at their joint news conference in Montreal in December, 1982, when Mulroney announced his support of the incumbent in the leadership review. Privately he told Clark: "Joseph, if 66 per cent was good enough in 1981, it's goddamn well good enough today." (Richard Arless, Jr., Montreal Gazette)

Above: In May of 1968, the spring of Trudeaumania, Tory leader Robert Stanfield goes on a walking tour of Montreal's Man and His World accompanied by Mulroney, at twenty-nine an up and coming Montreal lawyer and Conservative backroom boy in Quebec.

Left: June 19, 1962, the day after John Diefenbaker's historic majority is reduced to a precarious minority, and the Chief talks with reporters on the tarmac at Winnipeg. Behind the Prime Minister is a twenty-three-year-old law student, Brian Mulroney, travelling back from Saskatchewan with his boss, Agriculture Minister Alvin Hamilton.

Bottom left: With Frank Moores as Mulroney is about to go down the tube at the 1976 leadership convention. Should Mulroney, the third man, go to Clark or Claude Wagner? He did neither, releasing his delegates. Moores, after his retirement from the Newfoundland premiership, would later move to Montreal and play an important role in Mulroney's second leadership bid. (Montreal Gazette library)

Left: One more stop: Brian and Mila Mulroney deplane at Castlegar, British Columbia, with two weeks to go before the 1984 election.

Above left: The former Mila Pivnicki. In her view, they became partners in politics in the 1983 leadership campaign, as she unquestionably became one of his biggest assets in the 1984 national campaign.

Above right: "One thing I've learned," he had said as he entered the 1983 leadership campaign, "and that's to keep my eye on the ball. It's going to take me all the way to 24 Sussex Drive."

Below left: With Robert Cliche at the Quebec royal commission investigating the construction industry, the inquiry that made Mulroney into a public figure in the winter of 1974-75. (Mac Juster)

Below right: With Senator Guy Charbonneau, financial chairman of Mulroney's 1983 leadership campaign and a key player in the leadership review – the least well known but by no means the least influential member of Mulroney's inner circle.

Top left: Waiting out another ballot on June 11, 1983, with Dave Angus, the "Golden Goose," who would become chairman of the PC Canada Fund.

Left: Sam Wakim greets Michael Wilson after his arrival in the Mulroney box, June 11, 1983.

Below: Mulroney fulfils one campaign promise, to put the North Shore of Quebec on the map, by christening his 1984 campaign plane Manicouagan I. It's July 26, 1984, the morning after his clear-cut win over John Turner in the English-language debate, and a buoyant Mulroney shamelessly hams it up on the flight deck of his chartered Boeing 727. (Hans Deryk, UPC)

MANICOUAGAN I

Top right: Aboard the 1984 campaign plane with press secretary Bill Fox, former Ottawa and Washington correspondent of The Toronto Star. Wherever Mulroney went, Fox was usually one step behind. (Scott Grant)

Middle right: The three aides who had heard Mulroney's stump speech through the spring and summer of 1984 in every tank town and on every rubber chicken rostrum in the country – Mila's assistant Bonnie Brownlee, Mulroney's executive assistant Bill Pristanski, and Fox. (Scott Grant)

Bottom right: With Charley McMillan at the Mont Ste. Marie caucus in 1984. As Mulroney's senior policy adviser and polling analyst, McMillan was in some ways the key to his thoughts.

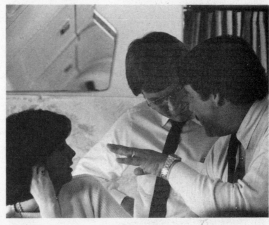

Below: At the Taverne aux Amis in Baie Comeau where, as Mulroney explained, he used to hang out for the cultural life and the pickled eggs. (Doug Ball, Canadian Press)

Left: September 4, 1984: Mulroney surrounds himself with his oldest friends and closest advisers to watch the victory in the guest house of Le Manoir. Left to right: Terry McCann, from the St. F.X. days, policy adviser Charley McMillan, and communications adviser Roger Nantel from Montreal. In the background, Pat MacAdam. (Scott Grant)

Below: The public moment of victory: the applause in the Baie Comeau recreation centre went on for at least seven minutes before Mulroney could begin to acknowledge the ovation. "Chers amis," he began time and again, only to be engulfed in another ovation. "You have to understand the symbolism of this to these people," he explained later. The electrician's son had been elected Prime Minister. (Scott Grant)

6

THE CLICHE
COMMISSION

There were more than sparks when Yvon Duhamel drove a bulldozer into an electric generator at the James Bay hydroelectric construction site on March 21, 1974. Duhamel, the business agent for Local 791, the Union of Operating Engineers, was setting in motion a chain of political events that would leave the government of Quebec no choice but to appoint an inquiry into the violence and corruption in Quebec's $6-billion-a-year construction industry. The sensational revelations of the Cliche Commission, in the fall of 1974 and the winter of 1975, would be more than a high melodrama detailing union chicanery, management complicity, and government impotence to stop either. It also revealed, to a shocking degree, that the government knew what was going on and permitted itself to be taken hostage by the disreputable elements of the trade union movement. The spectacular revelations of the Cliche Commission, and there has never been anything quite like it before or since in Canada, reinforced the perception that Robert Bourassa was a weak leader who was not overly concerned with the moral imperatives of public policy. In that sense, the Cliche Commission contributed significantly to his defeat at the polls in 1976.

Perhaps most significantly, the hearings of the Cliche inquiry turned one of the three commissioners, Brian Mulroney, into a public figure. "It's the Cliche Commission that put him on the map," Bourassa said without hesitation after he had regained the leadership of the Quebec Liberal Party in 1983. By this time, the two men were fast friends; indeed, they had always remained on friendly terms even when the Cliche Commission was putting his government on the rack in the winter of 1974-75. It was not, Bourassa was quick to add, as if Mulroney wouldn't have turned up as a public figure at some turn in the road, "but the Cliche Commission was the occasion of it."

Mulroney himself agreed that the Cliche Commission made him a public figure. "I think that's right," he said in May of 1984. "The commission was ten years ago, and it's probably most unlikely that I could have done what I've done on the public side without that boost from the commission."

The Cliche Commission made Mulroney a star in French Canada and gave him entrée to the news media in the English-speaking provinces. Robert Cliche, his one-time law professor, made sure of that. "For English Canada, Brian was the commission," recalled Lucien Bouchard, his close friend from Laval who had served as its chief counsel. "Day after day, for the television interviews, Cliche would push him forward, and say, you look after the English."

In Quebec, television audiences and newspaper readers were fascinated by this management lawyer and pinstriped Tory who spoke to them, through the filter of the media, in such colloquial French. By the time the commission had completed its work, it was a given in Quebec that Mulroney was a francophone, notwithstanding his Irish name.

And as the hearings developed a life of their own, the people of Quebec were paying very close attention. A poll taken for the commission in August of 1974 indicated that only 25 per cent of the respondents were aware of its work. By the following February, when all the Premier's men were in the witness box, the figures were reversed. Fully 75 per cent of Quebecers in the poll were aware of the commission and its work.

The construction industry in Quebec, from James Bay in the north to the Olympic site in Montreal, was easily the most important sector of the province's economy. In the boom year of 1973, it accounted for 12 per cent of Quebec's gross domestic product. Because the construction industry represented big dollars and important trades, there was a fairly constant state of tension among Quebec's big union centrals as they contended for the allegiance of the various trades. But the most important by far was the FTQ, the Fédération des Travailleurs du Québec, or the Quebec Federation of Labour, under the leadership of Louis Laberge, the most colourful and, in spite of everything, the one trade union leader in Quebec who afterwards continued to inspire a degree of affection among the general populace.

Things had never been better for the FTQ and the locals affiliated with it than in the mid-1970's. "These were boom times," recalled Irwin Block, who covered the Cliche hearings for the *Montreal Gazette*. "The unions were booming, the separatist movement was booming. It was a time for big cars and vacations in Florida." And it was a time when Laberge's influence reached its apogee, not just within the trade union movement, but in the rarefied atmosphere of the Premier's office. As Bourassa's top aide, Paul Desrochers, would himself testify before the Cliche Commission, he had discussed the possibility of granting the FTQ a ten-year monopoly on the James Bay site in return for a promise to keep the Project of the Century free of strikes.

As Desrochers discussed this over lunch with Laberge in a Montreal restaurant called Chez Son Père, the conversation and the lunch were shared by a man named André "Dedé" Desjardins, head of the FTQ construction wing. Not to put too fine a point on it, Dedé Desjardins was a tough character, not unacquainted with some of the strong-arm tactics that gave trade unionism a bad name. The Cliche report would ultimately denounce him as "a danger to the state and a nuisance to our society, as well as for trade unionism."

That a man like Desjardins was having lunch with the Premier's top adviser was indicative of how far the government was prepared to go in making itself a hostage to the whims of the union leaders. Desjardins was not the only undesirable character holding union office. There were others, for instance, Raynauld "Ti-Blond" Bertrand, business manager of the plumbers and pipe fitters union, Local 144, who ran a little loan-sharking operation on the side. His partner in this lucrative little sideline was Romeo "Bull" Theriault. Other charming gentlemen included René "Le Gros" Mantha and Yvon Duhamel, the man who got on a bulldozer one day, 600 miles north of Montreal, and began the rampage of James Bay, destroying generators and fuel tanks and burning the men's sleeping quarters on the site. He got ten years in prison and Quebec got the Cliche Commission.

Bourassa was committed to the idea of an independent inquiry, one without any connections to the Liberal administration. "We wanted to be more pure than them," Bourassa said many years later, "more pure than the PQ."

He needed a chairman who could command the respect of all sides, and in time he decided on Robert Cliche. "And it took a management guy," Bourassa said, "someone respected by all sides, and Brian was respected on both sides."

Julien Chouinard, who had been one of Mulroney's professors at Laval, was by now the powerful secretary of the cabinet in Quebec. If it was Desrochers who garnered most of the headlines, and in the coming months he would get rather more than he bargained for, it was Chouinard who ran the administrative affairs of the government, totally out of the public eye and unknown to all but the senior civil servants and ministers who had to deal with him on a day-to-day basis. Ironically and unhappily for Desrochers, the construction crisis occurred just as he was about to leave the Premier's service and return to private life as a vice-president of Le Permanent trust company in Montreal. It would be left to Bourassa, Chouinard, and Labour Minister Jean Cournoyer to fill in the blanks. Chouinard thought of his former student, and Cournoyer thought of the young management lawyer who had settled the epic strike at *La Presse*.

When Cournoyer took Mulroney to lunch to ask him if he would be inclined to serve, he said that depended on a number of things, including the choice of the chairman and the key commission staff. Subsequently, Bourassa himself called to ask the same question, and Mulroney's answer was the same. The Premier said he was down to Lucien Saulnier or Robert Cliche for chairman of the inquiry. Mulroney pointed out that Saulnier, as the long-time chairman of the Montreal Executive Committee and subsequently the first head of the Montreal Urban Community, the metropolitan government, was too identified as a management figure. As for Cliche, Mulroney allowed as how this would be an excellent choice. "You won't," he suggested, "have any trouble getting people to work with him."

Certainly, there would be no problem getting Mulroney to work with him. With the appointment of the commission on May 3, 1974, Mulroney was also off the hook to take an active part or run in the 1974 election that was about to be upon them. Five days later, the minority Trudeau government fell with the defeat of John Turner's budget and the Liberals went into the election with the numbers needed to win in Keith Davey's hat. Inflation may have taken off in the wake of the 1973 tripling of petroleum prices by the international oil cartel, but in a Trudeau-Stanfield showdown, Trudeau was bound to win every time. The Liberals went around selling the slogan that the issue was leadership and the problem was inflation. The Tories replied that the issue was inflation and the problem was leadership. It wasn't selling that year, nor was Stanfield's program of wage and price restraints, least of all with Trudeau going around the country telling voters that, zap, they would be frozen under a Conservative administration.

In Quebec, Stanfield's perseverance brought the PCs up to 21 per cent of the vote from 18 per cent in 1972. The problem was that Trudeau's share of the Quebec vote also rose, from 48 per cent to 54 per cent, and sixty seats along with it. The Créditistes, though declining in numbers, still managed to cling to eleven seats in what would be Réal Caouette's last hurrah. Stanfield, for all his efforts, all the weekends he had spent in Quebec, had only three seats to show for it. His Quebec caucus consisted of Roch LaSalle, Claude Wagner, and Heward Grafftey, who could all fit comfortably into the back seat of an Ottawa cab – on any day they happened to be speaking to one another. Mulroney, who had been a member of the 1972 Tory triumvirate and chief Quebec organizer for the first six months that followed, was able to sit the election out. His activities consisted of making a few phone calls to try and beef up the Tory media coverage, and raising a few dollars to try and pay the campaign bills. For the rest, he was genuinely on the sidelines, with an armload of preparatory work to do at the commission.

For one thing, there was the choice of the commission counsel. First Cliche brought in Jean "Bulldog" Dutil, a lawyer from his beloved Beauce whose political connections, such as they were, were with the Union Nationale. Then Mulroney brought in Lucien Bouchard from Chicoutimi as the associate counsel. Bouchard was not eating very well in those days. He had joined the PQ in 1971 and worked actively for the election of Marc-André Bédard in Chicoutimi in 1973, as a consequence of which he was not looked upon with favour in his law firm, which consisted of a bunch of Grits. It might have been a different story had the PQ won then instead of three years later, in which case the firm might have been looking for someone who could make the big phone call in Quebec. As it was, the Liberals were returned with 102 seats out of 110, the greatest landslide in Quebec history, and this particular firm of Liberal lawyers had not much need of Bouchard's service. "I was treated pretty coldly," Bouchard said, and so he struck out on his own, not a very assured way of making a living. In May of 1974, Bouchard was sitting alone in his office when he got a call from Mulroney in Montreal. "We're choosing a lawyer," he said, "and the government wants to give us a turkey."

Bouchard thought about it for about two seconds before he said yes.

What you had then were the essential elements of some pretty extraordinary chemistry: in Cliche, a country judge of folkloric qualities; in Mulroney, a big-city management lawyer who knew when to hit and when to duck; in Guy Chevrette, a teachers' union executive who was emotionally shocked by what he saw being carried out in the name of trade unionism; in Dutil, a bearish country lawyer; and in Bouchard, a small-town advocate with an ever-apologetic tone for the way in which he asked a leading question. Put all of these guys together, and you had a lot of trouble for whomever was being investigated.

Mulroney was no stranger to royal commissions. As he himself noted, he had spent fourteen months in 1966-67 appearing before the Picard Commission on the Montreal waterfront. He knew that the choice of commission counsel could be critical to their work. "A lot of Montreal lawyers, you know, live on inflated reputations," he observed ten years later, "and they don't put in the time, and I was concerned about that, knowing full well that the lawyers and the police would have to play a major role in this."

Dutil and Bouchard proved to be felicitous choices. Dutil knew the judge, while Bouchard knew both Cliche and Mulroney. They fell in like thieves.

Before very long, it became pretty clear to all concerned that while Cliche was the master showman, Mulroney was running the show. "Cliche didn't like details and neither does Brian," Bouchard observed, "but Brian had a gift for finding in details things which were essential." And very quickly, as Bouchard said, "it became Brian who ran the show."

The Cliche Commission afforded the first glimpse of the Mulroney management style, which tends to be improvisational, oriented to crisis management, with the details left to subordinates. And because of that, the choice of subordinates, Bouchard and the others, was critical if they were to get along and get the job done. "I was satisfied that chemistry was going to be the name of the game in this thing," Mulroney said, "and that the commissioners should do what they were supposed to do, the commissioners should be the chief executive officers and set the policy, provide the leadership, then let the lawyers and the police and the other staff devise the strategy and get the facts."

That process of gathering the facts took nearly five months, from May until September. For Mulroney and his commission colleagues, it was a lost summer, but not a waste of time. "Because we hadn't been doing anything publicly," he said, "I think there was a general view in the milieu that we were taking it easy, as all royal commissions are supposed to do, which of course was not to know us very well, because we were working fourteen, fifteen hours a day, all summer. So that we would be well prepared for September, and indeed we were."

Even so, when the commission began its public hearings in Quebec in mid-September, there was no sense in the Quebec media that they were on to a sensational story. "I didn't even want to cover it," recalled Irwin Block, who by the mid-1980's was the senior political writer for the Canadian Press in Montreal but was then a labour reporter with the *Montreal Gazette*. Then, as Block said, "all this wonderful copy started to roll out," and every reporter covering the hearings at the Centre de Réhabilitation had himself a free pass to the front page. It was a story, as Block said, "of a sort of reign of terror" by the unions, with the complicity of management and the acquiescence of the government. And as the parade of witnesses began, it became an easy story to cover. The commissioners were the guys in the white hats. The witnesses were the guys in the black hats.

"You didn't need anything to promote it," Mulroney said a decade later. "All you had to do was bring your facts together and lay out your evidence in an airtight manner. And part of the strategy was the manner in which we did it. And there was a great drama as we built from point to point, from file to file.

"A lot of thought went into the strategy of this thing," he continued, "because a royal commission is of no value unless it sensitizes public opinion to the point where public opinion demands immediate changes in the statutes. And that is what we did. We realized that if we had no impact, then they'd just bury the report, and that would be that. But if, on the other hand, we ran away with the marbles, the government would have no choice but to implement the report, which is what they did."

Nevertheless, as Irwin Block pointed out, the commission "had very good relations with the media. It was the good guys versus the bad guys, and they were the good guys."

There were two reasons for this: Cliche and Mulroney. "Brian and Cliche liked journalists and liked their company," Bouchard said. They knew the job of a reporter was to get the story out, and get it on time, and they made sure the press got both, something early enough every day to sell it to the desk for the front page, or for a lead item on the evening news. "We were supposed to ask our good questions before the deadlines," Bouchard would recall. If Bouchard hadn't got down to cases with an important witness by mid-afternoon, with morning newspaper and supper-hour newscast deadlines rapidly closing in, he would look up and "see Brian or Cliche pointing at his watch."

By January of 1975, when the commission was sitting in the Quebec Police Force headquarters on Parthenais Street in Montreal, the Cliche Commission was the biggest story of the day. "You could have dropped an H-bomb somewhere," Mulroney said, "and it wouldn't have driven this story off the front pages of the Quebec press."

By this time it was not just the revelations of union strong-arming and management going along. It was a question of the government's involvement, of how much the Ministers of Labour and Justice knew of what had been going on in the construction industry, and how little they had done to stop it. It became a question of Desrochers' dealings with the FTQ leadership before leaving the Premier's office in April of 1974. And finally, it became a question of Bourassa's knowledge of these events. It became a question, to paraphrase Senator Howard Baker's bottom line on the Watergate hearings, of what the Premier knew and when he knew it. In the climactic stage of the commission's public hearings, it was quite evident that there was now, as Mulroney put it, "a crisis involving the Premier of Quebec."

"It was the post-Watergate period," Bourassa later pointed out. And to the Quebec press, he was looking increasingly like another Nixon. Certainly the mood of the Quebec media in those days could hardly be described as sympathetic in his regard. Since there was no opposition to speak of in the National Assembly, the press effectively appointed itself to that role. And since many reporters had *péquiste* proclivities, they were not uncomfortable in it.

Paul Desrochers, subpoenaed to appear on February 28, spent a long day in the Parthenais witness box. It was a painful experience for him, both literally and figuratively. He had a permanent back injury from an old war wound, and it was difficult for him to stand there, more difficult still to hear the questions about his conversations with FTQ leaders. A week later, the commission sat in Quebec for two final days, with two star witnesses, Labour Minister Cournoyer and Justice Minister Jerôme Choquette. Cournoyer, who would become a popular Montreal hotline host after his defeat in the 1976 election, demonstrated considerable theatrical flair of his own, answering the commission's questions with bold affirmations of his own. "If I'd had anything to be afraid of at the time, you wouldn't be here yourselves," he said, reminding the commissioners that he had played a prominent role in their appointment.

And then there came the last star witness with the surprise appearance of Jerôme Choquette, inevitably referred to in news reports as the jut-jawed Justice Minister. Choquette's testimony caused an immediate sensation when he contradicted a statement by the Premier that both of them had known for only three weeks about an alleged 1970 influence-peddling case, involving a civil servant who reportedly paid a cabinet aide $2,000 for an appointment to the Minimum Wage Commission. This rumoured payoff seemed a long way from James Bay or any other

94

kind of corruption in the construction industry, but it came within Cliche's mandate because, as Block explained to his *Gazette* readers at the time, "the Minimum Wage Commission administered the construction industry decree before the creation of the Construction Industry Commission."

Choquette testified that he had informed Bourassa of the case in September of 1970, two weeks before the storm of the October crisis broke over the government. "I believe the Premier had forgotten our earlier conversation," Choquette suggested in his voluntary testimony.

"In my mind," Mulroney said, "Jerôme Choquette was first class in this thing throughout. He was Minister of Justice. He had done a great deal himself in trying to get to the bottom of this. Jerôme is a much-maligned figure, and he ought not to have been. I thought he was first class. He didn't try to put any pressure on us."

But there was certainly some pressure for Bourassa to explain the discrepancy in their recollections as to when he had been informed of the case. Within hours of Choquette's testimony, he called a news conference at the provincial capital and insisted he still couldn't remember being informed of the case in 1970. "Both the Justice Minister and I have tried to remember when he told me, but we just can't find the moment," Bourassa explained. It was the simple truth, but at the time it sounded like a pretty lame explanation.

Bourassa was offering this explanation in a news conference rather than from the witness stand before the commission, which had decided against calling him. "It wouldn't have bothered me to go in the box," Bourassa said many years later, "except it would have been in the style of Judge Sirica calling Nixon."

But it would have bothered Mulroney, and had already bothered him a lot. The question of whether the Premier of Quebec could, and should, be summoned before the Cliche inquiry had precipitated a major crisis within the commission. In an argument that went on for several evenings, Mulroney made it perfectly clear to his colleagues that if they insisted on issuing a subpoena to the Premier, he, Mulroney, would quit. This set him on a collision course with his close friend Bouchard, by now the commission's chief counsel. "My plan was to put Bourassa in the box," Bouchard acknowledged. "It was the logical follow-up to Choquette."

Mulroney was having none of it. "I just said absolutely no, that this was improper, that that was in excess of the jurisdiction of the commission," Mulroney said in 1984, "and that I had no intention of going along with that request under any circumstances."

Among other things, Mulroney "felt that the commission's credibility was intact because it had never overplayed its hand. It had never made a mistake, either on the evidence or on strategy, and all the opponents of the commission and the commissioners, and there were many, would have seized upon a tactical error to say, 'See, we've been telling you all along that these jerks are nothing but a bunch of showmen trying to make themselves popular.'"

There was another reason, in Bouchard's appraisal, for Mulroney's adamant opposition to calling the Premier. "Brian didn't want to screw the government," Bouchard said, "and neither did Cliche, because, for them, it was the state."

They did not consider that their mandate extended to bringing down the democratically elected government of Quebec. As Cliche himself acknowledged privately some months later, the government was perceived as being weak. And neither he nor Mulroney perceived it as being within their mandate to bring about its downfall.

Nearly a decade later, Mulroney downplayed a suggestion he had threatened to resign over the question of issuing a subpoena to the Premier. "I didn't have to threaten," he said. "I made it very clear that they would never sit again with me as a commissioner."

Mulroney's objections were technically based on what he termed "the propriety of issuing a subpoena to a Prime Minister while the House was sitting, and beyond that, the propriety of issuing a subpoena in any case."

The issue of the commission's right to subpoena the Premier was less important than their desire to maintain a united front, as they had all through the summer and fall of 1974 and into the winter of 1975. Cliche, Dutil, Bouchard, and the other out-of-towners on the commission were living at the Queen Elizabeth Hotel. Mulroney would go down and join them there for breakfast, whereupon they would proceed over to the hearings on Parthenais Street. Back at the hotel at the end of the afternoon, they would review the day's proceedings, watch the supper-hour newscasts, and go into a round of evening meetings planning the strategy for the next day's hearings. Eventually someone would have some supper sent up, usually followed by copious amounts of cognac. "We lived together at the Queen E.," Bouchard said, "working until eleven at night and having dinner until two in the morning."

And with these kindred spirits in the room, it wasn't all serious business. It was during this period, and in this way, that Cliche and Mulroney became exceptionally close. Other than his own father, no man had a greater influence on Mulroney's outlook and character. When Mulroney spoke in later years about the need for a tolerant society, he was reflecting not only his own minority experience but articulating Cliche's idea of improving the Quebec and Canadian way of life. Mulroney used to say of Cliche that the only thing he couldn't tolerate was intolerance.

"There was that," Mulroney recalled, "there was his principles, and there was also his outlook on life, always positive. There was no malice in him, and he wasn't big on retribution. He used to talk a great game, but I used to say to him, 'You're not really a good hater.' But his outlook on life, his enthusiasm, were just remarkable."

In the ten-year interval between law school and the royal commission, the former professor and his one-time student had come into occasional contact in Montreal. Cliche had been persuaded by his friends to leave the Liberal Party and take on the Quebec leadership of the NDP in time for the 1965 election. One of the people who had talked him into it, as Cliche later told the story on himself, was Pierre Elliott Trudeau, to whom he would merrily refer as "Quebec's revenge on Canada." By 1968, Cliche was leading the NDP into his second election, and Trudeau, by several strange twists of fate, was leading the Liberals as the newly sworn-in Prime Minister. In spite of his own Conservative loyalties, Mulroney did what little he could to help Cliche win a seat in the House of Commons. In this sense, he was trying to help both his friend and his own party, for to whatever extent Cliche might loosen the Liberals' iron grip on Quebec, the Tories might be able to get a hand in. "Absolutely," Mulroney recalled sixteen years later, when Cliche was dead and Trudeau had announced his retirement. "We were trying to get him elected."

Cliche ran against Eric Kierans in the riding of Duvernay in the populous Montreal bedroom community of Laval. Since the riding was heavily unionized and heavily francophone, Cliche was given a good chance. And there was some help from Mulroney's political mentor, Daniel Johnson, by now the Premier of the province. It was a close enough thing for the Liberals that Trudeau paid the riding the honour of a visit on the last day of the campaign, June 24, 1968. A few hours later, when television viewers saw the Prime Minister standing firm against an onslaught of Coke bottles, Kierans' slender margin of 2,500 votes was assured. Cliche's narrow loss did not alter Mulroney's impression of what he might have done.

"This was a great man," he said. "And had he been able to get into the House of Commons, he'd have undoubtedly captured the attention of the Canadian people in a remarkable way, which of course is why Trudeau did so much to defeat him."

When Mulroney himself finally got to the House of Commons in the fall of 1983, he went out of his way to refer to Cliche in his maiden address on the Manitoba minority rights question. As he did so, speaking of "my friend Robert Cliche," he turned to the NDP benches on his left, as if to remind them of what they had missed out on. Across from him, Pierre Trudeau looked on approvingly.

"It was no accident he spoke of Cliche in his maiden address," said Lucien Bouchard. "He was one of the men that really marked him."

And the commission left other marks on the men and the issues it touched. Within a week of receiving the 600-page report, Bourassa introduced sweeping legislation to clean up the construction industry. The evidence of the report was overwhelming and irrefutable. After sixty-nine tumultuous days of public hearings and a parade of 280 witnesses, Cliche and Mulroney had put the story on the public agenda and kept it there until the government took decisive action. "They broke the back of this clique," as reporter Irwin Block summed up their work.

"It was an accomplishment of some significance," said Mulroney. "Because you see the report was handed down on the second of May, 1975, and there hasn't been any trouble in that industry in nine years.

"So that was a royal commission report that has quite properly gone down, in an objective analysis of the content, that was the finest royal commission ever to sit in Canada, at any time, under any circumstances," he continued, unburdened by any false modesty. "So that was quite an accomplishment to take part in. To have done it in record time, at the lowest cost, to have it all out in 364 days, was an accomplishment of no small nature, so that to the extent that when mid-1975 came around, that people could say, 'Well, you're not a Member of Parliament, what have you done?' Well, 'I've been a royal commissioner,' that was an accomplishment."

There was no doubt that before the Cliche Commission, Mulroney did not consider himself a public person; afterwards, he did.

The experience made other careers and changed other lives. Chevrette went on to become a Parti Québécois candidate in the 1976 election, finally becoming a cabinet minister after the PQ was returned to power in 1981. Bulldog Dutil had already gone off to the provincial bench to become head of the Quebec crime probe. Lucien Bouchard was on his feet now, and when the PQ took office, his friend Marc-André Bédard became Justice Minister, something his former Liberal law partners might have considered before forcing him out of the Chicoutimi firm. Bouchard would become chief negotiator for the Quebec government in its dealings with 300,000 public employees.

Robert Cliche would go back to his basement office in Quebec's old Palais de Justice, where he was associate chief justice of the provincial court, across the street from the Château Frontenac and within commuting distance of the hills and streams of his beloved Beauce county. It was time for him to turn the page, he said in an interview in August of 1975. Three years later, he would be dead at the age of fifty-eight. When he heard that Cliche had died, Mulroney wept when he came on the telephone to another friend. By now he was president of Iron Ore, and he got it organized for himself and Chevrette to get down to Cliche's funeral in style, flying in a helicopter.

Lucien Bouchard had his own memories of Cliche, of the time they were leaving a Montreal hotel to go up to Mulroney's home at the top of the hill in Westmount. "We want to go to Mr. Mulroney's place," Cliche instructed the driver, as if he were getting into a cab in St. Joseph-de-Beauce. "He's Mr. Bronfman's neighbour, you know." Bouchard also remembered Mulroney and Cliche after dinner, shameless showmen that they were, singing the songs of Yves Montand.

Bouchard had another unforgettable memory of Cliche, of the many times, in the middle of something else, he had turned to Mulroney and said: "Now Brian, Prime Minister, don't forget, Brian, Prime Minister." And Mulroney, with, as Bouchard said, "all the modesty of this that's well known," would say, "Don't worry, Robert, don't worry."

7

THE CANDIDATE

Brian Mulroney came out of the Oxford Stationery as he did every Sunday afternoon, carrying the *New York Times* under his arm. He crossed to Nick's restaurant on the other side of Greene Avenue in Westmount. Michel Cogger and Jean Bazin were not much interested in the news of the world that last Sunday of July in 1975. They wanted to discuss the possibility of his running for the Conservative leadership. By the time the conversation was over, Mulroney had authorized Bazin to take the next step of writing up his arguments. This was important, because nothing is deemed to be serious in politics until it exists on paper.

Bazin wrote a five-page, single-spaced memo entitled "Project Leadership Campaign: Phase One." In this first phase, Bazin wrote, they had to get across the idea that "it's serious." And one of the people they had to convince of the seriousness of the idea was the prospective candidate himself.

"It was important," Cogger said many years later, "to satisfy Brian that we wouldn't be laughed at."

After all, Brian Mulroney was only thirty-six years old. And he had never run for or been elected to any office in his adult life. He had just completed an exhilarating but exhausting year on the Cliche Commission, which established his public profile in Quebec. But it didn't put any money in the bank for his law partners, some of whom resented Mulroney's local celebrity status only slightly less than his absence from the firm. The idea of his running off across the country on a six-month leadership campaign was not likely to be well received at the Factory in Place Ville Marie.

Besides, he and Mila had been married only a little more than two years. They had been living only a year in their first home, an exquisite red-brick house on Devon Avenue in the upper reaches of Westmount. The bay window in the living room overlooked Devon Park, a little patch of green from a John Little painting. Their infant daughter Caroline was just over a year old, and twenty-two-year-old Mila was expecting their second child the following February.

Everything about the idea of a leadership campaign seemed hopelessly doomed from the beginning. It was just the wrong time in Mulroney's life. But Bob Stanfield had been determined to quit since the previous July and his third electoral loss to Pierre Trudeau. So, in early July of 1975, Stanfield gave his notice. "I thought it was a mistake," Mulroney said many years later. "I called him up and said, 'Lookit, we're eventually going to make it.'" What he didn't know at the time, Mulroney added, was the extent of Mary Stanfield's illness and the cancer that would eventually claim Stanfield's second wife.

Not long after Stanfield's decision, Brian and Mila Mulroney dropped down to Michel and Erica Cogger's century-old farmhouse in Knowlton, less than an hour's drive from Montreal in the Eastern Townships.

The Mulroney and Cogger baby daughters splashed together in a children's pool. Their fathers talked of the leadership. "I'm looking at my candidate," Cogger said. That, Mulroney said later, was the first time he could ever remember someone discussing it with him. While it must have flattered his ego and tickled his fancy, Mulroney had a more likely career option to discuss. He had been approached over the previous winter by Bob Anderson and Bill Bennett, who sounded him out on joining Iron Ore as executive vice-president. The company was beset by labour and productivity problems and desperately needed someone who could communicate with its workers in Sept-Iles, Labrador City, and Schefferville. Anderson, from the head office of Hanna Mining in Cleveland, was impressed with what he had heard about Mulroney. Bennett, the former assistant to C.D. Howe, was reaching the end of the road as IOC president, and the company was looking for an heir apparent. Mulroney was clearly intrigued by the opportunity. He discussed it with Cogger, went in the house to telephone Robert Cliche and get the judge's opinion, and then came out to take it up again with his Laval classmate. "My response was not very powerful, but it was realistic," Cogger said. "There would be other Iron Ores, but the leadership came up only once every ten years."

But the conversation did tell Cogger one thing: "If he was looking at IOC, he was ready for a change of career."

Cogger had driven down to the Maritimes and discussed the thing with Lowell Murray, Graham Scott, and Michael Meighen, all good friends of his. Murray, by now executive assistant to Richard Hatfield, was godfather to Cogger's child. Graham Scott, of Stanfield's office, he had known from his time as associate national director of the party and his days on the Stanfield bus in 1972 and 1974. Meighen, a member in good standing of the Laval gang, had been installed as party president the previous fall with some help from his classmates at the law faculty.

Visiting Murray at his cottage at Grand Lake in Cape Breton, Cogger found him surprisingly cool to the idea. "He said that Brian couldn't yet aspire to that job because he hadn't put his mind to the questions before the country," Cogger recalled many years later. "Lowell in those days belonged to the group who perceived themselves as the soul and conscience of the party." Of course, Murray also belonged to Dick Hatfield.

Neither were Meighen and Scott overwhelmed by the idea, but by mid-August Mulroney himself had begun to take it up and was seriously scouting his prospects. Now Cogger, Bazin, and the others had to come up with the names of some potential supporters who would lend a bit of prestige and substance to the notion. "Since we wouldn't get it from caucus," Cogger said, "we had to get it from somewhere else." They got it from private-sector people like Don McDougall, the young president of Labatt's, and Paul Godfrey, the chairman of Metro Toronto. Out West, they lined up Paul Norris from Edmonton, where he was well known in party circles as Peter Lougheed's bagman. In Saskatchewan, Mulroney brother-in-law Dick Elliott had his brother Bill, who lined up an audience with Dick Collver, then head of the provincial party. In Montreal, Mulroney had no shortage of friends in the business establishment who were willing to lend moral and financial support. After the Cliche Commission, he could also count on making a big splash in the media any time he wanted to jump in.

In Toronto, it was a different story, both in the media and in the powerful precincts of the Conservative Party around Osgoode Hall, Queen's Park, and the Albany Club. "Come down to Toronto," Sam Wakim told his former roommate, "and give her a flyer."

Wakim was hardly a member of the Tory establishment in Toronto, but he could open one or two doors and was not shy about kicking a few others down. In the fall of 1975, he happened to be president of the Thomas More Lawyers Guild, to which most of the leading members of the Toronto Catholic legal community belonged. Every September, they would begin the legal season with a mass celebrated by the Archbishop of Toronto, followed by a dinner at Osgoode Hall. In September of 1975, the guest speaker was M. Brian Mulroney, a Montreal lawyer, who addressed his Toronto colleagues on the experiences of the Cliche Commission in Quebec.

That was the door Wakim opened. The door he knocked on was the Empire Club, whose president, Alan Leal, was the deputy minister in the office of the Attorney General of Ontario. Did he have an open date, Wakim wanted to know, for his friend Mulroney to come and talk on the Cliche Commission? He did indeed, on October 16. By then, Mulroney had been working the press pretty good, and his arrival in Toronto on the day of the Empire Club speech was heralded by a front-page *Globe and Mail* story, under the headline "Mulroney latest entry in PC race." The paper's Montreal correspondent, Richard Cleroux, informed its readers that Mulroney had already set up headquarters in Montreal, would be announcing in early November, had gained a good measure of fame in Quebec, and had "the healthy, good looking, clean cut appearance many Conservatives were looking for in a leader."

With this kind of build-up in the morning paper, Mulroney had a large crowd of curious onlookers and media representatives in the luncheon room at the Royal York Hotel. As advertised, he spoke mostly on the Cliche Commission, on how the commissioners had addressed the problems of the Quebec construction industry, for that was his reason for being there. "The Cliche Commission," as Wakim observed many years afterwards, "gave him legitimacy as a public figure."

The answer to the chronic labour and productivity problems of Canada's work force, Mulroney told the receptive crowd of blue suits, was a lack of leadership in the country. "Leadership, that is the question today," leaving the audience with a musing about Canada fulfilling "the splendid promise of her youth." In the evening, Mulroney went on to the Albany Club, where Wakim had arranged a cocktail party with Metro Toronto riding association executives.

The reaction to Mulroney's two Toronto appearances was generally favourable, and this was critical in his decision to enter the race, for at this point not even Mulroney, cockeyed optimist that he was, thought he had much of a chance of winning. "But I wouldn't have done it," he said of his first time around, "if I had thought I was going to do poorly."

On November 13, second last to enter the race, Mulroney formally announced his candidacy at the Queen Elizabeth Hotel in Montreal. "I start from the premise of an indivisible Canada," he began. "That is to say exactly the same thing in French as it does in English." There was no room in his choice of words, as he made clear himself, for the kind of ambiguity that arose from the Deux Nations episode of 1967-68. He then stated the electoralist themes that he would stake his political life on, then as later. "It doesn't take a doctorate from the University of Montreal," he declared, "to know that it's out of the question for the Conservative Party to form a government without substantial support from Quebec." As he spoke, the Tories, flush from an unexpected by-election victory in the East End Montreal riding of Hochelaga, had increased their Quebec deputation to four seats, which would turn out to be the high-water mark of the decade. The Tories, who won two seats in 1972 and three in 1974, would fall back to two seats in the 1979 election and one in 1980.

In 1975, as he would in 1983, Brian Mulroney set out to sell himself as the electoral remedy to the Conservative malaise in Quebec. "I'm in this race to stay," he said. "I'm in this race to win."

But in mid-November, he was still a long way from being a serious contender, much less the man to beat. He left Montreal, as he said, with "nothing more than a clipping from the *Gazette* and an Air Canada ticket in my pocket." In Vancouver, columnist Allan Fotheringham dubbed him "the candidate from whimsy." In one of his own more whimsical moments, Fotheringham had written in his *Maclean's* column that Mulroney would emerge as the next Tory leader. And when did he begin to take the idea seriously himself, Fotheringham asked the visitor from over the Rockies. "The second time I read it in your column," Mulroney replied.

But by mid-December, Mulroney was beginning to believe in miracles. On December 16, he went home to Baie Comeau, where someone had affixed a large sign at the entrance to the town. "Bienvenue chez toi," it said. Welcome home, indeed. They had a reception in Le Manoir Hotel, a magnificent hostelry worthy of a railway resort. It had been built in the grand style for Colonel McCormick and the newspaper executives from Chicago, and was restored as such after a fire. From his suite upstairs, Brian Mulroney could look out the window to the white clapboard house on Champlain Street where he had grown up.

Now it seemed as if half the town had turned up to hear him speak – boyhood chums, old girl friends, all the people who had remained behind. And Mulroney gave the speech of his life, never equalled before or since. He improvised a speech that was by turns funny, sentimental, and inspirational. Canada was a network of Baie Comeaus, he said, built on the frontier spirit and the sacrifice and courage of the parents of the people in the room.

"It is a great country," he said, "where the son of an electrician can seek the highest office in the land."

Something had happened in the room. Some people were fighting back tears and others didn't bother. He had explained to the women in the room why they made baloney sandwiches for their husbands, and to the men why they carried lunch buckets, precisely so that their sons and daughters wouldn't have to. "Mila always said it was the best speech I ever gave," he said many years later. "It just popped out of my head."

By the time he closed off the pre-Christmas phase of his campaign, something was going on. "I don't think in the beginning we thought we could win," Cogger said. "But then, number one, it began happening for us, and number two, the other guys were not making big inroads with the delegates."

Mulroney, Cogger, and their wives, both very much with child, repaired to Peter Thomson's place in Nassau for a Christmas break. When Cogger had to break off his holiday to attend to a family matter, Mulroney came back with him. On New Year's Eve, he went to the Forum to see the greatest hockey game played in that building in modern times, a 3-3 tie between the Montreal Canadiens and the Soviet Red Army team with its great goaltender, Vladislav Tretiak. Mulroney sat behind the Canadiens' bench, in full view of about 10 million of his fellow Canadians, as the guest of Jacques Courtois, then president of the Canadiens and a prominent Conservative in Montreal circles.

It was the kind of free media exposure that Mulroney needed to make himself known to the delegates and reach them over the heads of the caucus, where he had only three committed supporters in Jim McGrath and Jack Marshall from Newfoundland and Heath MacQuarrie from Prince Edward Island. It was not much out of a club of ninety-five. And contrary to the impression that he was the darling of the party establishment, Mulroney was a long way from being the favourite among the power brokers who would name and control the delegates-at-large from across the country.

He had already been roughed up in this regard when the Wagner-controlled Quebec executive named a straight Wagner slate of twenty-one delegates-at-large at a December 6 meeting of the provincial executive in Montreal. Mulroney charged ten days later at a press conference in Baie Comeau that the fix was in, as indeed it was, since his name was not on the list. Neither was

Cogger, nor Courtois, nor Lévis Larocque, chairman of the 1974 provincial campaign. And since the delegates had already been chosen from his own riding of Westmount, Mulroney was out of luck. Not only did he lack a seat in Parliament, his opponents were perfectly justified in pointing out that he wasn't even chosen a delegate to a convention at which he hoped to be elected leader. For Mulroney, it was a humiliation and a lesson he would not soon forget. In 1983, he would control the Quebec executive and name his own slate to the exclusion of his opponent.

Not only was Mulroney shut out of the delegates-at-large, he was having a tough time loosening Wagner's stranglehold on the remainder of Quebec's 550-odd delegates. Apart from the North Shore and the West Island of Montreal, Mulroney was picking up only scattered Quebec support. A delegate survey in *La Presse* on January 10 indicated that Wagner would capture about 80 per cent of the 444 elected delegates from seventy-four Quebec ridings. It wasn't a very scientific survey, being based on reporters' calling up as many delegates as they could reach, but it didn't turn out to be very far wrong.

But in the very week that the *La Presse* survey indicated Mulroney was having difficulty making inroads in Quebec, his campaign was taking off in the rest of the country. With a DH-125 leased from Execaire in Montreal, he took off for a run through New Brunswick and the Gaspé Peninsula. In Moncton, the seven-passenger aircraft somehow landed in a freezing rain on a skating rink that passed for a runway. At the Beauséjour Hotel, he gave a regurgitated version of his Empire Club speech before a convention of New Brunswick road builders. Then it was on to Fredericton and a late-afternoon meeting in Jim Ross's restaurant. There was no meeting with Dick Hatfield on this trip through Fredericton. They had exchanged some tough words at a private session on Mulroney's last time through in mid-December. Hatfield accused Mulroney of not telling everything he knew about the Wagner trust fund, and the candidate angrily maintained he had nothing to do with the actual financial arrangements, though he knew perfectly well who had set it up.

Hatfield did not remember it as such a tough conversation, but he did recall many years later that "he took it very hard. I did know the story on Wagner. What I was afraid of, and what I told him, was that he was denying he was involved in it, when he was involved, and there was nothing wrong in that. The only thing he had going for him was that he was clean and honest and so on. And he didn't need this." Perhaps more to the point, suggested

Hatfield, "what really made him annoyed, is that he could have been seething because I wouldn't support him. He saw Lowell at the same time." And Lowell Murray wasn't going anywhere, least of all to some place where his boss wasn't.

From Fredericton, Mulroney flipped over to Saint John. As the plane was coming into Sam Wakim's home town, the burly Toronto lawyer excused himself and went to the washroom. When he came out, Mulroney noticed he was no longer wearing his vest. "You don't go into the East End of Saint John," Wakim explained, "wearing a three-piece suit."

Where they went was the Admiral Beatty Hotel, one of those places where the chairs in the lobby had seen better days. The local delegates and press were invited to a meeting where an increasingly confident Mulroney said, "I'm going to put these Grits on the street."

The next morning, he flew in a smaller chartered plane to Bonaventure on the Gaspé coast. There were ten-foot snowbanks on the sides of the road and more snow billowing across it, and he was driving to New Carlisle to meet a single delegate in his home, a single delegate who controlled the others in a riding where the party had fallen upon hard times. The man was taken by Mulroney's charm, ordered his son to put on the kettle, got out his deKuyper gin and best crystal, and served his guest a stiff "ti-blanc" at 10:30 in the morning. Not wanting to be rude, Mulroney gulped down the hot gin and went on to a luncheon meeting with Gaspé delegates in an old hotel on the coast. Then it was back over to Chatham on the New Brunswick side, where he had gone to high school and where he recognized some familiar faces at a quick meeting at the air base. The smaller plane was still to take him to Bathurst for the drive to Caraquet. Reaching Caraquet at nightfall, he spoke to a group of Acadian delegates who were taken by his bicultural charms. And finally, he caught up with another group of delegates, and his DH-125, in Charlo. In two punishing days, he had covered all of the media and most of the delegates in New Brunswick and the Gaspé Peninsula. But he paid a price for it. The delegates were starting to be more interested in his planes than his policies.

But it was the way Mulroney had chosen to go, and it gave him the kind of flexibility and mobility he thought he needed. An hour after leaving Charlo, he was home for the night in Montreal, where he picked up Dave Angus for a fund-raising stop the next morning in Toronto at the office of Stephen B. Roman, the chairman of Denison Mines.

"Who's winning this thing?" Roman asked.

"Steve," Mulroney said, fixing him with one of those cocky blue-eyed stares, "you're lookin' right fuckin' at him."

At that point, Mulroney may well have been moving to the front of the pack. From a swing on the DH-125 through northern Ontario earlier that week, the *Globe and Mail*'s national columnist, Geoffrey Stevens, had gathered enough material for three pieces in the bottom left-hand corner of his paper's editorial page, known in the trade as the choicest piece of real estate in Canadian journalism.

In the second column that had appeared on that Friday morning of January 16, the headline had proclaimed that Mulroney was "A Strong Contender." "He has a quality which is difficult to describe," Stevens wrote. "It's a quality of reasonableness, an ability to convince people he shares their opinions, even when he doesn't. He does this without shading or slanting his own views to suit those of others, without blunting his opinions, without making them so bland as to be universally acceptable and universally meaningless." Stevens concluded:

> When you get right down to it, there is no discernible philosophical difference between Brian Mulroney and Robert Stanfield. Both men know there are no simple answers to complex questions. Mr. Mulroney is more articulate, more persuasive. And he has that way of making people believe he shares their views when, through his reasonableness, he has led them to share his. A handy asset for a would-be national leader.

Mulroney's reaction, reading this on the plane on the way down from Montreal, was entirely predictable. "This," he said, waving his folded copy of the *Globe and Mail*, "is great stuff." He would be less enchanted by the third instalment in the next day's Saturday paper, when the journalist would discern something faintly presumptuous about the boy from Baie Comeau flitting around in a private jet, asking his friend and aide Stephen Leopold for "a cigarette, please."

Mulroney got out of Toronto on Saturday by the skin of his teeth. At a meeting of Metro women delegates he was reminded that Toronto considers itself the policy capital of the world, when a woman asked him about his science policy. His rather lame reply was that Canada was research-poor and needed more research and development, a theme he would know more about when he raised it himself in the 1983 leadership campaign. In answer to another question on how to curb government waste, he suggested it wouldn't hurt to mothball a few government jets.

And then he went out to the airport to get on his own. In the hotel elevator, he acknowledged that he had led with his prominent chin on that one. But then, as Bob McKenzie would observe many years later, "Brian has never been afraid of skating on thin ice. He likes to get out there and give it a whirl."

If he was picking up in the rest of the country, Mulroney had some miles to travel in Quebec. In Montreal the next evening, he drew a big crowd of 1,850 to a fund-raising dinner, not all of them paid by any means. Of the 450 delegates and alternates in the room, a majority of them were supporters of Claude Wagner. Still, Mulroney could claim it was a show of strength, both in Quebec and across the country. The turnout, he said, was "proof positive that Quebec is not the private sanctuary of a single man." In the context, it was evident that he was talking about Wagner, not Pierre Elliott Trudeau. But Mulroney did not make a good speech that night. Neither his prepared text nor his extemporaneous remarks had much in them. In a sense, he had misjudged his own occasion.

By now Mulroney had proven that he could draw a crowd, as his organizers had demonstrated that they could paper the house, but the candidate's needs were simpler in the last month. He needed delegates from Quebec to go with his gains in English-speaking Canada. In one three-day swing in the first week of February, it was difficult to measure how he was doing. Snowed out of the Gaspé by a terrible storm, he turned back and made for Black Lake and Thetford Mines before creeping along to Quebec City for the night. In Maurice Duplessis's old suite in the tower of the Château Frontenac the next morning, Mulroney fed the Quebec press corps with croissants, coffee, and a line about how Wagner's Quebec majority was "melting like a snowbank in May."

It was wishful thinking in regard to Quebec, where it was still the dead of winter for Mulroney. But the spring of his campaign was breaking over the rest of the country. "We're going to win this thing," he exulted in Le Chef's old suite that evening after a day of campaigning in and around Quebec. On the telephone, someone had just leaked word to him of a poll *The Toronto Star* would be running the next day, which showed he had moved up to second place at 14.9 per cent, behind Wagner at 17.2 per cent. Moreover, the Peter Regenstreif survey indicated Mulroney was the second choice of 25 per cent of the delegates, compared to only 12 per cent for Wagner.

By the time he got to Montreal the next evening and Ottawa the following day, he had attracted the kind of media mob that follows a front-runner. In an article alongside an interview in Saturday's *Le Devoir*, publisher Claude Ryan personally signed a laudatory piece under the headline: "Brian Mulroney, new meteor in the Conservative sky."

Unfortunately for Mulroney, there was more truth than Ryan intended by it, for his spectacular campaign was about to come to earth with a crash. *The Star* poll indicated to the media that he was a man to watch, and to the caucus and power brokers that he was a man to stop.

In Ottawa on February 6, reporters pressed him for any knowledge he might have of the Wagner trust. Whatever Mulroney might have known about it, he wasn't talking. But Peter White was, without attribution, to Bob McKenzie of *The Toronto Star*, for which he later offered no apology. "I was personally responsible for getting Claude Wagner into the Progressive Conservative Party," White said in 1984. "And I was willing to help get him out." To White, it wasn't the trust that was offensive but the fact that Wagner wasn't telling the whole story. But neither were White's motives wholly disinterested. He was trying to advance the cause of one candidate, Mulroney, and damage another, Wagner. It was a dirty errand, a job for a point man.

The story of the Wagner trust surfacing again may well have hurt the former judge, but it didn't help Mulroney, whose camp was regarded, not without reason, as the source of the latest information. And then, as Geoffrey Stevens noted in his *Globe* column on February 12, "Brian Mulroney's campaign seems, paradoxically, to be heading into trouble at the very moment it is achieving its greatest success." Delegates did not seem persuaded by Mulroney's protestations of ignorance regarding the Wagner trust, they were beginning to be offended by his high and expensive style, and, "more seriously, a definite anti-Mulroney backlash is developing among senior organizers for other candidates." Instead of the interesting dark horse, he had become the man to beat. And quite a few people in high places were determined to do so.

The only fear that Jean Bazin had expressed way back in August had been realized. "There is a risk," he had written to Mulroney, "that a campaign such as this will take off too quickly and reach its apogee before the 22nd of February." That risk had come to pass. Brian Mulroney, though he did not then know it, had peaked too soon.

On February 12, Mulroney quit the road and holed up for a few days at David Angus's country house on the Hermitage Club grounds near Magog in the Eastern Townships. He worked on his speech, a finely crafted address that was more of an acceptance speech than anything else. His organizers, and Mulroney, were trying to follow the script from the Trudeau convention in 1968, right down to the silhouette posters and the train ride from Montreal to Ottawa, with the big welcome at the station.

"We're well ahead," Mulroney confided on the train on February 18. "We'have 585 votes."

If he had, he might have won. But already his convention week was going badly for him even before he hit town. The *Gazette* carried a story that day detailing a $10,000 donation from Power Corporation, complete with quotes from Dave Angus. It couldn't have come at a worse time for Mulroney, who was fighting the impression that he was the candidate of the vested interests, the friend of the rich, the member from Power Corporation. And when he got into Ottawa, things only got worse.

Arriving at a downtown hotel, Mulroney did a second walk-through for the benefit of a television cameraman who had missed it the first time. The story spread around town in half an hour as evidence of the plastic man. And there were complaints that the Mulroney people had basically rented every big hall in town. "What a month before had been excitement, newness, and style had become slick, crass, and expensive," Cogger said later. "While some of it was well founded, some of it was nonsense. Hatfield said to me later, 'You should never have hired Bachman, Turner Overdrive.'" Which they never had, actually. They had spent $10,000 to hire Ginette Reno for a Friday night concert in the Coliseum adjoining the Civic Centre, which they had rented for the nominal cost of taking up the roller-skating track. Mulroney himself had ordered the Reno show cancelled, but the order was never received down the line. It wouldn't have mattered anyway. "By then," as Cogger said, "if you had said we were buying the Château Laurier, people would have believed it."

And then the powers-that-be in the party were deciding they would not be for Mulroney. Former Ontario Premier John Robarts had warned Cogger that he had never seen an unbrokered convention, and now the brokers were meeting in Ottawa and moving among the delegates-at-large. Mulroney tried to dismiss the suggestion that he could be stopped by the kingmakers. "At this convention, there are no kingmakers," he kept saying. "The delegates are king."

On Thursday night, after John Diefenbaker had received the tribute of the party, the old Chief made a speech in which he lashed out at the presumptuousness of anyone seeking the leadership without parliamentary experience. "When old Dief said that," Mulroney later recalled, "I looked around the hall and saw the vigour with which that statement was applauded by the supporters of all the other candidates and I knew that was it. I said to myself, 'I'm going to get hammered badly.' That's when I knew the gang bang was on." Mulroney turned to his wife and said, "Honey, we're dead in the water."

Afterwards, Mulroney never believed that he lost it on some performance in a policy workshop, or even because of his well-written but poorly observed speech. Still, he never stopped campaigning. Even after the speeches on Saturday night, he made the rounds of all the hotels and spoke in the lobbies to anyone who would listen. Even on Sunday afternoon, he worked the floor, going over to pump the hand of Bill Davis, who understandably looked as if he was shaking hands with a leper.

The first-ballot numbers were not so bad: Wagner, 531; Mulroney, 357; Clark, 277; Jack Horner, 235; Paul Hellyer, 231. If Quebec hadn't failed Mulroney, if he had only 100 votes more, he would have been first and Wagner second. Yet Mulroney later said that the convention was going to elect neither of them. "It was a convention for a third man," he said. And that third man was Joe Clark.

When Mulroney went off the ballot after the third round with 369 votes, only Clark, with 969, and Wagner, with 1,003, remained. Mulroney might have made one or the other leader. But he sat on his hands instead. Even if Mulroney had been inclined to go to Wagner, he said, "Most of my delegates wouldn't have followed. And I did the only honourable thing, the only thing I could do, just as John Crosbie did later on."

It would be many years before Mulroney would look at it as a learning rather than a losing experience. "That was tough," he said nearly eight years later. "I'm not going to try to make out that it wasn't. You can become vindictive about it, or it can become part of a growing experience." It was four years before the bitterness passed, and four more before he could say: "When I look back on it, I was thirty-six or whatever, to the extent that I'm qualified for the job, that anyone can be, I'm infinitely better qualified today."

His younger brother Gary, a fine arts teacher in Montreal, later thought that 1976 was the "worst thing that ever happened to him and the best thing that ever happened to him." His mother thought of it as a growing experience for both Brian and Mila Mulroney. And Sam Wakim, his friend through it all, later said "that without '76 there would have been no Mulroney in '83, and he showed his capacity for growth in the meantime."

He certainly remembered the lessons and the mistakes of the first campaign, none of which would be repeated if the chance ever arose again. But that kind of serenity would not be easily achieved. First, there was the bitterness to be lived and the campaign debts to be paid. When he left Ottawa and went home to Montreal the next day, no one could say if and when he would be back. It was too early to say whether the man had missed the moment, or the moment had missed the man.

8
RIGHT UP
ON TOP

"I think these babies have got themselves a deal," Mulroney said later.

He was hardly back in his law office before he had a call from Bob Anderson, then second in command of the Hanna Mining Company, in Cleveland. "I'd like to talk to you," Anderson said, after commiserating with Mulroney on the outcome of the convention.

Hanna was the American mining and steel company with a controlling interest in the Iron Ore Company of Canada, which took ore out of the hills of the North Shore of Quebec and Labrador, turned it into pellets for blast furnaces, and shipped the product out of Sept-Iles and up to the Great Lakes and the smokestack industries of Middle America.

Anderson and Mulroney had talked before, in the spring and summer of 1975. The IOC had serious labour problems and was incurring equally serious operating losses. Moreover, its president, Bill Bennett, was reaching retirement age and, with his superiors in Cleveland, was scouting around for a successor.

Bennett had given Mulroney a strike to settle as far back as 1969, when they lived for ten days in adjoining suites of the Château Frontenac. This did not go unnoticed among the people up from Cleveland and New York. Bennett occasionally called on Mulroney's services after that, and during the Cliche Commission he invited him to dinner at Ruby Foo's.

Anderson flew in from Cleveland with Carl Nickels, one of his senior vice-presidents. Over drinks and dinner, they talked about the royal commission and the problems in the construction industry, of which the IOC people had more than a passing acquaintance since they had a horrendous cost overrun on a smelter they were trying to build in Sept-Iles.

"The violence in the construction industry was now localized

in Seven Islands," Mulroney later explained, "and that was con-
tributing to the worsening of labour relations throughout the
whole town. I mean, they were carrying guns on the streets of
Seven Islands. The Iron Ore Company was trying to put up new
plants and they couldn't because of the violence in the construction industry. The construction industry people would come
inside the plants and infect the steelworkers with the same
kinds of attitudes. I mean, they couldn't start the plant. They
couldn't finish building it."

It soon became apparent that Mulroney was not just being
invited out for Chinese food, he was being sized up for a job at
Iron Ore. And he was quite happy to go on at some length when
they asked him what was wrong with the company. "I told them
it was going down the chute because it wasn't being properly
run, and that management had to show some strength in communications capacity." In other words, they had to get someone
up in Sept-Iles and Schefferville who could communicate with
the union leadership and rank and file in their own language –
French.

"How the hell are you going to run anything when it's on
strike?" Mulroney asked years later. "Be it a chocolate factory or a
mine. You can have the best product in the world, but if nobody
is working, or somebody is throwing monkey wrenches into your
$200-million plants, you're dead. So we discussed the debt in the
Iron Ore Company. They gave me the full breakdown of how bad
it looked. And that was that."

Then in the summer of 1975, when Mulroney was weighing a
run for the leadership, Anderson approached him with a firm
offer to join IOC. Mulroney declined with thanks, explaining that
he had decided to run for the leadership because "this thing may
only come around once in a lifetime and I'm going to give it a go."

When Anderson called in the days following the convention,
Mulroney put him off again. He had campaign debts; Mila was
about to have their second child; and he had to digest the bitterness of his defeat, much less get it out of his system. But he did
promise Anderson an answer by the beginning of June.

In the next three months, Mulroney negotiated a back-loaded
five-year contract that made it increasingly attractive for him to
stay right to the end, certainly well past the next federal election. The final offer from Iron Ore, with its equity and pension
benefits, would assure Mulroney of lifetime financial security.
The next time he reached for the brass ring, he would not have to
worry about what would happen to him if he lost or what would
happen to his family if anything happened to him. It was all

there in the five-year deal with "these babies" from Cleveland. In early June, Mulroney called Bennett and told him he had decided to accept the offer to come in as executive vice-president. Then he called Anderson in Cleveland. "You got yourself a deal," Mulroney said.

It was understood that Mulroney would remain executive VP for a year and then, if things worked to the satisfaction of both sides, take over from Bennett at his retirement. "I said, 'You take a hard look at me,'" Mulroney later explained. "I said, 'I've got a lot of learning to do, and this is brand new for me. It may turn out that I don't like it at all. It may turn out that you don't like me. If you don't like me, I want the time to get turned around.' So it was to be an agreement that I could walk away from, with time."

There were two things about Mulroney in the Iron Ore years. The obvious one, and it was immediate, was his new affluence. The second thing, which only became apparent much later on, was how much he was learning and growing on the job. The Iron Ore presidency meant prestige and standing in the Montreal business community. With it went a membership in the Mount Royal Club, a fishing camp in Labrador, a couple of company planes, and four box seats behind the Canadiens' bench at the Forum. What also went with it was the means to purchase the house on the hill, the big place on Belvedere Road that the Mulroneys moved into at the end of 1976.

He was discussing this one day with Bob Lewis, then Ottawa bureau chief of *Maclean's* but also an expatriate Montrealer. Lewis said he'd heard Mulroney had a new joint somewhere in upper Westmount and inquired as to its exact whereabouts.

"You know, right up on top?" Mulroney asked.

"Yeah."

"Well, right up on top."

Anyone who had grown up in a company town, or anyone who knew Montreal, understood what he was saying. In most company towns, if they didn't have a hill for the management homes, they would build one. In Montreal, some people might regard Mulroney as somewhat *arriviste* for moving to the top of the hill, just as they might sneer at his propensity for wearing Italian loafers. In his own mind, it didn't matter. He had arrived.

But he had some painful adjustments to make, not just to the routine and rhythm of a bottom-line man, but he had to accept the fact that he had been defeated by Joe Clark. "He was up and down, reliving it," recalled Tommy Montgomery, his mentor at his old law firm. "He couldn't leave it alone. I thought he might be permanently damaged by it, though he managed to function all right. But he did have a period of black depression."

In his bleakest moments, he occasionally worried about "kicking the bucket" as a young man. He once told Montgomery he had a dream he was going to die. He would occasionally check into the hospital for general tests, only to be told he was a perfectly healthy, if somewhat run-down, male specimen of the species.

And always there was the brooding over his defeat.

Years later, he could look back on it with a surprising degree of objectivity and equanimity. The Iron Ore move had been good all-round, he would say, good for him, good for Mila. "It helped get the convention, the political stuff, it started to remove it," he said. "You have to remove yourself from old situations, and old habits, otherwise you relive the stuff, which everyone of value in a leadership convention is condemned to do. You can't change it."

This was after the 1984 Liberal leadership convention, when those who had lost to John Turner were experiencing the same pain and disappointment. "I mean," he said, "we're all the same, we're all condemned to relive the damn thing. I mean, it would take a pretty frivolous guy, when you think about it, who would commit himself and his dollars and his energy and his future, to something, and then to lose, and to walk away from it and say, 'Well, it really wasn't important.'"

In his own case, leaving his law practice took him away from his former haunts and opened up a new world to him. Anderson and his colleagues in Cleveland couldn't care less about the Conservative Party or Joe Clark. They were more concerned about getting things turned around in the IOC. And that wasn't going to be easy, except that compared to the way things had been going, they could only get better. Iron Ore had endured nearly sixty work stoppages of one kind or another in the previous decade. It hadn't paid a dividend in ten years. It had a huge debt. And it had a terrible labour relations problem with its 7,000 employees.

Mulroney could go back to the North Shore as the son of a unionized electrician from Baie Comeau and as someone who could communicate the company message to the workers. It was also apparent to his new employers that Mulroney could make the big phone calls to all the right people on both sides of the parliamentary aisles in Ottawa, Quebec City, and St. John's, the three government towns where the IOC did business.

"I don't think Brian was hired to be the complete CEO," observed his friend Paul Martin, himself chief executive officer of the CSL shipping group. "They hired him for those strengths, and he did

117

grow." Martin noted that he often heard it said around town that Mulroney was essentially a communicator and a lobbyist with no intrinsic executive skills. "If you're going to disqualify Canadian businessmen because they're only partial CEOs," Martin said, "then you could eliminate half the membership of the Mount Royal Club and two-thirds of the Toronto Club."

He was in a good position to observe Mulroney's growth. Martin had come to Montreal in 1966 as executive assistant to Maurice Strong, then president of Power Corporation, and he stayed on when Paul Desmarais took over the store. Martin said of Mulroney, "You'd see it in a conversation," how he had grown. "He had gone from how do you solve a labour problem, to the problem underlying it, to how to improve productivity and the financial ramifications of all those things."

Desmarais, who was also well placed to observe the growth in Mulroney, offered much the same appraisal. "The IOC experience," said Desmarais, "gave him a better understanding of what business is about."

In a way, the IOC was a microcosm of the Canadian economy, resource-based, sensitive to world economic trends, reliant on its dealings with government in a complex federal system. And to get the product out, IOC was reliant on the felicitous functioning of the Canadian transport system. The ships would sail up the St. Lawrence, past four and a half centuries of Canadian history, to the Seaway at Montreal and the Great Lakes beyond: the hinterland supplying the heartland. The iron-ore pellets that had left the docks of Sept-Iles would come back to the streets of Sept-Iles as Chryslers.

Buying fleets of cars for the company, Mulroney learned that Detroit's product was more expensive than the Toyotas he could buy from Tokyo. So he had to inform himself about the problems of the North American steel industry. And with Detroit idling, he had to try to find new world markets for Labrador ore, an inferior grade to the competition from Brazil and Sweden. Altogether, it was quite an education for Mulroney.

As he also discovered, it was quite a responsibility. "The problems were huge," he said later. "But interestingly enough, the problems were all rooted in people, as they invariably turn out to be, mostly rooted in people. In a dozen different ways. By that I mean people running the wrong people in the wrong places, to wrong attitudes to poor productivity, to poor labour relations, to poor you name it."

What he learned, he acknowledged, was how to run a ship from stem to stern. "I learned and assumed responsibility over a period of time," he said, "as the chairman of the executive management for day-to-day and long-term management of the company. Personnel responsibilities, promotions, demotions, rewards, labour relations, productivity enhancement, all our financial side, the whole thing."

As he said, he had gone in a very short period of time from a law firm to a royal commission, to a big industrial shop. Despite some animosity and a good deal of scepticism, among both management and the workers, about this outsider being parachuted into the top job, he figured he would just have to win them over. There was nothing new to him about that.

Mulroney set about the process of achieving peace and productivity on the North Shore. By the end of 1981, the company had achieved a profit position of $100 million on its $1-billion investment. There was no doubt that the shareholders were pleased, and Mulroney was able to get the board to authorize a $250 Christmas bonus to each employee, as well as a $100 monthly increase in the pension benefits of surviving spouses. The steelworkers' union protested about this unilateral paternalism, and of course they sounded like a North Shore version of Scrooge. The workers happily accepted the money.

Mulroney had always known that cash money was an important consideration for getting people to work in small towns, which was one of the reasons he was so upset with Allan MacEachen's budget of November, 1981, which proposed to do away substantially with northern benefits. Mulroney had learned a good deal about tax law and about the impact of budgets, certainly more than the young officials in Finance who had given MacEachen such bad advice.

By the end of 1981, after five years at Iron Ore, the lawyer and prospective politician had become a business executive in fact as well as in name. By then, said Paul Desmarais, he had "a good understanding of business." From the Sept-Iles experience, Desmarais said, "he had his own private view of a mixed economy, of people working, of capital working, of people managing, productivity and the effects of new technology on his workers. All these things, when he reads about them now, they will not be words in a book. They're something he's lived through and understands."

He had also learned a good deal about the impact of inflation on monetary policy, and of monetary policy on exchange rates. "Your sales and profit margin require constant monitoring," he explained, "because we were paying for goods and services in Canadian dollars and selling them in American dollars. Obviously to me, the exchange rate became something of great value to understand and operate under."

He also learned something about paying down the company's long-term debt. "When you've got a company with assets of a billion dollars and $475 million in long-term debt," he said, "you've got a problem, so your debt repayment schedule becomes your number-one preoccupation."

He acknowledged that he had been "frustrated sometimes" by the rigid routine of the executive suite, with a calendar over the fiscal year, from one annual meeting to the next. "When you come in, you don't understand that," he said. "And then you don't understand how until you have done it – why there is certain documentation required and when it's required, and so on. Why these meetings must take place. But once you get into it, I could remember some years later, being able on New Year's Day to plan my year. I knew pretty well what I was going to be doing."

While Mulroney denied that was ever bored with the job, there were periods when he had too much time on his hands. He threw himself into a round of volunteer activities in 1977, as vice-chairman and then as chairman of Centraide, the United Way community fund-raising venture in Montreal. He then presided over the St. F.X. development campaign, which went $4 million over its $7-million objective. One of the small pleasures was in being able to fly down to the Canso jet strip in the morning, drop into St. F.X. for lunch, and drop off $1 million in cheques. When it was considered that some twenty-five years before he had arrived there carrying a cardboard suitcase, it was a fairly satisfactory turn of events.

After the election of the Parti Québécois in 1976, Mulroney, as a vice-chairman of the Council of Canadian Unity, became involved in the founding of the Pro-Canada Committee, the first umbrella grouping of the federalist forces. Their founding meeting at the Château Frontenac was hailed by the keynote speaker, Claude Ryan, as an historic event. That the Pro-Canada umbrella ultimately collapsed was inevitable. For one thing, it was an unwieldy coalition of fourteen groups, from the federal Liberals to the provincial Créditistes, not to mention national unity groups in all shapes and sizes, from the populist Quebec-Canada Movement to the elitist Positive Action Committee. More to the point, when Ryan became leader of the Quebec Liberals with legal responsibility to lead the "No" forces into the referendum, he understandably shut down the Pro-Canada umbrella.

From the founding of Pro-Canada at the end of 1977 to the 1980 plebiscite, Mulroney was more concerned with the refer-

120

endum issue in Quebec than with the prospects of the Conservative Party in the election. He wasn't going to run in 1979 anyway, and with his five-year contract he had a convenient out. He had so informed Clark and the leader quite graciously offered Mulroney's own explanations for staying home.

Whatever bitterness he might still have harboured in private, Mulroney was determined not to be perceived as a sore loser in public. He acted as chairman of Clark's Montreal dinner just before the election was called, an event that drew some 2,000 people to the Queen Elizabeth Hotel, a far cry from the 600 stragglers Mulroney used to paper the house with in the days of Bob Stanfield.

When Clark's government fell in December there was renewed pressure on Mulroney to run in the February, 1980, election. This time his old friends Cogger and Bazin, as part of the Clark organization, pressed him to enlist as a candidate. Clark himself reached him in Florida at Christmas and asked him to run. Putting an optimistic interpretation on the party's polling data, Clark suggested the Tories still might be returned with a minority. But Mulroney had heard of a Carleton University poll for Southam News that placed the Tories in a hopeless situation, some 20 percentage points behind the Liberals.

Mulroney stayed in Florida in December and January, and in February he was still at Iron Ore. Yet, he was enough of a Tory partisan to hope that Clark would pull it out. "There must be some benefit to us in this embassy stuff," Mulroney said some three weeks before the election, after the story broke of the Canadian embassy staff in Tehran spiriting six Americans out of the country in the midst of the hostage crisis. There might have been enough to encourage the Tory vote to go home, but, as it developed on February 18, no more.

With the defeat of Clark and the Liberal restoration, Quebec and the country turned to the referendum campaign, which for a time the sovereignty forces appeared to be winning. Mulroney played a modest role when he got caught up in one of those wonderful exchanges of insults that fill the letters-to-the-editor pages of the French press in Quebec. Louis Laberge, whom he had seen across many a negotiating table, had called the federalist "No" committee a coalition of reactionary forces. And he named names, including Brian Mulroney. Even Dedé Desjardins, of Cliche Commission fame, got into the act by writing a letter to *La Presse* in which he lambasted his one-time nemesis.

"I couldn't believe how lucky I was getting," Mulroney said later. "When Dedé got into it and attacked me, this was terrific. I kept it going, because when you've got Dedé and Louis going against you, you're real lucky."

Mulroney and Laberge carried their quarrel right into the CTV referendum-night studio in Montreal, where they engaged in a shouting match worthy of the best tavern brawl. It may not have been the most dignified spectacle in the world, but for Conservatives looking in across the country it was a rather loud reminder that Mulroney was still alive and kicking.

Then, in September, he made his first important speech in Montreal in the four and a half years since his defeat. The audience was a carefully chosen non-partisan forum of chartered accountants. The message was an elegantly worded but thinly disguised attack on the Conservative Party's role in the referendum campaign. It was only a modest role, he said, "and in this province, we have much to be modest about."

Reminding his audience of the party's chronic weakness in French Canada, he suggested a seven-point program for establishing a presence in the minds of Quebec voters, beginning with the early selection of candidates for the next election. Since the party had no base in dozens of ridings, it should look for candidates with their own networks of friends: school commissioners and credit-union managers, candidates who could come with their own built-in organizations.

"The kind of attention he received from print and television reporters," observed Bill Johnson in the *Globe and Mail*, "was that usually given a candidate declaring for a party's leadership." Johnson concluded that Mulroney, "at 41, is clearly a voice that will be heard."

At that point, he was being seen more than heard. His speech reminded Tory partisans, especially in Quebec, that he was still out there. It was close enough to the coming February 28 leadership review that the outing would be remembered, far enough away, and on high enough ground, that he could not be accused of grasping for Clark's job.

For the review in the Ottawa Civic Centre, Mulroney and his wife sat near the back of the hall, routinely applauding Clark's speech and voting before heading back to their suite at the Château Laurier. His own instincts and intelligence told him that the review forces were coming on strong. The estimate of review operatives on the day of the vote was that they had 35 per cent. It came in at 33.1 per cent, enough to cripple Clark's leadership but not enough to force him to ask for a convention. Ironically, in the view of Mulroney sympathizers like Rodrigue Pageau, Clark waited until 1983 to make the decision he should have made in 1981. In Pageau's view, Clark would have turned back any and all comers in 1981, including Mulroney. "It was too soon for Brian," Pageau said. Bill Davis was in the middle of an election campaign; John Crosbie was not yet organized; and Peter Lougheed would never have left Alberta.

Mulroney had his own problems in 1981, and they involved staying out of a by-election in Joliette, where Roch LaSalle had resigned to run and lose provincially that spring as leader of the Union Nationale. In the weeks before Trudeau set the by-election, Mulroney's name was the source of frequent speculation. In sitting out the 1979 and 1980 elections, he could cite his five-year contractual obligations to Iron Ore. But in the summer of 1981 those five years were up. As he himself said in the 1983 leadership debate in Toronto, and as he later repeated to Pam Wallin on CTV's *Canada A.M.*: "I became a free agent only on June 1, 1981."

Somehow, none of his opponents ever seized on the flaw of this logic to point out that his argument should have propelled him into the race for a by-election called only in early July. In fact, Mulroney was keeping his powder dry at Iron Ore. In the fall of 1981, he came to Clark's rescue by taking over a fund-raising dinner to which, as he did not fail to remind his sources in the press, only eighty-two or so tickets had been sold. But in so doing, he was also ignoring the advice of some of his friends that he should simply let the dinner go down the tube. "I don't think we can do that," he told one of his closest political confidants, "for the good of the party."

A week before the dinner, Mulroney travelled to Baie Comeau to make a widely publicized speech calling on Quebec and Newfoundland to come to terms on the question of Churchill Falls, urging Quebec to re-open the negotiations on the price of Upper Churchill power and Newfoundland to get down to cases with Quebec on developing the power resources of the Lower Churchill.

He also urged Pierre Trudeau and René Lévesque to end their constitutional squabble, offering them the services of an Iron Ore guest house as a negotiating venue.

It was in a place that would be heard of again, called Schefferville.

9

THE RITZ COMPACT

No one would ask what Joe Clark and Brian Mulroney were doing in a place like this. But a good many people wondered what they were doing there at the Ritz-Carlton together, holding a joint news conference to proclaim Mulroney's endorsement of the incumbent.

Mulroney read a three-page statement, first in French, then in English. The review process was "an ennobling instrument of democracy," and the delegates to Winnipeg could make their choice "freely and thoughtfully, as was intended by the reform of 1966." As for himself, he had travelled the country exchanging views with his fellow citizens, which was "my privilege as a Canadian and . . . my duty as a Conservative." But he now thought that Canadians wanted a change of government and "Mr. Clark's re-confirmation as leader is an important part of this process. His subsequent re-election as prime minister will be good for Canada." That, with one more reference to "proceeding to the confirmation of Mr. Clark," was it.

It wasn't much. But, on December 6, 1982, it was all Clark was going to get. Understandably suspicious of Mulroney's motives, reporters asked if he had instructed his supporters working for review to cease their activities. "I have no supporters," Mulroney replied, "only friends."

It was a careful distinction. There was a nuance in Mulroney's answer to another question, about whether he would run under Clark's banner at the next election. Let Mr. Trudeau issue the writs, went Mulroney's enigmatic reply, "and I'll be there."

It was the most sincere and truthful utterance of the public part of the event. Before they had come down to meet reporters shoehorned into a small salon of the Ritz-Carlton, Mulroney and Clark met for a good hour upstairs. As Mulroney later recalled it, he advised Clark that he was not entirely out of the woods and repeated the message at a second private meeting afterwards.

"Where do you think I am?" Clark asked.

Mulroney replied that the endorsement should move him from one-third to two-thirds support in Quebec. "Joe," Mulroney said, "there are 35 per cent of the people in the province of Quebec in the Conservative Party who wouldn't support you under any circumstances. This will bring you up to 65 per cent, roughly 65 per cent."

"What do you think about the convention?" Clark asked.

"Well, Joseph," Mulroney replied, "if 66 per cent was good enough in 1981, it's goddamn well good enough today."

As Finlay MacDonald was his witness, Mulroney swore "that's exactly what I told him, in exactly those words." As for himself, Mulroney had told his closest friends and advisers the day before that he was "getting out of the traffic."

He made this observation several times in the course of meetings with two different groups of advisers on December 5. The second meeting, which has been written about elsewhere, was held in the living room of Mulroney's home on Belvedere Road, on the Sunday afternoon, and about two dozen Mulroney loyalists attended. But by then the decision to get out of the traffic had already been announced at a previous meeting of Mulroney's inner circle that had gathered for lunch at Guy Charbonneau's duplex apartment in Westmount Square.

Besides Charbonneau and Mulroney, only Frank Moores, Peter White, Elmer MacKay, Sam Wakim, and Michel Cogger were present. Cogger announced at the outset that he would not state his views. And Wakim would follow Mulroney anywhere. The others were not so reticent. Not only was Mulroney making a mistake, they told him, he was making it worse by appearing with Clark, leaving himself open to the accusation that he was a ruthless opportunist and a shameless hypocrite. "There was ferocious opposition to it," Mulroney later remembered, "and bitter words were exchanged at that meeting."

Charbonneau's assessment of the mood was more senatorial. "Some of the boys," he acknowledged, "were pretty disappointed." Or, as Frank Moores put it: "If he was asking for a consensus, he sure as hell went against the consensus."

Each of the six members of the inner circle had his own reason for being there. MacKay, attending his first meeting of the group, was the link to the caucus. He was not persuaded by Mulroney's arguments. "I felt at that stage that the review process had to go on," MacKay said. "And I felt at that stage that Joe's claims had to be reinforced by another test." While MacKay could see Mulroney's reasons for stepping aside, he was horrified that Mulroney proposed to do so in a very public joint news conference with Clark. "I just thought he should have put out a press release, stating his general support for Clark, without going to such lengths," MacKay said. "I was concerned it might send out signals that were not appropriate. He went too far, I thought, and created problems for himself. A lot of the boys were quite upset. They felt that Brian had dealt the whole review mechanism a blow. But Brian made such a production of it, he looked unnecessarily hypocritical. He was caught between the invidious choices of looking hypocritical and opportunistic."

Mulroney offered several arguments in support of his decision. He said he didn't want to see any damage done to the party, that as far as he could see there was no great desire to push Clark out nor any great desire to keep him, but that the two groups were on a collision course and he proposed to get out of the road. Besides, the focus had to swing back on what review was all about, and the only way to do that was to depersonalize the debate. Furthermore, he said he didn't want Quebec to get blamed for an anti-Clark putsch. Then as later, Mulroney was both sensitive and touchy on this point. John Crosbie's friends might organize the Newfoundland delegation for review, but he wouldn't get blamed for it. Conservative premiers Bill Davis and Peter Lougheed might sit on the sidelines, but no one could accuse them of not being on the high road. Mulroney wanted some room for himself on the high road.

Peter White, who like Cogger went back more than twenty years with Mulroney, was one of those people who could look him in the eye and tell him to get to the point. White could also take the long view of things, and he didn't like the smell of a news conference. He thought it would hurt Mulroney at Winnipeg, with the delegates in a leadership convention, and with the voters in an election, and he said so. Even after Mulroney had become leader, White still felt uneasy about the event and thought that it was a factor in Mulroney's trust problems that showed up in later polls.

In a real sense, White had been the creator of the review circle around Mulroney. As early as the winter of 1982, he recalled, "I kept saying, 'Brian, we've got to have a meeting.'" And so they began to have sessions of the inner group every two weeks or so at the Mount Royal Club or across the street at the Ritz.

Peter White wrote the kind of memos Mulroney appreciated,

at once detailed and pertinent, with short paragraphs and sharply enumerated points. Of his own volition, White had drafted a six-page, single-spaced, legal-sized memorandum to Mulroney in February of 1982. He outlined a scenario that would unfold in three phases, "Before the Call," "After the Call," and, finally, during "Convention Week." It was a pragmatic and prescient piece of work.

In the first phase, he called for "regular meetings of [the] core group, every week or second week, probably in this city [Montreal]." And, as White noted, "security is also very important, and nothing must be done to precipitate Phase Two." Once a convention had been called, Mulroney should have clearly developed strategies and objectives for Phase Two, for meeting the delegates and keeping the lines open to the other camps. As for his prospective candidate's tour activities, White warned: "Beware media disenchantment and backlash. Emphasize no messiahs. Go underground after announcement and let media come to us."

There was nothing particularly treasonous or treacherous about the White memo. He was only proposing an agenda and a posture in the event that Mulroney, in one of his own favourite expressions, got another kick at the can. "We all expected there would eventually be another leadership campaign," White said.

And in the winter and spring of 1982, Mulroney went about the business of consolidating his Quebec base and letting the news media and rank and file have a second look at him. In one five-week period in April and May, he made five speeches. The events were perfectly legitimate, fund-raisers staged by local associations who wanted a speaker with some box-office appeal. "I had literally a hundred invitations, and I accepted five or six of them," Mulroney said. He wouldn't have called it a cross-country speaking tour, even though it took him across the country. But by making a series of speeches on major economic themes, he hoped to dissipate the perception that he was merely a talking head, and not one with many ideas in it.

"You want policy? Here's some goddamn policy for you," he said as he tossed a text at Bill Fox, later to be his press secretary but then the Ottawa bureau chief of *The Toronto Star*. They were sitting in Mulroney's room in the downtown Holiday Inn in Ottawa. In a few hours, Mulroney would go downstairs to deliver his first speech in the capital since his defeat in 1976. It was April 22, 1982, six years and two months later to the day, and Mulroney did not have to be reminded of the importance of his speech to the Ottawa-Carleton riding association. In the national press gallery, there was a highly developed disdain and this was one of the few precincts left in the country where he was not well accepted. Since he did not think highly of the press gallery, he had made no serious efforts to ingratiate himself with them. If they wanted to see him, as some of them occasionally did, they could come and have lunch with him in Montreal.

The Ottawa press corps had always acknowledged he had style; now he was determined to show them some substance. They wouldn't pay much attention to his ideas, least of all to a forty-five-minute text on Canada's productivity problems, but afterwards no one could say he didn't have any ideas.

So he set out to beat one of the bad raps left over from 1976. And he was determined to do it on the productivity question, an issue in which he could raise a policy profile that was his own.

"The definition of productivity is pretty uncomplicated," he began. "It is what you get out for what you put in, in capital resources and labour. Productivity is not a judgement on how hard people are working. It is a measurement of efficiency – how intelligently and innovatively industry uses each of the elements that go into creating a product or service. That measurement, GNP per worker, determines total income."

Mulroney rattled off a few productivity bullets: Canada was afflicted with negative productivity growth in the first two years of the 1980's; the country had dropped from second to twelfth place in productivity among the twenty-four-nation Organization of Economic Co-operation and Development. And to demonstrate that he knew of which he spoke, Mulroney gave the example of the iron ore that leaves Labrador, crosses the Pacific Ocean to Japan, and comes back in a Toyota Corolla that costs over $500 less than a comparable Chevy Cavalier, complete with rebate, made in Oshawa from the same Labrador ore.

Altogether, it was a solid performance. Of course, the news leads all referred to Mulroney's requisite denials that he was running for anything, while implying that he was. But at least he couldn't be criticized for not saying anything. He had learned one important rule of the media game: you have to give them something to not write about.

In the leader's office as well as over at party headquarters on Laurier Street, the Clark people weren't particularly interested in Mulroney's policies, either. Nor were they persuaded by his plea that he was merely raising money on the party's behalf and speaking out as a concerned citizen.

Six days after the Ottawa speech, Mulroney was in Toronto at a fund-raiser for John Bosley in Don Valley West. Bosley was known to be a Clark loyalist and Mulroney later said, "That's why I went there," to deflect suspicion that he was part of a cabal. Mulroney was back in Toronto a week later at a Westin Hotel fund-raiser for the Tory association of Broadview-Greenwood, where there was a by-election coming up later in the year to fill a vacancy left when Bob Rae moved to the Ontario legislature to lead the New Democratic Party at Queen's Park. Mulroney may have been raising funds to help pay off campaign debts in the riding, but he was also giving the national media in Toronto their second look at him in a week.

Then it was on to Vancouver on May 17, where over 500 people turned out for a North Vancouver-Burnaby dinner at the Hotel Vancouver. "I took a lot of static over that fund-raiser," said Chuck Cook, the MP who had invited Mulroney. "The PC Canada fund threatened not to give tax receipts."

Mulroney was furious and remained angry for months. "I was very upset," he said, "after all I had done for the party." He was left shaking with rage by a Southam news story that he had run up a big tab for room service. "It was just venomous what was done," he said. Mulroney should not have been surprised that the Clark people used every bit of leverage at their disposal to defend the incumbent, including discrediting a would-be dauphin. What the Clark agents may not have realized was that nearly every bit of derogatory gossip about Mulroney was picked up on the Hill by Pat MacAdam, who seldom wasted any time in passing it back to his former schoolmate. In any event, by the time he closed off his spring swing in Fredericton, Mulroney had hit a campaign stride with a speech full of bullets and bombast aimed at the Trudeau government's management of the economy and reckless deficit spending.

"What would I do?" Mulroney asked. "I'd cut everywhere and under every circumstance. I'd cut consultants, outside accountants, advertising, public service compensation, waste, unproductive travel, indexed pensions and fringes, capital construction programs, capital overruns, and just plain bureaucratic excess – to name but a few examples."

Leaving aside the rhetoric, Mulroney proceeded to lay down the planks that would comprise his leadership platform in a year's time: on the National Energy Program, the Foreign Investment Review Agency, a national industrial strategy, productivity enhancement, and research and development. The R&D theme would become another of Mulroney's hobby horses. If Canada would double its R&D commitment to 1.5 per cent of GNP, he asserted, this would "ultimately provide one million new jobs and generate $20 billion in new manufacturing sales. I believe that we require some dramatic tax reform regarding investments in high technology. If this country can afford to give total write-offs on third-rate pictures you wouldn't even show in your own basement, we can certainly do no less for high-tech industries which will ensure a viable future for our children."

Mulroney's policy pronouncements on the economy could hardly be said to have generated a sensation in the country, but he had dealt with the criticism that he had no ideas. And he had satisfied himself that if and when there was a next time, he had his stuff together.

Mulroney made two important decisions in the summer of 1982. He went to lunch and he went fishing.

As he did nearly every day when he was in Montreal, Mulroney walked through the open double doors of the Mount Royal Club, one of those places that lowered its flag for deceased members and made women come in by the side door. Mulroney generally took a private salon upstairs, partly because he did not like people eavesdropping on his conversations.

On one mid-July day, he had an important private conversation with Guy Charbonneau, for whom he had secured a Senate appointment during the brief season of Joe Clark's administration. Over Mulroney's objections, Clark had named Arthur Tremblay from the Quebec City area instead of Pierre Boutin, a wealthy Grande Allée figure who had been raising and giving money to the party for years. Tremblay was a retired civil servant of considerable distinction, having been Deputy Minister of Education during the 1960's and Deputy Minister of Intergovernmental Affairs before his retirement in 1977. Though he was associated with Liberal regimes, he knew the Parti Québécois crowd quite well and was meant to give Clark the inside track on the Lévesque government's referendum question and appropriate posture for the federal government. It was a defensible, even laudable nomination, an argument for an appointive upper chamber, where people could be kept around for the quality of their advice. But Clark also wanted to fill a second Quebec vacancy with Alfred Rouleau, nearing the end of his career as president of the $12-billion Caisse Populaire Desjardins, the jewel of Quebec's credit union movement. Not only had he never done anything for the Tory party, there was a very narrow limit as to what he could do for Clark.

Charbonneau had been raising money for the party in Quebec and across the country since 1956, through thick and thin, in nine elections between 1957 and 1979. When Mulroney lobbied for Charbonneau's Senate nomination with Clark, the Prime Minister assured him he would go in the second wave of appointments. "What if there is no second wave?" Mulroney asked. Charbonneau got his appointment on the same day as Tremblay. Charbonneau was a rare bird in Quebec Conservative circles, a graduate of Collège Brebeuf and a contemporary of Pierre Trudeau.

Charbonneau did not really fit either mould. Although he had known and liked Trudeau for over forty years, Charbonneau considered him a bit of a socialist. In his ideological makeup, he was closer to the denizens of the oil patch, more at home at the Petroleum Club than the Liberal salons of Outremont. Neither did Charbonneau seek the limelight. He was delighted when he was not named once by Patrick Martin and his co-authors in *The Contenders*, their book on the 1983 leadership. In fact, Charbonneau was one of Mulroney's closest advisers, as well as a personal friend. As they sat down for lunch that July day, Charbonneau wanted to give some straight advice and get some clear guidance from his prospective candidate. Winnipeg was only seven months away, and the Clark forces were already well organized in Quebec.

"Look, Brian," Charbonneau said, "if you want to lead this party some day, you better do something."

Mulroney had a problem. He didn't want to be seen as the agent of Clark's downfall. But neither, if the incumbent was in genuine difficulty in other parts of the country, did he want to hand him Quebec on a silver platter. Clark's salaried operatives were already at work in the Quebec ridings, selling memberships and sewing up a good number of ridings.

Mulroney and Charbonneau achieved an understanding. If people wanted to work for review, there was nothing he could or should do about it. That was all Charbonneau needed to get a review operation under way in Quebec. With Michel Cogger, Rodrigue Pageau, Jean-Yves Lortie, and Jacques Blanchard in the Quebec City region, they began getting their own delegates appointed to Winnipeg.

The summer operation leading up to Winnipeg served as a warning to the Mulroney forces, or should have, as to how tough the going would be the following spring. "We controlled the provincial executive," Charbonneau said, "but Clark, through the national director, controlled the people who were paid." Charbonneau's solution was simple. They would get organized themselves. Even then, it was an uphill battle. Pageau, who had known Mulroney since the time he was working for Daniel Johnson in the late 1960's, was a fiery whirlwind of a man who threw everything behind the effort to dislodge Clark. The problem, as he later acknowledged, was that "Clark had an overt campaign organization in place." Pageau and the others set to work and by the middle of August they had stopped the run-off to Clark in Quebec.

In the meantime, Mulroney had gone fishing over the last weekend of July with an interesting cast of characters he assembled at Innotech Aviation in Dorval for the flight to Labrador City and the IOC fishing camp at Lac Koberdoc on the Quebec side, an area with ravaging streams known to yield four- and five-pound speckled trout to even the most unskilled angler. The Iron Ore jet, a DH-125, Mulroney had picked up from Nelson Skalbania when the Vancouver businessman started his losing streak. The passengers he had picked up in a quarter of a century as a Conservative activist.

There was Dalton Camp, who knew a thing or two about leadership review, since he had invented the process. There was Finlay MacDonald, the man who invented Bob Stanfield and who by now was the head of the PC Canada fund. There was Bill Neville, formerly Clark's chief of staff. Mulroney had used his influence with the Bank of Commerce, of which he was a director, to ease Neville's return to the private sector as a vice-president at the bank. There was Dave Angus, the Montreal maritime lawyer who had been financial chairman of Mulroney's 1976 campaign. He would sit out the 1983 campaign as a director of the PC Canada fund, keeping an eye on things there for Mulroney. And there was Sam Wakim, still with Mulroney twenty-seven years after they had met on the St. F.X. campus.

They weren't just going up there for the trout. "The conversations lasted a lot longer than the fishing," Finlay MacDonald said. "Brian's problem was whether to get in or out. He didn't want to be seen as the spoiler in the thing. Everyone loves a conspiracy but everyone hates the conspirator. It was a subject that Dalton could speak to with some degree of experience. He could bell the cat, but in the process he kissed good-bye to his own political prospects."

Mulroney later thought rather too much had been made of this fishing trip. "I thought it was a lot of fun," he said. "First of all, it was a lot of laughs. But I do remember one night where Dalton was reviewing the thing about leadership review, you know, his own involvement in it, and he made the observation, something to the effect that 'I'm living proof,' you know what happens when people with the best faith in the world try and improve leadership in the party. And I remember him making that comment, or something to that effect. I saw a lot of press speculation after that that it was some kind of turning point. Actually, it wasn't." It may not have impressed Mulroney as such, but he did make an impression on Camp. "The only guy who can stop Clark is right here," Camp observed, "and the only guy who can pull Clark through is right here."

Camp had always seen Mulroney as likable enough and always acknowledged his charm, but essentially he thought of him as a bit of a pol and a bit shallow. Then one night Mulroney gave an impassioned discourse on the importance of free trade unions and the responsibilities of an enlightened management. This had nothing to do with party politics, but it had everything to do with Mulroney's formative experience as an executive. He had filled out since 1976, in mind and spirit. "It was the first time," Finlay MacDonald said later, "that Camp ever took Mulroney seriously as a future leader. His comment afterwards was, 'I think he can make it.'"

In the fall of 1982, though Mulroney kept four more speaking engagements, he appeared to his closest associates to be edging away from a confrontation with Clark. In early October, Mulroney summoned Cogger, Pageau, and a couple of others to lunch at the Ritz. While he was not unaware of their activities, Mulroney was now inclined to pass on the leadership review if the Tories could win two out of three upcoming by-elections on October 12, the day after Thanksgiving. "The principal knock against Clark," Mulroney said, "is that we can't win under him. All right, we've got a test coming up. If the guy wins two out of three, that's good enough for me. That means we can win seats."

Come October 12, the Tories did win two out of three. "That's why I felt that was that," Mulroney said later. "That's when I first started thinking about giving Clark, to the extent that I could, to persuade people to give him more active support."

The day after the by-elections, Brian and Mila Mulroney went off to Europe for ten days with their friends Paul and Jackie Desmarais. They rode the new Orient Express from Paris to Venice. And they had a lot of fun.

The leadership situation was not very far from Mulroney's mind. "I knew he had been thinking about it a lot," Desmarais said in February, 1984. "But he didn't talk about it a lot. I suppose at that time he thought Joe was going to win in Winnipeg. I can't say we even discussed the possibility of Joe losing." They did discuss the possibility of Mulroney entering politics at some point down the road, either at the next election or the one after that, in which he might emerge as Clark's Quebec lieutenant and position himself for another run at the leadership. "And," Desmarais pointedly added, "he knew he was having problems in the IOC, that things were going badly and they would have to face reality."

It was nearly the end of October before Mulroney got back to Montreal, and by then he had other things on his mind. The IOC board had decided to shut down the company's money-losing operations at Schefferville. With the American steel industry running at below 40 per cent capacity at the bottom of the worst slump in fifty years, there was no lineup of iron-ore boats in the harbour at Sept-Iles. Mulroney informed the Lévesque government on November 1 and federal Mines Minister Judy Erola before the next day's announcement that Schefferville was shutting down. Suddenly the rap on Mulroney, as the man who shut down a town, appeared to diminish his political currency.

It did not enhance his efforts to tie up loose ends with Clark. Some time before the Schefferville closings, and before his trip to Europe, Mulroney had received a call from Claude Dupras, a Montreal engineer and former president of the provincial association, who had been active in his 1976 campaign. They went back a long time. And when Dupras ran for Parliament in St. Henri-Westmount in 1980, Mila Mulroney worked in his committee room and her husband threw a party for him. They had a difference of opinion over the constitutional debate in the fall of that year, when Dupras thought Mulroney rushed in with undue haste in support of Trudeau. Moreover, Dupras considered that Clark's position deserved his support, and after that he rallied to the leader's side. Now, in the fall of 1982, Dupras thought he could play a conciliatory role. "I like the two guys," Dupras said, "and I wanted to bring them together."

On November 21, the party would be having its annual Montreal fund-raising dinner at the Queen Elizabeth. "In the beginning," Dupras said, "I had called Brian and said, 'Why don't you present Clark?'"

Mulroney said he would think it over. In the meantime, it was decided by Dupras's committee that Roch LaSalle would introduce the leader. By mid-November, Mulroney was getting back to Dupras. Over lunch at the Mount Royal Club, he read the introduction he had written up for Clark. It seemed to Mulroney to be

134

a generous and proper introduction, without being hypocritical and subservient.

"It's not good enough," Dupras said.

"What do you mean it's not good enough?" Mulroney shot back.

"You've got to have a ringing endorsement of Clark."

"Are you out of your goddamned mind?" Mulroney shouted back. "This is a generous, solid text of endorsement, but it's not the kind of thing you're looking for."

Dupras wouldn't budge. It wasn't good enough. Besides, the programs had already been printed. LaSalle would do the honours.

Mulroney was more than angry – he was hurt. In a considerable rage, he took the matter up with Finlay MacDonald, who had just gone into Clark's office as chief of staff. "Whatever transpired between Dupras and Mulroney, Clark had no knowledge of," Mac-Donald said later. "Mulroney phoned me, and I called Clark. He was kind of puzzled by the whole thing."

Within a couple of days, the incident got into the press as another blood feud between the Mulroney and Clark clans. The damage, such as it was, had been done. But while Mulroney was seething, he was now back in touch with Finlay MacDonald, and it wasn't long before they were working out the details of another kind of deal.

As a trustee of the Schenley football awards, Mulroney had to be in Toronto during Grey Cup week. On Friday, November 26, he met MacDonald at Winston's, the mecca of the expense-account lunch. Mulroney took out two pages of handwritten notes on legal-sized foolscap. "This is what I'm prepared to say," Mulroney said, and he read it aloud.

Finlay MacDonald was delighted. "I thought," he said, "it solved all the party's problems."

Mulroney may have had some idea of how his decision to support Clark would be received when he phoned Pat MacAdam from Toronto to let him in on it. "If you want to show you're onside," MacAdam said, "why don't you take Clark to the Forum?"

On the Monday before Charbonneau's intimate Sunday brunch, Mulroney had the senator into his office to explain his decision. "He figured he had a lot of support from Quebec, and he had been getting a lot of calls from across the country," Charbon-neau said later. "People liked Clark but they didn't think they could win an election with him. But if he opposed Clark, what would it do to his chances, three, four, five years down the road? Although a lot of supporters were working for review, it wouldn't do him any good in four, eight, or ten years, whenever the leadership came open. He had to make up his mind."

Informed of Mulroney's decision at Charbonneau's apartment, most members of the inner group were frankly appalled that he had chosen to appear at a joint news conference with Clark rather than simply issuing a press release. "The only thing I was afraid of was his credibility," Charbonneau said, "and this was proven out subsequently by our polls."

Mulroney later said he wasn't "wedded to the idea" of a news conference. "That was an idea Finlay and I came up with, but it wasn't cast in concrete. I think it was more fortuitous than anything else." It happened that Clark would be in Montreal that Monday to appear before the Laval Chamber of Commerce. Afterwards, the news conference appeared to rebound on both sides, and on Finlay MacDonald from both sides. "As a result," MacDonald said, "the Mulroney people thought how could anyone with that much experience be so naive, for I had clearly endorsed the thing. And on the Clark side, either I had been conned, or I was obviously closer to Mulroney, a mole."

If the Clark people could have been present in Mulroney's living room the previous afternoon, they would not have thought it was a set-up job. If the inner circle at Charbonneau's place had taken the news badly, the enlarged group up on Belvedere Road was simply thunderstruck.

"Look, Brian," Pageau told him, "everybody here respects your decision to withdraw, it's your career, but the majority of people are here because they want a change."

Impassioned speeches were made, pleas were entered, but Mulroney's mind was quite made up.

"I guess the message at his house," said Cogger, "was that he was saying to the guys, 'I recognize your right to do this, but you can't do this on my back.'"

And Mulroney repeated in French what he had said in English down at Charbonneau's place: "Je m'enlève du traffic."

Rodrigue Pageau then asked a critical question. "Does your commitment to Clark commit other people?"

"No," Mulroney said, though he made it clear that he wanted no activities carried on in his name. "I didn't want anyone organizing in my name," Mulroney later insisted, "and I counselled them not to organize at all."

"On that basis," Pageau replied, "I will continue, we must continue."

At this point, Pageau said, "One hundred per cent of the group

136

went over to my place." Or as Cogger put it: "We all adjourned over to Rodrigue's."

Leaving Mulroney's house, Pageau turned to have a final word with him. "If the result in Winnipeg is what we want," Pageau said, "I hope we'll be able to come back in this same room and ask you to run."

10

FROM WINNIPEG
TO SCHEFFERVILLE

Joe Clark was out of the woods, or was he? The Mulroney announcement had the desired effect of focusing the issue on review and on the incumbent. It raised expectations as to how well Clark would have to do in Winnipeg, and the Clark camp did nothing to lower them. The word went out to the Ottawa press gallery that Clark could now expect to receive up to 80 per cent of the vote in Winnipeg. On the very night of Mulroney's decision, Clark's chief Quebec organizer, Marcel Danis, appeared on television to announce that they had expected to do well there anyway.

The Clark people had one problem getting the message out. Not everyone was buying it. Just one week after Mulroney's endorsement of the leader, the *Globe and Mail* ran a page-one story headlined "Anti-Clark forces say they'll win review." It carried the byline of Lawrence Martin, who had just returned to the paper's Toronto newsroom from a stint as its Washington correspondent. Martin was the classic loner, a reporter who had neither a need nor a desire to run with the pack. He had to endure not only the enmity of the Clark camp but the scepticism of many of his own senior colleagues. He later called it the loneliest period of his career, and Martin had been through some solitary times, first as a reporter writing from Montreal about the developing Olympic cost overruns and then for his exposés of the activities of the security branch of the Royal Canadian Mounted Police.

While the Ottawa press gallery was generally unquestioning of the Clark claims, Martin was writing early and often from Toronto that the leader was, as he quoted Dalton Camp in his December 14 piece, not out of the woods at all. Despite the howling protests of the Clark camp, Martin kept writing it and his editors kept running it. The importance of Martin's *Globe and Mail* articles should not be overlooked in any examination of the Tory leadership crisis, for here was a reporter with the solitary courage to stick his neck out on a big story. And once his stuff started to appear in mid-December, it began to generate its own momentum. Dissenting Tories, who had given up on the Ottawa media, began to get in touch with this tall, thin man, whom most of them had never heard of, let alone met.

It was generally acknowledged by press and pundits, by friend and foe alike, that Clark would have to improve on his score of 1981, when 66.4 per cent of the delegates had voted against review. He would have to improve, however marginally, on that 2-1 score. But it was generally agreed that if he came in over 70 per cent, he would be all right, and their polling indicated they would have just enough to cross the finish line on empty. "Most of our polls," MacDonald said, "had it around 72.5 per cent."

But that didn't account for a margin of error known as liars. It also took no account of the alliance that had formed in the back rooms of the party. While the news media focused on a Toronto advertising man named John Morrison as the leader of the review forces, the others weren't getting their names in the papers and they certainly weren't giving interviews. The real leader was Frank D. Moores, former Premier of Newfoundland, former party president, former member of caucus, friend of the premiers, and friend of Brian Mulroney.

"It's been a hectic two years," Moores said after Winnipeg and Ottawa. "The thing was to work hard without anyone knowing about it."

The Winnipeg operation would cost money, cash money. If they were going to help delegates pay their way to Winnipeg, they couldn't have credit-card numbers and cancelled cheques floating around. The Moores group was an alliance of convenience. Moores and Charbonneau were clearly hoping for a Mulroney candidacy. Bob Wenman, a British Columbia MP, was for John Crosbie. Chris Speyer, the Cambridge, Ontario, MP, was there to represent David Crombie's interests.

The Moores group was rounded out by Elmer MacKay, by now the leader of the mutinous caucus elements. Notwithstanding Mulroney's declaration, the anti-Clark forces in caucus did not cease their activities. On the contrary, they redoubled their efforts for review. Nor were the Clark loyalists unaware of their activities. In one rather unwitting but conspicuous display, about twenty-five MPs met one night in MacKay's office, across the way from Geoff Scott, a Clark loyalist. George Hees, who was not of the same persuasion, walked into Scott's office by mistake and asked in his booming voice if this was where the meeting was.

"In a way we hadn't intended," MacKay said, "it was a show of strength."

In a way he had intended, there was another show of strength. MacKay was quietly gathering letters from MPs calling for a leadership convention in the event that Clark did not improve on his score of 1981. By the time of Winnipeg in the last week of January, MacKay had some forty-eight letters locked away in a safe place. And after Winnipeg, MacKay was confident he could have obtained the three more signatures he needed for an absolute majority of Conservative MPs. Even before he got to Winnipeg, Joe Clark had lost the caucus.

By this time, the existence of the Moores group had become known to a few reporters, but it was not appreciated how well organized or financed they were. With a quarter of a million dollars in cash spread around the country, they had managed to get their pro-review delegates to Winnipeg. Now it was a matter of getting them registered and hoping they had enough votes to push Clark into a convention.

When they went over their numbers in their informal command post in Moores' suite at the Westin Hotel, they were pretty sure they had between 35 and 40 per cent for review, depending on how many provincial Tory legislators came out for Clark. They had no way of knowing how many provincial legislators would turn up from across the country. Among Clark loyalists in the provincial legislatures, there was a marked tendency to stay home since Clark was supposed to be in the clear, and Winnipeg was a long way to go for a cup of coffee, and on the last weekend of January, not a very warm one at that. Among provincial members inclined to vote for review, some simply stayed away because their premiers were nominally supportive of the leader.

When the CBC checked the registration records after the convention, it found that only eighty-five provincial legislators had turned up out of 341 who were eligible. Peter Lougheed was in Hawaii and most of his caucus was on a beach, too. Only eight out of seventy-five Alberta legislators voted at Winnipeg. The record showed that only seven of seventy Ontario members turned up in Winnipeg, in spite of the loyalty of Bill Davis, which was more apparent than real. Only eight members of Dick Hatfield's thirty-eight-member caucus made it out from New Brunswick. These were the people who could have saved Joe Clark's hide, and they didn't.

"For Joe Clark, the irony is biting," Peter Mansbridge observed on his Sunday CBC newscast a week after Winnipeg. "If the votes had been delivered and delivered for him, there would have been

140

no leadership convention because those votes would have given him a 70 per cent approval, the acknowledged figure he needed to stay on the job."

In the weeks after Winnipeg, Mulroney carried a transcript of the Mansbridge commentary around in his jacket pocket. He also had a clipping from the *Vancouver Sun* in which Clark stoutly maintained that he had received two-thirds of the Quebec vote, and that it wasn't Quebec's fault.

In fact, the Quebec split was about 50-50. On this point, there was general agreement in the Clark and Mulroney camps only much later on, when it no longer mattered who or what was being quoted. Looking back a year after Winnipeg, senior Clark Quebec organizers Mario Beaulieu and Jean Bruneau acknowledged that Quebec had been a 50-50 proposition. From the Mulroney side of the fence, Cogger and Pageau did not disagree. "At Winnipeg, it was probably a 50-50 split out of Quebec," Cogger said. "At least, I always claimed it was a 50-50 split."

As early as their December 5 meeting at Mulroney's house, Pageau estimated "we could count on 275-300 delegates" from Quebec. Even after Mulroney took himself "out of the traffic," those delegates were still going to Winnipeg in a mood to vote for review. As for Pageau and the others, they hadn't even taken the rest of the afternoon off after their meeting with Mulroney.

But even with as many as 300 pro-review votes from Quebec, there turned out to be nearly 500 from the other provinces, and they couldn't all have come from Newfoundland junior colleges and the radical fringe of Morrison's review group in Toronto. In fact, most of them came from Metro Toronto and other Ontario ridings. It was just hard to find them. In the bar of the Albany Club, they might say one thing, but then in the cloak room they would often say quite another. As Dalton Camp had observed in mid-December: "Ontario is the key to the convention, and I don't know anyone who has a reading on Ontario."

For the longest time on the evening of January 28, it was hard to get a reading on anything. The television networks left the definite impression that Clark was in the clear. He had made a strong speech, though it remained to be seen how many delegates would spend the last weekend of January in Winnipeg to be swayed by a speech. The CTV network ran an exit poll that indicated Clark had the support of about 78 per cent of the convention. The mood on the floor was a mixture of jubilation and relief that the issue had been settled in a clear-cut manner. Flora

141

MacDonald, a staunch Clark loyalist, even danced a Highland fling.

In his suite at the Westin, Mulroney wandered off into his bedroom to pack his bags for Florida, where he planned to spend the next week preparing the Iron Ore brief before the Quebec National Assembly hearings on the Schefferville closings. "I was absolutely satisfied that Joe would get his 66 per cent, minimum, and that he would hang on," Mulroney said. "You know, after the convention and so on, I thought that the convention was a disaster but that he, personally, was going to get his vote. I was personally convinced of that."

But then it became apparent that something was wrong, as it had been apparent for some time to Clark in his holding room. "Why do you bring me the same result?" Clark asked the man bearing the envelope with the results. He had a decision to make, and it was clear that the caucus was not far from being uppermost in his mind.

"He couldn't have gone back after Winnipeg," Moores said. "Elmer had all those letters in his safe."

MacKay did not disagree that it wouldn't have been easy for Clark in caucus. "Sure, he could have hung on," MacKay said, "but it would have been the bloodiest fight the party had ever seen. The people who were opposing him were pretty strong-minded guys." As Clark weighed his decision, it dawned on people who had been in counting rooms before that it doesn't take three hours to add up a simple yes-no vote. "I never heard of anyone waiting an hour to give good news," Cogger said. Finally, Pat Carney and Jean Guilbeault approached the podium. She announced that Clark had 1,607 votes, or 66.9 per cent.

"Well then, Joe's okay," Mulroney said with neither surprise nor elation in his voice. "He did better than he did the last time."

There were 795 votes for review, or 33.1 per cent. In two years, Clark had travelled the country, become a stranger to his own daughter, gone up nearly nearly 20 points in the Gallup, but had risen only half a percentage point in his own party. Still, he had gone up. If he had gone to the podium and simply thanked the crowd for their support, "it is not clear," as Cogger said, "that anyone would have had anything to say about it." Nevertheless, Clark announced that the mandate wasn't good enough, and he was asking for a convention at which he would be a candidate to succeed himself.

"I was flabbergasted," Mulroney said later. "I was absolutely stunned. It never, never once occurred to me that that would be the decision." MacAdam, Wakim, Cogger, and Charbonneau, who were with him, all thought he looked quite surprised and taken aback by Clark's announcement.

Down in Frank Moores' suite, the alliance of convenience was already celebrating and disbanding. On television a few minutes after the vote, a glum Flora MacDonald was being interviewed. "Let's see you dance now," a jubilant Moores said in the general direction of the TV.

Mulroney had to finish packing. He hadn't changed his destination, but he had already changed his plans. His plane was waiting for him on the ground at Winnipeg, warmed up and ready to take him to Florida. Over the next week he would pull into focus the IOC brief before the Quebec Parliamentary Commission, which was scheduled to sit Feburary 10-11, not in the Red Room of the Assembly overlooking the Grande Allée, but in a school gymnasium in Schefferville. The Quebec government was going to put on a show, and on the morrow of Clark's decision to call a leadership convention, Schefferville loomed even larger for Mulroney – it was not impossible that his own political hopes could be buried along with the town.

So it wasn't to get a tan that he hunkered down in Florida in the last days of January and into the first week of February. A stream of company officials and assistants paraded through, bearing enough documents and data to load an iron-ore train. Mulroney's job was to synthesize all this material, to tell the company's story, to put the best possible slant on the closings, and to make some constructive suggestions for the future of the town.

He had already tried to deflect criticism that the company and its president were impervious to the cares and concerns of the townspeople by announcing $10 million in severance payments for the loss of jobs in Scheffervile. The 152 permanent employees would each receive $16,400, plus relocation assistance. Anybody who wanted to stay on could buy his company house for one dollar. In the circumstances, it was a good deal, good enough that the director of the United Steel Workers, Clément Godbout, was able to tell *Le Soleil*'s Raymond Giroux that it was "an important gesture" and an example of how the government might enact legislation to "civilize company shutdowns."

That Mulroney should have announced this package at a Montreal news conference, two days before the vote in Winnipeg, was understandably cause for suspicion as to his motives. Whether the scepticism of the media was well founded, the fact remained that after Winnipeg, especially given the outcome, Mulroney could not be accused of paying off his workers to advance his own political prospects. By the time he returned from Florida at the beginning of the second week in February, he was carrying a fifty-five-page brief. And by the time he flew into Schefferville on Wednesday, February 9, the eve of the two-day hearing, he was ready to put on a show.

The first person waiting for him at the airport was *Gazette* reporter Claude Arpin, who had a choice of either walking back to town in a blizzard or accepting a lift and an invitation to lunch with the IOC president. At the Iron Ore guest house, an historical site because Maurice Duplessis had died there in 1959, the company chef Santo Mazzolini had prepared a shrimp salad. Mulroney, sipping a Virgin Caesar, promised the reporter that "these guys are going to see a professional at work."

The decision to close Schefferville had been taken at a special meeting of the IOC board in Cleveland after Mulroney's return from Europe in late October. The board had several options to consider. "They all," Mulroney said later, "involved how much money do you want to lose. We'd been carrying Schefferville as a dead loss. It was costing millions."

The problem was twofold: weak markets and the competitive position of low-grade iron from the hills of Labrador in comparison to the high-grade product from Brazil. While IOC's competitive position in world markets was relatively weak, its American markets were protected by long-term contracts with the consortium of six American steel companies who held a controlling interest in the company. The problem in the fourth quarter of 1982 was that the American steel industry had been knocked on its rear end by the worst economic downturn in half a century. Bethlehem, National, Republic, and the other American steel giants were looking at less than 40 per cent of their rated capacity. If they weren't running their blast furnaces, it followed that they didn't need iron ore to feed them. "The first day of extractive operations at any mining town hastens the arrival of the end," Mulroney noted near the end of his brief. "That is an immutable fact of life and there are no exceptions to the rule."

Mulroney never got that far into his brief. He was just getting wound up when the presiding MNA, Jean-Pierre Bordeleau of the Parti Québécois, reminded him that he had run over his allotted twenty minutes. Undaunted, Mulroney wheeled out of the witness chair, grabbed a pointer, and began an hour-long explanation of graphs and charts detailing rising and falling demand for the product, profits and dividends, and taxes paid to municipalities over the years. Finally, he came to a bunch of recommendations for the future of the town. A national park could be established in the area, a northern institute, a mining and metals institute, a correctional institute. There were even possibilities for tourism.

"What extraordinary opportunities," Mulroney declared. "Everybody in Montreal is complaining because there's no snow at Mont Tremblant. The Americans have ended up on Sherbrooke Street with their skis. They have no snow and we have snow coming out our ears. All it would take is a little federal-provincial co-operation, a big publicity campaign and the people of Schefferville would have it in the bag, I guarantee it. Skiers spend money, just as hunters."

Listening to this, Liberal member John Ciaccia nearly fell out of his chair. Here it was, he said later, forty below zero outside, a howling wind practically blowing down the school, and Mulroney was talking about a ski resort. "It was a masterful performance," Ciaccia said later. "On balance, he looked good and the government looked bad."

Mulroney wasn't finished. When the commission came back after lunch, the members had some questions for him, beginning with Energy Minister Yves Duhaime, who wanted to make the political point that hard times on the North Shore were not unique to the PQ administration, but had also been a curse of the previous Liberal government with the closure of the huge ITT-Rayonnier operation. "It's part of the Liberal record of the 1970's," Duhaime insisted.

"Mr. Minister," Mulroney replied, "I must tell you with respect that you place me in a somewhat delicate situation. There are political implications in your question, and God knows how much I shy away from political questions."

The audience roared with laughter. Mulroney was on a roll. He certainly didn't shy away from saying that Marxist-Leninists had for a time taken over the Steelworkers Local 5569 in Sept-Iles and called an illegal strike (as opposed to the legal work stoppages that Mulroney would tell audiences he hadn't had any of during his years at the helm of Iron Ore). When he had finished, after two hours of close questioning, Mulroney went away to an ovation from the people of a town he had closed down.

A few feet away from the witness chair, backbencher Elie Fallu turned to his PQ colleague Robert Dean, one-time organizer of the epic Pratt & Whitney strike in the mid-1970's and a hero in the trade union movement. "Christ," Fallu was overheard to say by one of Mulroney's aides, "this guy's going to sweep the province."

The three ministers present hadn't laid a glove on Mulroney, not that they had tried very hard. When the IOC president referred to "my friend, Mr. Marois," he meant Labour Minister Pierre Marois, then a very senior member of the Lévesque government, whom he had known for twenty years. The Minister of Fish and Game was none other than Guy Chevrette, "Ti-Guy," who had served with Mulroney as a member of the Cliche Commission. Even Duhaime wasn't particularly aggressive with Mulroney. "We have just heard," Duhaime said as Mulroney left the witness chair, "a long, well-documented exposé by someone with an obvious talent to become a parliamentarian."

The reviews in the press were hardly less flattering. "Brian Mulroney steals the show" was the headline in *Le Soleil*. "Mulroney scores points at probe" went the headline over Arpin's *Gazette* story the next day. And over an analysis by veteran Quebec correspondent Gilles Lesage, *Le Devoir* headlined that "Mulroney withdraws with honor from a war that never was."

It was, as Mulroney later said with no immodesty, "quite a performance." Where his political career could have ended up in a snowbank in a remote mining town, he now left his Schefferville worries behind as he flew home on Friday. And he could get down to the business of organizing his campaign, satisfied that he had done his utmost to minimize the negative fallout from Schefferville.

The phoney war period of February and March was an interval of real importance in the Conservative leadership battle that was not greatly appreciated. It was a time for raising money, putting the elements of national organizations in place, and lining up important endorsements; above all, it was a time for waiting on Peter Lougheed and Bill Davis and their intentions.

In Florida, as he worked on the Schefferville brief, Mulroney professed not to be worried about the prospect of either of the Big Two premiers making the race. "Peter Lougheed's not going anywhere," Mulroney said in those last days of January. He didn't think Bill Davis was going anywhere, either, though he was somewhat less categorical about that.

And if one or the other came in, Mulroney thought he would be well positioned to pick up support from the other premier's region. With a Lougheed candidacy, Mulroney might have emerged as the candidate of the East. If Davis had made the race, Mulroney might have been able to foster a new Quebec-West axis against an Ontario candidate. Certainly Davis was anathema in the West, dating from his opposition to Lougheed's oil-pricing policies in 1979 and more recently owing to his support for the Trudeau patriation package. In Quebec, in spite of whatever assurances Davis might have received from his friends in Montreal, the Ontario Premier would have faced very heavy going over his refusal to enact Section 133-status to make French a recognized language of the courts and legislature of Ontario. Davis had always taken the position that it was preferable to provide legal and educational services to his province's half-million francophones than to risk a backlash by the largely symbolic gesture of granting French a constitutional status. But symbols were largely what the politics of Quebec were about, and whatever the practical merits of the Davis position, he would have received a terrible going-over in Quebec.

However unlikely Mulroney thought it that one or the other would come into the race, he would clearly be a lot happier if they both stayed home. He had no appetite for running against Lougheed, who had always treated him well, almost as a favourite nephew. And as the campaign wore on, Lougheed would send along an occasional long handwritten note of encouragement and advice.

As for Davis, though they had never been close, Mulroney did not relish the prospect of running against the four-time Premier of Ontario or his formidable organization. Still, there came a time when, despite all his disclaimers, Davis was sorely tempted to step into the vacuum that appeared to exist in the early to middle stages of the campaign. After Easter, there was all the negative fallout on the front-runners from the rough and tumble of the delegate selection process. Many Tories had a yearning for someone who had held himself above this fray, a made-in-Ontario statesman.

The Davis rhetoric, the kind of speech he brought down to the Canadian Club of Toronto on April 25, was the sort of bottled bafflegab that could have been uncorked at a Chamber of Commerce picnic. "The truth of the matter," he told an approving audience of blue suits at the Royal York Hotel, "is that we in Ontario take great pride in being Canadians because we have enjoyed great success as a result of being Canadians. Unfortunately there is, in other parts of the country, a belief that our success has been at someone else's expense."

If you cracked the code, Davis was admitting that people in the rest of the country didn't like Ontario. As for himself, Davis said he had no plans, and no plans to have any plans. Davis raised obfuscation to an art form. But a week later, on what *The Toronto Star* had proclaimed "D-Day" in its early editions, Davis said "no" in uncharacteristically unequivocal terms, admitting that it would have been a divisive, uphill fight. The mood and the numbers simply weren't right for someone who saw himself as a unifying figure and who would have needed something approaching a draft rather than a streetfight.

"I personally never believed he was going to enter the race," Mulroney said much later. That being said, he could acknowledge his relief that Davis stayed home. "Had he entered the race," Mulroney said with some candor, "he would have automatically, unquestionably, gone into number-one position, in my judgement, and may have won. Because he did have the capacity to grow. Unquestionably, had Bill Davis decided to get into it, he would have, I think, been number one at the convention, and probably would have won. Certainly could have won, let me put it that way."

But the Mulroney camp had polling numbers of their own that indicated it would have been very tough, if not impossible, for Davis to win the convention, and they were more than happy to share these numbers with Queen's Park. A week or so before the Davis announcement, Michel Cogger sent Charley McMillan down to Toronto with the result of the second Gallup wave. McMillan passed them on to Davis's executive assistant, John Tory, who had been a youth supporter of Mulroney in 1976. It was generally assumed that Tory passed the numbers on to his boss.

From Winnipeg in late January to Toronto in early May, it took Davis more than three months to give a final and definitive "no." For Peter Lougheed, all it took was the time to fly from Honolulu to Edmonton.

With characteristic lack of equivocation, Lougheed had already made his decision in Hawaii and announced it after his return to Edmonton at a February 1 news conference. "The answer is no," he said. "I believe I have a responsibility to continue to serve the people of Alberta." Period.

"So many people were pressing me, from so many parts of Canada," Lougheed said later. Some people, he continued, "say no just to be convinced." And he knew that some potential supporters "wouldn't accept the no." Nevertheless, his mind was quite made up "in Hawaii to go back to Alberta and make it unequivocal." He wasn't going to put "good friends in a box" of raising money and delegates for him. Coming as it did only four days after the Winnipeg vote, it was even too early to nip the Draft-Lougheed movement in the bud. Alberta MP John Thomson had thirty of his fellow caucus members lined up and ready to go for Lougheed. Petitions were circulated, editorials were signed in the Alberta press, all to no avail.

The only place Peter Lougheed was going was to New York with his wife Jeanne for their annual weekend at the Pierre Hotel with his Harvard classmates Philippe de Gaspé Beaubien, Roger Beaulieu, and their wives.

Philippe de Gaspé Beaubien, the head of Quebec's big Télémedia broadcasting network, was not known for being of the Conservative persuasion. But Roger Beaulieu was a long-time Tory activist and fund-raiser in Montreal. He was also the senior managing partner of Martineau, Walker, which he had built from a small outfit of thirteen lawyers in the 1950's into one of the biggest boardroom law firms in Montreal, with over 100 lawyers spilling over more than three floors of Place Victoria's Stock Exchange Tower. One of the firm's occasional clients was the province of Alberta, and one of his closest friends was Peter Lougheed. Beaulieu had been an ardent promoter of a Lougheed candidacy with the Premier, notwithstanding his lack of French. At least, he hoped Lougheed wouldn't make his decision on that basis. They had one discussion over breakfast in Edmonton on February 4, and Beaulieu later recalled "he was pretty well decided at the time that Brian was the man."

These three old friends and classmates had another discussion after lunch at the Pierre on February 20. Lougheed was quite firm, if not without some wistful thinking, in his decision not to go. Other names were discussed. Finally Lougheed asked: "What's wrong with Brian?"

Two days later, Roger and Andrée Beaulieu happened to be going to dinner and hockey at the Montreal Forum as the guests of Brian and Mila Mulroney. The Quebec Nordiques were the guests of the Montreal Canadiens. Around the dinner table in the Mise-au-Jeu restaurant, the discussion edged gently toward the leadership. Mulroney was in one of his nervous moods. He said he was inclined to back Lougheed if the Alberta Premier chose to run. It was a generous and astute statement, one that Beaulieu was glad to hear and one that was likely to get back to the Alberta Premier. But Beaulieu made it clear "that Brian didn't have anything to fear from Peter getting into the act."

From that evening on, Mulroney had Lougheed's ambassador to Montreal in his corner, raising money and making phone calls. To those who took the trouble to read these things, it was a clear and unmistakable signal. Mulroney could go into the month of March secure in the knowledge that not only did he have nothing to fear from Lougheed, but the Alberta Premier was backing him in a quiet sort of way.

"We're going to do a little business," Mulroney said on the day of his coming-out party in Montreal on March 9. "And then maybe we'll do a little politics."

11

JAWS II

On the morning after his forty-fourth birthday, Brian Mulroney bounded out of the lobby of the Château Laurier to begin his second run at the Tory leadership. It was Monday, March 21, the first day of spring, which struck him as a favourable omen. And he had taken elaborate care to address the criticisms that lingered from his previous campaign.

If he had avoided Ottawa like the plague in 1976, he would announce his candidacy from the National Press Theatre in 1983. And he was prepared for whatever questions the Ottawa press gallery might have left over from 1976. It would be a tough test of his mettle, but once he got by it he could get the press gallery off his back and get the hell out of town. If he had been faulted by media and Tory activists alike for flying around the country in private jets in 1976, he would tour the provinces in a "rusty station wagon" in the spring of 1983, starting now, as he left the hotel to go down to the Wellington Street press building on the other side of Parliament Hill.

But as Mulroney swung through the lobby doors, he saw something that stopped him dead in his tracks. The first car at the Blue Line cab stand was none other than a big black Cadillac. "Probably the only goddamn Cadillac cab in the city of Ottawa, and I have to get it," Mulroney later recalled as he told the story on himself.

"Hop in," the driver yelled. Someone explained lamely that they were just going a couple of blocks, and maybe the guy would rather wait for an airport fare. But the cabbie insisted, until Mike McSweeney, who would be travelling with the candidate, paid the guy off not to take the fare. The irony of the inadvertent screw-up, McSweeney said later, was that his father was general manager of the Blue Line cab company and could have got them the rustiest cab in town. In any event, as Mulroney said later, "we got ourselves an appropriate Plymouth," and he was on his way. The Ottawa press corps was waiting for him. But he was ready for them, too. And as Peter White had put it in a memo to his Laval classmate, the twin aims of the candidate's first appearance were "accentuating positives and rectifying negatives" of his image. The positives pretty well spoke for themselves; the negatives would have to be squarely addressed by the candidate, and any he left out the press were sure to take up.

On the negative side, White listed eleven points, starting with: "Lacks political courage, has never run." White's advice to his candidate – resign the presidency of Iron Ore; announce up front his intention to seek a seat in the next election, irrespective of the outcome in June. As to his lack of parliamentary experience, Mulroney should "highlight lifetime of work in party." As for his never having submitted his full financial report from the 1976 campaign, White urged his candidate to say that he was "protecting contributors from public disclosure, refusing to go back on his word." As for the negative perception since Winnipeg that he was "deceitful, duplicitous and treacherous," White's advice was succinct: "Ignore," he urged in his February memo. "The issue is leadership, not Winnipeg."

Most of these points would come up at the press conference, and Mulroney would answer them in his own way, as he had in an interview published that morning in the *Montreal Gazette*. Yes, he had said, sitting in his sun room the previous Friday morning, he would resign the Iron Ore presidency and pledge to run in the next election, whatever the result in June. He was out in front of that issue, and he intended to stay there.

As for never disclosing the sum and substance of his 1976 expenses, it was because of his refusal to do so that Mulroney had forfeited a $30,000 subsidy from the party to each of the candidates. For Mulroney, it was an appropriately sour note on which to end the campaign. To make things worse for him, the party official who wouldn't give him the money was none other than Michael Meighen, one of the Laval gang and later two-time candidate in Mulroney's riding of Westmount. When Meighen ran for the party presidency in 1974, Mulroney had been in his corner.

"The rules were that the amounts would be divulged to the party for internal use only," Mulroney insisted seven years later. "After I raised money and advised donors of the limits of publicity, a new wrinkle was added ex-post facto which required that these names would be published. Inasmuch as I had already given my word to my donors, it was evident I couldn't break it." One of the things he professed to be worried about was the Liberals settling up with consulting engineers, lawyers, and advertising firms who might have contributed to a Tory cause. He said he knew of no instances of donors, whose names had been published, who immediately lost contracts with the feds in Montreal and Quebec City. "Given the vindictive streak of the federal Liberals, and having witnessed this myself," he maintained, "in good faith I could not leave them naked. As a result, I paid a heavy price for that. Anyone who wants to analyse that will see it's the case. I had nothing to gain, and a lot to lose, including the $30,000."

As to his lack of parliamentary experience, Mulroney would say that all candidates brought assets and liabilities with them: some were bilingual and some were not; some had business experience and some had none. His seven years at Iron Ore were an experience he planned to emphasize in the campaign, though he could have done without the Schefferville closings. The problem was that Iron Ore wasn't very well known in the country outside Quebec and Newfoundland. And so for the next three months, in living rooms and rec rooms across the land, he would spin out an IOC cassette. When he had moved into the company as executive vice-president in 1976, it had endured fifty-nine work stoppages over the previous decade, hadn't paid a dividend in years, and was burdened with a heavy debt. "With the great team we put together," he said that Friday morning in his sun room, "we began the process of civilizing relations with our employees and with governments. We're now in year six without a work stoppage of any kind, with 15 union locals in three different jurisdictions, in two provinces, in both official languages every day. Employee income, profits and productivity are up, accident rates and labor strife are either dramatically down or have disappeared."

That was the Iron Ore story, or at least his side of it, as he would explain it to delegates across the country in the next three months. As for the desirability of business experience, he would encounter few Conservatives who would disagree with his appraisal that "one of the great things about the nature of business is the process of accountability. The balance sheet holds you responsible before government, employees and the shareholders."

At home that morning with the *Gazette* reporter, he was already warming to what would become his principal rec-room theme, the spiel that he would repeat so often that some of his own advisers would become sick to death of hearing it: "There are 102 seats with a francophone component of more than 10 per cent. In 1980, the Tory party won two. That means the day the writs are issued, we knock on Trudeau's door and say here's our gift to you. I'm saying that while I have an instinct of generosity, it doesn't extend to giving Pierre Trudeau 100 seats."

The Tory party's chronic problems in French Canada attained the dimensions of a tragicomedy in Quebec, where it received only 12.6 per cent of the vote and one seat in the 1980 election. And this is how Mulroney would end the spiel. In Quebec, he would say, "We lost our deposits in fifty-six seats, we finished third in forty-one seats, behind the NDP in thirty-nine seats, and behind the Rhinoceros Party in two."

Brian Mulroney's problem as he flew out of Montreal that Friday morning wasn't seats or popular vote. It was delegates. And to get them, or at least to get at them, Mulroney meant to take the long way around by a twisted, bumpy back road. He called it the boony strategy. And the rules were simple. Don't fly anywhere you can drive, and when you do fly, go commercial. This time around nobody was going to catch the candidate in a private jet.

Mulroney showed that he meant business in the first week of the campaign. In Saskatoon, someone had chartered a small plane to fly the Mulroneys on to Regina. When Mulroney got wind of it, he informed his aide Mike McSweeney that he was not getting into a private plane and ordered him to go out and rent a car. And so the three of them, McSweeney and Mulroney in the front, and the former Mila Pivnicki in the back doubtless wondering how she had got roped into this gig, drove the 150-mile stretch between Saskatoon and Regina. Mulroney's apprehensions may have been well founded, and they were certainly reinforced when he heard a television crew was to have taped his arrival. After that, it was almost verboten to mention the words "private" and "plane" in the same context around Mulroney headquarters. "We call them those things with wings," Michel Cogger joked in his Ottawa office one spring afternoon. And those things with wings, when their use was even contemplated, had damn well better have props instead of jet engines.

The delegates and party activists meeting the Mulroneys this time around would get a different impression of him, flying economy, carrying his own luggage, and so on. And they would get that impression largely first hand, because he was not planning on travelling with a big entourage of media. Getting his name in the papers or his face on the news was not a problem for Mulroney this time. He didn't need to make himself known to the media. They already had a rather fixed impression of him as

154

slick and superficial. If he could not dissipate that impression with the Ottawa-based media, he could at least avoid them and do his best to persuade the delegates that he wasn't the plastic man he was made out to be. And the best way of doing that, as he would later say in another context, would be to meet the delegates in their homes at their convenience.

"They didn't know him," said his Manitoba co-ordinator, Janis Johnson Moores. "He did literally four times the work of anyone in our province." Typically, instead of bringing the delegates from one rural riding into Winnipeg for a big meeting, Mulroney went out to meet them in a farmhouse. In New Brunswick, he toured the province in a van. The last time he had been to Caraquet, N.B., in 1976, he had left one private plane in Chatham and taken a smaller one to get into Bathurst.

And this time his wife was travelling with him. To no one's great surprise, she would prove to be a considerable campaign asset, not only for her winning way with people, but for her knowledge of her husband's moods and her own political intuitions. When they landed in some small city or town, there would be just the two of them, and McSweeney. No press aide, and no press entourage. For the first two months of the campaign, from mid-March to mid-May, the candidate went underground. And with a few exceptions, such as *The Toronto Star*'s Bob McKenzie, who had known Mulroney for nearly twenty-five years, reporters were not encouraged to tag along. They would even have a terrible time finding out where Mulroney was at a given time. Calls to his Montreal office were generally referred to the Toronto tour office and sometimes passed on to Ottawa, where Michel Cogger was the candidate's only authorized spokesman with the press gallery. Since the Ottawa crowd weren't seeing or hearing him on their own newscasts, since they couldn't find out where he was half the time, they soon assumed either that he wasn't going anywhere or that his campaign was completely screwed up, or both. For the time being, that suited Mulroney's purpose.

But before going to ground, Mulroney and his aides had purposely and purposefully organized a little party called "The Friends of Brian Mulroney," on March 9 at the Queen Elizabeth Hotel in Montreal. "We're going to go," Mulroney had told his friend Fernand Roberge during a lunch at the Café de Paris in the Ritz-Carlton Hotel. "I want you to arrange for a party for me at the Queen E in two weeks." Roberge, who had quit smoking over a year earlier, reached across the table for one of Mulroney's duMauriers.

Though not a part of the Laval mob, Roberge was a Quebec

155

City native who had known Cogger and Bazin there, and gravitated to Montreal at the same time as them, which was how he came to know Mulroney in 1966. He had been general manager of the Bonaventure Hotel when Mulroney staged his big dinner there in January of 1976, and soon moved uptown to take some of the staid and stuffy airs out of the Ritz while maintaining its character as one of the great carriage-trade hotels of the continent.

Roberge, as general manager, brought his friend Mulroney onto the hotel's board. And in the spring of 1983, Roberge guarded one of the best-kept secrets of the "frugal" campaign. Since Mulroney couldn't go across the street to the Iron Ore Company, and since he needed an office when he was in town and a place for his secretary, Ginette Pilotte, to crank out his speeches and letters to delegates, Roberge gave him a two-room suite in a corner of the sixth floor. An office at the Ritz did not exactly blend with the image of rusty station wagons, but only Roberge and his room-service waiters knew about it. And since Mulroney had instructed him not to tell anyone, he didn't. "It took a helluva long time before Rodrigue Pageau found out about that suite," Roberge said of Mulroney's chief Quebec organizer.

So on that late February day, Roberge reached for a cigarette and got to work to fill Mulroney's request for a crowd of 1,500 people.

The purpose of the evening was twofold: to show that Mulroney could turn out a crowd, and to announce to the world that Montreal was his town, Quebec was his province, and he was not about to cede either to the Clark organization.

"It was to send out a signal that we were alive and well," Mulroney said later. "You see, Clark had had his hands on the organizational apparatus for seven years and had a lot of people on the payroll. The party had spent a great deal of money, mostly on payroll and organizational functions, which certainly made the party, such as it was in Quebec, responsive to his desires. And we had to strike back at that kind of thing. And we wanted to send out a signal to our troops around the province and elsewhere that we were going to be people of substance at this convention."

On the morning of the event, Mulroney began his day by reading a story by the *Gazette*'s Claude Arpin disclosing that 8,000 invitations had been sent out and that as many as 5,000 people were expected to converge on the midtown hotel at the height of the afternoon rush hour, creating a chaotic traffic jam. "Of course," Mulroney said in some bemusement, "you can always count on our guys to talk too much." But he did not sound unduly upset, for by this time he knew it was going to be a good event, and that he could tell a few thousand of his closest friends that they could anticipate a positive decision in the near future.

As for the friends chosen to make a born-again declaration of support on stage, the idea was to demonstrate that Mulroney's appeal cut across party lines and across public life.

There was Paul Desrochers, one-time chief organizer and special adviser to Robert Bourassa. Desrochers had been reproached by the Cliche Commission for his dealings with the Fédération des Travailleurs du Québec. They had put him in the witness box at the beginning of 1975, and yet here he was endorsing Mulroney's candidacy for the Conservative leadership. It was to be the last public appearance by a man who eschewed public appearances. Four months later, at home in Hawkesbury, Ontario, Desrochers would take his own life.

There was Phil Cutler, the labour lawyer from the union side of the table who had tangled with Mulroney in more than a few cases. There was a telegram for his "unforgettable friend," from Lucien Bouchard, by now the chief negotiator with Quebec's public employees for René Lévesque's Parti Québécois administration.

There was Bobby Orr, the retired hockey star whom Mulroney had got to know through Ross Johnston, the president of Standard Brands in New York. Orr endorsed their products. He endorsed the St. F.X. development campaign. And now he endorsed Mulroney's candidacy, telling him to "go for it."

The event achieved most of its objectives. Michel Cogger and the organization registered the names of everyone who showed up. "It gave us a nice base of volunteer pool and dollars," Cogger said. "And it showed Brian had not lost his ability to draw a big crowd. In other words, you could go underground afterwards and when people said, where's the style, you could point to that."

The only argument was over the size of the crowd. Both the *Gazette*'s Claude Arpin and the *Globe and Mail*'s John Gray made it out to be an audience of about 4,000 people. But CBC's *The National* the night before left it at "more than one thousand." After the newscast went off the air, the phone rang in *The National* newsroom in Toronto and a familiar, deep baritone voice informed the desk that they had missed the biggest story in the country: 3,000 people had disappeared in Montreal. The slightly annoyed caller was the candidate's brother, Gary Mulroney. But since he never identified himself, the people in Toronto thought it was the candidate himself. It would not have been the first time he complained about his coverage, as it would certainly not be the last.

From the beginning, he also meant to run a decentralized campaign based in the provinces, and he planned to make most of the big decisions himself. Some five years earlier, he had drafted a fourteen-point memorandum of do's and don'ts for Claude Ryan when the Montreal newspaper publisher was getting into the Quebec Liberal leadership race. Now Mulroney meant to put those observations into practice for himself. This, as Peter White later observed, "is usually a recipe for disaster, but this time it worked out."

For one thing, Mulroney was extremely reluctant to name a national campaign director. There were a number of reasons for this. For one, with a provincially based organization, there would be no need for an omnipotent campaign manager, who would inevitably offend the delicate sensibilities of workers in the regions, especially if the orders were coming from Toronto. Second, Mulroney was holding the nominal position of campaign director open for someone from the Big Blue Machine, preferably Norman Atkins if Bill Davis decided not to come in, for if Atkins or Paul Curley would move onside with Mulroney, that would be seen as a signal of a prevailing wind from Brampton.

And finally, the people who were apt to be named campaign director could not be appointed. Michel Cogger bore much of the criticism for the failures and excesses of the 1976 campaign, even some he didn't know about. He could hardly be campaign director again. Nor could it be Peter White, not least because of his connection with Conrad Black. "He had been the candidate of Power Corporation the last time out," White later observed. "He wasn't going to be the candidate of Argus this time around."

And so Mulroney flew into Toronto for two days of meetings at the Bristol Place Hotel with his organizers from across the country. They were in a bullish mood. At one point, the campaign directors from each province reported on their first-ballot expectations. "The way I figure it," Charley McMillan cracked, "we've got 4,500 votes on the first ballot."

They weren't there yet, not by a longshot. Even as the big boxcar numbers were being bandied around the table in Toronto, a Gallup affiliate was carrying out its first secret poll for the Mulroney organization in the period of March 17-25, the days leading up to and following his announcement. Though the sample was based largely on Winnipeg delegates, and this had a heavy built-in bias for Clark, it showed Mulroney had a long way to go, with only 13.5 per cent of the sample compared to Clark's 44.2 per cent. At that point, Clark was also the second choice of 8.1 per cent of the sample. Clearly, his strategy would be to re-elect as many of his Winnipeg slates as quickly as possible, and they might then have enough to put him over the top on the first or second ballot. Mulroney was the clear second choice of 15.4 per cent of the sample. Further back in third, but still surprisingly in third place in the Mulroney sample, was former party president Peter Blaikie at 6.9 per cent, who was also the second choice of 10 per cent of the delegates. Blaikie had announced on March 18, at the beginning of the survey, and this may have created a bubble, but his bilingual abilities made him a possible compromise candidate and a prospective recipient of both ABC and ABM support.

Blaikie was a bit of a joker in the leadership deck. Though a fluently bilingual Montrealer, he was handicapped by the lack of a Quebec base and his supporters across the country tended to be those who were against either Clark or Mulroney. Though Blaikie had been president of the party for the previous two years, he had no network of supporters beyond his own circle of personal friends. He found it difficult to raise money. His campaign organization, based in Montreal, was too narrow for a national race. With his towering figure, sculptured good looks, and booming bilingual voice, he came on too strong for many strangers, and for some, the more they knew him the less they liked him. Still, he was regarded as a potential threat in the Mulroney camp, a contender for the same ABC votes as well as for the ABM constituency. Jean Bazin, for one, was nervous about the prospect of a Blaikie candidacy.

Many of the Mulroneyites were privately relieved in late April when Blaikie took himself out of contention, saying he was not well enough versed on the issues. "Have you ever heard anything so ridiculous in your life?" Mulroney scoffed. "Peter saying he's not well versed on the issues. Of course he's well versed, as well versed as any of us, it's just that his campaign wasn't going anywhere." But then Mulroney's voice softened. It was tough, he knew, putting yourself on the road every morning at 6:30 when you know you're not going anywhere, when the delegates are standoffish, the press is unfavourable, the creditors want to be paid, and there's no money in the bank.

There had been a strong clash of personalities between the two men from the same time and place angling for the same job. When Blaikie became national president at the 1981 meeting in

Ottawa, Mulroney's private assessment was blunt: "If Peter Blaikie can parlay the presidency of the association into the leadership of the party, then good luck to him." When Blaikie's chance came, he lacked the years in the party he had joined only in 1976, he lacked the base in his home province of Quebec, and he lacked the experience and discipline to keep going through the heavy going of a three-month leadership campaign. But his abortive month-long campaign proved helpful to Mulroney in two respects. As a fluently bilingual candidate, Blaikie drew attention to that issue. And like Pocklington, as another candidate who did not hold elective office, he helped defuse that

Even if Mulroney remained unelected, there was one important difference in tone and substance from the 1976 campaign. This time, he was not without caucus support.

From his post in Gordon Towers' office, Pat MacAdam was Mulroney's eyes and ears on the Hill. Or rather, he was Mulroney's eyes, and Rick Logan, operating out of Bob Coates' office, was his ears. Coates, one of the surviving Diefenbaker loyalists, and Elmer MacKay were among the leaders of the review forces and later would become two of Mulroney's leading supporters in caucus. Another was George Hees, who had first come to Ottawa in a 1951 by-election and was by now the dean of the Tory caucus. Hees was one of many MPs Mulroney saw during a two-day stay at the Château Laurier the Tuesday and Wednesday of the week before he announced. "Brian," Hees told him, "let's cut the bullshit. I just want you to know right off the top I'm with you all the way. Now what else do you want to talk about?" Then and later, Hees would receive from Mulroney what he never had from Clark – a little bit of homage and respect.

In the end, some twenty MPs and a few senators moved onside with Mulroney, and the stigma that had attached to his 1976 campaign, that he had no support in caucus, was removed the second time around. It bothered Mulroney that his caucus support was perceived as coming from a bunch of mental midgets or right-wing dinosaurs, as compared with the moderate progressives around Clark. "The implication was that the people with talent and virtue were supporting Joe," Mulroney recalled, "and that I had the poor bedraggled souls that no one else would want. Of course nothing could be further from the truth and that bothered me, not for me personally. But the implication, the broad generalization that would come forward from the press gallery in Ottawa, was inaccurate and unfair." Bedraggled souls or not, Mulroney still had enough bodies from caucus to take the heat off.

Mulroney was soon finding that it wasn't much of an issue this time around. He had resigned the Iron Ore presidency and announced up front that he would be seeking a seat in the next election. For most delegates, that was the end of it. Among some of Mulroney's close friends, there was some concern as to whether he would make good on that promise if he lost, or whether he would have left Ottawa to return to a comfortable corporate perch in Montreal. It was generally assumed he could have returned to Iron Ore, whose owners in Cleveland appeared to be in no hurry to fill the presidency. It was even rumoured that he could have become publisher of the *Montreal Gazette*, whose proprietors at Southam Inc., in Toronto, seemed to be in no hurry to fill a vacancy that had occurred in March. Over the 1983-84 Christmas holiday, when Mulroney was in Florida, a close friend got around to asking the hypothetical question of what he would have done if he had lost. He replied that he would have had to get back to work in Montreal, though he did not say where. As for the 1984 general election, after the promises he had made, he acknowledged that he would have been obliged to run somewhere in Quebec if he was to have any long-term political future and not be dismissed for all time as a fleeting opportunist who turned up only at leadership conventions and withdrew in a sulk when denied the great prize. But getting elected in Quebec, under the banner of Joe Clark or John Crosbie, might have proved difficult even for Mulroney. And having made the pro-forma effort, he mightn't have been heartbroken had he lost.

There were some striking and fundamental differences between Mulroney at the end of his 1976 campaign and at the outset of his 1983 run for the leadership. Older in a superficial sense – his grey hair was evidence of that – Mulroney was also fundamentally a more mature man, better equipped for the rigours of a ninety-day campaign.

Though he wouldn't have said so at the time, his defeat in 1976 had turned out to be a lucky break. It gave him the opportunity to achieve the financial security that he had always wanted before entering politics.

The seven years also gave Brian and Mila Mulroney a chance to put their private life on a solid footing and to enjoy the important child-rearing years of their family life away from the goldfish bowl of Ottawa. This may have been especially important for the former Mila Pivnicki. At twenty-two in 1976, and the mother of two infant children, she might have been overwhelmed by the experience. As for Brian Mulroney, at thirty-six, the rounding-off experience of his business years lay ahead of him. And he had some sadness, as well as a good deal of bitterness, to put behind him.

One day, the terrible bitterness was gone. He simply stopped making disparaging comments about Clark. He had also stopped drinking. As near as one close friend could make it, this occurred some time in the spring of 1980. Joe Clark was out of office, the victim at the polls of his own obstinacy in government, now denied the job for which Mulroney still considered himself better equipped. Now there still might be another chance for Mulroney. Whether it came after the next leadership review or the next election or the one after that seemed unimportant. At forty, he would take to noting that Pierre Trudeau had entered politics only at the age of forty-six and had become Prime Minister at forty-eight.

Mulroney's long-term political prospects were not diminished by the fact that he had given up drinking. When Conrad Black heard about it from Peter White, his half-humorous, half-serious observation was that now Clark had better start taking Mulroney seriously. Mulroney never made a big fuss over this. He never said anything about it. But friends and associates soon noticed that he was drinking soda water or tomato juice with his lunch, or that he was no longer having a cognac after dinner. If asked about it, he would just say that he felt better, as he certainly looked better. And those of his friends who had ached for him in his bitterness now rejoiced for him as it became clear that he was putting all that behind him. For the longest time, Mulroney was terribly sensitive to any mention in the press that he had given up drinking. What might have been a human failing had become one of his private personal triumphs, and he didn't see where it was anyone else's business.

Until March of 1983, the story had a happy ending. And in the spring of 1983, many of Mulroney's friends wondered and worried what losing again would do to him. The bitterness would have been there, but they needn't have worried about the drink. It was part of Mulroney's past. And he was even ordering his lieutenants to go off the hard stuff for the duration of the campaign. "I've told our guys that I don't want any booze in this campaign," Mulroney said in March of 1983. "For a very good reason, that on the night of June 11th, I'm going to throw them the biggest damn party you ever saw."

It was the beginning of what one Mulroney adviser had dubbed "the coffee campaign." As he flew into Ottawa on the eve of his announcement, Brian Mulroney was observing his forty-fourth birthday. And whatever lay down the road, he would never be in better physical and mental shape for the rigours of a leadership campaign.

Mulroney's first inclination had been to declare earlier in the month, but when he finally settled on March 21, he made one phone call – to John Crosbie, who was planning to announce the same day in a service club speech in Toronto. Mulroney wanted to apologize for any inconvenience this might cause Crosbie and to make sure his nose wasn't too far out of joint. "It was clear to me," Mulroney said later, "that the mood between candidates was going to be important, and that because of a number of matters it would not be favourable to Clark."

Win or lose, he meant to call all the shots himself. And one thing no one would accuse Brian Mulroney of in this campaign would be travelling in style, even in a cab that looked like a limo. In front of the Château the next morning, the luckless owner of the innocent Cadillac was paid a few bucks for his trouble and waved on. Brian Mulroney climbed into another car, and gave the address of the press building at 150 Wellington Street, where his campaign sequel, Jaws II, would open in a few minutes.

12

THE BATTLE OF QUEBEC

It was a straight, simple proposition, as Mulroney explained it to his Quebec organizers during a rare Saturday morning appearance at his Montreal campaign headquarters on Delormier Street in the East End, in the shadow of the Jacques Cartier Bridge. First, you sign people up as members, and then you get them out to vote. Then, if more card-carrying members voted for your delegate slate than the other guy's, you win the riding's four senior and two youth delegates. There are seventy-five ridings in Quebec, and seventy-five times six equals 450 delegates from the associations.

You could call this slate warfare, or trench warfare, but in every riding the principle was the same, as it was in some fifty-six campus clubs that sprouted miraculously from the barren ground of Quebec in the winter and spring of 1983. Not only were the province's seven universities and forty-one community colleges organized, but the Mulroney and Clark forces also contended for votes at secretarial schools and the like.

The delegate contest in Quebec was apt to be organized as a battle of slates for a number of reasons. First, as Clark organizer Marcel Danis pointed out, the party was not big enough to sustain more than two candidacies on a province-wide basis. In good years, the Tories counted themselves lucky to carry 10,000 members on their rolls across the province, about one-tenth of the federal Liberal rank and file in Quebec. In at least three dozen ridings and probably more, the Progressive Conservative Party did not exist during – never mind between – elections. In these rotten boroughs, there were few regulars to monitor the selling of memberships.

Moreover, there were only two candidates, Clark and Mulroney, who were interesting to the vast majority of Quebecers: Clark because he had worked hard to make himself fluently bilingual and because his courageous position on the constitutional patriation package had won him high marks from the provincialist *bleus* of Quebec; Mulroney because he was a favourite son, and in Quebec, blood runs thicker than water. Since his French was so idiomatic, and since his French culture was so broad, it was widely assumed that his mother or grandmother was a francophone. He wouldn't have been the first Quebecer bearing an Irish name to have been fully integrated, even assimilated, into the francophone community. Because of their religious affinities and their mutual dislike of the English that carried across an ocean, the Irish and the Québécois mixed and married. There are O'Connors and O'Keefes in Quebec who don't speak a word of English. "As a francophone from Baie Comeau," Mulroney was asked in a 1981 appearance on Réal-Jean Couture's Sept-Iles hotline show, "how do you feel as the head of a multinational company?"

"Very comfortable," Mulroney replied. This perception, which Mulroney never did anything to dispel, was his free pass into the politics of Quebec as a favourite son. Nor had anyone, even his fiercest detractors in the rough and tumble Quebec trade union movement, ever dared to call him one of "les autres." He was one of "nous autres."

Even acknowledging Clark's organizational strength in Quebec, Mulroney had to do substantially better than the man from High River. He needed to do well in the Quebec associations not only to solidify his base but to fortify his argument that he was the man to make a breakthrough in Quebec. He would be hard-pressed to make this case among delegates from the common-law provinces if he couldn't even achieve a majority from Quebec.

"The big change since '76," Mulroney said in 1981, "is that I'd have all of Quebec."

It wasn't to be. Clark, as Michael Wilson observed, had a lot of practice at organizing conventions. He had the prestige of incumbency, even when he had renounced the office. And he had a lot of appeal in Quebec, to a degree that was not appreciated in English-speaking Canada. Quebecers would never vote for him, at least not against Pierre Trudeau, but they had come to respect him. It was not by accident that Clark, after a sunning stint in Florida, started his campaign to succeed himself in Montreal on St. Valentine's Day.

The meeting, at the Club Canadien on Sherbrooke Street East, was the perfect demonstration of Clark's strength with the Quebec intelligentsia, and of his weakness with the party rank and file. While Conservative activists waited downstairs, Clark met privately in an upper room with Senator Arthur Tremblay, his adviser on the constitution. Louis-Philippe de Grandpré was there, not because he was a Tory, even in his home riding of Outremont. The former Supreme Court justice said he was simply there as a citizen supporting Clark. So was Solange Chaput-Rolland, the columnist and former member of the Task Force on Canadian Unity. It was all very well, but neither one of them had a delegate vote or could even vote in a delegate-selection meeting.

Downstairs, a man named David Bernstein, a three-time loser in the riding of St. Denis, was selling tickets to his own fund-raiser in the month of March. He would work hard to deliver his six delegates to Mulroney. Marcel Masse, the former Union Nationale cabinet minister, came and went. Now a vice-president of the huge Lavalin engineering firm, he was known to be waiting for Bill Davis. If necessary, he would end up with Mulroney. "At the present time," Masse said in answer to a reporter's question, "I would say that 100 per cent of the party supports Joe Clark, since he is the only candidate." This guy could have answered questions in Richard Nixon's White House. "Excuse me," he said, "I have to go."

And there was Jean-Paul Cardinal, senior managing partner of Michel Cogger's century-old Montreal law firm, soon to be disbanded. A long-time *bleu* who had been the government of Quebec's lawyer during the reign of his friend Daniel Johnson, Cardinal was a renowned raconteur and one of the funniest men in Montreal. "Is there a way," he said in an aside as he bounded up the front stairs, "of being for both Clark and Mulroney at the same time?"

"One thing is sure," he added, "the Conservatives will find a way to screw themselves."

This was the world of Quebec Torydom that reporters loved to write about, with more warring factions than the streets of Beirut and more moles and other assorted double agents than a shelfful of George Smiley books.

Of the 200-odd people in the room, Clark might have been able to count on half of them. No matter, Clark was in superior form that night, fit and tanned from two weeks in the sun, buoyed by a Gallup Poll that put the Tories at 49 per cent, and buoyant to be in Quebec, where he always seemed to enjoy himself. The presentation seldom varied. He was the Alberta boy who understood the aspirations of Quebec. "I may be from Alberta," he said this night, "but my heart is in Quebec."

And no one ever doubted it.

There was a lot at stake in Quebec's potential 725 votes, when the youth and automatic delegates were included, enough to put Joe Clark over the top on the first ballot or enough to put Mulroney in the race. It should have surprised no one that the delegate battle proved to be rough. But nobody was ready for the trench warfare that began on March 25, the Friday night of the first weekend of delegate-selection meetings.

With control of many of the constituency associations, the Clark organization scheduled more than two dozen delegate-selection meetings for the first weekend alone. And it was not child's play on either side. In Longueuil, south of Montreal, Mulroney supporters were checked for their credentials and held up at the church door. In neighbouring Chateauguay, Mulroney's riding organizer had his house ransacked during a Friday night nomination meeting. On Sunday, a busload of Mulroney supporters were brought in from a men's hostel to vote for the Mulroney slate in St. Jacques. It was Jason Moscovitz's CBC television piece, on the men from the Old Brewery Mission, which created a nationwide sensation and led to the empanelling of a committee to review riding meetings in Quebec and across the country. Mulroney tried to deflect the criticism, noting that these were men who were down on their luck, that many of them had served their country, that they were mostly permanent residents of the mission whose names were on the electoral list. But there was no putting a good face on it, and privately he acknowledged as much to his public relations strategist, Roger Nantel, whom he now brought on board full-time, telling him that the Brewery-type incidents had to stop.

Mulroney was also aware that the trench warfare would continue into the month of April. It would be tough, it would be dirty, but they would just have to get through it. The basic question for Mulroney and his organizers was whether to let the Clark slates pass or to fight them every inch of the way. Even with all the bad publicity, even with all the allegations of dirty tricks, even with all the expense of paying thousands of new memberships, it was never a difficult decision.

"I knew I was going to have to take some heat," Mulroney said early in 1984. "It didn't bother me in the least. I knew I was going to be the underdog. We galvanized our troops. And they had absolutely exhausted their budgets, and that meant they had shot their bolt. They shot their bolt in Quebec, right off the bat, and we kept growing with every subsequent Sunday. But it was a tough one."

Over the first ten days, including the long Easter weekend in the first week of April, nearly 400 Quebec delegates were chosen in forty-five ridings and forty-one campus clubs. With nearly a month to go before the delegate selection terminated on May 1, only thirty ridings and a dozen or so campus delegations remained to be chosen in Quebec. Clark's lightning strategy appeared to be paying off. Of the ridings selected at the opening bell over the last weekend of March, Mulroney's Quebec organizer Rodrigue Pageau later estimated that "we took seven."

For Mulroney, with his cockeyed Irish optimist's way of looking at things, the opening weekend's pre-emptive strike, while ostensibly a victory for the Clark forces, "ultimately did them in." As far as Mulroney was concerned, Clark's first-strike strategy was "the best thing that happened to us in the whole campaign." Correspondingly, he saw the opening weekend's rough skirmishing as "the death knell" of Clark's campaign.

"There was no doubt in my mind," Mulroney said later, "that he couldn't win after that." Mulroney later maintained that he was all that stood between Clark and a first-ballot victory, that the other candidates were not unaware of this and were quietly grateful to him for it, notwithstanding some of the pronouncements by David Crombie and Michael Wilson, who may have been genuinely scandalized by what was going on in Quebec and some other provinces. Crombie called it a "moral crisis." Wilson's sensibilities were also offended. "The other candidates," said Mulroney, "quite properly tried to take advantage of the issue."

Crombie demanded and got a special Saturday meeting of the candidates or their representatives to deal with the dirty tricks issue. The meeting resolved nothing, other than giving Crombie a tiny, perfect, white hobby horse to ride out in front of the media hordes gathered on the pavement in front of the Conservative Party's Laurier Street headquarters in Ottawa. For the rest, the meeting changed nothing, and the trench warfare in Quebec resumed after the brief Easter truce. The national and local media were hot on the story, sending reporters to cover every Quebec meeting as if it were a Stanley Cup final, where they might otherwise have been content to receive the results over the telephone, like a high school hockey game. There were reports of fourteen-year-olds turning out to vote for Mulroney in Verdun, of a soccer team being bussed in by the Mulroney forces in West End Notre-Dame-de-Grace, of tavern habitués getting out to vote in East End Rosemont, of a meeting cancelled in South Shore Chambly by pro-Mulroney scrutineers who bounced an $888 cheque for as many Clark memberships.

It was with a mingling of horror and fascination that many

Tories in the Conservative home counties of Ontario watched and read reports of the delegate-selection process in Quebec. The difference between the two provinces was that the Tory party existed in Ontario and the party rank and file turned up at meetings. But even in true blue Ontario, riding associations were not immune from allegations of dirty tricks, with the Clarkians being accused of bussing in Korean immigrants in Metro Toronto ridings, though as citizens it was their perfect right to join a political party and the Tories had a need to expand their ethnic base, especially in Metro Toronto. In other ridings, Peter Pocklington's friends from the Amway crowd were accused of pyramiding memberships to pack nominations. But most of the heat was in Quebec, and Mulroney decided to hunker down and wait out what he termed Clark's scorched-earth policy.

Mulroney said later he got his Quebec organizers together one morning and laid it out for them: "We're going to fight hard and mind our own business. We're the underdogs. And we're going to deal with our colleagues on the co-ordination committee to forge alliances for the second, third, and fourth ballots, and we're going to force them [the Clark campaign] to spend every nickel. Plus some. Because now we know they're into the banks and we know they've shot their bolt. They selected all their ridings that first weekend, and anything they're going to get they're going to fight for. And it's going to cost them an arm and a leg."

As for all the bad publicity from the Old Brewery incident, Mulroney later insisted: "It didn't bother me, it genuinely didn't." When the smoke of the battle cleared, after all, he had the essential votes he needed to stake his claim that he was Quebec's candidate at the convention.

But he mightn't have had them without Rodrigue Pageau, whom Peter White quite accurately characterized as "a rock" of the Quebec campaign. Pageau, together with Cogger and Mulroney himself, masterminded what may have been the key stratagem in the leadership race in the spring of 1983, and that was taking over the Quebec association in the winter of 1982.

Ostensibly, the issue to be settled that last weekend of February, 1982, at Montreal's CEGEP Maisonneuve was whether the Conservatives should form a provincial party to put down roots in the province. Clark, as an Albertan, stood aside from the question. Mulroney spoke in favour of an idea he had long advocated within Conservative councils. And Jean-Yves Lortie spoke passionately against it. He came to praise the Union Nationale, not to bury it, even though the party of Maurice Duplessis and

Daniel Johnson was clearly a spent force in provincial politics. Mulroney voted for the idea of studying the proposition further and lost; Lortie voted against and won.

Then the Mulroney forces got down to the serious business of electing Lortie and Ed Ross as vice-presidents of the provincial association. It was another one of the strange twists and turns along the Tory road in Quebec.

In 1976, Jean-Yves Lortie had been Roch LaSalle's number-one Quebec organizer for Claude Wagner. Lortie's organizational acumen, holding his delegates until the last moment across the river in Hull, was the stuff of which party legends are made. Six months later, Lortie stood as Wagner's candidate for the provincial presidency. LaSalle, with Mulroney's backing, carried the day as Clark's candidate. By the time of the 1981 leadership review, Lortie was again producing his delegates from Quebec. The review forces were in touch with him, as they would be again. By 1982, Lortie had come full circle as a member in good standing of the Mulroney clan in Quebec. A Montreal bailiff, he might not fit with the Tory blue suits, but he had a way of delivering that Mulroney was not unaware of. All things considered, he would rather have Lortie working from his side of the street.

By 1983, and the review in Winnipeg, the ineffable Lortie had become rather too famous for his own good. With his Brillo hairstyle, he was impossible to miss moving among his delegates on the floor, and French-speaking reporters flocked after him for quotes that were too quotable. So in the spring leadership campaign, he never showed his face at the Mulroney campaign office in the heart of his turf in East End Montreal. Yet he kept organizing the ridings in the eastern half of the city and delivered handsomely in June. On the day of the vote, he was nowhere to be found on the floor of the Civic Centre. He was sitting in the third to last row near the roof of the building. He had his walkie-talkies and he had his numbers, and he expected to win. A final irony of this seven-year saga is that Clark's chief Quebec organizers, Mario Beaulieu and lawyer Marcel Danis, had been Mulroney supporters in 1976. All things considered, as between the lawyer and the bailiff, Mulroney would take Lortie, who had proven that he could deliver more than a subpoena.

The Clark loyalists did not miss the significance of the events on Sunday, February 28, 1982, as Lortie and Ed Ross won their vice-presidential posts. Jean Dugré, who was Jean Bazin's former brother-in-law, was acclaimed as treasurer. Thus, the Mulroney clan had wrested control of the provincial executive from the Clark loyalists. Outgoing president Danis, though he wore a pained expression that Sunday afternoon, said nothing. After all, his law partner, Robert Brunet, had been installed as his successor.

But Peter Blaikie, the national president, did not feel bound by such constraints. "As far as I'm concerned," he announced in an impromptu news conference, "war has been declared. There is an obvious attempt to take control of the association, and it relates to the leadership." It was a rather bald way of putting it, but Blaikie's assessment was absolutely bang on. The problem for Blaikie was that it wasn't his people taking control, it was the Mulroney clan.

They were looking to Winnipeg and perhaps beyond, as the literate Tory pundit Dalton Camp, alone among his colleagues, perceived in his newspaper column: "The appointment of delegates-at-large, for example, will be made by the newly elected Mulroney-leaning executive, and these represent a tidy bloc of votes." Thirty-eight votes, to be exact, both in Winnipeg and in the great beyond of Ottawa.

The fight for Quebec's delegates-at-large in the spring of 1983 was the political equivalent of a four-point game in hockey. The episode had the overtones of one of Peter Sellers' Inspector Clouseau films, except that where thirty-eight delegates were concerned, it was a deadly serious business. On April 10, LaSalle and three other members of the twenty-four-member provincial council availed themselves of their right to demand a bimonthly meeting on April 30, where delegates-at-large would be chosen. The provincial president, Robert Brunet, Danis's law partner but by now an open Mulroney sympathizer, in turn availed himself of his emergency powers to move up the meeting eight days, to April 22, effectively disenfranchising four regional vice-presidents who would be elected only on April 27. Even at that, the April 22 meeting was a close thing. The Mulroney slate of thirty-eight delegates, including the candidate and his wife, was elected by a majority of 13-11. The Clark representatives played the game under protest and went ahead anyway with their meeting April 30 at the same location, the party's Quebec headquarters on the eighth floor of a mid-town high-rise on President Kennedy Avenue in Montreal. In the absence of the Mulroneyites, they upheld their own protest and proceeded with the election of their own slate – twenty-nine Clark delegates, eight Mulroneyites, including the candidate, his wife, Jean Bazin, plus Peter Blaikie's wife, Maja.

So now the Mulroney and Clark forces were into a nasty credentials fight, a battle that would be carried to Ottawa in front of

171

Jean Riou's nine-member credentials committee. Appearing for Mulroney, Bernard Roy argued in vain that the credentials committee had no jurisdiction, since it was empanelled to hear complaints on elected rather than appointed delegates. For most of a day at national headquarters in Ottawa, Roy tried to make Mulroney's case, to no avail. And it was clear that the 5-4 committee vote to hear the case was breaking down along leadership lines, with the Clark loyalists enjoying a slight edge over the ABC faction. When the final arguments were heard, Roy for the defence, as it were, and Michel Côté for the Clark slate, no one would predict the outcome. It was another cliffhanger. But this time Ontario MP Scott Fennell, who had been siding with the Clark faction, changed his vote. The Clark appeal was rejected by a slender 5-4 margin, and Mulroney had his thirty-eight delegates. Mulroney's reaction, when informed by Roy, was a deep baritone sigh of relief.

For Mulroney, it seemed to be more than thirty-eight delegates. It appeared to be a sweet revenge for the humiliation of 1976, when the Wagner-controlled provincial executive named an at-large slate that left Mulroney completely out in the cold. He was not even a delegate to a convention at which he was presenting himself as a leadership candidate. Mulroney had begun to get even on the afternoon of February 22, 1976, when he was eliminated after the third ballot. With a crush of delegates from both the Clark and Wagner camps shouting his name, Roch LaSalle had pushed through the throng to his box.

"Brian," LaSalle had called up, "we need you."

"Roch," Mulroney had replied, "I don't have a vote."

The Clark loyalists threatened to take their case all the way to the national executive, but there the ABC were in the majority, and Peter Elzinga made it clear he wouldn't even hear a further appeal. By the closest of margins, Mulroney had won the four-point game.

There was one more factor in the Mulroney clan finally winning the bloody battle of Quebec, and that was the youth delegates, organized primarily by Pageau in the office and by Jean Dugré in the field. Outremont was a typical example of a riding where the Mulroney forces worked their youth vote to overcome Clark's advantage among senior delegates. According to the rules, elsewhere as in Quebec, members under thirty years of age were eligible to vote for the four senior delegates as well as the two junior delegates. In many if not most instances, youth members also voted on campus for their three student delegates. Thus the

172

Tories had enshrined a new principle of democracy: one man, three votes.

In Outremont, the Clark loyalists should have prevailed. Mario Beaulieu, the major-domo of the Clark Quebec organization, lived there, as did Michel Côté, Clark's legal counsel in the province, and Henriette Guerin, a Quebec representative on the national executive. But there was Bernard Roy, standing in the schoolroom door, barring the way of the Clark youth members, checking their credentials. Pretty soon, with the Mulroneyites carrying the youth section by twenty votes, it became clear that they had a majority of the hall. Mario Beaulieu did the prudent thing. He took his name off the Clark slate so as to avoid a personal defeat that would embarrass his leader.

Beaulieu had been with Mulroney in 1976, but after Clark named him chief Quebec organizer in 1982, he remained loyal to the leader in Winnipeg and beyond. Through all this rough combat, there was no doubt in the minds of Pageau and the Mulroney people that it was Beaulieu, and not the talkative Danis, who was keeping Clark in the game. For Beaulieu, it was a question of loyalty over personal preference. "It was not the easiest day of my life," he said nearly a year later, "when Brian Mulroney called me and I had to say no. But Clark was acceptable to us in Quebec, acceptable and accepted."

Beaulieu, one-time Finance Minister in Daniel Johnson's Union Nationale government, stayed with Clark, as did Jean Bruneau, another old *bleu* who had worked the 1968 federal election with a twenty-nine-year-old organizer named Brian Mulroney. It was largely because of their efforts, and the fund-raising of Bob de Côtret and Pierre Roy, that Clark was in the game in Quebec. Roy, an insurance executive, raised $40,000 for the Clark cause in a single lunch. It was a time-tested approach, in Montreal as in other cities. They threw an intimate lunch for Clark at the exclusive Club St. Denis, with twenty guests at $2,000 a plate. It wasn't enough. Clark's Quebec campaign finished with debts that still exceeded $100,000 at the end of January, 1984, and had to be cleared off by another intimate supper, this time with Mulroney as the guest.

"Let's face it," Beaulieu said with no undue modesty, "if it hadn't been for us, Joe wouldn't have done nearly as well. He would have been lucky to get 25 per cent of the Quebec vote." As it was, Mulroney had to fight Clark every inch of the way.

For the most part, it was as Mulroney prescribed in the meeting with his senior campaign officials in early April – a logistical question of signing up members and getting them out. For his part, he spent only four days campaigning in his home province after the completion of the delegate-selection process on May 1.

Mulroney flew into Montreal for a news conference that Sunday morning carrying a copy of *The Toronto Star*, which proclaimed in no uncertain banner-headline terms that David Crombie and he had been the stars of the previous day's debate in Toronto.

Even before they got to Massey Hall, Mulroney had been sowing the seeds of trouble for Joe Clark, asserting that Clark's endorsement of the original Vancouver amending formula, with full compensation for provinces opting out, would put money from the federal treasury in the pocket of the separatist Premier of Quebec. Before he gave away his aces, Mulroney said, "Before I give away a plugged nickel, I want to know what René Lévesque's going to do for Canada."

It was a bit simplistic, but for the sake of argument, it served its purpose. All that week leading up to the Massey Hall debate, Clark was dogged by the issue and forced to clarify his position on the amending formula. By the weekend, editorials had appeared in the Toronto press, and by the time the candidates got on stage, the issue blew up in Clark's face. And since John Gamble had raised it in rather demagogic terms, Clark began to reply in French and was hooted down for his trouble. Afterwards, much was made of this, but Mulroney pointed out that both he and David Crombie, as well as Michael Wilson, received loud applause for switching into French. And much later, Wilson pointed out that the tickets had been divided up equally among the seven candidates. "You must remember," Wilson said, "that six out of seven people in that hall came to bury Joe Clark."

The Mulroney people released an optimistic breakdown of Quebec in which they gave themselves 491 of some 750 eligible delegates. But the Montreal press was more interested in his constitutional position, or lack of one, after he had scored Clark's endorsement of the original Vancouver amending formula with full compensation for provinces opting out of federal-provincial programs. This was the formula that René Lévesque had bought in the accord of the dissenting premiers of April 16, 1981, and it was the formula, with only partial compensation in education and cultural programs, that would be enacted following the First Ministers' agreement of November 5, 1981. It was the deal offered now by Clark, even though he was not in power, even though Lévesque was offering nothing in return, and even though it

174

required unanimous consent of the other partners to change the amending formula.

Mulroney later remembered the Sunday news conference as the day of "my intellectual skirmish with the local press." Once again, given a choice between examining a candidate on economic issues and falling back on the constitution, the assembled Montreal media opted for the constitution. The issue continued to dog Mulroney as he headed downriver to Trois-Rivières, Quebec, Rimouski, and Rivière-du-Loup.

Finally, on a Quebecair flight, he wrote down nine points, as he said, "on the back of a Quebecair barf bag." That did not seem to satisfy anyone, least of all the intelligentsia, but at least he had reiterated his basic commitment to minority language rights on the one hand and the need for the flexible application of language laws on the other. For the rest, he held himself open to another round of constitutional negotiations, but made the point that it would not be a very useful exercise with the Lévesque government as Quebec's bargaining agent.

Still, the Quebec tour was essentially meaningless, except for the pictures it produced of the rusty station wagons. In open delegate meetings, Mulroney seemed to have little luck in persuading Clark delegates to come over to his side. One woman in Trois-Rivières observed that in the Church you have to be a priest before you become a cardinal. Mulroney later maintained they had pulled "the old back door trick" of bringing the delegates up to his suite when reporters' backs were turned and winning them over in one-on-one conversations.

This may have been wishful thinking on his part. It was a long, grungy week in Quebec. But there was one half-hour in it that was worth saving, on the morning a Quebecair flight stopped to refuel in Baie Comeau. Since Mulroney had all six delegates from his home riding of Manicouagan, there was no need for him to go into town. But he did ask the pilot if he could get out, take some air, and stretch his legs. In the small terminal, he was surrounded by a bunch of students going to Alberta on an exchange program. Some of them were the kids of people he had grown up with, and like this friend of their fathers', they were starting the process of growing up and moving away from home. For a few minutes they chattered at him and he signed autographs. Then he, and they, were gone.

175

13

HOW THE
WEST WAS
(FINALLY) WON

In most respects it was the most physically and psychologically punishing week of the campaign. It was Brian Mulroney's week in Alberta. It was also John Crosbie's week on the cover of *Maclean's* magazine. And it was the week of a Southam News poll that had Mulroney way behind Clark, 35 per cent to 19 per cent, in committed first-ballot support, 39-23 when the leanings were added in, and only eight points ahead of the fast-closing Crosbie. As always, the worse things looked, the more optimistic Mulroney became. Nick Hills, he said of the general manager of Southam News, "is gonna have a heart attack, right on the goddamn spot," when the numbers went up on the big board on June 11. As for the *Maclean's* cover, Mulroney dismissed it as hype, though he was rather hoping that the woman sitting across from him would write a piece on this western swing that would make the cover of the following week's edition. That decision was out of Carol Goar's hands. Her job, as the magazine's Ottawa bureau chief, was to bounce around Alberta for three days from the foothills to the high Rockies and back again.

In three brutal days, Mulroney would go from Red Deer to Edmonton, to Fort McMurray and Grande Prairie in the northwest part of the province, to Medicine Hat near the Saskatchewan border, and to Lethbridge and Calgary before moving on to Victoria and Vancouver. There was only one way to do it, in one of those unmentionable things with wings, and it did have props. A small group of reporters soon worked out a running gag that "the candidate is travelling in a small private aircraft, that's S-M-A-L-L." By this time, Mulroney was prepared to bump aides from his plane to make room for four eastern reporters who were waiting for him on the afternoon of May 17 as he came tripping across the lobby of the Black Knight Hotel in Red Deer, the capital of the Bible Belt. "I'm telling you," he said, "you should have been in

Saskatchewan." He looked glad to see some decidedly familiar faces.

This was going to be a tough audience in Red Deer, a dinner crowd of some 300 small business people. If there weren't many delegates in the room, they were all Tories. The local and regional news media would be there. At least Mulroney had the local MP, Gordon Towers, in his corner.

"The next election's not going to be decided at the Lakehead," he said. "It's going to be decided right here in downtown Red Deer."

And he went into a variation of his pet electoralist theme. It would be election night in Canada, and Knowlton Nash and Barbara Frum would be discussing the results coming in from the Atlantic Provinces, where the Tories would be holding their own. "Pow," Mulroney said. "They hit the Gaspé coast, and the whole thing sinks. And Knowlton says, 'What do you think of that, Barbara?' and she says, 'I don't know, let's ask Larry Zolf.'"

The problem, of course, would be the Liberal juggernaut rolling through French Canada. If this struck some listeners as rather too bald an appeal for votes, Mulroney would try to dress it up in a historical perspective. The Tories, he said, should remember the teaching of their founding father, Sir John A. Macdonald, who spoke of "the grand alliance, East and West, English and French, and when either of those elements are missing, you're doomed to opposition, and opposition is where we have been." Mulroney would acknowledge that Macdonald may never have said that in exactly those words, but nobody ever thought to look it up.

When he had finished, they gave him a hat, the biggest ten-gallon hat in town, but it was still a size and a half too small for his outsize size-nine head. The man making the presentation said that in those parts a big head was supposed to be a sign of great intelligence. Mulroney does not like hats and never wears them even in the dead of winter, but he had a feeling for this beautiful western hat and held it on his lap as the six-passenger Piper bumped its way from Red Deer to Edmonton Municipal Airport, which is so close to downtown you hardly need to take a cab.

Charley McMillan was waiting for his candidate on the ramp. That his top policy adviser was picking up the tour was indicative of the importance Mulroney attached to his agenda for this week. The next morning, he would be submitting himself to the Inquisition, as some critics had dubbed the five-member committee of Peter Lougheed's Tory administration who were interviewing

177

candidates as they came through the Alberta capital.

It was the first time McMillan had joined the tour, and the impact on the candidate's performance was immediate and evident to anyone who had been following Mulroney in the boonies. After McMillan's briefings on western issues, Mulroney's answers on the National Energy Program and the Crowsnest Pass Rate came into much sharper focus. The ambiguity and the fuzziness fell away. "We had planned way ahead for that," McMillan said. "Brian had said a month before he wanted a comprehensive briefing on western issues."

And now, in a late-night session in Edmonton's venerable Hotel Macdonald, McMillan briefed his candidate for the next morning's session with the Lougheed group over at Government House, the former residence of the lieutenant-governor on a bluff high over the North Saskatchewan River. The Lougheed meeting lasted for more than two hours, and when it was over Lougheed had Mulroney stay back for a private chat. As Mulroney recalled it, the Premier told him to "keep it up, you're doing just great." Mulroney had more detailed advice from Lougheed in the form of private letters in the Premier's own broad handwriting, and he had received some support in the matter of delegates, organization, and issues.

On his first time through Edmonton in the last week of March, Mulroney had met privately with Lougheed's chief of staff, Bob Giffen. "There were a number of ministers that I had hoped to see while I was there, who were unavailable," Mulroney said later. "I can assure you that they were available very quickly when Bob Giffen got on the phone."

Lee Richardson, who ran the Premier's Calgary office, was very much onside and would later become deputy chief of staff in the Opposition Leader's office in Ottawa. Helen Hunley, the former Alberta Health Minister, was the campaign chairperson. The Premier's own son, Steve, would eventually turn up wearing a Mulroney badge at a meeting for the Calgary delegates, letting it be known that he would serve as the candidate's Alberta floor manager.

Finally, there was Peter Lougheed himself, his prudent instincts and private way of doing things reinforced by the necessity to avoid offending the two favourite-son camps of Joe Clark and Peter Pocklington. Lougheed could not, would not, show his hand.

And so he carried on with the committee interviews, which themselves became the cause of a minor campaign controversy when Michael Wilson abruptly announced that he would not be appearing before the Inquisition, which he found an affront to the democratic process. Leaving aside the principle of it, it was quite clear that there might be some votes in it for Wilson back in the Tory home counties of Ontario, where the trustees of the Big Blue Machine had a well-developed aversion to the blue-eyed sheik of Saudi Alberta. Privately, the Mulroney strategists were delighted by Wilson's gesture. "Every vote for Wilson in Ontario was one vote less for Crosbie," said Charley McMillan.

The Mulroney and Wilson camps happened to cross paths in the lobby of the Hotel Macdonald that May evening, and it was quite clear they were exchanging pleasantries rather than hostilities. Mulroney's problem, when asked about it the next day, was to defend Lougheed's right to run his committee any way he pleased, without giving undue offence to Wilson. "I didn't find anything offensive in the process at all," Mulroney said later. "I was sort of alarmed when people started to put out the line that it was some kind of ideological purity test or something. It was no such thing. It was a simple situation where we get together and talk about problems that effect the Premier of Alberta and his colleagues. Now I'll allow that it was rather more structured than other meetings with other premiers. But no more than that."

Mulroney was well prepared for the concerns of the Lougheed committee, and the NEP, his idea of the country, the role of the West, and their particular regional perception that it was difficult to communicate with the permanent public service in Ottawa, whom they suspected of having socialist tendencies. On a scale of ten, Charley McMillan gave his candidate an eight. Peter Lougheed was impressed, and the word that he was soon got out on the jungle telegraph.

For public consumption, Lougheed maintained his posture of neutrality. "The best thing for a premier would be to stay neutral," Lougheed said in a rare interview with a visiting reporter from the mysterious East a few hours after the committee grilling of Mulroney. On the morrow, John Crosbie would be the last candidate through, and the exercise would be complete. But even if Lougheed had come straight out with an endorsement of Mulroney, it would not have had an appreciable impact on the first ballot. Clark commanded a considerable degree of loyalty, if not affection, from his fellow Albertans, and Pocklington was not without significant support, especially in the Edmonton area. "We were in difficult territory," Mulroney later acknowledged. "But it was second- and third-ballot stuff . . . that's what the whole thing was about. . . . We were still working on alliances out there."

In search of second-ballot support, Mulroney knocked himself out from one end of the province to the other and halfway back again. From Edmonton, he flew to the northwest part of the province and an early evening meeting at Grande Prairie. *The Toronto Star*'s Bob McKenzie, who had been watching Mulroney speak for more than twenty years, had never heard him in better form. Small towns and small-town folk sometimes had that effect on him, as they had in his sentimental appearance in Baie Comeau during the previous leadership campaign. "Looks like Baie Comeau," Mulroney said with his nose pressed up against the window of the Piper Cheyenne as they flew into Grande Prairie. And he made one of those Baie Comeau speeches, about sacrifice and courage and pioneer spirit, and how the country was composed of towns like that. There were no cameras present and only two reporters. Mulroney was sitting on the edge of a table talking to a small group of delegates and alternates. He was stiff and nervous at first, but gradually, as he sensed the audience warming to him, he warmed to his improvised theme.

Mulroney said that the first time he had been to Grande Prairie about twenty years ago, he had run into a man at the airport named François Aquin. And he explained that Aquin, then a young Liberal, later became the first separatist member of the Quebec National Assembly when he left Jean Lesage's caucus to sit off by himself.

"In a strange way," he said, "that's what June 11 is all about. In a very circuitous way, you and I are going to solve François Aquin's problem together. And in fact, we're going to give the François Aquins of this generation a real live federalist option."

"What struck me," McKenzie said later, "was the way he was able to talk about Quebec and separatism in the West, that there was something wrong with the country if a man of François Aquin's talent didn't believe in it. It wasn't like Trudeau, beating up on Quebec."

Mulroney, bone-tired from a day that had begun too many speeches and coffees ago in Edmonton, was nevertheless hitting a certain stride, rather like a marathoner, with his sense of well being as he goes through "the wall" of his own exhaustion.

"Pierre Trudeau all by his lonesome," Mulroney said in another of his practised lines, "has been in power longer than all the Conservative leaders since the end of World War One. Bennett. Mannion. Bracken. Drew. Diefenbaker. Stanfield and Clark. Put them all together, and Trudeau has been there longer than the whole bunch of them."

The Grande Prairie crowd, including delegates from across the British Columbia line in Dawson Creek, were for the most part committed to Clark, Pocklington, and Crosbie for the first ballot. But like the delegates from Williams Lake, B.C., where Mulroney had spent a Saturday night in the month of April, they were struck that Mulroney was not the plastic man they had read about.

From Grande Prairie, Brian and Mila Mulroney hopped back into Kip Scott's Piper and were jounced and bounced all the way down to Medicine Hat, where the tour was booked into a $30-a-night Travel Lodge. It was close to midnight when Mulroney got in at the end of another eighteen-hour day. He hadn't eaten, and the restaurant was closing up. Mulroney was starving, and when he is in this state, food takes priority even over newspapers and the national news. He always seems to be hungry but never eats very much or very well. A junk-food addict, he would take to eating chocolate bars for quick fixes of energy. So in Medicine Hat they ordered up a king-sized pizza, spread it out over his bed, and Mila Mulroney divvied the thing up.

The next morning, Mulroney was up for a 7:30 breakfast meeting with area delegates who had come out for scrambled eggs and sausages. Then it was on to Lethbridge for two hours of downtime at the Lethbridge Inn, a stunningly beautiful hotel with a tree-lined courtyard and swimming pool. The hotel's design was spectacularly simple. The rooms were turned inside out, so that instead of looking out on the highway and shopping centre, they gave on a created oasis-like environment. Even Mulroney's Alberta organizer, Doug Lomow, was enchanted by the setting. After three days of making a difficult tour run on time, and with an important stop still ahead in Calgary, Lomow abandoned his candidate and jumped into the swimming pool. In a corner room on the ground floor, Mulroney took a phone call from Peter Pocklington, who wondered if he could drop up to Edmonton. Pocklington had just received his latest polling results and it was becoming increasingly clear to him, as he told Mulroney, that "you're the only guy who can stop Clark."

An hour later, in his second shirt at his second event of the day, Mulroney was on again with his song-and-dance routine about the 102 seats in French Canada. "You give Pierre Trudeau a gift of 100 seats and he's going to beat you ten times out of ten," he said. "What I'm saying is for every seat I win in Quebec, and I'm going to win a chunk, Pierre Trudeau is going to have to win two in Alberta." And he threw in his western wrinkle, about how the remedy for western alienation began with winning seats in the East on election night, so that the lights weren't turned out at the Lakehead. "I'm getting to the point," Mulroney said, "where when I throw out the line, I wonder how long before it clicks." He was clicking with the Lethbridge Foothills delegates and alternates, clicking on all cylinders. What would he do about such-and-such, somebody asked from the back of the room, "if you become prime minister."

"Now don't be a pessimist," Mulroney shot back with another of his familiar replies. The delegates wanted to get a look at him and get some idea of what he stood for. On important western issues, such as oil-pricing, he would always say that he hoped he had a reasonable grasp "for an easterner." But by then he had surprised them with another one of his wrinkles for western audiences. "I first came to Lethbridge," he would say, "in 1962 as the private secretary to the Minister of Agriculture." And this told audiences that he knew the West and had paid his dues in the Conservative Party. It was a very good way of addressing regional sensitivities, which in Alberta are as striking as the Rockies rising suddenly out of the road to Banff.

Mulroney found that regional issues and sensibilities had varied across the country: delegates were concerned about the economy in Ontario, the NEP and the Crow in the West, Pacific Rim issues and the nuclear question in Vancouver, the importance of the central government in Atlantic Canada, and with Quebec journalists there was always the infernal constitutional question. But everywhere, Mulroney said, he found one common denominator, "jobs, jobs, jobs," and everywhere he went, he pounded the podium with it. For the rest, he said, "the delegates set the agenda. It's the living-room syndrome, they want you right there in their living rooms. You give an overview, and then they set the agenda."

"This time," as University of Calgary communications professor Tom McPhail observed, "he was taking the long way around. It was what we call small-group communications or inter-group communications. The mass media were the third priority, not the first."

The boony strategy always struck some people as a bit bizarre, given Mulroney's flair for television. "This is the craziest goddamn campaign you've ever seen," observed Steve Phizicky, a producer with CBC's *The Journal*. "Here's a guy made for television and nobody can find him, and Crosbie, who's a born comedian, walking around with a pickle up his ass. It's as if nobody wants to make use of his talents."

Mulroney had remembered reading about a survey as to why Tory delegates had voted the way they had in 1976, and it was because of their personal impressions of the candidates. McPhail had sent him a copy of a study he had written with his former Carleton University colleague Alan Frizzell, ironically enough the man who had supervised the fieldwork for the Southam News poll Mulroney had been lustily denouncing all week. "It wasn't," Mulroney said later, "worth the powder to blow it all to hell."

He acknowledged, though, that it didn't make his life any easier that week. "There was the Southam poll as we started out and then there was the hoopla about the *Maclean's* cover on Crosbie. And we were in difficult territory."

As the Piper Cheyenne made one final hop to Calgary on that Thursday afternoon, Mulroney was in a buoyant mood, telling stories about Robert Cliche's days as Quebec leader of the NDP, and how Cliche used to tell the story on himself of how Pierre Trudeau, then in the NDP, had encouraged him to try it, saying he was behind him all the way. "He was behind him all the way, all right," said Mulroney, by this time doubled over with laughter. Then he became serious again as he discussed the business of delegate-hunting. This time, he wasn't measuring the success of his campaign only in newspaper inches. "What counts is what's in this goddamn briefcase," Mulroney said, thumping his leather case beside his seat. "And that's votes."

But as the small plane drew to a stop in Calgary, Mulroney left the boony strategy behind in the plane. "I figured we had gotten just about what we were going to get by concentrating exclusively on the boonies," he said much later. "And the time was just about there to raise the profile."

And so before a meeting with Calgary-area delegates at the Four Seasons, he met with the Calgary news media. They tossed their most difficult questions, unaware that Mulroney had already heard them all out in the boonies. The strategy had served the same purpose as opening a show in New Haven before taking it to Broadway. Down the hall, he worked the roomful of delegates, something for which he needed no practice, and at which the former Mila Pivnicki had become just as adept.

This was a different crowd from the boonies, moneyed and elegant, the same kind of people you ran into at Liberal meetings back East. Some of them probably had been Liberals back East. It was quite clear that no one in the room was voting for Joe Clark. And on the last ballot they would vote for his opponent.

The votes that Mulroney had in his briefcase were the results of the second Gallup Poll of delegates conducted before the Toronto candidates' meeting in the last week of April. It indicated Clark had 35.2 per cent first-ballot support, with Mulroney at 25 per cent and Crosbie back at 8.8 per cent. McMillan's conclusion was that "Brian's campaign has momentum and strength; Joe is faltering."

As a Lear jet climbed quickly and raced the setting sun over the Rockies, Mulroney opened his briefcase on his lap, fumbled with his new spectacles, and started quoting the figures to George Hees, who had met up with his candidate in Calgary and was going out to campaign with him in Victoria and Vancouver. As always, Hees was in an upbeat, expansive mood, giving advice to his candidate. "I never once had a good conversation with Joe Clark," Hees said without rancour. But after all, he had been Transport and Trade Minister in the Diefenbaker government, and might have been of some use to the Clark people. "Joe Clark?" Hees said with amused contempt. "Why, you wanted to send him down to the corner store to buy a pack of Sweet Caps."

But there was one point on McMillan's page of conclusions that Mulroney wasn't leaning forward to show Hees or anyone else. "Clark's second ballot support has not appreciably improved," McMillan had written. "Brian's has decreased, probably due to the Clark-Mulroney hostility and dirty tricks image. Crosbie has been the big winner, especially among senior delegates and youth."

Shoring up the youth vote was the principal purpose of the trip to the coast, where a quick overnight pass through Victoria had been tacked onto a stop in Vancouver. Mulroney bedded down for the night at the old Empress Hotel and had his dancing shoes on at 7:30 the next morning for a meeting with Vancouver Island delegates down in the basement of the hotel. The breakfast fare was standard orange juice, croissants, coffee from a big urn, and questions from the delegates.

As he had even in the Bible Belt of Alberta, Mulroney spoke a few sentences in French, to make the point that he could, and to make the point that he would. There were no questions on bilingualism, as indeed there had been none in Alberta, but the tone was less sceptical and more worldly, and the context was the boundless blue Pacific. It was one of those breathtaking days that make you wonder why supposedly intelligent people like Allan Fotheringham come East.

With half a planeload of MPs in tow on the boat plane, Mulroney flew over to Vancouver and two hours of private meetings with youth delegates at the Holiday Inn on the Vancouver harbour. In a holding room down the hall from Mulroney's suite, MPs Chuck Cook and Walter McLean worked the gentle arts of parliamentary persuasion on the young Vancouverites. In one small knot of youth delegates, Cook quietly pointed out that Mulroney would come in handy in the event of another Quebec referendum. For eighteen-year-old Greg Thomas, bilingualism was simply one of the new facts of Canadian political life. He would go back to Clark before going to Crosbie. In fact, the Mulroney organization had assumed that Thomas, a former national youth president, would be in Clark's camp. But Peter White had called him early and asked if he was "open to blandishments," and Thomas, a very precocious young man who had worked for one of the Sterling papers in B.C. at the age of sixteen, actually knew what the word meant. He was indeed, and so he flew to Montreal in the very early going for dinner with Mulroney at the Ritz.

Thomas had a long list of questions and even wanted to know Mulroney's idea of the meaning of life (the answer was that you do the best with the talents you've been given). When he went away he was onside, and he brought most of the B.C. youth with him. Mulroney led the youth vote with 39 per cent in his second Gallup sample, but in Vancouver some of them were caught up in the Crosbie hype and concerned by his poor showing in the Southam survey.

It was a natural impulse of young people to go with their friends and go with a winner, and that week, Brian Mulroney did not look like a big winner. So the Vancouver-area youth came in for special treatment in Mulroney's room. Hardly anyone noticed the spectacular view across the harbour to North Vancouver. At noon, the Vancouver media were very much invited to and present at a public meeting, with most of the same young people, where Mulroney unveiled the "eleventh commandment" of his campaign, to speak no ill of other Tories.

In five hours on his third trip into B.C., he had nailed down his support that had propelled him into second place in the province behind Clark. His superb B.C. organization, headed by Vicki Huntington, made sure those votes stayed nailed down and got to Ottawa. She rode with him on the way to Vancouver airport, and they agreed that he had come a long way from when he started there in the last week in March with not more than twenty-five B.C. delegates.

In the first-class departure lounge at the airport, Mulroney was recognized by someone from Quebec. "Est-ce que c'est notre prochain premier ministre?" asked a fellow Air Canada passenger to Montreal.

"You better believe it," Mulroney replied. "You can bet the damn mortgage on it."

But as the Boeing 727 turned away from the Pacific and climbed back over the Rockies to Montreal, Mulroney was headed into the greatest danger of his campaign.

Charley McMillan was waiting for him back East with some bad news. While Mulroney was campaigning on the coast, McMillan was in Toronto receiving the results of the "third wave," which drew quite a different delegate profile than the one Mulroney was still carrying in his briefcase. McMillan and Michel Cogger made a decision not to tell their candidate what was in the new sample until the next morning, for Mulroney, as he came home for the Victoria Day weekend, was both elated and exhausted. They were reluctant enough to disturb his mood, more reluctant to disturb his sleep.

Saturday morning, McMillan called from Toronto. "We've got some real things to talk about," he began. The "new swing," as he called it, showed that Clark had slipped a further two points to 33.2 per cent, that Mulroney had slipped a point or so to 24 per cent, but that Crosbie had zoomed up from less than 9 per cent to 21.6 per cent. More to the point, he had overtaken Mulroney among the youth and was now the second choice of 27 per cent of the delegates, twice as many as were committed to Mulroney. Although the *Maclean's* cover was on the newsstands and the Southam poll in the papers during the last part of the May 12-19 polling period, that wasn't enough to explain the Crosbie bubble.

Mulroney didn't believe it because he hadn't seen it. And he didn't want to believe it. "We just had to let it sink in," McMillan said. "And we kept telling ourselves the goddamn thing's in three weeks." As of then, though, the convention appeared to be slipping away from Mulroney, with Crosbie looking like the winner if he could maintain the narrow first-ballot spread.

"Crosbie is gaining," McMillan wrote later in a May 25, eyes-only memo to Mulroney and Cogger, "from the Clark-Mulroney in-fighting and from his media hype. At the moment he would come in second in a three-way fight and beat either Clark or MBM in a two-way fight."

The Victoria Day weekend was supposed to be Mulroney's time of relaxing before the final home sprint through Ontario in the last ten days of the campaign. It was not a very good way for him to begin the weekend, and the poll clearly preyed on his mind.

It wasn't difficult for McMillan to visualize his candidate prowling around the house, chain smoking his way through another two packs of duMauriers, getting on the phone to the boys across the country, and watching the news every night. There was nothing to be done about the coffee and cigarettes. But McMillan wished there was a way to keep him off the phone and away from the television.

The Sunday of Victoria Day weekend is one of the slowest news days of the year. There wasn't even much to be said about the leadership, since most of the candidates were at home with their feet up. Mulroney's problem was that his feet were up in front of *The National* as it came on at its weekend time of 11 o'clock. There wasn't much campaign news to report. In a stand-up piece taped Saturday for the Sunday night news, Mike Duffy suggested that Mulroney was "trying to set up" a Stop-Clark coalition and that "he wants an agreement among the candidates, that they'll unite on the floor of the convention behind the man with the best chance of stopping Clark." Without such an arrangement, Duffy suggested, "Mulroney believes that Clark will probably win the convention." Duffy added that with former Toronto mayor David Crombie faltering, "Mulroney is trying to convince Crombie to pull out and endorse him even before the convention begins. He believes a Crombie endorsement would quickly be followed by support on the floor from Mike Wilson, Peter Pocklington, and John Gamble." Duffy added that Mulroney "knows from the 1976 convention that if you wait until you get on the floor of the convention it will be too late to make deals, and that's why he's spending this long weekend on the telephone, putting together an anti-Clark coalition."

Duffy's only error was in saying Mulroney himself had been "on the phone," leaving the impression that the principals had been talking directly, which, other than the case of Mulroney and Pocklington, was not true. The rest of the story was perfectly reasonable speculation, but Mulroney, unaccountably furious, denounced the piece as "a total fabrication" and threatened on Monday to take "the appropriate legal action" against the CBC and its reporter.

The effect of Mulroney's statement was to keep afloat for the whole week a story that would otherwise have sunk like a stone thirty seconds after the Sunday night broadcast. For days, the press came alive with quick-fix stories of sanctimonious denials from various camps that they had been talking, as well as progress reports on the Mulroney lawsuit. Finally, Michel Cogger put an end to it, explaining that his candidate had more important things to do than sue Mike Duffy. The Duffy story became secondary to the issue of Mulroney's bad judgement, of whether

187

or not his inexperience was showing. In the end, Mulroney was able to shrug it off with a comment that he was prepared to make a modest contribution to the Mike Duffy defence fund.

Months later, however, Mulroney maintained that it wasn't the Gallup results that had upset him but an interview with Duffy on the local television station in Edmonton the previous Wednesday. Mulroney had gone back to the Hotel Macdonald to change for a noontime meeting with Edmonton delegates. On the local midday news, there appeared Mike Duffy, not as a reporter but as an oracle from the East. As well as reporting on Mulroney's meeting with Lougheed, Duffy was prompted by the local broadcaster to go on about how Crosbie was coming on strong. Mulroney, already smarting from the Southam poll and the Crosbie hype in *Maclean's*, smouldered with anger for another five days, and when he saw the Sunday night piece he simply exploded. "All I wanted to do was put him under the spotlight," Mulroney insisted. Duffy didn't come back on the leadership beat for a week or so, and when he did, Mulroney admitted, "he was very fair."

The following weekend, Duffy wasn't even in the country; he was in Williamsburg, Virginia, as scheduled, along with a busload of Ottawa correspondents covering the Economic Summit of Industrialized Nations. In the hospitality room of the Canadian hotel, reporters debated the significance of the Mulroney gaffe far into the night, but by this time, they had a far more significant blunder to look over. On Thursday, May 26, John Crosbie came a cropper with the admission that he couldn't speak French but that that was no bar to his understanding the aspirations of French-speaking Canadians. This had been his line for months, and he had been getting away with it. But then Crosbie carried on with one of those impulsive statements that were his trademark: "I cannot talk to the Chinese people in their own language, either," Crosbie said in a scrum in the lobby of the Holiday Inn in Longueuil, across the river from Montreal. "I can't speak to the German people in their own language." It was quick-fix time again for reporters who had lolled around Prince Edward Island with Crosbie on Tuesday, followed him up to Quebec City on Wednesday, when the language issue began to simmer, and trailed him down to Montreal on Thursday, when it came to a boil.

In a way, it wasn't Crosbie's fault. His campaign directors should never have allowed him to come into Quebec a second time, after it had been apparent on a previous swing that he was awkward and uncomfortable. At a May 2 press conference in

188

Montreal, Crosbie received a going-over from the media that was, if anything, rougher from the English-speaking representatives than the French. What would he do in the event of a referendum? Come in and campaign with an interpreter, he said. Would he negotiate sovereignty-association with René Lévesque? Winston Churchill, he replied, once said that he wasn't elected to preside over the dissolution of the British Empire, though come to think of it, he did. It was a terrible performance and Crosbie, having got out of Quebec alive, should never have come back.

Where he had turned the issue to his advantage, with the argument that 20 million unilingual Canadians had the right to aspire to the top job in the country, the bilingualism question now rebounded on him. "Crosbie says lack of French doesn't make him a criminal," proclaimed the *Globe and Mail* over three columns on the front page of its Friday edition. Now Crosbie had forced the delegates to focus on an issue many of them would rather forget, of his own incapacity to speak French and his propensity to toss off the kind of careless remarks that can cost elections.

Brian Mulroney couldn't believe his luck. In Ottawa later in the day for the launching of his book, a collection of speeches, Mulroney was handed a wire-service account of the Crosbie incident. Then someone played him a tape of Crosbie's exchange with reporters. "Why they ever put him into Quebec again is beyond me," he said later. "I couldn't believe it."

Since Crosbie had addressed his own weakness, Mulroney was able to implement to the letter the strategic recommendations of the memo he had received only the previous day from McMillan. "Our strategy should be to stall Crosbie from further growth and focus on his areas of support – seniors, youth and in Ontario," McMillan wrote. "By convention week, we need a Clark, MBM, Crosbie ordering where we manage the spreads and second ballot support." McMillan's further recommendation was to drop the boony strategy, play down the frugality theme, which wasn't showing as an issue, and build up momentum.

Mulroney had already taken these decisions, and decided to spend most of the last two weeks in media-saturated, delegate-rich Ontario. In Toronto, on May 31, he met the Ontario provincial caucus at Queen's Park, taped an interview with *The Journal* for later broadcast, and flew back to Montreal to appear before the editorial boards of *Le Devoir* and *Dimanche-Matin*. Then he made a final swing through Thunder Bay and Ottawa, where he taped CTV's *Question Period* for the weekend before the convention opened. In terms of the media, he had had the last word.

In terms of Crosbie, he had the last word as well. You had to be a corporal before you could be a general in the army, Crosbie had said in Thunder Bay on June 1, the day before Mulroney came through. "Which army are we talking about?" Mulroney fired back. "I've been a corporal in this army, while John was in another army," the Joey Smallwood regiment of Liberals from Newfoundland. As for Crosbie's assertion that parliamentary experience was necessary, Mulroney alluded to the ill-fated Crosbie budget and "the defeat after thirty-six days in Parliament of the government it took us sixteen years to elect. If that's experience," Mulroney said, "I'll stick to my good old common sense from the North Shore." For good measure, Mulroney advised the delegates to beware of candidates, like Crosbie, who flew around the country in private jets. The candidate they could trust flew Air Canada economy. "Just to show you how frisky I was feeling," Mulroney said later, quite unabashed. "Cheeky" would have been more like it.

Finally, after eighty days on the road, he came home to Montreal for the last time on the night of Friday, June 3. It was for a meeting in a church basement in the East End, and it had been organized as a youth party. But it loomed as an absolute disaster: no podium, no sound, and no crowd.

"Brian almost didn't get out of the car," McMillan said. Here he was, coming home after three months on the road, to close his campaign with a bad event. After they organized enough people to surround him as he entered the hall, he went through with it, spun a few quick cassettes, and got the hell out of there. For once, Mulroney didn't see the news. "It was great," MacAdam informed him of the CBC report that showed the candidate surrounded by young admirers.

They had got away with it. And Mulroney's good luck was only just beginning.

14

OF SPEECHES
AND LEAKS

Charley McMillan had some new, improved numbers to show his candidate. It was the first Saturday of June, the last Saturday before the convention. In his room at the Ritz, McMillan was reading a *Gazette* review of Mulroney's book when he received what amounted to an 8:15 wake-up call from the author. Any time McMillan was ready, he could wander on up to the candidate's house on the hill in Westmount.

If polls are nothing more than snapshots of public opinion at the time they are conducted, Mulroney would want to frame this one. The Gallup associate, Nationwide Market Research, had been in the field from May 30 to June 2, Monday to Thursday of that same week, polling the preferences of a sample of 250 delegates. It was like getting a sixty-second Polaroid instead of having to wait a few days for the Kodak prints to come back from the drugstore.

The poll indicated that Clark was just short of 37 per cent, that Mulroney had grown four points to 28 per cent since the previous Gallup wave in mid-May, and that Crosbie had slipped four points, to 17 per cent. "We walked through the numbers and discussed what it meant for convention week," McMillan said. "And it meant everything was back on track."

The numbers indicated that Clark was stalled, that Mulroney was peaking at exactly the right time, and that Crosbie had peaked the week of the previous Gallup wave, when he had appeared on the cover of *Maclean's* as "The Tory to Watch." Since then, Crosbie had committed his memorable campaign blunder, about not speaking French and not speaking Chinese or German either. The Crosbie gaffe, reported in the *Globe and Mail* on Friday, May 27, effectively stopped the Crosbie bandwagon that had been rolling through the Tory heartland of Ontario. He had unintentionally focused the delegates' attention on the issue of bilingualism, which many of them would have preferred to forget. He was also reminding them of his unpredictability. If they made him their leader, who knows what they might read when they picked up their morning paper.

So now Mulroney had what he needed, room to grow in front of him and room to breathe behind him. The results of this poll would also figure prominently in Mulroney's agenda for convention week.

One of the lessons he had assimilated from the 1976 experience was the importance of a candidate setting his own agenda for the media and, through the media, conveying a positive image of a growing campaign. In 1976, he hadn't even got off the train from Montreal before his convention troubles began. As he rode to Ottawa on the morning of February 18, 1976, a front-page *Montreal Gazette* story told of a $10,000 contribution to his campaign from Power Corporation. All through the campaign, Mulroney had been dogged by the perception that he was the candidate of Paul Desmarais. Then, on the first day of the convention, it followed him right into Ottawa in a story authenticated in print by his own financial chairman, Dave Angus. In Ottawa, he made the mistake of making a second entrance to a hotel for the benefit of a television crew, thus reinforcing his image as a creature of the media. His orders to cancel a $10,000 Ginette Reno concert were ignored. On the whole, it was a bruising experience; but if Mulroney bore the scars, he had at least learned the lessons. This time would be different.

"My expectation," he said, "was that the Clark people would try and dominate the week starting on Tuesday, because they were all Ottawa-based, they had all the MPs, you know, the strength that comes with having been leader and so on, and they were going to try and generate enough momentum that week. So there were a couple of things we were going to do."

First, as previously planned, the policy side of the Mulroney campaign would put out a study McMillan had ordered up from Data Resources of the impact of Mulroney's economic policies on productivity, research and development, and fiscal incentives. "They took my book and my speeches," Mulroney said, "and they did a computer run on it, what it would mean to the economy."

The Data Resources report was given to the press on Tuesday. On Wednesday, the *Globe and Mail* ran a favourable editorial under the headline, "Mulronomics to the rescue." By the time of his appearance in the economic policy session on Thursday, Mulroney's organization had thoughtfully photocopied the *Globe and Mail* piece and placed one on every chair on the convention floor. The delegates wouldn't have read the Data Resources report or been aware of the optimistic assumptions that were fed into the computer model. But at this convention, nobody could say Mulroney had no policies.

Mulroney was already enjoying a sensational week elsewhere in the *Globe and Mail*. Over the previous weekend, he had decided to leak his latest poll results. And there they were on the Tuesday morning of convention week, leaping out from the top of page one.

For Mulroney's chief fund-raisers, Senator Guy Charbonneau of Montreal and Don Matthews of London, Ontario, the splash in the Toronto paper came not a moment too soon. The Mulroney campaign, if not broke, had a short-term cash crisis on its hands. "We need a hundred and ten by Tuesday," one of them said privately on Sunday. That was $110,000. Hearing this, McMillan wondered why he had been asked to stay back after a Sunday meeting of the national campaign committee in Ottawa. He was not long in finding out from the bagmen, who had been joined by convention chairman John Thompson and campaign director Paul Weed. Potential contributors, they explained, didn't understand the boony strategy. As a consequence, the big money was sitting on the sidelines. They needed to make a splash, and fast. "You've got to get us a major news story," one of the group told McMillan.

"Do you want the front page of the *Globe, The National*, or both?" McMillan asked, only half in jest.

"The *Globe* will do fine," someone told him not at all in jest.

It was something for McMillan to think about on the drive back to Montreal with Frank Moores and his former wife, Janis Johnson. Together, Moores and Johnson made quite the odd divorced couple: they remained friends and were able to make common cause for Mulroney, he as the backroom operator and she as the up-front director of his Manitoba campaign who also gave the candidate a window on women's issues. Furthermore, she was Mila Mulroney's only friend from the political side of their life. Moores dropped Johnson and McMillan at Mulroney's home on Belvedere Road near the summit of Westmount and continued on to his own place down the hill on Clarke Avenue. His present wife Beth, who doubled as his assistant in his offshore oil ventures in Montreal, had pulled together the gadget and newsletter side of the Mulroney campaign. It was Beth Moores and a group of Montreal advertising people who had settled on the signature logo for the Mulroney posters, pamphlets, buttons, stickers, shopping bags, and other materials. The

logo was a blow-up from a composite of Mulroney's broad signature, which delegates would have seen in letters from the candidate. In some of the posters and buttons, his surname was
dropped. The idea was to humanize Mulroney, to address the
negative perception that he was slick, superficial, and sleazy.
"The slick thing about it," said Roger Nantel, "was that it wasn't
slick."

"The plastic goddamn image," Frank Moores later admitted,
"was the biggest thing we were fighting."

Mulroney had two problems that night – cash and credibility. He
and McMillan hit on a way of solving both at the same time.
They would leak the Gallup. It would alert reluctant contributors
to the fact that Mulroney was well positioned in second place
with a comfortable lead over Crosbie. And a timely leak would
get Mulroney's convention week off to a big start.

Mulroney decided to call Lawrence Martin of the *Globe and
Mail*. "He told me it was going very well for him," Martin recalled.
"More to the point, he could prove it. He said he would have
Charley give me a call later on."

Martin had been on top of the delegate count since before
Winnipeg. Fresh from his tour as the paper's Washington correspondent, Martin came to the Conservative leadership review and
race of 1983 with no fixed view of how it would unfold. He was
also working outside the perspective of the Ottawa press gallery,
where most political contacts can be made within a four-block
radius of Parliament Hill. In an early piece on the review on
January 4, Martin disclosed that the Clark camp had devised a
seven-point scale for rating the delegates' sentiment for and
against review. The *Globe and Mail* ran the story at the top of
page one under the headline, "Clark steps up his effort to avoid
leadership test."

Beyond the orbit of the press gallery, Martin was soon developing his own network of contacts, especially in Metro Toronto,
where Clark's leadership was being vigorously contested. One of
the people who noticed the new byline on the Tory leadership
watch was Charley McMillan, the York University prof and Mulroney policy adviser. In the months between the Winnipeg and
Ottawa conventions, McMillan would occasionally meet Martin
and discuss the emerging delegate shakedown with him.

"I have something that might be interesting for you," McMillan
told Martin when he reached the *Globe* reporter at home in
Toronto that Sunday evening. They agreed to meet at noon the

next day in room 1451 of the King Edward Hotel. The room was Peter White's, which he kept on a permanent basis for his frequent swings down from London to Toronto, where he operated out of an office in the Commerce Court.

McMillan, travelling with nothing more than a couple of dirty shirts and a waft of computer printouts in his briefcase, grabbed the ten o'clock Rapidair from Montreal and arrived a few minutes before noon. Before meeting Martin, McMillan hurriedly phoned Gallup president Frank Kielty to notify him he was about to leak the poll. Kielty protested that Mulroney's deal with Gallup had been that polling data not be leaked to the press. "Screw the deal," McMillan replied.

From dozens of pages of computer printouts, he was hoping to interest Martin in two aspects of the poll. First, the attitudinal stuff on the most important factor in the delegates' decision: 14.4 per cent chose winnability; 12.8 per cent cited ability to achieve party unity; only 7.2 per cent mentioned policies and an even smaller 6.4 per cent mentioned bilingualism. Integrity came in at 5.2 per cent and charisma and image right at the bottom of the list at less than one per cent. Mulroney scored on winnability. Of all the candidates, he ranked first at 36 per cent as the most likely to defeat Pierre Trudeau, followed by Clark at 33.6 per cent and Crosbie at 18.4 per cent. When the question was asked with John Turner as Liberal leader, Mulroney was still first at 34.4 per cent, closely followed again by Clark at 33.6 per cent and Crosbie back at 18.8 per cent. This meant that, in attitudinal terms, Mulroney was running ahead of his own delegate strength. Many delegates implicitly recognized Crosbie's liabilities of being unilingual and temperamentally unpredictable.

"That's very interesting," said Martin, who made it clear he was much more interested in the boxcar figures, which showed Clark at 36.8 per cent, Mulroney at 28 per cent, and Crosbie back at 17.6 per cent.

"If this is true," Martin said, "it's the story of the campaign."

"I don't know whether I can give you that," McMillan replied. Martin was adamant. Moreover, he would have to confirm the numbers with Gallup and McMillan would have to be identified as the source and quoted in the story. Finally, Martin said he couldn't go with such a big story on his own. McMillan would have to come down to the *Globe and Mail* newsroom and explain the figures to his bosses.

After clearing it with Mulroney in Montreal, McMillan agreed and Peter White accompanied him down to the paper's Front Street office to "make his bona fides." The senior editors had never heard of Professor Charles McMillan, but businessman Peter White had been at Bishop's College School in the Eastern Townships with Norman Webster, then the paper's assistant editor, and ducked into his office to say hello. National editor John Fraser was also present when they met in the office of Cameron Smith, then managing editor.

"They thought it was a big story," White said later, "and they treated it as such."

The *Globe and Mail* editors might also have been interested in the stuff McMillan didn't let them see. These were two sheets, one detailing the ABC factor at 23.6 per cent but also showing the ABM factor close behind at 20.8 per cent. The other sheet showed the results of limited ballots, and one scenario in particular in which a Crosbie-Mulroney run-off revealed the Newfoundlander beating the Baie Comeau Irishman by 44.4 to 35.6 per cent.

But the *Globe and Mail* had itself a big story with the first-ballot scoreboard, for the Gallup numbers showed Mulroney several points closer to Clark, and several points further ahead of Crosbie, than any other survey had turned up. If proven out in the Saturday afternoon shake-out, the leak would indeed prove to be the story of the campaign. After confirming the numbers with a slightly chagrined Frank Kielty over at Gallup, the paper went with Martin's piece as the "line" story on page one.

"Mulroney gaining in latest poll," blared the headline.

By this time, Charley McMillan had rushed home to Forest Hill, thrown some clean clothes into a suitcase, waved good-bye to his wife Kazuyo, and grabbed a supper-hour shuttle to Ottawa. He was going for an exacta payoff by offering the same information to David Halton, the chief political correspondent of the CBC.

Halton was interested but his editors in Toronto weren't buying any candidate's leaked poll, even one carrying the prestige of a Gallup affiliate. Tired and strung out, McMillan went to Frank Moores' suite at the Château Laurier, poured himself a stiff Scotch, and called Mulroney at home in Montreal around quarter to ten.

"I think we blew the thing on *The National,*" McMillan said.

Mulroney told him to forget it. Sam Wakim had just called from Toronto with the bulldog edition of the *Globe and Mail* in hand. The story was on page one.

McMillan's worries weren't over. There was a rumour flying around the capital that CTV also had a poll, and if the numbers were at variance with Gallup's, then the issue would be confused and all his work might prove to be for nothing. It was with some anxiety, after sweating out the CBC's *National* and *Journal* broadcasts from ten to eleven, that the men in Moores' suite switched over to the CTV *National News*. The private network had a poll, all right. They had the Gallup from the first edition of the *Globe and Mail*.

"This," suggested Michel Cogger, "just goes to confirm the superiority of the private sector."

The story created an immediate sensation on Tuesday morning. As the Mulroney camp had hoped, the Clark people predictably dismissed it as being a cooked survey. Other news media scrambled to catch up to the story. Southam News, which had their own poll coming out within forty-eight hours, developed a new angle by calling Gallup president Frank Kielty, who acknowledged that the margin of error might be larger than usual because of the relatively small sample. "Mulroney aide Charles McMillan could not be reached for comment," Southam reported, "although he was quoted in published reports as saying 'it shows Mulroney is in a strong position to win and Crosbie is a distant third.'"

Southam had its own nest to feather and reminded readers that its previous poll by the Carleton School of Journalism was based on "a sample twice that of the one done for Mulroney. And it indicated Crosbie is in an excellent position to close on Mulroney on the second or subsequent ballots, being by far the most popular second choice of the delegates." This was a reference to Southam and Global TV's mid-May survey that had the Clark-Mulroney-Crosbie splits at 35-19-14. The Wednesday story on the Southam wire also set up readers for the next day's poll package.

But Mulroney was now covered where polls were concerned. If he showed well in the Southam survey, so much the better. If he didn't, there would be a stand-off in the polls, and, between Gallup and the Carleton School, the delegates and the media could determine for themselves which had the greater credibility.

As it was, Mulroney showed reasonably well in the Southam survey, which was headline news in Thursday's *Montreal Gazette* and *Ottawa Citizen*. The Carleton sample of 530 delegates had Clark at 37 per cent, Mulroney at 24 per cent, and Crosbie at 16 per cent. When the undecideds and leanings were added to the sample, the adjusted numbers became 39-26-17. But the key finding of the Southam poll, the one that McMillan put into the Mulroney rumour mill on Thursday, was that Crosbie would lose a showdown with Clark by a 49-42 spread. The message to un-

197

decided ABC voters was clear: only Mulroney could stop Clark.

Meanwhile, Mulroney had been back in Montreal since the previous Saturday morning, working on his speech. The problem was to craft a speech he felt comfortable with, summarizing the basic themes of his campaign, without repeating his "102-seats-in-French-Canada" spiel, which all the delegates had heard in their basements.

The other problem, as Charley McMillan discovered, was writing for a candidate who had begun his political life as a speechwriter, and one who was fascinated as a youngster by the rhetoric of Churchill and as a law student by Theodore Sorensen's speeches for John F. Kennedy.

More than a quarter of a century after his first political involvement as a student writing speeches in the 1956 Nova Scotia election, Mulroney was still writing his own stuff on his second time around as a candidate for the leadership in 1983. As his entourage discovered in the second week of June, he could be both demanding and obstinate, and in that sense he could be his own worst enemy. While McMillan tried to work on a vision-of-Canada speech, Mulroney initially insisted on an approach that was so mundane the opening paragraphs contained a laudatory reference to one of his supporters, George Hees, as the dean of the Tory caucus. Listening to the candidate read this draft in his sun room on Sunday night, McMillan and Janis Johnson were frankly appalled. Mila Mulroney wasn't exactly thrilled with it, either, and he had come to rely on her political instincts. "The first draft was so bad," McMillan said, "that he killed it immediately."

The problem was to work up a speech that addressed itself to Mulroney's idea of the country and the Canadian people without getting him too far off the electoralist and economic themes with which he felt at home. He was going to be under a lot of pressure, since he was perceived as having blown his speech in 1976 and because he was in the nominally disadvantageous position of speaking first at the Friday night speeches. On the second point, there was general agreement by Mulroney and his advisers that it could be to his advantage to speak first: he could set a high-road tone at the beginning of what might be a long and hot evening. Both of these presentiments turned out to be bang on. Mulroney knew also that he couldn't blow it this time, and that meant he couldn't take too many rhetorical risks that might fall flat with the crowd. "I was trying to avoid a home-run swing," Mulroney said later. "What I wanted was a stand-up double, a ground-rule double right off the top of the fence."

198

From Sunday until Friday, McMillan and Johnson fought a mostly losing battle with their candidate and with national and convention organizers over what Charley called "El Speecho." The organizers wanted their word about fine-tuning the draft. After midnight on Wednesday, with the candidate himself presumably tucked up for the night, a starving McMillan had just ordered a chicken sandwich and a bottle of Scotch from room service at the Château Laurier when he received a summons from convention manager John Thompson and campaign director Paul Weed. "The Big Blue part of our fucking campaign wants to hear the fucking speech," he said as he stalked off down the hall. The problem, as far as the organizers were concerned, was that McMillan had put too much vision of Canada and not enough electoral facts of life into his revised drafts of Mulroney's own text. "We're still five, six hundred votes short," Cogger explained to a disheartened McMillan later that night. The speech was not a time for the high road. Mulroney would have to explain the dismal facts of electoral life to the delegates one more time.

Cogger need not have worried. His candidate was of the same mind. By Friday afternoon, lounging around his fifth-floor suite at the Château, he had a draft he was satisfied with. And while there may have been some of Charley McMillan in it, it was mostly Brian Mulroney. He read the text for Mila and Janis Johnson and then got dressed to go back down to the convention.

It would be the toughest moment of the convention for Mulroney, coming at the end of a long day in which he had already appeared in two policy sessions, one on foreign policy and one on social policy. The news media had been looking for him to trip up in the foreign policy session in the Coliseum adjacent to the Civic Centre, for it was the area in which he was least expert and could claim neither elective nor appointive experience. But he had got through it without being tripped up on El Salvador or Guatemala, or the Cruise-Pershing emplacements in Europe versus Soviet SS-20 missiles.

In the social policy session back in the Civic Centre voting area, Mulroney had been more than adequate with his statements on the "sacred trust" of health care and old-age security programs, as well as the need to bring women into a more prominent role in the affairs of the party. Whether these declarations bore any delegate fruit, Mulroney had been doing an important bit of fine-tuning. His campaign was soft among women delegates, who were apparently more suspicious of his slickness than they were taken by his charisma. On the policy side, Mulroney had been concerned to correct any impression that may have been abroad that he was simply a big business candidate with no social conscience. Since his campaign was not overrun by Red Tories, he needed to emphasize this point.

But a curious and significant incident had occurred in this workshop, which had nothing to do with policy. When a bunch of Mulroney's supporters stormed into the hall with placards, they were lectured by workshop chairman Marcel Lambert that no posters or demonstrations were permitted in the policy sessions. Mulroney tried to smooth the waters, reminding his followers that Lambert was a former Speaker who was used to more decorum. He then turned to Lambert and apologized for the excess of enthusiasm by his friends. Other candidates had friends, too, Lambert replied somewhat huffily. This inspired a chorus of boos not against the candidate but against the platform chairman, and Mulroney had to wave down the hostility. And he sensed that, unlike 1976, the mood was friendly. "Now," he said later, "we were unquestionably on a roll."

It was much the same in late afternoon and early evening when Mulroney, admittedly "pretty nervous," walked out from the holding area under the centre-ice exit. There was no organized demonstration, no balloons and no band with him, only an organized spontaneous demonstration by hundreds of his supporters who had successfully staked out most of the floor to the centre and left of the podium. With a good-luck pat on his wrist from Mila as he walked her offstage, he went back to the podium. "I was very grateful for the fact that we were speaking first," Mulroney would recall, "because the heat just hit you like a baseball bat as soon as you walked in."

He spoke to his pet economic themes of productivity enhancement and research, saying this was the way to "recapturing that golden wave of opportunity that has been lost for the past fifteen years." And he came back to the need "for an elevated sense of social compassion. Of all the challenges of government, none is more sacred, none binds us more as Conservatives than to care for those who are unable to care for themselves."

Then he got down to the real business of the speech, his electoral themes. "Your response," he said, "will affect this party not for a day, but this country for a generation. With few exceptions," he continued, "we as a party have excelled at winning conventions and losing elections. You've got to ask yourselves why. All of you, everyone in this room is a winner in his private life, in his professional life, in his community life. In provinces, in eight of the ten provinces we've formed governments on a sustained and ongoing basis. You are here today because you are

200

winners and held in esteem by your communities. Why is it that when we put on our hats as federal Conservatives and go into another room, everyone in the country says that we're a bunch of losers. Why is it?"

The hall had fallen silent. The delegates had heard this theme from Mulroney before, and they knew the answer that was coming. It was, he said, "our area of weakness in French Canada, time after time, decade after decade, election after election, depriving the country of prominent Conservatives such as yourselves of serving in government and influencing the course of our history."

It was the heart of Mulroney's speech, and the nerviest part of it, driven home with the sound of a sledgehammer to a spike. "That was the message," he later acknowledged. "The convention was about winning and losing elections. There were two things I had to demonstrate out there, first the winners and losers thing, and second was the leadership pitch, and I could do that in half a dozen different ways, but the key was private-sector experience and an easy degree of bilingualism."

When he got off, Mulroney had cause, in one of his own favourite expressions, to be "well pleased" with his performance. He hadn't lost anything, and he hadn't choked. Maybe it wasn't the Gettysburg Address or Kennedy's New Frontier speech of the 1960 Democratic Convention, but he had said what he wanted to say in the way he wanted to say it. And it was enough. As Tom McPhail of the communications group put it, in reference to a famous address from the 1968 Liberal leadership convention: "If speeches won conventions, Joe Greene would have been Prime Minister of Canada."

When he reached his dressing room under the west exit, Mulroney could relax and enjoy himself. Now it was essentially up to the organizers and delegates to give him the spreads he needed. And up to his connectors to make sure his deals stuck.

15

OF WHEELS
AND DEALS

Winning a convention, Peter White was saying, "is a process of coalition building." In
Brian Mulroney's camp in the spring of
1983, the coalitions were built through a network of connectors.
If you knew someone, or if you knew someone who knew someone, you got in touch and stayed in touch. It wasn't written down
anywhere, there was no perfect salesman's kit, but it was the first
rule of the campaign, and it was in force whether Mulroney's
operatives were dealing with other candidates or simply trying
to woo and win delegates. In the Mulroney camp, there were
three key connectors: Peter White, Michel Cogger, and Frank
Moores. Four, if you counted the candidate himself.

White and Cogger, of course, went back with Mulroney to his
Laval days. Moores had been in the Mulroney camp since before
the 1976 convention, where he placed Mulroney's name in nomination. When Mulroney became president of Iron Ore, the largest
employer in Newfoundland, they became even closer. Whenever
Mulroney was in St. John's, he would stop into the Premier's
official residence, a mansion built for the chancellor of Memorial
University that Moores decided would make an ideal residence
for the Premier. Here, when Moores was getting out of politics in
the winter of 1979, he spent four days closeted with Mulroney
and Dalton Camp figuring out an elegant way to do it.

When Moores set up his consulting shop, Torngat Investment,
his office just happened to be a block away from Mulroney's on
Sherbrooke Street in Montreal, next door to the Ritz and across
the street from the Mount Royal Club.

Moores was an ideal connector to the other camps because he
knew nearly everyone in the Conservative Party and hardly
anyone disliked him, even when he was being an operator, which
was most of the time. He had been president of the Conservative
Party after Dalton Camp had done his Diefenbaker deed and had

the task of binding up the party's wounds, or trying to, and getting the lines out to the warring factions of Torydom. And as a retired premier, "a retired undefeated premier," as he liked to say, Moores maintained a lifetime honorary membership in Canada's elite club of ten, the Premiers' Conference. He had struck up particularly close relationships with Peter Lougheed and Dick Hatfield. And as a former MP before his premiership, he still had lines into the Conservative caucus.

Most of all, Frank Moores had lines into Newfoundland and the big 165-member delegation that John Crosbie had pieced together in every outport and community college of the island. Crosbie had been in Moores' cabinet before going off to Ottawa in a 1976 by-election. Moores later maintained that he never concealed his true allegiance from his fellow Newfoundlander. "Crosbie knew I was a conduit between the two camps," Moores said many months later. During the leadership campaign, Moores had made a point of persuading Mulroney "not to go to Newfoundland." Eventually, Moores knew, Crosbie and most of his delegates would be coming their way anyway. "If it didn't get to the stage where they had to come to us," he said, "then we weren't in it anyway."

The other key connector was Peter White, who, as he put it, "had appropriated several roles to myself." First, he put together Mulroney's youth network, which, in Cogger's view, "saved our ass." Then, as White explained, he "shepherded" publication of Mulroney's book, *Where I Stand*, a collection and collation of his speeches that was sent to the delegates the last week of May and reviewed in one big eastern paper, the *Montreal Gazette*, only the Saturday before the convention. In an informal way, White acted also as a Mulroney troubleshooter in Toronto and for the organization of the convention.

Most of all, though, White used his business and establishment connections into the rival camps of Peter Pocklington and Michael Wilson. They were two very different candidates and had two strikingly different campaigns. Pocklington was the flamboyant and flashy outsider; Wilson was the quintessential establishment man, decent and deferential. If he was a bit on the dull side, nobody doubted Mike Wilson's sincerity. Decency of character was one of his biggest assets, never properly exploited by his organization because it got going too late to go anywhere: Michael Wilson, up from Bay Street, was the candidate of the business and political establishment that spelled its name as Ontario, and Ontario had been waiting for Bill Davis.

Peter White understood both styles and was equally comfor-

table with Amway salesmen pyramiding Pocklington memberships and the blue suits of the London Club complaining about
these parvenus in windbreakers muscling in on their action.
Peter White felt at home in both worlds because he had inhabited
both worlds. He had been adventurous enough as a student to go
off and study in French at Laval. And yet, after coming of age in
Quebec's Quiet Revolution, he found his way back into the comfortable embrace of the business establishment. So, at home in
London, he got to know Bill Campbell, Pocklington's man from
Amway, and Bob Howard of the London East PC association, who
was active in the Pocklington campaign and would eventually
help edge the candidate over to Mulroney.

On a couple of occasions, White even went out to Edmonton
to see Pocklington in his office. As always, the conversation
would get around to delegate counts. "I would try to introduce a
note of realism," White would recall. "He would ask, 'How do you
think I'm going to do?' And thinking he might get 200, I would
say 300, and he would get very upset, thinking he had no less
than 600. I later found out he didn't like talking to me."

White's candidate never made that mistake. "One of the biggest
surprises of this convention, Peter," Mulroney told Pocklington
on the phone from Lethbridge in mid-May, "is how well you're
going to do on the first ballot." To Pocklington, making contact
with Mulroney from Edmonton, it must have sounded like music
to his ears. Here was a man looking for respect and getting it,
from one of the leading contenders. He would get it after June 11,
as well. When Mulroney appeared in the Commons visitors'
gallery two days later, Pocklington was seated beside him. And
Mulroney, when he stood to take a bow, had a hand on Pocklington's shoulder. After that, they struck up a friendship. In December of 1983, after a hectic week of formal entertaining at the
newly renovated Opposition Leader's house, the Mulroneys invited about sixty of their close friends to Stornoway for dinner a
week before Christmas. There were two noteworthy aspects in
the presence of Peter and Eva Pocklington: first, that they were
included with the Mulroneys' personal friends, most of whom
had come down from Montreal and Toronto; and second, that it
was a Saturday night, *Hockey Night in Canada*, and Pocklington
was not at the Northlands Coliseum to see his Oilers play.

The deal with Pocklington was closed between the two candidates themselves. Where White played a more important role
was with the Wilson camp. White fit in here, too. From his Argus
Corporation connection, he had impeccable entrée into the Bay
Street-Albany Club world of the Toronto branch of the Conserva-

tive Party. By convention week, as he later said himself, he "had got to know Mike Wilson very well."

This was a bit like saying that Kim Philby got to know the workings of the British Secret Service before he went over the wall. Peter White, classmate and adviser to Brian Mulroney, was no stranger to the Wilson camp. Though not working directly in it, he had come to know the players, from the candidate and his press attaché Sandy Millar on down the line. White's dealings with the Wilson camp, he said later, were "always on the understanding that I was supporting Brian."

White had lines out to Wilson early in the game, even before there was a game. In April of 1982, Wilson was White's guest at the Canadian Press annual dinner in Toronto. White was there as a director of CP and because of his proprietary interest in Sterling Newspapers, the little organization he and Conrad Black had started out with the *Sherbrooke Record* back in 1969. Frank Moores was there because of his interest in Brian Mulroney. White sat him down beside Wilson and the two of them got on famously. Other Wilson and Mulroney sympathizers were spread around Peter White's two tables. The intention, as White frankly acknowledged, was to create an affinity between the two putative campaigns. "There was a relationship there," he said after Ottawa, "that we built up over the previous two years." When Mulroney spoke to a Toronto service club, Wilson was at the head table. When Wilson later appeared before a Montreal luncheon club, Mulroney repaid the favour.

The next time Frank Moores and Wilson sat down together at a dinner table was in Montreal over a year later, just a month before the convention. Moores' agenda pinpoints the time as the evening of May 9 and the place as the Beaver Club of the Queen Elizabeth Hotel. Wilson, between events in Montreal, came in after Frank and Beth Moores had finished their meal and spent about half an hour with them. By the time Wilson got up from the table, they had what Moores considered to be a deal. "We shook hands on it," Moores said later. "As far as I was concerned, that was it."

As far as Wilson was concerned, that wasn't it at all. "I just dropped by for a drink," he maintained. "It was mainly chit-chat. Frank did his level best to make me feel good, you know, that it was too bad he had prior commitments to Brian because I was a great candidate and so on. He laid it on pretty thick. But no, there wasn't any understanding that I would go to Brian. He may have been reading between the lines of some of the things said."

Many months later, Wilson insisted he had made up his mind

to go to Mulroney only on the morning of the vote, during a meeting of his high command at the Château Laurier. "We went around the table once and there was no consensus as between Brian and Crosbie," Wilson said. Regarding his own intentions, "I deliberately tried to keep them guessing," meaning his own people as well as those counting on his favour.

Moores and Michel Cogger thought they had another deal, too, with David Crombie lieutenants Chris Speyer and Tom Watson. Early on the Thursday evening of convention week, Moores and Cogger went to see Speyer and Watson in Speyer's room of the Château Laurier. "We had an absolute total commitment," Moores later insisted. "We shook hands on it. It was all done."

"There was only one person who could make the deal, and that was David," Speyer said. "There was a group of us that he consulted, but in the end it was his decision to make."

Anyway, Speyer said, the main purpose of the meeting with Cogger and Moores was to tie up the loose ends of Mulroney's prospective visit to Crombie's tent. For his part, Speyer maintained the idea for the visit came from Peter Simpson of the Mulroney camp. Midway through the meeting, Watson went out to clear it with Crombie on the phone and it was fine with the candidate. "As a matter of fact," Speyer said, "there was to be a meeting, a private meeting later that night between David and Brian."

Moores and Speyer had previous dealings in the run-up to the Winnipeg review, when the Cambridge MP was Crombie's representative on the alliance of convenience known as the pro-review forces. Cogger, in Ottawa as Mulroney's chief counsel and spokesman throughout the spring, had frequent dealings and many drinks with Speyer.

Cogger always took special care not to offend the delicate sensibilities of the Crombie camp. "If our people's loyalty to Brian could be measured up to here," said Cogger, drawing a line at his chin, "the Crombie people were up to here," as he drew another one over his head. Cogger, like Sam Wakim in Toronto, always went out of his way to heap praise on the Crombie campaign, and would never pass on the polling data unless Speyer asked for it. So they shook on it, Moores and Cogger from the Mulroney clan, Speyer and Watson from the Crombie camp. That was early Thursday evening, before later on Thursday evening.

What happened then was the incident in Crombie's tent, down from Confederation Square. Mulroney, accompanied by a horde of cameras and a claque of supporters, arrived after a patio party at the Holiday Inn and a quick ten-minute visit to Peter Pocklington's reception at the Château.

The very public meeting with Crombie had supposedly been laid on. "I mean, what the hell," Cogger maintained later, "they invited us over. They even asked for a copy of our song, so we sent them a cassette." Mulroney himself "didn't like the smell of it from the beginning," and his reservations were more than confirmed by the look of embarrassment and hurt on Shirley Crombie's face as the crowd of delegates and media encircled the Crombies and the Mulroneys. "She was not happy, to understate the case," Mulroney recalled, "and I felt that (a) we shouldn't have gone there, and (b) we had better leave immediately."

Mulroney had been informed the previous day, on his arrival in Ottawa, that "it was all set up and we were expected to drop by." But he wasn't crazy about the idea. "I could see that David's campaign wasn't going very well, and that we were on a roll," Mulroney said, "and I didn't want to give the impression of intruding."

At the same time, Mulroney had an invitation to stop by Pocklington's reception on Thursday night, and "it was put to me that we should first stop by and see Peter and then go across to David's tent. And then I was told, in both cases, that this idea met with the approval of the candidate and, indeed, they looked forward to it." Mulroney later maintained he had "made up my mind not to go to the Crombie tent."

But then on Thursday afternoon, after a party with the Alberta delegation in Rockcliffe, Mulroney was strenuously urged to go through with the visit to Crombie. The man lobbying him to do so was his convention manager, John Thompson of Toronto, not to be confused with John Thomson, the Alberta MP whose residence they were pulling away from in a rented executive bus. "He told me it was all set," Mulroney recalled. "This was a signal and that it had all been worked out, and that it would be very badly perceived if I didn't go, that Crombie was fully aware of it and looking forward to it. So were Shirley Crombie and Chris Speyer. Faced with that, I said 'All right.'"

Mulroney still didn't like it. Neither did Pat MacAdam, who was liaison with caucus. MacAdam was all too aware of David and Shirley Crombie's easily bruised feelings. The former Mila Pivnicki did not like it either. "Mila and I tried to head it off," MacAdam said later. "We implored Brian not to do it, to go instead to a women's barbecue at Lakeside Gardens. But the train had left the station. We thought it was going to be a low-key event."

As it turned out, with a surging crowd shouting "Brian and

David," with the media crowding around and jostling Shirley Crombie, the reaction of MacAdam was representative. "We were," he said, "just aghast."

The still photographs of the event told the story, with an anguished-looking Crombie trying to squirm out of Mulroney's rather clumsy embrace. Back in his suite, Mulroney called Cogger, Wakim, Charley McMillan, and Roger Nantel into his bedroom and explained in rather vivid terms that there had been a screw-up. Mulroney also called Chris Speyer on the phone back over in Crombie's tent to make an apology *cum* protest for the mixup.

"I only went over there," Mulroney recalled telling Speyer, "because I was told there was a genuine invitation that had all been arranged. I wasn't trying to crash anybody's party, or put either David or Shirley in an uncomfortable situation. I feel embarrassed by this." Speyer, said Mulroney, "assured me there was no problem, but indeed there was."

"I told him that David was pretty upset, that we were all pretty upset," Speyer said. The Crombie people, he explained, "had been expecting Brian and Mila and maybe their official representative, not the mob that turned up."

Later that night, Mulroney "sat down and wrote a handwritten letter to both Crombies in which I conveyed my regrets for any inconvenience the incident had caused, and that was that."

In any event, it was quite clear that Crombie was not going to "pull a Mitchell Sharp," as the convention idiom had it, withdrawing before the vote and throwing his support to Mulroney, as Sharp had done for Pierre Trudeau at the outset of the 1968 Liberal leadership convention. "Oh, I think David wants to stay in," Mulroney told one reporter who knocked on the door of his suite late that evening.

Had the mood of the convention been different, had the Crombie incident occurred on the first day instead of at the end of the second, there might have been more negative fallout. As it was, the foul-up occurred around nine o'clock on Thursday, by which time it was too late for the national newscasts and the morning papers. Besides, most reporters had done the usual thing – they had gone off to dinner. Incredibly, Mulroney's media luck was holding. In the next morning's *Globe and Mail*, the headline on Lawrence Martin's lead story on page one indicated that delegates were "taking a second look at Mulroney." The lead backed up the headline:

With John Crosbie's campaign showing signs of stalling,

anti-Clark Tories were taking a hard look yesterday at Brian Mulroney as possibly the only candidate in a crowded field who can stop Joe Clark from regaining the leadership of the party.

Although his supporters expressed optimism, the momentum of Mr. Crosbie's campaign seemed to have been slowed by delegate polls released in the previous two days.

A Clark strategist reported that the former leader had expected to face Mr. Crosbie on the final ballot, but now expected it would be Mr. Mulroney.

Delegate tracking by the Clark team since Mr. Crosbie ran into trouble on a visit to Quebec two weeks ago indicated Mr. Crosbie's support had dropped four or five percentage points, the strategist said.

Martin, who was already regarded as an enemy of the people in the Clark camp, was no great favourite on Friday of the Crosbie campaign, which was betting all the chips on second-ballot strength. As for the Crombie incident, it went unreported, since Martin's piece had been written to deadline as a stand-up story well before the events of Thursday evening. The only reference at all to Crombie was buried deep in Martin's 900-word piece. "Mulroney strategist Sam Wakim," it read in the second to last paragraph, "was saying that his candidate's chances were good with Mr. Crombie."

It was left to Crombie's own convention tabloid to break the story. "Let's not make a deal," read the bold headline. Crombie himself, appearing in the foreign policy workshop before Mulroney, cracked that any candidate was welcome to come to his tent for a beer. Finally, the *Ottawa Citizen* turned up with the story as front-page news. But by then, reporters had stopped scrounging for screw-ups, colour, or different angles. Friday night would be speech night; Saturday morning would bring the vote. The misunderstanding in Crombie's tent was consigned to an item in Saturday's convention notebooks. The damage to Mulroney, of fostering the impression that he was a sleazy opportunist, was minimized.

Still, if there ever had been an understanding with Crombie, it was far from certain at this point whether it was still on. A few minutes before three o'clock on Saturday, Cogger could see for himself that it was definitely not on. Standing in front of Crombie's box, he raised himself up to his full height of 5'4" to get a splendid view of the backs of cameramen and reporters in front of him. Cogger then borrowed a cameraman's stool from Toronto television journalist Fraser Kelly and could finally see for himself that not only was Crombie not coming to them, he was staying in. From Speyer and Tom Watson, as well as from Ontario Attorney General Roy McMurtry, another Mulroney connector with Crombie, there were only shrugs and averted glances. "I think it was not to happen," Cogger later said a bit wistfully. "And if not, the thing on Thursday was a very convenient place to hang it."

John Laschinger stepped out on the back veranda of a modern townhouse in the New Edinburgh section of Ottawa. Inside, a Thursday night cocktail party was in progress in Allan Fotheringham's living room. The columnist and gadfly had suggested jokingly that he was bringing everyone together to make peace, deals, and history. There was none of the above, but there were Finlay MacDonald from the Clark clan, Janis Johnson from the Mulroney organization, and Laschinger from the Crosbie campaign.

Laschinger's mind was not on socializing and small talk. On the balcony, he turned to press aide Diana Crosbie, no relation to their candidate, and muttered something about jumping off, as well he might have, though he would have done nothing more than twist an ankle or aggravate an old football injury from his days with the McGill Redmen. At the end of the second day of the convention, the Crosbie campaign was perceived as having run out of steam. If so, it certainly wasn't for lack of trying on Laschinger's part.

Thanks largely to his battle plan, Crosbie had moved up from a distant third to the point where, if the convention had been held in mid-May, he would have been the probable winner of a showdown with either of the front-runners, according to Mulroney's previous poll from Gallup. As Crosbie's campaign director, Laschinger had a highly sophisticated computer delegate-tracking system in place, and he invited the world in to see it. Crosbie's media operation was superb. Anybody who called Laschinger usually got a call back within an hour. "Lasch" was regarded as practically one of the boys by the press corps, who remembered him from the 1974 Stanfield campaign, when he had been on the bus, and from his subsequent tour as national director of the party before he disappeared into the Ontario civil service, which he had left to run the Crosbie campaign. Though Laschinger had been quoted in May as saying Mulroney was dead in the water and "this guy's going nowhere," the sort of remark Mulroney was not likely to forget, Laschinger later moved into Mulroney's 1984 election campaign as operations manager.

For those who had been through the previous leadership convention, there were striking similarities between the Mulroney campaign of 1976 and the Crosbie campaign of 1983. Both began from narrow provincial bases, Mulroney with the Westmount and business establishment wings of the party in 1976, and Crosbie with Newfoundland in 1983. No matter how many important friends Mulroney had in 1976, no matter how many Newfoundlanders tried to spread the message in 1983, it just wasn't enough. As with candidate Mulroney in 1976, candidate Crosbie had to build and rely on a media strategy in 1983 to make himself known, to create a favourable impression, to generate momentum. As with Mulroney in 1976, Crosbie spent lavishly and foolishly in 1983, running up bills far in excess of budget. On the Monday night of convention week, Crosbie threw a $30,000 fish fry for early-arriving delegates and media. There were no votes in such an extravaganza, and if Mulroney had thrown that kind of party, he would have been crucified in the media as a born-again big spender.

In spite of his best efforts to live down his big-spender image of 1976, Mulroney's victory did not come cheap. While he talked about "my rusty station wagon," one of his friends used to kid him that it cost a lot of money to get all that rust on brand new cars. And Mulroney's Ottawa operation, like Crosbie's and Clark's, was big and expensive. The difference was that the press wasn't invited in to see it. There was a storefront, all right, and a kiosk on the Mall, but the real nerve centre of the operation was spread out over three floors of an office building on Laurier Avenue, across the street from the Roxborough Hotel where Cogger and the other Mulroney Mafia had been staying throughout the spring.

From the candidate on down, they took no chances. Mulroney actually overdid the frugality bit, arriving unannounced at his hotel at midday on Wedneday in a rented Chevette, with his Quebec advance man Peter Ohrt at the wheel and Mila tossed in the back seat. The arrival scene was quite a contrast from Mulroney's sweeping into town by train in 1976, when a huge crowd of supporters was rounded up to meet him at the station. This time it was Mulroney who went out to the airport to greet arriving delegates on Wednesday afternoon. He was casually dressed, in an open-neck shirt and blazer, as he would be for most delegate-oriented events of the week. They were trying to break down the plastic image, though not to the extent of jogging, as recommended by convention manager John Thompson in a memo later

211

published by Patrick Martin and his co-authors in their convention book, *Contenders*. It was there that Mulroney saw it for the first time, though it had been intended for him. "I never saw the thing in my life," he maintained. That, plus the Crombie fiasco, was enough to put Thompson in Mulroney's bad graces.

But Thompson was credited with the idea of the Mulroney lapel shamrock, which reminded English-speaking delegates of his Irish rather than his Quebec origins. The shamrock also contributed to a team feeling in the Mulroney camp, and they quickly became the hottest item at the convention. "One youth delegate told me he would break his arm for one," Peter White said. Thompson also commissioned the Mulroney song, "Win Together," which emphasized the two themes of winnability and party unity. Mulroney did hear this in advance, playing a cassette in his kitchen one May morning for Frank and Beth Moores. Before long, they were all humming it. At $3,000, it was a bargain. The rest of Beth Moores' convention gadgets came to nearly $40,000, including $5,700 for fans, which came in handy, and $19,500 for 8,000 golf visors, which later proved to be a hot convention souvenir. But they dropped scarves from the list. They were part of the bad memories, the silk-and-satin look of 1976. Besides, they would have cost $10,000.

On the nocturnal side of the convention, the Mulroney campaign had the usual beer-and-pizza youth parties, women's parties, pool parties, caucus parties, Rockcliffe parties, and just plain parties. And there was one special hospitality suite over in the Chaudière Hotel in Hull, where Peter Lougheed and the Alberta delegation were housed. Fernand Roberge, the manager of the Ritz in Montreal and Mulroney hospitality director at the Ottawa convention, made sure the Alberta delegates got a warm Quebec welcome and not someone refusing to speak English to them. "We wined them and dined them," Roberge said. "Sometimes until three and four o'clock in the morning." By seven in the morning, Roberge and his hospitality committee would be meeting to review the gains of the previous day and to target their Quebec switchover operation for the coming hours.

And on the fourteenth floor, Peter Lougheed was tucked away with his Harvard classmate, Roger Beaulieu, very much a personal friend of both the Premier and the candidate. There was no doubt in anyone's mind that Lougheed was supporting Mulroney. By the Saturday morning Alberta caucus, when Mulroney turned up to speak, Charley McMillan said, "You could almost feel the hostility breaking down, melting."

As Mulroney later said, "The mood was completely different

from 1976." The connectors had done their job. They had kept the lines open and created a good feeling. All through convention week, they had been meeting first thing in the morning, Moores and White and Cogger, McMillan and Rodrigue Pageau and Elmer MacKay, and campaign director Paul Weed. By Saturday morning, they had no need for a meeting. The cards were being dealt. It remained only to be seen how they turned up.

16

THE BOYS

In the front row of Mulroney's box, Michel Cogger was part of the joyous celebration before the announcement of the fourth-ballot showdown, and yet somehow he stood apart from it. "I realized that this was a beginning," Cogger was to say some months later, "but I was struck by the fact it was an end. Nobody in his right mind thought of Brian as his personal property. But I thought a bunch of us, who were his best friends, were delivering him to the world and saying, here, and so that we were losing him. I felt that we were turning a page, that something was ending."

Cogger had been through all the battles, had been a party to all the intrigues, and hatched a good number of them himself, going back to the Congrès des Affaires Canadiennes at Laval. Through it all there were two aspects about Cogger that never changed. One was the hard edge of a born political operator, and the other was an irrepressible sense of humour that got him through a lot of close scrapes.

In many respects, the 1983 leadership campaign had been difficult for Cogger, since he was inextricably linked with the excesses and failures of the 1976 effort. At one point, when Mulroney told him he wanted to bring in new blood, Cogger was unable to resist asking what was wrong with the old blood. Where he had been campaign director seven years earlier, Cogger had to content himself with being Mulroney's "chief counsel" and authorized spokesman out of the Ottawa campaign office, to which he commuted every week from his home in the Eastern Townships of Quebec, a pattern he would continue after Mulroney became leader.

Without organizational burdens, Cogger was free to roam about Ottawa and Montreal as a troubleshooter. As events had demonstrated, his talents were not in the administrative area, and he had no proofs to furnish as to his closeness to the boss. "He doesn't need a title," Mulroney would say later. "He can sit anywhere he wants."

As it developed, Cogger had been involved on the messy side of the leadership review process. Since he had to work at it practically full time for months, and since he also had to eat, he had drawn money out of his business partnership with Walter Wolf, a wealthy Swiss resident and naturalized Canadian who ran in the fast lane of the Grand Prix racing set. Cogger had negotiated on behalf of Labatt's Breweries to bring the Grand Prix of Canada to Montreal's Man and His World site on Ile Notre Dame in 1978, and he had struck up a friendship with Wolf, who had a racing team. Wolf, who apparently liked to dabble in politics as well as racing, was no admirer of Joe Clark. So, as Lawrence Martin later discovered for the *Globe and Mail*, he did not discourage Cogger and Frank Moores, who was a director of Wolf's firm, from working on the leadership review. Even after this embarrassing story broke, Cogger could not stifle his sense of humour. When there was speculation that John Turner would have no problem raising $2 million for the 1984 Liberal leadership campaign, Cogger could not resist asking, "Where's Walter, now that we really need him?"

Cogger had an understanding of Mulroney's moods from instinct, as well as from experience. Like Mulroney, Cogger had a complex personality, being a bit of an operator on the one hand, a hopeless romantic on the other. As with Mulroney, it sometimes seemed that he played the game mostly for the fun of it but could not help becoming attached to the people in it. Like Mulroney, Cogger had spent many years in the back rooms of the party, throughout the wilderness years of Robert Stanfield and Joe Clark. Mulroney was one of those responsible for moving Cogger over from the Liberal Party after law school, and in late 1967 Cogger became associate national director of the party when, in his own words, "there was no one to associate with" in the Ottawa office, since it would be some months before the appointment of Malcolm Wickson as national director for the 1968 campaign.

The whole experience was a comic disaster, typified by the chartered Stanfield plane, an aging DC-6 aptly called *Misajumax*, after his four children. While Pierre Trudeau was seen sliding down the foldaway staircase of his DC-9, the misbegotten *Misajumax* once lumbered into the airport at Rivière-du-Loup, where there was no ramp for the Conservative leader to disembark. The Tories had a prestigious candidate in the area in former Laval professor Julien Chouinard, who would later go to the Supreme

Court. But it was not enough to have principles, as Wilfrid Laurier once observed; it was also essential to have organization, and on the ground in Quebec, even with the Union Nationale of Daniel Johnson in power, the Conservatives had practically nothing. When the Stanfield entourage arrived at a big arena in the riding of Matane, there were no more than 100 people waiting for them. Cogger should have known – the Quebec Tories had also hired a school bus with a flat tire. In the 1972 and 1974 campaigns, he went out on the Stanfield tour as associate press secretary, primarily to handle the French inquiries that were lost on Rod McQueen. Though Stanfield lost twice more, Cogger met his second wife, Erica, who was travelling with Mary Stanfield, in the 1972 campaign. When they were married, in the courthouse at Cowansville in the Eastern Townships in 1974, Mulroney was his witness.

After the 1976 leadership, Cogger moved onside as an adviser to Clark and was one of those present in the transition period in 1979. Afterwards, as Cogger admitted, he enjoyed being an adviser to the Prime Minister, and even if it was a limited, part-time role, it was not one he was inclined to give up without a fight after the fall of Clark's government in December of that year. Cogger was even prepared to lean pretty hard on Mulroney to run as a candidate in the February, 1980, election. But after Clark's defeat at the polls, Cogger became a quiet advocate of review in January of 1981. Or, as he put it in an inelegant but succinct turn of phrase: "What the fuck, let's get it over with."

When it came to the 1983 review, Cogger and Rodrigue Pageau had been the key operatives in Quebec. And in the 1983 leadership campaign, nobody was fooled by Cogger's modest title as Mulroney's counsel. When Charley McMillan would write up his periodic analyses of the campaign's private polling data, there were generally two eyes-only copies, one to the candidate and one to Cogger. When the bad poll of the Victoria Day weekend came down, it was Cogger who went up to Mulroney's house to take him through it and try to keep him on an even keel.

While Cogger looked down at the surging crowd from the railing of the Mulroney box, Jean Bazin stood just behind Mulroney. If you didn't know it was him, you would have wondered what Dan Rather was doing there. By now, Bazin had been accustomed to being mistaken for the American newscaster, especially whenever he went to the United States on business. At Washington's National Airport in the fall of 1983, one man came up to him with his son, asked him how he was, and told his boy to say hello. Bazin said fine, and hello. In the spring campaign of 1983, Bazin had been almost invisible in the day-to-day business. Yet he remained then what he had always been for Mulroney, a moral voice in the affairs of his candidate. As long as Bazin was around somewhere, down the hall as he had been all week, then somebody was there to tell Mulroney to do the right thing.

At Laval, Bazin had been a year ahead of the Mulroney gang, and his involvement in campus politics took him further afield. In the national Conservative student federation, Bazin became vice-president in 1961-62 and a young Albertan named Joe Clark became president. "We flipped a coin," Bazin recalled, "and I lost." After graduation, he served a year as president of the Canadian Union of Students.

Unlike Cogger, who had teamed up with Lucien Bouchard on the socialist side of student affairs, Bazin had always been a Tory, coming from an old Quebec family of Conservatives. In campus politics at Laval, Bazin, Mike Meighen, Peter White, and Mulroney had been identified with the Conservatives from the beginning. Journalist Evelyn Dumas, later an adviser to René Lévesque, knew them in those days and once observed that they seemed determined even then to take over the Conservative Party, such as it was in Quebec.

In those days of campus politics, as Bazin said, "we took on the left." And the people on the left included Cogger, then editor of the student newspaper, *Le Carabin*, and Lucien Bouchard, then an NDP activist who would one day become chief negotiator for the Lévesque government with the public service unions. Whether of the left or the right, they would become the Laval part of the Mulroney Mafia. Bouchard was at home in Chicoutimi on this June evening, watching the party scene unfold on television. Of all the people close to Mulroney, Bouchard knew him best in a spiritual and cultural sense.

Meighen was roaming back and forth between the party on the floor and the broadcast in the CBC television booth, where he had been enjoying a very pleasant afternoon as the expert from the Mulroney camp. Meighen had some experience of Mulroney's thin-skinned nature after the 1976 campaign when, as party president, he had to deny Mulroney a $30,000 PC subsidy for refusing to divulge the sum and sources of his campaign expenses. "I think he's forgiven me for that," Meighen said after the big win in 1983.

Meighen fell into the pattern of Mulroney getting cross with his friends when he considered that they disappointed him. Over

217

some real or imagined hurt, he mightn't speak to someone for weeks or even months at a time, and then as abruptly as he had become sore, he would be on the phone again, offering hockey tickets, getting together fishing trips, calling about lunch, or organizing a dinner in somebody's honour. So when Meighen finally announced his engagement in 1978, it was Mulroney who organized his bachelor supper at the Mount Royal Club in Montreal, bringing together the Laval gang as well as a good many mainstream Tories. In a sense, it was Mulroney's way of acknowledging that he could be a terrible sorehead, as it was also his way of admitting that for all the times he quoted the Kennedys about getting even rather than mad, he was not very good at nursing a grudge. Or as Cogger once put it, late one night after the 1976 defeat: "Brian tries to be vindictive, but underneath it he's a soft touch."

He could also, as Meighen well knew, be a shameless flatterer. Even before his own accession to the leadership, Mulroney mentioned to Meighen on at least one occasion that the next leader of the party would probably come from Ontario. As much as anything else, it was his way of saying he appreciated the efforts Meighen had made as his Ontario chairman. Well before Winnipeg, Meighen had been to see him and indicated that Mulroney would have his support in the event of a leadership convention. And though Meighen would be the last to claim any organizational acumen, he knew all the right people in Toronto and lent an air of legitimacy, if not many votes, in the Ontario Tory establishment.

Peter White could make the same kind of claims, but he was a good deal less visible than Meighen, even now, as the moment of victory neared. He chose to stay down on the floor rather than go up in the Mulroney box. He had no need to be there because, as he said, Mulroney knew perfectly well what White had done for him, and they would have a chance for a word later in the evening when White visited his suite at the Château.

Two members of the Laval group were nowhere to be seen. Sonny Mass was running the switchboard in Mulroney's dressing room, and he hadn't left room 60 for the entire ten hours of the vote. But he could see what was going down on television, and he was happy just to be there, just to be alive. Only three months before, he had been lying in a room in Montreal's Royal Victoria Hospital, undergoing treatments for a cancer relapse. Later, he would always remember that on the first day of Mulroney's campaign, just before he left Montreal for Vancouver, Mulroney had called him at the hospital to cheer him up. As a Quebec City boy,

Mass had something else in common with Mulroney besides the Laval law faculty. They had both come to Montreal in the mid-sixties as strangers, making their own way in its closely connected legal, political, and social circles. On many a Friday afternoon, Mass would receive a telephone call reminding him of a special meeting of the "board" at five o'clock. And in those carefree bachelor days, the Mulroney gang would hang around a noisy Place Ville Marie bar called Le Carrefour, which translates as "the crossroads" but was known around town, not without affection, as "the Swamp." It was known, among other things, for generous drinks and lots of female company.

Bernard Roy knew all about that from his days upstairs in the Place Ville Marie complex, where he and Mulroney practised law together at the Factory. By now, Mulroney had been gone from the firm really since the Cliche Commission, while Roy had stayed on and become the head of its important litigation department.

Destined to become Principal Secretary to the Prime Minister, Roy was known in Montreal legal circles as a pretty tough nut, a reputation he enhanced during the rough-and-tumble delegate wars in Quebec in the spring of 1983 when he had stood in many a schoolroom door as Mulroney's legal agent. Now he was in the voting area underneath the centre-ice exit of the Civic Centre. He was there as Mulroney's chief agent, along with Gary Ouellet from Quebec City. As they counted the last ballot, Ouellet noticed that their candidate won every last one of the ballot boxes. In their brief meeting in the voting area, Roy noticed that Mulroney betrayed only one sign of tension from the long day – his tongue had gone white. But as soon as they let him out of this room, Roy could give the signal as arranged. He would not wear his glasses. Mulroney had won.

Jean Bazin had spent a few moments trying to get another kind of signal straight with Joe Clark, as the man from High River made his unannounced walk down to the Mulroney box. Charley McMillan and Bazin, the two members of the Mulroney camp who knew Clark best, frantically signalled that Mulroney wasn't there. Finally Bazin squeezed his way through the crush and explained that "Brian's not here, he's in the shower. We'll arrange a meeting in the middle."

Bazin had known Clark almost as long as he had Mulroney. It was Bazin who was the first member of the Mulroney camp to go over and make peace with the Clark people on the night of

February 22, 1976. For a time, he served as Clark's chief Quebec organizer, a job for which he had no great talent, and in time he became a key member of Clark's 1979 transition team. When the job was finished, Bazin would often turn up in Ottawa a couple of days a week as a consultant, but nothing more than that. After the 1980 defeat, he dropped from political view to concentrate on practising labour law in the Montreal firm of Byers, Casgrain. He bought a substantial pile of bricks a few blocks away from Mulroney on Sunnyside Avenue, near the summit of Westmount. To all his friends and to all appearances, Bazin seemed fed up with politics.

But after Winnipeg, he was there again in the second Mulroney campaign. He had no title this time and, like Cogger, no need of one. As chief Quebec organizer of the 1976 campaign, Bazin had blamed himself unduly for their poor showing against Wagner. But if he was not the world's greatest organizer, and in this respect he was not alone in the Mulroney inner circle, there were other reasons for having Bazin around. First and foremost, he knew the mesh of Mulroney's mind and personality, knew how to soften the impact of a Mulroney burst of anger as he passed a message down the line. If Mulroney said to tell so-and-so that he was a double-crossing son of a bitch, Bazin might suggest that Brian was a little upset. Bazin had considerable diplomatic qualities, which would stand him in good stead when Mulroney named him national campaign co-chairman with Norm Atkins, principal trustee of Ontario's Big Blue Machine. Bazin had been dealing with the Toronto crowd for twenty years, in law as in politics, and by now he knew better than to get too upset when the Toronto people got up one of their "national" committees.

Bazin was also one of the people who knew Mulroney's personal habits. At one point in the campaign, the only way they could get Mulroney from Chicoutimi over to Ottawa in time for an evening event was to charter a private plane. Mulroney was at first adamant that he would not do so. Bazin mentioned that he might miss the news. Mulroney took the plane.

But the best reason for having Bazin around was for the moral quality of his advice. He could always be counted on to tell Mulroney that something was just plain wrong. In the tough going against Wagner in 1976, Bazin constantly implored Mulroney to stay on "le high road," advice that was not always followed. After the poor reception of Mulroney's 1976 convention speech, a disconsolate Bazin walked down a back staircase of the Civic Centre looking like he was about to be physically sick. It

220

was a very different scene now as he stood behind Mulroney. "Ti-Baz" was one of those who noticed the release of tension in his old friend, as he would notice a new quality of serenity come over him in the days ahead. And Bazin would know why. "He's not grasping for the job anymore," Bazin explained in one of his unguarded moments. "He has it."

A few feet over, Sam Wakim had literally been breaking down barriers to the adjacent Crosbie camp. He was exactly the man to take down the railing between the two boxes, though he wouldn't be anyone's first choice for low-key buttonholing. In the nearly thirty years since Brian Mulroney had sat down at his table at St. F.X., Wakim had become his best friend. They had been through it all together, the joy rides and pranks of their college days, down through the 1976 campaign and the ensuing bitterness. In the Iron Ore years, Wakim would always come in from Toronto for Mulroney's "political" fishing trips. He got himself nominated and elected in the Toronto riding of Don Valley East in 1979, and in the short days of the Thirty-first Parliament he never even got to deliver a maiden address and never had the chance to come back after the 1980 election, when the tide was going the other way and carried him out with it.

Mulroney knew perfectly well that Wakim could be a bull in a china shop, but he delighted in the effect of seeing his big, swarthy friend from the East End of Saint John jump into action. Above all, he prized in Wakim a quality that was not always apparent to the denizens of the Albany Club, and that was his common sense, his grasp of national issues.

So while he was not temperamentally suited to go on Mulroney's staff even had he been so inclined, Wakim could serve in a private capacity as one of Mulroney's friends who could stand back and take a look at things. Quite apart from keeping an eye on developments in Toronto, he was always concerned for Mulroney's larger interests. Hardly a day went by, wherever Mulroney was, that he wouldn't ask for someone to get Wakim on the phone. And when Mulroney was in Toronto, which was often in the pre-campaign period of 1983-84, it was usually understood that Wakim would eventually turn up, with his wife Marty or just by himself, trailing a cloud of foul cigar smoke. For as long as they were together in a room, they would always be Sambo and Bones, the oldest and best of friends.

In the 1976 convention, Wakim had climbed into the Mulroney box only as his candidate was going down after the third ballot. "This could cost me my job," he mentioned to one bystander, and perhaps in a way it did, for he wasn't working much longer with the big Toronto firm of Stikeman, Elliott, Robarts, and it would be years before he would find another corporate perch at the Bay Street firm of Ian Outerbridge.

Fred Doucet, wearing a porkpie hat with a number on it, had spent most of the day in the Mulroney loge. He had been chairman of the Nova Scotia campaign, and afterwards he always maintained that they had done better there on the first ballot than most other people reckoned. Certainly it was no secret that Nova Scotia Premier John Buchanan, while nominally neutral, was quietly supportive of Mulroney. In the candidate's version of it, Buchanan had told him in the very early going that he would support Peter Lougheed, but since everyone knew that wasn't on, he was supporting Mulroney. Buchanan did turn up at a St. F.X. convocation where Lougheed was to receive an honorary degree that had been arranged many months earlier by Mulroney. As a member of the university board who had raised $11 million, Mulroney had found that money talks and that politicians love to dress up in academic robes, deliver statesmanlike homilies, and receive honorary doctorates.

Doucet, as the university's development officer, had waged the three-year campaign at Mulroney's side and had received the appointment at Mulroney's insistence that he needed somebody in the job he could work with. This may have been Mulroney's rationale for naming Doucet chief of staff in the Opposition Leader's Office, a position for which he may have been poorly suited by temperament and experience. Before many months had passed, Doucet had fallen to quarrelling with campaign director Norm Atkins in the party office, and by the winter of 1984, the two senior people on the Mulroney team were scarcely on speaking terms.

He had some problems also with a company called East Coast Energy, in which the ubiquitous Walter Wolf had been an investor. By some accounts, the offshore exploration company had a serious cash-flow problem. By others, it was simply broke. Mulroney himself had invested in the company, placing his shares in a blind trust after June 11. A few weeks before, in his appearance before Lougheed's inquisition, he said he knew from his own experience about the negative impact of the NEP. He may well have been referring to East Coast Energy.

But those difficult days in the Conservative Leader's Office

222

were not something Doucet could have foretold on the night of June 11. For him, his friend's win meant an opportunity for a fresh start in life, a chance to break out of the routine of a small-town campus that may have become too settled even for a man who came from a Cape Breton hamlet with no running water. To Doucet would fall the privilege of riding back to the hotel with the winner.

Pat MacAdam was already there. He had scarcely left room 581 all week. He was handling the phones at that end, along with Ginette Pilotte, Mulroney's personal secretary for nearly ten years. For MacAdam, too, this day meant a new beginning to his life. He described himself as coming from a line of dour Scots in Glace Bay, and sometimes he looked it himself. But he was actually more of a brooding Celt. When he was relegated to a minor role in planning the Ottawa end of the campaign in 1976, he never complained to anyone about taking orders from the Westmount gang in Montreal. After that, he didn't hear from Mulroney for a year and a half until one day, in exasperation, he sat down and wrote him a long letter, as he said later, "pouring out my frustration" for the way things had gone wrong. He didn't even bother to get the street number of Mulroney's new office, simply mailing it to the Iron Ore Company, Sherbrooke Street, Montreal. He soon heard back from Mulroney, and they were friends again.

By this time, MacAdam was teaching government at Algonquin Community College in Ottawa, and he would later dabble in a small business as the operator of the double-decker sightseeing buses that took tourists around the capital. He was also about a year from going on the wagon, which was the first decisive step he took in changing his life. By the early 1980's, he was back on the Hill as an assistant to a couple of Tory MPs. MacAdam had worked in the national office in the mid-1960's, was identified as a Diefenbaker loyalist, and even in Mulroney's office he would have his wall covered with mementos of the Chief.

Before Winnipeg and after, MacAdam had been Mulroney's main operative on the Hill. During the campaign, he had run Mulroney's press clipping service and would read him the main stories in the important French and English papers early every morning when Mulroney was not in the East.

There were two reasons he had stayed back at the Château this day. One, as he said, because somebody had to do it. And two, because he was too nervous to go down to the Civic Centre. By mid-afternoon, he had decided to put the champagne, twenty-four bottles of Dom Perignon, in a bathtub. He and Ginette Pilotte lost count of how many trips they made down to the ice machine with those little plastic ice buckets to put a bathtub full of champagne on ice. In the Opposition Leader's fourth-floor suite of Centre Block offices, they would have the two offices closest to and on either side of Mulroney and would control the access to him. If you wanted to see him, you literally had to go through one of them.

MacAdam had the little office through the hideaway door in the panelling of the leader's office. Pilotte was on the other side. A minor feud in the office, as to who would control Mulroney's agenda, was eventually resolved in her favour. In her mid-thirties, she had not made the easiest decision of her life to follow him up from Montreal, but she was wholly devoted to his interests and could cope with his tendency to change things at the last minute. Anyone who dismissed her as "just" a secretary was making a mistake. Anyone who treated her badly was making a bigger mistake, especially if her boss heard about it. And she knew enough about him not to be too intimidated by him. "I hear you've quit smoking," she told her boss on the telephone one April day in 1984, two weeks after he went off the weeds.

"I haven't quit, I'm trying to," he replied.

"Well, then," she said, "there'll be nothing left for you to give up except swearing, and then I'll quit."

As he recounted the conversation to Wakim one night in a Toronto hotel room, Mulroney practically fell down laughing.

After the Mulroney old-boy networks from college and law school, there were the people he had met along the way: in law, business, and politics.

For Frank Moores, this had been a long and difficult day. He was not a double-crosser, and he felt uncomfortable spending the afternoon in the Crosbie box. But one of the moments that broke the tension of the day for Mulroney was when he looked over his shoulder and saw Frank and Beth Moores shouting "Crosbie! Crosbie!"

"I thought I'd never get here," Moores allowed after voting on the fourth ballot, finally pushing his way into the Mulroney area. For him as well, this was a different ending than the one in 1976, when he had supported Mulroney and when he had tried to find an elegant way of getting his candidate off the ballot without doing him any harm. "The party wasn't ready for him in

1976, and the country wasn't ready for him," Moores said. "Brian wasn't ready for it, either." By 1983, in Moores' view, Mulroney had matured into a disciplined politician who would not shrink from the tough decisions of office any more than he had from the disagreeable aspects of a leadership campaign. In this regard, as was well known by now, he had received considerable help from Moores.

What was not well appreciated at the time was the importance of the role played by Guy Charbonneau, the man whose Senate appointment by Clark had been secured by Mulroney and who had played such an important role with Moores in pulling together the anti-Clark forces of Winnipeg. In 1976, he had told Mulroney that he didn't think it would come together for him, but he had always thought it was there for him in 1983. As his financial chairman, Charbonneau had to bring the campaign through some tight cash corners. This was a victory party he meant to enjoy, unlike the May 22 election in 1979, when he had been summoned to Yellowhead riding to spend the day with Joe Clark. All he drank then was a Dubonnet. Tonight, he meant to have a glass of champagne.

Elmer MacKay was the third member of this triumvirate of political men. MacKay had been with Claude Wagner in the 1976 campaign when he met Mulroney for the first time at a Halifax forum. Sometime after the 1981 review in Ottawa, he became a proponent of a change of leadership. What had bothered him, as Regional Development Minister in the short-lived Clark government, was the way nothing got done. Proposals got talked around the cabinet table, and back into cabinet committees, and down to officials for reconsideration.

Months ago, MacKay had offered his seat of Central Nova to Mulroney in the event he became leader. "I'd have offered the seat anyway," MacKay said later, "just to get him into the House."

Rodrigue Pageau had worked himself until he was ready to drop. He was the unsung hero of Mulroney's Quebec delegate operation, the man who had held the line. He had also found himself working over, under, around, and through Ronald Bussey, the nominal chairman of the Quebec campaign, who was an experienced municipal politician but new to the kind of trench warfare they experienced in Quebec. Pageau, a practising *bleu* since the days of Daniel Johnson, had no such qualms about the necessity of doing a disagreeable job. He had first met Mulroney in Quebec in the mid-1960's and always remembered discussing with Pierre Boutin, who didn't get the Senate seat that Arthur

Tremblay did, that Mulroney or possibly Meighen had the makings of a prime minister one day. Chief organizer for the Union Nationale during its brief revival in 1976, Pageau reluctantly agreed to become Clark's campaign manager for Quebec in 1980, which was like knowing when you set sail that you've reserved a seat on the *Titanic*. Even so, Pageau had always dreamed of a Conservative Party in Quebec that worked with the legendary efficiency and unity of the Liberals. In Roger Nantel's public relations office in Old Montreal, Pageau kept a copy of Christina Newman's *Grits* on a coffee table. "C'est mon Bible," he would say.

Pageau was more than worn out on this day. He was also, though he didn't know it, a sick man. Within weeks, he would undergo surgery for cancer of the gallbladder, an operation that left him in a weak and depressed state. When he was well enough to leave hospital in mid-summer, Mulroney would take him out to lunch one day at Les Mas des Oliviers, a favourite restaurant of Pageau's on Bishop Street. On this June night, he went back to his hotel and flopped into bed.

Roger Nantel was right beside his public relations partner in politics. Nantel had some experience of politics before the Conservative Party, as Jacques Parizeau's press adviser in the 1970 Quebec election. Nantel had been careful to warn Mulroney about his brief political past before pitching in with him in 1976, but the candidate had simply waved off this consideration. Nantel wasn't the first former *péquiste* he had met in politics, for he had been at school with dozens of them before the PQ had even been born. Nantel liked to refer to himself as the token nationalist of the Mulroney group, and one acquaintance later teased him about having captured him on video tape singing "O Canada" at the conclusion of the convention.

Janis Johnson was moving back and forth between room 60 and the floor area. She was the lone woman in Mulroney's inner circle of advisers and a close friend of Mila's as well. The last time around, in 1976, she had been married to the Premier of Newfoundland and was just recovering from having their child. By now, she had resumed her family name and moved back to Manitoba, where she had built Mulroney's campaign from ground zero to about 40 per cent on the last ballot. The weekend before the convention she had moved into the Mulroney place on Belvedere Road, screened telephone calls, and heard the speech until she was sick of it.

Like Charley McMillan, she would have preferred a speech

with more vision in it, but in the end she understood why he had to go with a re-packaged version of his stump speech. By summer's end, Johnson would move into the party office as national director to prepare the 1984 election alongside Norman Atkins, who was watching this scene unfold from the air-conditioned comfort of the CBC anchor booth, where he and Paul Curley had spent a good part of the afternoon getting in free plugs for the Big Blue Machine. In 1984, Big Blue would finally have an opportunity to deliver across the country. There was no question about Atkins' authority to call the shots in English Canada, and if there had been, it was settled at a 1984 mid-winter meeting of the national campaign committee when Mulroney declared that, from then on, Norm Atkins was in charge. In Mulroney's mind, there was a simple reason: "This guy's good."

There was only one person Atkins would have to get things straight with, and that was Charley McMillan, the York University economist whom Hubert Bauch of the *Montreal Gazette* had styled "Mulroney's intellectual bodyguard." Somebody else had called him the brain trust. And Michel Cogger, to Mulroney's slight annoyance, had dubbed him "our token intellectual."

McMillan was more than Mulroney's polling and policy adviser. In many ways, he was the key to Mulroney's thoughts. He was also about the most disorganized man you ever met, chronically behind schedule, always running for a plane, always carrying his office as well as his shirts in his briefcase.

But he knew how the inside of Mulroney's mind worked, knew how to vulgarize a concept by putting in what he called "bullets" or by writing up a framework for a speech that Mulroney could work around.

He had first met Mulroney at a Tory policy conference in Niagara Falls in the autumn of 1969. McMillan had done his Ph.D. in management at Britain's Bradford University and was then teaching in the new business school at the University of Alberta. His twin brother Tommy, later an MP and Mulroney's Minister of Tourism, was then working for Robert Stanfield and got Charley to fly down. Mulroney was there as a member of the policy advisory committee.

By 1976, McMillan was teaching at York and doing a bit of market research on the side. The client was Labatt's and its president was Don McDougall, another Prince Edward Islander who was then an early backer of Mulroney. "The discussion of beer lasted about eighteen seconds," McMillan said later. "He asked me what I thought of the various candidates, and I said not much of any of them. But I said one of the people who interested me was Mulroney, that he would be my longshot."

Before long, McMillan found himself attending an organizational meeting at Toronto's Bristol Place Hotel, and by mid-campaign he was doing Mulroney's polling analysis. It was McMillan who flew down from Toronto and drove down from Montreal to deliver the bad news of the last poll in mid-February, 1976. They were sitting around the basement of Dave Angus's place at the Hermitage Club. "It showed he had no growth," McMillan later remembered. "It showed the polarization of left-right at that convention. It showed the Red Tories couldn't win, unless there was a crossover, and that would have to be Horner or Stevens. He just sat on the couch and said something like 'interesting data.'"

This time it had been different. With the exception of the bad poll in May, the convention was setting up to break in Mulroney's favour. All they needed was the right ordering and the right spreads. It was too late to do anything about either, but McMillan spent most of the day on the telephone anyway.

Nobody could easily replace McMillan in Mulroney's esteem, whether it came to analysing polls or summarizing policy options. Above all, McMillan knew when to drop everything else and concentrate on one job. And above all, Mulroney knew when to pay attention. When he would say something like "tell Charley I'll speak to him later," it usually meant that while he might not like it, McMillan was right.

David Angus was standing in front of the box with Bill Fox. As they looked up, they agreed that it was a very different scene from 1976. Angus, a Montreal marine lawyer, had been hooked on Tory politics since John Diefenbaker had come to Princeton to give the convocation address to his class in 1959. He had known Mulroney well since the waterfront commission of the mid-1960's in Montreal and was one of the first to hear from him about the possibility of running in 1976. It was a July day in 1975 and Angus was planning to play golf at the Hermitage Club when the phone rang. Mulroney wanted him to come into Montreal to have lunch at the Beaver Club. Angus allowed as how it better be pretty damn important. "What would you say if I ran for the leadership?" Mulroney said.

"I'd say you're out of your mind," Angus replied.

Mulroney admitted that was his first reaction, too, but he added that some heavy hitters had been talking to him.

In the end, Angus agreed to serve as his financial chairman. He had a talent for raising money that had earned him the sobriquet of the Golden Goose. It was Angus who had to carry the can for the papers getting word of the Power Corporation donation, even though it hadn't been his idea to leak the story. In 1983, Angus had remained on the PC Canada Fund as Mulroney's mole there. This time there were no hassles about disclosure of campaign expenses, partly because the people making the decision were men, like Angus, who knew that if you had to tell who donated how much, they wouldn't give it to you in the first place.

Later on the night of June 11, Mulroney would ask Angus to stay over for a dinner he was giving for his friends and senior campaign workers the next night. He later agreed to become chairman of the PC Canada fund, with approval on spending the money he raised. It was a unique concept and a good one in that the person in charge of raising the money, knowing how hard a job it was, would be careful how he spent it.

And finally there was Bill Fox, then the thirty-six-year-old Washington correspondent of *The Toronto Star*, who had always been Mulroney's first choice to be his press secretary. They had never discussed it because Mulroney was concerned not to compromise his integrity. "Foxie would make a helluva press secretary," Mulroney told Angus on a flight from Montreal to Toronto way back in January of 1976. Fox was then covering Mulroney out of the Southam News Montreal bureau and was drawn to him as naturally as one Irishman to another, with the affinities of a kid from Timmins, Ontario, for a boy from Baie Comeau, Quebec.

They were flying from Sudbury to Moncton one night in that campaign when Mulroney looked at the journalist sitting across from him and asked his opinion of the itinerary.

"What do you say, Foxie, do we go to Moncton or do we go home?"

"Brian," Fox replied, "I haven't been home in nearly three weeks."

Later, Fox always said that if his daughter was in this world, it was thanks to Mulroney. And many months after the 1976 campaign, a certain lantern-jawed Irishman held Christiane Fox on his knee and sang a lullaby at her christening.

On this June evening, Bill Fox allowed his colours to show to the extent of giving a thumbs-up sign, which was promptly returned.

Of all these people, who knew Brian Mulroney and loved him best, none of them other than Mila travelled with him after he became Tory leader. By the fall of 1983, this had become a problem. Mulroney had to spend at least half his time on the road, and on one swing into Antigonish in December of 1983, he looked tired, tight, and tense. Mila wasn't with him, and neither was anyone else he could talk to. Mulroney isn't at all like Trudeau in the sense that you could surround him with interchangeable political technicians who could go home at the end of the day. He needed to be with people he understood and who understood him. On the road, alone that week, he struck one person who knew him well as a lonely and unhappy man. There was no joy in it for him. He was playing it safe, going through the motions. He needed someone to travel with him. He needed Mila. And he needed someone like Bill Fox.

He hadn't filled the job of press secretary in the hope he could persuade Fox to come back. Though he loved his Washington assignment, Fox was not exactly thrilled by being away from his family, including three young children, and living in a small apartment in D.C. He knew also that someone from his time and place would be prime minister only once, and to help him get there would be a unique opportunity, especially so for a journalist, who would be able to see the workings of government from the inside. Over Christmas of 1983 they talked through friends, and on a mid-January Sunday in 1984 the phone was ringing when Fox got back to his apartment from watching a Washington Redskins playoff game. This time it was Mulroney, from Delray Beach in Florida, calling for the first time, asking for the first time. "I'm going to see the Pope, Foxie," he said. "You wanna come?"

Fox had always known this call would come some day, and though it was the most difficult decision of his life, it was also the easiest.

"The one thing I promise you, Brian," he said when they met a few days later in Toronto, "is that wherever you go, I'll go."

He would prove to be as good as his word. A one-time pulling guard at St. Pat's High in Ottawa, Fox soon began running interference for Mulroney, breaking up scrums with a quick "Thank you" to the media and a polite "This way, sir" to his boss.

More than that, Fox would prove to be the needed tonic for Mulroney on the road, regaling him with stories from other campaigns and other small towns he had known. To a mutual friend, travelling with them in southern Ontario in May of 1984, the transformation in Mulroney's mood was remarkable. Fox had lightened his spirit and his step, to say nothing of improving a press operation that had been a shambles before his arrival.

On another Saturday night two weeks before the convention,

Fox had been in Williamsburg, Virginia, for the economic summit. He went to dinner with his colleague Richard Gwyn, *The Star*'s political columnist. "What is it about you Irish guys and Mulroney?" Gwyn wondered at one point in the evening.

Fox had no need to answer the question. It had answered itself.

17

MILA

"I thought of him as an older man," she said.

And so he was, thirty-three years old when he met Mila Pivnicki in the summer of 1972. She was just turning nineteen, a college student spending her summer hanging around the pool of the Mount Royal Tennis Club in Montreal.

"I was sitting there reading the *New York Times* before having a swim," Mulroney said, "and Mila goes by. Bikini, what have you. Well, so I arranged to get myself an introduction, and by that I found out that Thursday was her birthday. She was just turning nineteen, for heaven's sake."

That Mulroney was there at all, on a Monday or Tuesday morning of the second week of July, was another one of those accidents along the way. He was in Europe in the spring of 1972, planning to spend about five weeks in Spain and the south of France when he got a phone call in Monte Carlo from Arnie Masters advising him of trouble on the Montreal waterfront. There was another strike in the port of Montreal, and his client, the Maritime Employers Association, had urgent need of his services. He came home for about seven weeks of work on MEA business before the strike was finally settled at the beginning of the summer. In the meantime, Bernard Roy had thrust a piece of paper under his nose putting him up for membership in the Mount Royal Tennis Club, as Mulroney later said, "unbeknownst to me."

So after the waterfront situation quieted down in July, Mulroney decided to "proceed to the club, take a couple of days off, you know, before going to work and then taking holidays. I go to the club, empty as hell. It's Monday or Tuesday morning, there's nobody there."

Except, as he noticed from his perch on the veranda, a dark-haired eighteen-year-old girl in a bikini, walking by the pool. All of a sudden, she recalled nearly twelve years later, it started to rain.

"Come upstairs and have a drink with me," he called down to her.

Before she knew it, he was asking her out to dinner. She said she didn't think she could, since she had to babysit at home.

"Good," he said, "we'll go to your house."

In those days, Mulroney was driving a big Oldsmobile Toronado, and the muffler had dropped off somewhere along the way. She could hear him coming from way down the street to her parents' house on Marlowe Avenue, just up the street from the tennis club and just across the city line in Montreal from the western limit of Westmount. Although she later admitted she was always "embarrassed" by the sight of the noisy Toronado, she found that she became increasingly interested in this man fifteen years older than herself. "Brian made me laugh," she would say later. "He had a fantastic sense of humour."

By Christmas they were engaged; by the following month of May they were married, with a reception thrown by her parents at the Faculty Club of McGill.

Neither Brian Mulroney nor Mila Pivnicki had any particular sense, in that summer of 1972, of being in any hurry to settle down. As he later put it, he regarded himself as neither a confirmed bachelor nor someone who was looking to get married.

"Neither one nor the other," he would say in 1984. "Just very happy with my station as it then was in life. I used to work hard and play pretty enthusiastically. I was just drifting there, you know, pleased with life and having a great time, and really not giving it much thought except, as time went on, I became more and more confirmed in my view that bachelorhood had a lot to recommend it."

Mulroney never regarded himself as any kind of playboy in those years because, as he said, "I wasn't. I had to work too hard. But I had a lot of fun. A lot of fun."

In those days he was living in an apartment on Clarke Avenue, below Sherbrooke Street, in Westmount. His mother would come once a week, shake her head at the pile of newspapers on the floor, and bundle his dirty shirts off to the laundry over on Greene Avenue, where she would buy him some groceries. "Brian never did very much in that way," Irene Mulroney said. "But he always hung up his clothes."

Though Mulroney would not become a partner at Ogilvy until January, 1973, he was getting into the big-money years in the early 1970's. Not to mention the fun he was having, with week-

233

ends at the country place of friends like Peter Thomson and his weekday crowd at the Carrefour. One story was later told in Montreal legal circles of the time Mulroney met a young lady on her way to Toronto. He gallantly accompanied her on the overnight train, then grabbed a shuttle flight to Montreal and was at work by nine o'clock, with the boarding pass still sticking out his shirt pocket.

As for Mila, she later said, "I never wanted to get married. I really had many plans for myself." She was then an engineering student at Concordia University's downtown Sir George Williams campus. She was interested in architecture. There were other things she wanted to do at the age of nineteen.

"The reason I got married," she later allowed, "is that I was madly in love with Brian. He was very generous. He had a good sense of humour. I also wanted a person who was ambitious, who knew what he wanted, because I knew what I wanted. I knew because of the age difference that he would not wait for me. When I weighed the choice, it was not a difficult decision."

The difference in their age was not something that he worried much about. "Other people did, but I didn't," he said, "because she had just a remarkable maturity, great judgement. I worried about the idea of getting married because I was so old. By that, I mean not old. But I had left home at the age of fourteen, so at this point in time I had been by myself for about twenty years. So I worried about whether I was too old to change my tune and able to accommodate some new realities. I worried about that. But I didn't worry about anything else. I was absolutely certain that she had some pretty unique talents and good sense of judgement, apart from her obvious attractiveness to me. So that was pretty clear-cut stuff."

She also knew what she was getting into. "He told me that one day he was likely to run for public office," she said. And so on May 26, 1973, they were married in Montreal. Bernard Roy was the best man, and the ushers were Michel Cogger, Lowell Murray, and Yves Fortier, as he liked to say, "as the token Liberal."

They had a delayed honeymoon in September of that year, during which a pregnant Mila lost her first child. They were to wind up the trip in London and Ireland, but first they went to Paris, Vienna, and Dubrovnik in Yugoslavia, the land of her birth.

Her father, Dimitrije Pivnicki, left Sarajevo in 1957 to establish his psychiatry practice at Montreal's famed Allan Memorial Institute, affiliated with the Royal Victoria Hospital. While Pivnicki familiarized himself with the routine of Ravenscrag, the mountaintop mansion that was the legacy of railway pioneer Sir Hugh Allan, he was sending money home to his family in Yugoslavia. When he left, his wife Bogdanka was six months pregnant with their son, John. Their four-year-old daughter, Mila, indicated her displeasure at her father's absence by dragging one foot behind her when she walked. "She missed her father so much," said Bogdanka. "We thought she might have polio."

After a year, Dr. Pivnicki was able to send for his family, and in early November, 1958, they sailed from the port of Riejeka, put in somewhere in Portugal where the harbour was on strike, and finally arrived, after a twenty-nine-day voyage, in New York on December 2, 1958.

Mila Pivnicki had no recollection of sailing past the Statue of Liberty, but she did remember being terribly sick on the way over. "We were really in the bow of the ship. All of us were violently sick," she said. Although they might have had to spend the entire North Atlantic crossing in steerage, the ship's doctor took pity on them and put them up in his clinic. Afterwards, Mila would always remember the antiseptic smell of the ship's infirmary. From New York, they rode to Montreal on the train.

In Montreal, the Pivnickis lived at first in an apartment on Pine Avenue, near the Royal Vic. Mila attended a succession of primary schools, Miss Edgar's and Miss Cramp's, a private school for girls, until grade five, and then went to Côte des Neiges and Rosedale schools in the public Protestant system, since as a member of an Orthodox denomination she was not then eligible for admission to the city's Catholic school system. She went to high school at Monklands and Westmount High, again in the Protestant system, finishing up with indifferent grades in the spring of 1970. "I wasn't a good student," she said. But at Sir George she buckled down to her civil engineering studies, and she likely would have obtained her bachelor's degree in 1974 if she hadn't married the previous year.

In the meantime, a friend named Gail Murphy had persuaded her to go to work for Michael Meighen as a volunteer in his doomed campaign to unseat Liberal C.M. "Bud" Drury in the 1972 election, the first time she was eligible to vote. "I literally did it because of a friend," she said later.

There was no doubt that in joining the Conservative Party she was going against the grain of most people her age in Montreal, as well as her parents, who like most Montrealers and most immigrants were staunch Liberals. "I wasn't going to vote for the Liberals just because my parents were," she said.

235

Oddly enough, though Meighen was one of Mulroney's friends from law school, he never ran into her as the campaign went to a readiness footing in the spring and summer of 1972, possibly because he was otherwise occupied as chief Quebec organizer that year and didn't spend a lot of time hanging around a committee room in Westmount.

It wasn't long after they were married that they moved out of Mulroney's bachelor digs into their first house, on Devon Avenue opposite a little park at the top of Westmount. The Mulroneys would live in bigger houses, but none nicer. With its bay window and view on the picturesque little park across the street, it was just as Mulroney described it: "beautiful location, beautiful house." For a young couple to have a house like that, he said, "You can't beat it. Perfect for a couple, absolutely perfect. For a family, a little bit different." But it was big enough for their needs as long as there was only Caroline, who came along on June 11, 1974, nine years to the day before her father's election as Tory leader. Once there was a second baby in the house, with the arrival of Benedict in March, 1976, Mila began to scout around for something a bit bigger.

She eventually found what she was looking for on Belvedere Road, a big stone house in need of refurbishing. They had paid something like $80,000 for the house on Devon, sold it for close to $100,000 two years later, and in the undervalued Montreal real estate market got the big place on Belvedere for $139,000. By the time they moved in at Christmas of 1976, he was the executive vice-president of Iron Ore and they could afford to have the house fixed up.

By then, they had lived through the Cliche Commission and the 1976 leadership campaign, which had aspects of a fairy-tale existence and at the same time could have been overwhelming for them. "I would think so," he admitted many years later. "I mean, it's a bit of a blur to me, so I can imagine what it was like for Mila."

She was all of twenty when their first child was born, twenty-one during the tumultuous winter of the Cliche Commission, and only twenty-two during the leadership campaign.

The first leadership campaign proved to be a learning experience for her, as well as for him. For one thing, she learned to watch what she said to the news media. After her husband's successful Baie Comeau meeting on December 16, 1975, he stayed on at Le Manoir while Mila, seven months pregnant with their second child, flew back to Montreal. Several reporters offered her a lift into town and invited her to dinner at Ruby

Foo's restaurant. Since the three reporters were only a few years older than herself, she seemed glad of their company, opened up, and talked freely of her marriage and life with Brian. She thought the occasion was obviously off the record, as did two of the three reporters, one of whom, Bill Fox, would later become her husband's press secretary. But the third reporter, Don MacPherson, drew on this informal discussion for a profile of Mulroney that appeared only six weeks later at the end of January.

When she read it on the op-ed page of her *Montreal Gazette* that morning, Mila Mulroney could have kicked herself. "It is late in the Year of the Woman," the piece began with a reference to 1975 being International Women's Year, "and the candidate is about to start his campaigning for the day with a policy statement on that very subject . . . 'Mila,' he shouts irritably at his dozing wife, who is to give birth to their second child two months later on, if he is lucky, the day of the vote, 'where are my shirts?'"

She was absolutely mortified. She thought that she had inflicted great damage on her husband's campaign. "I'll never forget it," she said more than eight years later, "because it was a crucial piece in the paper for Brian, and it made Brian out to be something he wasn't."

Specifically, a screaming male chauvinist pig.

"She was traumatized by that," Mulroney said. "She couldn't believe it. I can still remember being in Toronto that morning and I get this panic-stricken call at seven o'clock in the morning. It was Mila. She'd just read the story." Mulroney liked to say, then as later, that "Mila's a big Teddy Bear, Mila likes everybody," and he couldn't accept that a journalist would do a number on him through her.

In the days after his defeat in 1976, the fairy-tale aspect of their life came suddenly to a halt, and ahead there was the hard struggle of building a solid marriage. There were times in the next three years when even his most loyal friends wondered at her seemingly inexhaustible fund of forbearance and good cheer. For one thing, he was bitter; for another, he was sometimes bored silly by the job at Iron Ore. Because of either or both, he could be a damn unhappy man and a difficult one to be around. In those years, it was Mila who made the extra effort, sometimes simply by biting her tongue, and in so doing may have saved their marriage and helped him get his career back on a steady and promising course. As Bob McKenzie noted in his lengthy *Toronto Star* profile on the day after the Tory leadership, she had something to do with his swearing off the booze, which sometimes tended to exacerbate his bitterness.

"The defeat in '76 was a rude awakening for Brian," she said. "As he said, he realized he wasn't going to be Pope."

But it was a long time, at least three years, before he began to come to terms with that. "We really did overcome a lot," she said in 1984. "I got a pleasant surprise out of those days, of how we overcame, because it was tough."

As always, she knew what she wanted, and she knew how to get it. She wanted her husband, whole, and eventually that was what she got. "Brian knew what I wanted," she said, "a sense of regularity, to regulate his hours a little more." They started making a point of travelling together more, down to New York for weekends or to South America or Europe on combined business trips and vacations. Gradually, instead of the fairy-tale romance, they were building a rock-solid marriage.

There was something right about the arrival of their second son, Mark, in the spring of 1979. The election he might have fought was on, he was sitting it out, and the birth of their child may have reminded him there were more important things in life than being Prime Minister. For the first time, he put on a surgical mask and went into the delivery room to assist at the birth of one of his children. After that, he seemed to develop more affection and respect for his wife. It was in the two or three years before the 1983 leadership campaign, she felt, that "we became partners," instead of simply husband and wife. In the eleven years of their marriage, she observed in 1984, there had been "a tremendous evolution" in his attitudes. You had to remember, she pointed out, that he had been used to being alone, and "it took him a long time just to get used to having someone around all the time."

But there is no doubt that by the 1983 leadership race they had become partners in the campaign, and as it went on his respect for her political aplomb and acumen continued to grow. "Absolutely," he said. "Her judgement is superb. And you don't just trip over that one day. What happens is that it dawns on you that in some crucial situations, your wife is turning out to be invariably right. And so I hadn't realized that she had that interest in, that she had developed that kind of interest in politics, or in people, or people's problems or whatever, but indeed she had."

On his forty-fourth birthday, the day before he announced he was running in 1983, they took one decision that had an important impact on the campaign. They were at the Château Laurier for a small birthday party when Mila reminded her husband that she was locked into some things with the kids in Montreal and he would have to take the first swing, to Vancouver and back, by himself. At this point, their friend Janis Johnson came into the conversation and told them they were both crazy if she didn't travel with him.

"You can't do that," he remembered Johnson telling him. "Conservative delegates will not understand, when you hit Nanaimo or wherever, what the hell you're doing here while your wife's in Montreal." And that, he said later, "is what did it."

As Johnson recalled, he turned to Mila and said, "Pack your bags." Later on, Johnson said, "When she called me from someplace in Saskatchewan, she said, 'What have you got me into?'" What she got into was an eighty-day roadshow, on endless two-lane roads to an endless round of meeting delegates in small towns.

Before very long, it was clear to anyone who had travelled anywhere with Mulroney that it was a stroke of genius to have her along. She softened his tense edges, helped to dissipate the image of the plastic man, and quickly proved to be a born campaigner in her own right.

"I wasn't on the trail forty-eight hours and I had never seen anything like it," he said. "I had never seen the reaction that she was getting. She, not me. And it's gone like that ever since – she's a natural. She's great with people. They just love her."

And so Mila Mulroney, who hates to fly, would spend three days bouncing and jouncing around Alberta in a seven-seat, twin-engine aircraft, the colour draining from her face with every patch of turbulence over the foothills. It was quite clear that, all things considered, she would rather be in Palm Beach. But in the leadership campaign as later, her composure on the ground was remarkable in two senses. First, she had an observable impact on her husband's performance. Also, she had chosen to play the more traditional role of a politician's wife, which was reassuring to the old-fashioned elements in the party who had been discomfited by the aggressive feminism of Maureen McTeer. Often during the Clark years Tories could be heard complaining that his wife wouldn't even use his name. This even came up, in an indirect way, at a dinner Mulroney had for the MPs supporting his leadership bid.

"Are you going to remain under the name of Mrs. Mulroney?" a member of the small audience asked her. She dodged the meaner implications of the question with instinctive good humour. "Of course," she replied. "What would you expect when your maiden name is Pivnicki?"

You can't teach people that. It's known as "the touch," and as the leadership campaign went on it became clear that she had it.

"I was really proud of the confidence we had in one another," she said later on. In the course of three months of barnstorming around the country, they did become political as well as personal partners. Then as later, he came to rely on her instincts and her advice.

"There's something else," he said. "Her judgement, which is partly based on gut, partly on intuition, partly on reflex, is remarkable. Absolutely remarkable. For people, for issues, for political solutions. Just amazing. It's a good thing that people don't know how influential she is."

On the road, there was a discernible difference in his performance when she was around. For one thing, he was less tense, more himself. For another, she became an intermediary between the candidate and his entourage. Like any road managers, they would run him into the ground if given half a chance.

"She also knows when people are pushing me," he said. "She'll tell the staff, listen, the guy's been at it for seven days and nights. Give him an hour. Let him take a shower."

And in private, she could be his toughest critic. "If he makes a bad speech, I'm the first to tell him," she said. "If there's something that's out of line, I'm the first to tell him." As thin-skinned and insecure as Mulroney could be, he had learned to accept critical observations from his wife in the spirit in which they were offered. "I know that if she tells me something," he said, "her motives are totally pure. All she's trying to do is help me, that's all. There would never be a time in her life when there would be a thought other than that that would cross her mind. And I've learned that. So when she tells me something, my ears get this big, right off the bat."

There was another quality about her: "She's loyal like a tigress. Very defensive of me. You know, she defends me, but she is critical as hell." Thus, in a discussion of her husband's temperament and disposition, she could say in all seriousness that she didn't find him thin-skinned. "He's sensitive, there's no doubt about it," she said. "I like him that way. I wouldn't say thin-skinned. I would say sensitive."

She had been working hard on making him less thin-skinned and more sensitive, reminding him occasionally that her parents had come to Canada so that people could express different political viewpoints, argue like mad, and still be friends.

In mid-1984, he thought he was making some progress in this regard. "Two years ago I would have been called very thin-skinned," he said. "Not anymore." As evidence, he suggested that he had been receiving a bad press from *Le Journal de Montréal*, which had apparently ignored his successful visit to Ronald Reagan at the White House. "I'm there for three days and I'm not mentioned in *Le Journal de Montréal*," he said. "Not a picture, not a mention, nothing. A year ago I'd have exploded, but now I realize it doesn't matter because we're gonna win anyway. I still get angry, not angry, I get perplexed, when I see some things."

He hadn't even complained about a false article in the same Montreal tabloid that Mila had paid $80,000 for a house in the Eastern Townships, touted to be the tip-off that her husband would be running in Brome-Missisquoi. "Two years ago, I'd have been very upset," he allowed. "I'd have been phoning people and raising hell, and suing people and so on. I've learned that it doesn't matter anymore. So she's quite right. I'm not thin-skinned anymore. I've become inured to it. I read it, and if it's unfavourable, I put it aside. Or if it's favourable, I put it aside, too, and move on."

But he was still touchy about some things, such as the time his office was quick to deny a wire-service story in the spring of 1984 that the Mulroneys had spent $150,000 refurbishing Stornoway, the Opposition Leader's official residence. As Mulroney's office was quick to point out, about half the expenses had been incurred by the Department of Public Works, which had carried out some long overdue repairs on the place between the time the Clarks moved out and the time the Mulroneys moved in.

That the government was spending money on Stornoway made quite a change from the days the Conservative Party bought the old house on Acacia Avenue in Rockcliffe for George Drew. "When the party bought it," Finlay MacDonald recalled many years later, "repairs had to be approved by Grattan O'Leary." MacDonald remembered that "Mary Stanfield once filled him with Scotch" to get the purse strings loosened and some work done. Shortly after that, as he said, the government took the place over.

The Tories had been in Opposition for so long that, for them, Stornoway had achieved the mythic status of 24 Sussex. For Mulroney, it was a house they had to live in and one which, even after a lot of work, would never be as comfortable as the place they had to unload in Montreal. But if they were going to live there, even if only for a year or so, they were going to do it right. The house looked as it did when built in 1912 and when the Tories bought the place for $55,000 in 1950 – a stucco exterior with no front porch. From one Tory leader to the next, guests went in through the kitchen door. Finally, public works added a porch in 1983, at a cost of $38,000. For the rest, Mila Mulroney and her decorator, Giovanni Mowinckel, spent $79,000 redecorating the interior of the three-storey house in bright and bold colours.

When the Mulroneys finally moved in at the end of November, they spent their first night apart. Mila was alone with the kids at Stornoway and spent a sleepless night listening to the unfamiliar sounds of creaking floorboards in the old house. Her husband was at the Harbour Castle in Toronto, also getting a fitful night's rest down the hall from a suite whose inhabitants kept knocking on his door, asking if it was really him.

"You're damn right," he finally shouted across the door, "and I'm trying to get some sleep."

In their first three weeks in Stornoway, they threw a frantic round of eleven parties and had some 2,000 guests through the place, including a good many Conservatives who had never been invited there. She had said after her husband's leadership victory that she wanted to make Stornoway a place where all Conservatives and Canadians could feel at home and proud of the way it looked. By most accounts, she succeeded. Seven months after they moved in, they were still doing a lot of entertaining at Stornoway when they weren't out on the road. Every Wednesday morning, Mulroney would have half a dozen different caucus members to breakfast before they all went downtown for the weekly meeting of the full caucus. "They'd have an hour and a half with me," he said, "to raise problems, and so on, just chat." And during the last week of the parliamentary session in June, the Mulroneys had the entire caucus over for a barbecue. "But I mean a real dinner, drinks and dinner," Mulroney said.

She was sometimes criticized, and he sometimes teased her, as being a big spender. "When I got my first cheque," he told a small dinner party of friends in Montreal one night in 1983, "I pointed out to her that this was my salary as an MP, and she said, 'I have to live on that?' I replied that we both had to."

There was no doubt that he had willingly indulged her expensive tastes during the Iron Ore years. This occasionally raised some eyebrows, even among friends, who may have overlooked the fact that he had expensive tastes, too. "I've noticed she'll go out and she'll come back with things for the children, things for my mother, her mother, me," he said seriously. "Very little will she get for herself. She'll go out for herself when I put money right into her palm and say, 'I'd wish you'd go.' That's when she'll go. No hesitation, a big smile on her face, and good-bye. I kid her about the spending, but she's a good spender, a real sharp spender, that's what she is."

When they were on the road together, Mulroney was accustomed to asking after his wife's whereabouts. "Where's Mila?" he asked one night in Montreal. "It's all right, sir," replied Hubert Pichet, one of his executive assistants. "The stores are closed."

"When they hear my wife's in town," he replied between bites of a steak, "they stay open."

Mulroney was having what an aide called "one of his five-minute dinners." Since he had given up drinking, and especially since he stopped smoking, it seemed that he was always hungry. But he never ate very well or cared very much about it. In the year following the leadership, he became one of the country's leading authorities on room-service cheeseburgers and charcoal-broiled steaks. In Montreal at the Ritz one night, he took his wife and a few friends downstairs for a late supper at the Café de Paris. He said hello to the maitre d' and ordered steaks for everyone. It was left to his wife to gently remind him that some of the people at the table might like a glass of wine. "He has a boarding-school mentality towards food," she said. "We let him eat at his speed." With the demands of his travel and speaking schedule, she observed, "He eats five little meals a day instead of three big ones."

It was a different and demanding kind of life they were leading in the year after the convention, constantly on the road, removed from the realities of the real world and the creature comforts of home and the affection of their children. "I get really lonesome when I'm on the road," he said. "And then the baby calls, and I get lonesome just talking to him."

The baby would be Mark, who turned five in the spring of 1984, the most extroverted of the three Mulroney children, the one who had inherited his chin and the blue eyes that promised a lot of mischief. He was quick to acknowledge that Mark "has me on the arm," but of their three children, he thought it was Caroline who was the most like him "in her mindset." In another kind of way, he was most fascinated by his middle child, Ben, an uncomplaining, well-adjusted boy who seemingly didn't need to compete with his older sister and younger brother for the attention and affection of their father. Mulroney was particularly proud of his work at the Lycée Claudel, where he evidently stood at the top of his class. When the parents of someone else in his class organized a trip to the House of Commons, Ben didn't say anything about it to anyone, least of all to his father.

"He didn't say, well, if you want to see the House of Commons, my dad will fix that up," a dumbfounded Mulroney explained. "I didn't even know they were coming."

243

It was left to Mulroney's driver, Derek McSweeney, to inform his boss that Ben's class would be visiting the Hill, and it was left to Ginette Pilotte to make arrangements for them to be brought up to the Opposition Leader's Office, where Mulroney met them all and where Ben had a chance to sit behind his father's desk. "But he would never have complained," Mulroney said. "Which I thought, there's a role reversal here. I mean, hell, I would have been right on the goddamn blower, saying, 'Hey, my old man'll fix this up for you.' I'd have had them buy me lunch at the Parliamentary Restaurant."

In some ways, the first year in Ottawa had been a difficult adjustment for Mulroney. The most he would say about the town was that it was "good for the family," which is the sort of thing everyone says about Ottawa.

With his incessant travels, he found it difficult to say how much he liked the job. "The last year," he said at the end of June, 1984, "has not been a fair one to assess the job of Prime Minister and Leader of the Opposition. I'm having a year like I'll never have again, a leadership campaign, new in the House, into the Liberal leadership and into the election campaign, and you win or you lose."

For her part, when she wasn't travelling with him, Mila would spend a good deal of her time back in Montreal, shopping, doing errands with the kids, and visiting with family and friends. Her friends were mostly non-political women. "I think I have the best friends a woman could have," she would say. "What's a friend? Someone who understands you don't have to be in town all the time. Someone who realizes that sometimes you just run out of words."

These women were among the Mulroney's closest Montreal friends who attended a small dinner for them in December, 1983, at Bernard Roy's apartment in Habitat on Cité du Havre. They cleared the furniture out of one of the rooms, put Mulroney posters up on the wall, and ate a hot meal around a bunch of card tables. He was tired from two days of travel in the Maritimes and a day of meetings in Montreal, and he wanted to get some sleep before a rally the next day in Toronto that was to precede a big party fund-raiser back in Montreal. And so, around midnight, he made a move to go back to their hotel and get some sleep. "Mulroney," Mila protested, "I'm having a good time."

In a sense, there may have been some of the age difference between them showing. She said she didn't concern herself with that, but she also knew that when she would be forty he would be fifty-five and hopefully on his way out of politics. It was understood between them that there were other things they wanted to do in life.

Mulroney would sometimes talk about "living in Europe for a couple of years, hang around Paris, that kind of thing, get a few ideas into my head." She sometimes allowed herself to think of having a home in a place like Palm Beach, and going back and forth in the winter.

For the foreseeable future, their commitment and their life was in politics. This meant, as it did one cold Saturday morning in Niagara Falls, riding in the back of an open car in a parade. Mulroney kept telling her to wave, and she, with a smile pasted on, kept wanting a cup of coffee to keep her hands warm. "I was not thrilled," she said later. But she did it, as he did, because you do these things to get elected Prime Minister.

"I think we're going to be a very fortunate couple in politics," she said, "with a good working relationship." As far as anyone could tell, she had remembered the promise to her father on that day of their lives in June, 1983, when the results were in. Amidst the joy that reigned in the Mulroney box, the snow-haired Dimitrije Pivnicki clasped his daughter and made her promise to go on being herself, whatever else happened.

And when Brian Mulroney made his way to the podium, he went out of his way to thank her in a manner that struck his friends as his way of admitting, for the first time, how much she meant to him. "I want to thank one person so very much," he said, "Mila, who has made such a contribution to my life." And then, almost as an afterthought, he added, "and to the campaign."

A year later he would say: "I would never have won the leadership without her. No question about that at all. I mean that in crass, vote-counting terms. There were votes that came to me because of her, lots and lots of them because of her. There's no doubt in my mind whatsoever about that."

But the other words played back as the more meaningful ones: "Mila, who has made such a contribution to my life." Only their closest friends could appreciate what he meant, and how much he meant it.

18

FRIENDS AND ACQUAINTANCES, ALONG THE WAY

Brian Mulroney always remembered the day Pierre Trudeau couldn't get a seat in a bar. It was an afternoon late in 1967, and Mulroney was sitting around the Carrefour bar in Place Ville Marie with a few other people when Trudeau walked in with Anne Lemieux, daughter of the great painter Jean-Paul Lemieux, and a mutual friend. Trudeau was then Minister of Justice, and in a very few months he would be Prime Minister, but this was in the pre-Trudeaumania days, even in Montreal.

"Trudeau is going around and he can't get a seat," Mulroney recalled a few weeks after Prime Minister Trudeau had announced his retirement in 1984. "Nobody knows who he is in the whole place, so I go over to him and say, 'Come and sit with me.' If he'd done that four months later, there'd have been a riot. So that's really how little he was known."

A few months later there was a riot when Trudeau came back to Place Ville Marie to campaign as the new Prime Minister. Same place, except upstairs and outside. Same Trudeau. But about 50,000 people had come to hear him, see him, touch him. One of the people at the back of the crowd was a Conservative organizer, Brian Mulroney.

"I remember just as if it happened yesterday," Mulroney recalled. "I swear to God, there were 50,000 people there, all going squirrelly. This is for a guy, not one of whom would have recognized him a few months earlier in Place Ville Marie."

As Mulroney stood at the back of the huge crowd, he met up with Claude Ryan, then the publisher of *Le Devoir*. Since he had failed to endorse Trudeau at the Liberal Party's April convention in 1968 and was supporting Robert Stanfield in the spring election, it was not a very happy sight for Ryan. What's more, his brother Yves was running as a Conservative candidate.

246

"Have you ever seen anything like this in your life?" Mulroney asked Ryan, who allowed as how he hadn't. "Well, neither have I. Let's go get some lunch."

At the time, Mulroney was twenty-eight years old, but he had already known the likes of Trudeau and Ryan almost since the time he came to Montreal four years earlier. As he explained it, everyone in the political milieu in Montreal knew everyone else. "Quebec is small, when you get right down to it," Mulroney said. "Quebec is a fairly small province in terms of the number of people involved in the decision-making process on the political side, and so by and large a lot of people in Quebec know one another. Not all of them like one another, but a lot of them know one another, and I'm one of those. A relatively small group in Quebec, and we all know one another."

The people Mulroney would meet and get to know along the way were the political elite of two generations, Trudeau's and his own, in both Ottawa and Quebec on both sides of the floor. Then as later, Mulroney's friendships were not restricted or in any way bound by party affiliation. Since he was living in Montreal, the citadel of the Liberal Party both federally and provincially, it sometimes seemed most of Mulroney's friends were Grits.

"By God," Mulroney used to say, "I hope the Liberals have the decency to come to my funeral, because I've done more for them than the Conservative Party has ever done for me."

In early as in later life, Mulroney knew two kinds of people in politics, those he became acquainted with and those who became his friends. Trudeau belonged to the former category, along with John Turner. Francis Fox belonged in the latter group, as did Robert Bourassa.

The relationship between Trudeau and Mulroney, as Prime Minister and Leader of the Opposition, was too short to be nasty or bitter. But it lasted long enough, in the year between Mulroney's accession as Conservative leader and Trudeau's departure as Liberal leader, to be interesting and intriguing. The fact is that the two men rather liked each other, and always had, and shared many ideas of the country, and always would.

On the rare occasions when they clashed in the House, there was a forced quality of belligerence about it, as if they were acting to please their respective followers, as in a sense they were. Some people in his party thought he was being too easy on Mulroney, the Prime Minister confided in a private conversation with the new Conservative leader in late June of 1983. Some people in his party, Mulroney allowed, thought he was being too easy on Trudeau.

This exchange arose from a couple of interviews they had given that month. After the Tory convention, Trudeau had paid a visit to the editorial board of *Le Devoir* in Montreal, where he called Mulroney's win a victory for bilingualism, for Quebec, and for French Canada. In the days before the convention, Mulroney had appeared on CTV's *Question Period*. It was the last day of his eighty-day campaign before he returned to Montreal to prepare for the convention. Someone asked how he responded to the criticism that he was another Trudeau. Mulroney was either so tired that he dropped the partisan pose, or he was simply incapable of being mean where Trudeau was concerned. Trudeau had many faults, he allowed, but there were limits to partisanship. Trudeau was a Quebecer who loved his country, Mulroney said, "and so am I," and to the extent that made him like Trudeau, "so be it."

Among the people who saw these comments in the papers he claimed never to read was the Prime Minister of Canada. "Pierre Trudeau remembers that," he assured Mulroney during their conversation a few weeks later.

For his part, Trudeau had long thought well of Mulroney. The day before the Conservative leadership convention in 1976, he ran into Claude Ryan at the funeral of their mutual friend, Fernand Cadieux, who had been one of the intellectual lights of their generation. Afterwards, Trudeau offered Ryan a lift and the small talk got around to the Tory convention, where Ryan had endorsed Mulroney. "They don't," Trudeau said, "have the brains to elect him." Ryan later reported this conversation back to Mulroney, and it tended to confirm his high opinion of Trudeau.

On at least two occasions, Trudeau asked Mulroney to join his cabinet. After he became Tory leader, Mulroney was quite reticent to talk about the occasions on which he was courted by Trudeau. "I'll confirm that overtures were made, federally and provincially, to join the government," was all Mulroney would say.

But on one occasion after his defeat in 1976, Trudeau had Mulroney up to 24 Sussex Drive for dinner, just the two of them, and offered to bring him into the cabinet. The second time they talked, the Prime Minister repeated the offer. Both times the answer was no. It wasn't that Mulroney didn't like Trudeau or the idea of becoming a senior cabinet minister with an open path to the Liberal succession. It was simply the idea of changing parties that he could not sell to himself. As he said quite simply in 1984, "I'm a Conservative."

In the years between the two Conservative conventions, they would occasionally run into one another in Montreal, in the Forum directors' lounge at a hockey game, at a charity ball, or at some other social event. "I've seen them together on different occasions," said Montreal financier Paul Desmarais, who had them both over to his Palm Beach house on New Year's Eve in 1983, "and it's always been very civilized between them."

Mulroney was spared the corrosive scorn with which Trudeau had treated Robert Stanfield, and the withering contempt with which he regarded Joe Clark. "If they ever got into a real battle," Desmarais mused in the winter of 1984, "the gloves would come off. It wouldn't be a very gentlemanly fight. It would be a professional knockout fight."

It never came to that. There never was anything more than a couple of encounters that reminded National Arts Centre director Don MacSween, who knew them both well, of a couple of pups biting one another's ears.

In the 1970's, Trudeau used to remind Mulroney of Frank Mahovlich wandering aimlessly up and down his wing until somebody made the mistake of hitting him and getting him into the game. "It's like what Sammy Pollock used to say about Mahovlich," Mulroney would say of Trudeau. " 'Whatever you do, don't wake him up.' "

It was a rare occasion in the House when Mulroney chose to tangle with Trudeau. He preferred not to wake him up. "He's pretty tough, you know, pretty tough, and clearly head and shoulders above anybody in the government," Mulroney said in May of 1984. "God, he's so far ahead of the rest of them that it's embarrassing, and when he's not in the House, it's almost futile to try and interrogate anyone else because they're not in the same league. He can be very aggressive and unkind, and very churlish in his responses, but by and large he's good. You know, when he's wrong, he can be very good at being wrong, because he's a hell of a performer."

And when Trudeau was right, Mulroney knew, he could also be very good at being right, as when he smote René Lévesque and the "Yes" forces in the 1980 Quebec referendum in a historic speech at the Paul Sauvé Arena in Montreal. Lévesque had made the mistake of suggesting that Trudeau wasn't a full-blooded French Canadian and took after his mother's side of the family, the Elliotts. Trudeau simply murdered Lévesque with that, in a dramatic speech that brought the referendum campaign to an exciting conclusion. Mulroney was out speaking at some other "No" event that evening, but he heard bits of it on the radio, enough to know that it was just about the greatest piece of oratory he had ever heard.

There were two things about Trudeau that Mulroney always admired: the first was his style and the second was that he loved a good fight. Mulroney's own style was much more conventional than Trudeau's, but as he liked to say, "one thing about the old Trud, he's got a lotta class."

He noticed that in Trudeau's comments from Greece after Mulroney's by-election victory in Central Nova, saying the new Leader of the Opposition would be a worthy and formidable opponent. And he certainly noticed it in Trudeau's welcoming remarks in the House on September 12, 1983, when he spoke of Mulroney as a man "who sent shivers of pleasure down the spines of the matrons all the way from Oyster Pond to Mushaboo." And, Trudeau concluded, "as the great André Siegfried said: 'If you want to harm someone, too much praise is more effective than criticism.' I think there is a Machiavellian plot afoot among members of the press gallery who seem to be out to destroy in this way the new Leader of the Opposition – he can count on us to render the plot ineffective."

Trudeau thus set the tone for what would remain a good-humoured adversarial relationship with a man twenty years younger than himself, from a different kind of Quebec background, but holding certain tenets of the Canadian faith in common. Above all, Mulroney saw the country being composed of minority groups, and he viewed the central government as the protector and promoter of their interests. In that sense, he was Trudeau's political heir. "I have never hid the fact that, in my judgement, some of the things he set out to do were extremely honourable and he accomplished them well," Mulroney said of the retiring Prime Minister. "And so that kind of situation, the fact that the bitter hostility that you so often see between the Prime Minister and the Leader of the Opposition was totally lacking in our relationship."

This did not alter Mulroney's political judgement in the winter of 1983-84 that Trudeau was through, although as he said privately of the four-term Prime Minister, "He's had a damn good run."

John Turner was someone Mulroney met through "the Montreal connection" of the Junior Bar and mutual friends such as Yves Fortier, a partner at Ogilvy, Cope and a future president of the Canadian Bar Association. Fortier, very much a member of the Montreal Liberal establishment, was considered a hot political prospect in his own right if ever he decided to jump into it. He had one recollection from the late 1960's of "inviting Brian, who was very much a bachelor in those days, home for dinner." Standing around the kitchen with Fortier's wife, Carol, "We began talking about Turner. Brian said that man has one ambition and that is to become prime minister, but that there were a couple of people who stood between him and that. I asked who they might be, and he said they were right here in this kitchen."

Turner had fought and won two elections in his downtown riding of St. Lawrence-St. George by the time Mulroney came to Montreal in the summer of 1964. "I knew Turner in Montreal," Mulroney said, "but I can't remember when I knew him, just that I knew him and that he was an obviously successful young guy, doing well and highly regarded."

Mulroney was in Vancouver on business after the 1968 election when he ran into Turner, in town as Justice Minister to address the annual Canadian Bar convention. Turner invited him up to his hotel suite for a drink at the end of the evening. "Which I did," Mulroney said, "about ten or eleven o'clock, and we spent three or four hours, just the two of us."

Another time, when Turner was Finance Minister, Mulroney called him in the government lobby of the Commons to settle an important problem for the Maritime Employers Association, that of paying its bills and so keeping the port of Montreal open. By a complicated procedure, the National Harbours Board was to guarantee the MEA's payroll to help it through the difficult times in the early 1970's. "The National Harbours Board started to welsh on their guaranteed payment to the MEA to get us over the difficult times, because we had that buy-out to do and all that stuff," Mulroney explained. "It was pretty clear that without that guarantee, the banks wouldn't give us the money so we could make the payroll payment on Friday."

So on a Wednesday afternoon, Mulroney and MEA president Arnie Masters were sitting in the Maritime Employers' boardroom in Cité du Havre in Montreal, trying to figure out what to do next. Mulroney decided to get Turner on the phone and lean on him.

"I said, 'Listen, John, I'll tell you at this time tomorrow the port of Montreal is going to shut down, and when it does, you're going to get the blame, not because it's your fault, but because they're gonna blame you.'" Mulroney recalled. "And he said, 'What the hell are you talking about?' And I said, 'The NHB has just put a stop on the amount they owe us, which means we're going belly

251

up. When we go belly up, this thing's gonna land right on your desk. It's very unfair but that's going to happen.' He says, 'I'll be goddamned, you leave it with me.' He says, 'Where are you, I'll get back to you.' In my recollection it wasn't a half-hour before Turner called back and said, 'I'm sending a guy down there. There's a guy going down to see you in a car, and he's got a cheque, a certified cheque, for the payroll tomorrow.'"

After Turner left politics in 1975, Mulroney said privately that he would be remembered as a great Justice Minister for his creation of the Law Reform Commission and the quality of his appointments to the bench. In the late 1970's, when they were both moving in the world of corporate boardrooms, their paths would occasionally cross in Montreal or Toronto. Once they even had a long lunch together at Winston's, Turner's favourite Toronto restaurant. But it would be an overstatement to call them friends. When Turner came into the 1984 Liberal leadership race on March 16, with the statement that extension of minority language services, in Manitoba and elsewhere, was primarily a provincial jurisdiction, Mulroney jumped all over him. Before the day was out, Mulroney had read a transcript of Turner's Friday morning press conference at the Château Laurier, and before the end of that weekend, he had accused Turner of preparing to renounce the Liberal legacy on minority rights.

The issue was fraught with difficulties for Mulroney, who was trying to get his party to go along with him, and fraught with anguish for the Liberals, who in choosing Turner as Trudeau's successor were taking on someone with a very different idea of the country. While Trudeau kept silent on this matter, his opinion of Turner was almost as well known as his views on the minority rights question. When he ran into Mulroney at Chief Justice Bora Laskin's funeral in late March, the Prime Minister noted that Mulroney had been giving Turner the business on this issue.

Robert Bourassa was one of Mulroney's friends in politics, especially in a time when Bourassa didn't have many other friends. John Turner might invite Bourassa to dinner in the McMillan, Binch boardroom at the Royal Bank Plaza in Toronto. But that was in 1984, when Bourassa had no shortage of invitations. Turner might say, as he campaigned for the leadership in Quebec in the spring of the same year, that he had had "a good cup of coffee" with Bourassa at his home on the Outremont side of Mount Royal. But Mulroney had been buying a cup of coffee for Bourassa when hardly anyone else would.

They had become friends during the Cliche Commission, even though the hearings were politically harmful to Bourassa's prospects for re-election as Premier. After Mulroney's defeat at the 1976 Conservative convention, Bourassa let him know that he would be welcome any time in the provincial Liberal cabinet. After Bourassa's own defeat in November of that year, Mulroney was one of the few people who called him for lunch. "I wasn't getting too many invitations for lunch," Bourassa recalled. "Ho-boy, the phone wasn't ringing very much either."

One day, a month after his defeat, Mulroney and a mutual friend took the defeated and apparently discredited Premier for a long lunch in a private salon of Chez Son Père, a restaurant on Park Avenue that had been favoured by Bourassa during his years as Premier. Bourassa, whose future looked to be behind him at the age of forty-three, was very much concerned that day about his place in history. "Give it time, Robert, you've got to give it time," Mulroney told him. "In a few years, compared to these guys, you're going to look pretty good."

In a few years, both Bourassa and Mulroney would have to learn how to bide their time and wait for their second chance. "Later on, in 1980," Bourassa would recall, "he used to say to me that Paul Martin used to say that the worst mistake in politics was impatience." In this way, they used to counsel one another on the virtues of patience. On his own leadership swing through Quebec in 1983, Mulroney could see that Bourassa was winning the leadership in the same way he was – out in the boonies, without any fanfare and without any press. And Mulroney advised him to stay with the same strategy all the way to the Quebec Liberal Party's October leadership convention.

By then, the congratulatory call that came to Bourassa's room in the Motel Universel in Quebec City was placed from one leader to another, and the conversation was from one friend to another. They would talk again on the evening of September 4, 1984.

As leader of the Quebec Liberal Party, Bourassa had to maintain a strict neutrality in the 1984 federal election, but it was no secret as to his private preferences. Still, he knew he had to be careful. At the rank-and-file level, as Bourassa explained, "about two-thirds" of the federal and Quebec Liberals "are the same people."

That did not prevent the Bourassa Liberals and the Mulroney Conservatives from exchanging polling information on Quebec. It did not prevent Bourassa's chief organizer, Pierre Bibeau, from meeting on a regular and private basis with Bernard Roy, whom Mulroney had named his chief organizer for Quebec. It did not prevent Pierre Paradis and his entire organization from moving onside in one of Mulroney's prospective ridings, Brome-Missis-quoi in the Eastern Townships, which the aggressive young Paradis represented in the provincial riding of Brome in the National Assembly.

There was a general sense in Quebec, too, that Mulroney and Bourassa could put an end to what John Turner would call "the bitterness and the bickering" between Ottawa and Quebec and restore a climate of partnership between the two governments. The problem was in getting one or both of them elected.

All things considered, they could live with that problem, especially considering where both of them were on that gloomy December day in 1976. After he left Bourassa to drive back downtown, Mulroney shook his head at the way the former Premier had been abandoned by his Liberal friends and said that he preferred to see people when they were down. "I don't know why," he said, "it's just the way I am. I'd probably give a dinner for Joe Clark if nobody else would."

Certainly Mulroney was in the habit of giving money to lost political causes, and as the boss of Iron Ore he was in a position to do so. Whether it was Jerôme Choquette, on a quixotic crusade as leader of something called the Parti Nationale Populaire in 1976, or Guy Chevrette running up in Joliette for the PQ, or even Nick Auf der Maur, running as leader of the predominantly English-speaking Democratic Alliance, they all needed money to do it, and Mulroney helped them out.

"It was a lonely time," said Auf der Maur, a Montreal city councillor and journalist, and later an unsuccessful Conservative candidate in the riding of Notre Dame-de-Grace-Lachine East in the 1984 election, "lonely in the sense that no established person would have anything to do with us, and Brian gave us some money. Was he piling up future debts? I don't know. But it's an instinct he's got, it's part of his tribal makeup. It's a virtue he practises. Hell, I sound like his p.r. man, but he gets a kick out of making people feel good.

"He's a typical Irish fraud," Auf der Maur continued. "It's a positive thing, not a negative thing. He's not trying to make you believe in his fraudulence. You know exactly why he's doing it and how but you can't help but be charmed by it, and for reasons I don't know, only the Irish can do that."

Another Montreal journalist, Brian McKenna, was a producer with the CBC current affairs program, *the fifth estate*, and had spent three years with his wife, Susan Purcell, writing a biography of Montreal's legendary mayor, Jean Drapeau. "There was this review in *Maclean's*," McKenna recalled, "the first review of my book on Drapeau, and it hits you hard because writing is the hardest thing in the world, the magic of the book appearing and everything, [and] the first review is this mean-spirited and flip review. I'm sitting there in my office at the CBC, the phone rings and it's Mulroney. I didn't know him particularly well. He said, 'I want you to know that your book is a first-class piece of journalism, and that I've bought a dozen copies for my friends for Christmas.' "

More than that, Mulroney passed on the word that his friend Peter C. Newman, the magazine's editor-in-chief, had apparently liked the book. Two weeks later, McKenna recalled, "Newman singled it out as one of the best Canadian books of the year on his Christmas list. Brian's never written a book. How could he have known how I felt?" Somehow he knew enough of how McKenna had felt to put in a word with Newman, an old friend he had first met in Ottawa early in the 1960's when he was a youth adviser to the Chief and Newman was covering the Diefenbaker administration for *Maclean's*.

Newman was typical of Mulroney's friends in the media in one important respect: though very much a political animal, he had never been part of the parliamentary press gallery crowd, even in the years he was working there. Richard Doyle, for many years editorial-page editor of the *Globe and Mail*, was another friend and influential journalist cultivated by Mulroney. Allan Fotheringham was writing his column out of Vancouver when he first made Mulroney's acquaintance in the 1976 leadership campaign. Bob McKenzie, the senior Quebec correspondent of *The Toronto Star*, had met Mulroney during the Laval period and was still in the provincial capital nearly twenty-five years later. During the period of the Cliche Commission, Mulroney had become quite friendly with Michel Roy, later editor-in-chief of *Le Devoir* before becoming deputy publisher of *La Presse* in Montreal in the 1980's.

Roy would be one of those who could vouch for Douglas Fisher's complaint in a 1983 *Maclean's* column on Mulroney. "He has raised the leaking of information to preferred sources into an art," Fisher wrote of the man he had first met some twenty-five years earlier at the St. F.X. model parliament and whom he found unchanged in two respects – "the boyish charm" and "the almost total dependence on platitudes for ideas and clichés for vocabulary."

Since the column dealt partly with Mulroney's thin-skinned nature, Fisher might have been surprised by Mulroney's even-headed reaction to the piece. "I guess that makes me one of two in *Maclean's* this week," he said, referring to another, generally flattering piece in the same edition.

Don McGillivray, neither an old friend nor a sworn journalistic foe of Mulroney, would call him "a crony seeker" who would be in for some rude surprises in an Ottawa where Pierre Trudeau had killed cronyism by showing such contempt for and keeping his distance from the press. "There's a chance Mulroney will charm his way into the hearts of the press people," McGillivray conceded in a *Maclean's* column. "But it's a mighty slim chance."

There is no doubt that Mulroney had his friends in the news media when he came to Ottawa and that, as Conservative leader, he would be good to the people who had been good to him. That meant that when Bruce Phillips asked if he would do CTV's *Question Period* the day after the convention, Mulroney agreed, though he had nothing left in his voice but a whisper, though he had to get up at seven o'clock in the morning to do it, and though he had to wear what may have been his last clean shirt to the studio. Phillips had first met him at the Laval symposium on Canadian affairs and had always shown him some kindness, even and especially after his 1976 defeat. He was one of the few older members of the Ottawa press gallery that Mulroney had much time for. Among the new generation of parliamentary reporters, Mulroney admired talent, even when he found it in the smaller papers. In his view, the most aggressive and perhaps the best reporter on the Hill was Michel Gratton of Ottawa's *Le Droit*, who would become his assistant press secretary at the outset of the 1984 campaign. "He's got that Liberal caucus wired for sound," Mulroney said admiringly late in 1983.

Whether he liked or loathed a reporter, Mulroney usually read everything he could get his hands on. An early morning visitor to his home or hotel room would invariably see the debris of morning papers littered on the floor. By 8:30 most mornings, Mulroney would have read the *Globe and Mail*, the *Montreal Gazette*, *Le Devoir*, *La Presse*, *Le Droit*, the *Ottawa Citizen*, the *Toronto Sun*, and *The Toronto Star*. Before the day was out, he would have seen *Le Soleil*, along with selected western papers and perhaps the odd clipping from the *New York Times* or the *Wall Street Journal*. Most evenings when he wasn't out on the hustings, he would watch the CBC's *The National* or Radio-Canada's *Téléjournal*, whose anchorman, Bernard Derome, he regarded as the best in the business. Then he would usually watch *The Journal* and stay up to watch the news begin all over again on CTV. When he was in Ontario, he would have a third news channel to fiddle around with in the Global television network.

Mulroney is a news freak. Whether it comes in video or in the paper, he can't get enough of it and can't stand being away from it. Part of his problem in taking a holiday is being out of touch. And one of his pleasures of holidaying in the West Palm Beach area of Florida is that the Canadian papers are flown in the same day.

"Mulroney is a bit of a media groupie," McGillivray suggested in his *Maclean's* piece, "and has carefully cultivated a list of press pals as he climbed the slippery slope to the Tory leadership." While it is true that Mulroney had his cronies among the press when he came to Ottawa, it is also true that critics missed the point of it. Generally speaking, Mulroney liked the company of journalists and preferred them and their tweedy informality to the blue suits he had been spending his days with during the Iron Ore years or the blue rinse set he had been meeting in his campaign for the leadership. For all his talk about business as the agent of economic recovery and for all his memberships in the best clubs, businessmen generally bored him to tears. He would rather have a newspaper friend like Bill Fox to lunch at the Mount Royal Club. "But tell Foxie to wear a pair of shoes," he told a mutual friend with a laugh. "The last time he came he was wearing his goddamn Wallabies."

Even a friend like Fox might fall into temporary disfavour when he suggested, after an April, 1982, interview, that "old Bones" was doing more than just passing the time of day on the telephone. While episodes of his thin skin were much less evident after he won the Tory leadership, some of his friends wondered how he would handle the criticism when the cheering stopped. His wife preferred to think of him as sensitive, and some of his oldest friends knew he was still basically insecure, still eager to please. In that sense, he may still have been the young boy singing the songs for the Colonel. On the night of his swearing-in as a member of the House, which by all accounts was a tremendous day for him, he called one of his oldest friends who had been there to ask how he thought things had gone. One of his senior law partners, Tommy Montgomery, a man who loved him dearly, used to say that with all his talent Mulroney should be more self-assured. But that did not prevent him from exercising his own talent for developing new friendships.

"Brian converts people to himself, or tries to, all the people he meets," suggested Lucien Bouchard of the Laval gang. Jean Bazin, of the same Laval crowd, thought he knew why. "He is perspicacious, humanly and politically," Bazin said fondly of his friend. "He judges people well, he's a good judge of people. That helps him. He's very *attachant*, very likable, and because he's likable he's perspicacious."

On the Monday after he was elected Conservative leader, Mulroney went up to Parliament Hill to take a bow from the visitors' gallery. On the way he ran into Francis Fox, the Liberal Communications Minister and a close personal friend. Mulroney had been one of the people who stood by Fox in his personal ordeal when he resigned from the cabinet in 1978 after disclosing that he had signed another man's name to procure a therapeutic abortion for a woman friend. In that month, when Fox was between the devil and the deep blue sea, Mulroney had spent hours on the phone with him, bucking up his spirits. "I'll never forget what he did for me," Fox said. When they met in the Commons that day they exchanged warm greetings. For both of them, it was an emotional moment.

"It's the beginning of a new era," Fox told another friend later. "The end of one era, the beginning of another."

19

THE MEMBER
FROM CENTRAL
NOVA

All his life, Brian Mulroney had to win people over to himself: first, as an English-speaking kid growing up in a French town; then as a Quebecer attending college in the Maritimes; then as an anglophone studying in a French law faculty; and finally as a small-town boy come to Montreal to practise law. In the Conservative Party, he rose quickly through the ranks to stand at the side of two leaders, John Diefenbaker and Robert Stanfield.

Imposing himself, winning people to himself, was something he had been doing since childhood. Only once had he been rudely rebuffed, by the Ontario-based Tory establishment when he had been emboldened to seek the leadership in 1976. Later on, he could look at this defeat as a growing experience because, until then, everything perhaps had come too easily to him. As his soul-mate Lucien Bouchard observed, "Brian avait besoin de manger une claque." Roughly translated, he needed a slap across the face.

But he didn't forget the way he had been rejected by the Queen's Park crowd and in 1983 redoubled his efforts to win them over. In the campaign, he achieved only modest results. For weeks, he held open the job of campaign director for Norm Atkins in the event Bill Davis decided, as he finally did, not to seek the leadership himself. Mulroney's second choice for campaign manager, Paul Curley, also stayed on the sidelines in the formal sense, though he was known to be sympathetic to Mulroney in the final weeks. It was not that Mulroney thought these guys were the be-all and end-all of campaign organization, but they had the reputation of the invincible Big Blue Machine going for them, and Mulroney would have loved to have had them onboard, not just for their organizational skills but for the momentum they could have generated in Ontario. By most estimates, he had no more than 100 senior Ontario delegates on the first ballot.

Only his strength among the youth and campus delegates brought him up to a respectable score among Ontario delegates.

Most of all, Mulroney wanted to win over Bill Davis, something he had never been able to do in 1976 or since. Mulroney put all his considerable charm into this operation. Where the Queen's Park people had felt slighted by the Clark regime, they had their calls returned quickly by the Mulroney office. Davis began to be the recipient of Mulroney's phone calls, soliciting his advice on this or that issue or just shooting the breeze. The Mulroneys and the Davises began to see one another socially, not just at party functions in Ontario but over the Christmas holidays in Florida.

By the spring of 1984, the Mulroney charm was having its desired effect. Davis was not only onside, he was eager to work for Mulroney's election: "Bill has told his people that if he has to move the city of Toronto five feet to the right to get me elected then that's what they should do," Mulroney observed in May, 1984, after a visit from Davis. The occasion was a joint meeting of the two Tory Ontario caucuses at the Sutton Place Hotel in Toronto. Davis, who can be all business, was clearly disappointed that the two leaders were expected downstairs a few minutes after his arrival in Mulroney's suite and regretted that they didn't have more time for a private chat.

Winning over the hearts of the Conservative Party, even after the leadership, would prove to be a daunting task. Winning over the hearts of his countrymen, in the run-up to the 1984 election, seemed for many months to be a much easier task than it would prove to be in the end.

The first returns were more than encouraging, both in the polls and in the Nova Scotia riding of Central Nova from which Mulroney had chosen to make his entry into the House of Commons. The July, 1983, Gallup Poll showed a five-point jump in Conservative popularity since the June convention, increasing their lead to 55-27 over the Liberals. "How do you like that for a first sweep?" Mulroney asked one friend on the phone. In the September Gallup, the Tories rose to an unprecedented 62 per cent, an incredible 39 points ahead of the Grits, the highest rating and the biggest spread in the history of this poll.

Only eight months later, in the euphoria of the Liberal leadership campaign, Mulroney had ridden the roller coaster down to a 40-46 deficit. When press aide Bill Fox got word of the Gallup in Montreal one Monday night in May, he hastened to get his boss out of bed at the Ritz-Carlton. The next day they had a discussion on the Gallup and its implications, and Fox summed it up in a single sentence. "Well, boss," he said, "now we're going to find out who can play this fucking game."

The shocking turnaround in the Gallup produced two characteristic reactions in Mulroney. First, he didn't believe it, because it didn't correspond with what he had been seeing and hearing on his incessant travels around the country. And then he looked at it with his boundless, bottomless optimism.

Robert Cliche used to say that "Brian is such a goddamn optimist." Whenever something unfavourable about the Cliche Commission would appear in the morning papers, Mulroney would come bounding across the doorstep saying it was exactly what they wanted. So with the bad Gallup Polls in the spring of 1984. As Mulroney finally read them, the polls knocked him off that "damn 55 per cent pedestal," which was both unrealistic and untenable, and put him back at the floor figure of 40 per cent he needed to win the election. From there he hoped to climb back up to a good 44 per cent by election day. In this regard he had always been consistent, and realistic, in private. Two weeks after his election as Tory leader, he sat in the living room of his Montreal home and allowed that "I've told our guys our floor figure is 40 per cent." On a winter afternoon some eight months later, when the Liberals had begun the long climb back, closing the Tory lead to 52-36, Mulroney sat in his fourth-floor Centre Block office and insisted he had been telling people all along that the Liberals were not a 30 per cent party. "They're a 40 per cent party," he said. "The two parties are at 40 per cent, and the election will be won in between."

Most of all, he knew, it would be won with the kind of hard slogging in the boonies with which he won the convention, an approach that was perfectly suited to the by-election campaign in Central Nova.

Mulroney made two important decisions in June, 1983. One was to accept Elmer MacKay's offer of a seat; the other was not to set foot in his Parliament Hill office until it was rightfully his as a member. For the rest of the summer, his staff worked out of a small office adjacent to his fourth-floor suite in the Gold Key section of the Château Laurier, the same rooms from which John Turner would manage his takeover of the Liberal Party, and the government, a year later.

As for Mulroney, he left the capital at the end of June and would not return until two months later. He devoted the summer months of July and August to winning the hearts and votes of the people of Central Nova on the eastern shore of Nova Scotia, in New Glasgow, Stellarton, and other places he had known in his student days at Antigonish, over in Allan MacEachen's riding next door.

They fixed up a log cabin for him on the grounds of the Lodge at Pictou, and while the Mulroney kids settled in there for a good part of the summer, their parents went about the business of campaigning at every strawberry and church social in the riding. Mulroney enhanced his carpetbagger status by making light of it, as when he began his nomination address with the salutation, "fellow Nova Scotians," breaking up the place in laughter. And it meant, as he later said, meeting the voters "in their homes at their convenience." With their Nova Scotia common sense, they knew they would seldom see him again after August 29 and never again after the general election, but they knew the riding would always be well looked after. And with their highly developed Nova Scotia sense of fair play, they looked askance at the parade of Liberal Party wheelhorses and cabinet ministers, from Iona Campagnolo to Jean Chrétien, whose presence only enhanced Mulroney's status as well as adding a dash of interest to an otherwise mind-numbing succession of campaign outings.

When the polls closed on August 29, Mulroney waited out the formality of the count for more than an hour before going down to his New Glasgow committee room, formerly a Dominion store where it used to be mainly because of the meat. He actually lost the first poll that reported in from Tom Cleary's house in Roman Valley, but before long Mulroney was rolling up a big majority of 11,000 votes over his Liberal opponent, Alvin Sinclair, nearly tripling MacKay's 1980 majority. At that time, admittedly, the tide had been running against the Tories nearly everywhere in the country.

When he came to his committee room, the crowd of Scottish Canadians was singing "When Irish Eyes Are Smiling" about the same way you hear "O Canada" sung at Olympic Stadium in Montreal – not sure of the words, and not sure they should be seen doing this. "While I enjoyed that opening song," Mulroney began, "we Scots have our own preferences."

When the formalities of the victory speech had been observed and the obligations to the national television networks fulfilled, when the last hand had been squeezed and the last autograph signed, Mulroney stood in the back of the store in a dimly lit corner and talked with Gilles Lachance and a few of the boys from Baie Comeau who had chartered a couple of light aircraft and would fly home again at midnight. "We wouldn't miss this," said Blair Touchie, one of the boyhood friends.

At the other end of the country, as Mulroney stayed up to discover, the Tory tide was rising in Mission-Port Moody, an NDP riding that gave the first indications of a switch to the Tories. On his first swing out there, Mulroney had tried a line that would serve him well in future months. "A vote for Ed Broadbent is a vote for Pierre Trudeau," he would say, and then he would just sit back and watch the votes cross over to the Tory column in the polls. The apparent collapse of the NDP in the West, where it had won twenty-six of its thirty-one seats in 1980, was one of the keys to Mulroney's hopes of forming a majority government.

But on the night of August 29 he was more concerned, and more content, with his own showing in Central Nova, where his margin of victory exceeded even his own expectations. "How do you like them apples?" he said, glistening with perspiration as he stood in a disused refrigerator area in the back of the store. He knew that he wouldn't be coming back. He had practically told the voters as much and it hadn't done him any harm. After a press conference the next morning and a two-hour drive down to Halifax airport, it was on to Ottawa aboard an Air Canada 727 and a triumphant entry to the capital.

At nine o'clock the next morning, he would finally go up to Parliament Hill and claim the Opposition Leader's fourth-floor suite of offices.

"I don't know about this House stuff," Mulroney confided to a caller on the morning of Monday, September 12, a few hours before he was to take his walk down the green-carpeted centre aisle of the Commons. When he did so, arm-in-arm with George Hees and Erik Nielsen, his feet may not have touched the ground. With the galleries crowded by his family and friends, the chamber resounded with cheers and applause. "Listen to that," the ever-ebullient Hees whispered in his ear. "I've never heard it like this."

To Trudeau's words of welcome, Mulroney replied that he was "honoured by the thoughtfulness and generosity of his words today. I wait with bated breath for tomorrow."

That was as long as he had to wait for the Liberals to show their hand against him. The very next afternoon, Manitoba Liberal backbencher Bob Bockstael was on his feet asking the Prime Minister if the federal government intended to "reinforce its support," and "if so, in what manner," for the Manitoba NDP government's attempts to reinstate the constitutional status of the French language in that province, as provided by the Manitoba Act of 1870, but illegally withheld since the Manitoba Act of

1890. Since the first act had the force of a constitutional law and the second was merely a provincial statute, it was clear to the courts which was paramount. In Manitoba, Howard Pawley was striving toward a generous political solution with the Franco-Manitoban Society, an objective in which he was being frustrated at every turn by provincial Tory leader and former Premier Sterling Lyon.

Trudeau replied that he was "thinking perhaps of proposing a resolution" and would "probably seek an appointment" with the Leader of the Opposition to discuss a formulation agreeable to all parties. Trudeau had hardly sat down before Mulroney was on his feet, assuring him that "my door will be wide open," and, in a rather bizarre scene, they practically agreed right there on the floor that they would meet the next day. There's one thing about the language issue, Mulroney said later, and that's to "get it off the floor of the House of Commons, fast."

In the *Globe and Mail* the next day, the paper's Ottawa bureau chief, John Gray, suggested that the freshman Tory leader had tumbled naively into a trap set by the wily Liberals. Indeed, it had all the appearances of a no-win situation for him. As Mulroney often said later: "Here I am, not twenty-four hours in the place, I don't even know my way to the can, and the Liberals play their trump."

So it appeared at the time, for the Liberals were playing to an historic strength of their own party, minority rights, which was equally a chronic weakness of the Tories. On the available evidence, Mulroney would have trouble uniting his caucus around him on the issue, and he would have fits with the Tory party in Manitoba. Yet he was not caught as unawares as the Liberals might have thought. "Brian quarterbacked the Manitoba thing all the way," Charley McMillan later observed. "He was telling us down in Central Nova that we would have to be ready for this one."

The one thing Mulroney couldn't quite figure was Trudeau's attitude, whether he was sincerely motivated, as seemed likely on an issue he cared deeply about, or whether he was trying to set the new boy up. It would be nearly four weeks before Mulroney could assure himself of the Prime Minister's good intentions, which was just as well, because the Conservative leader needed all of that time to bring around the recalcitrant members of his caucus.

The first test of the Prime Minister's motives came when his office announced that it was at Mulroney's request that no photos were being permitted of the leaders meeting on the question in Trudeau's office. Mulroney angrily replied that this violated the confidential nature of the meeting, and when Trudeau quickly and personally apologized, Mulroney was assured that he was up to no mischief.

Privately, he acknowledged that he wanted no pictures taken of their meetings because of the bad reaction in the West when Peter Lougheed was seen clinking glasses with the Prime Minister to toast the 1981 federal-provincial oil accord. "Nobody," Mulroney said, "is going to catch me with a glass of champagne in my hand." He was not, in this instance, referring to the fact that he no longer took a drink.

If the Manitoba language question was loaded with evident dangers for any Conservative leader, it also afforded Mulroney the opportunity to quickly exert control over his caucus and to seek the high road for himself where the voters were concerned, especially those minority constituencies that had for decades vouch-safed the Liberals hold on power. The Tory caucus had long been known as a den of stubborn individualists who resisted or refused to bend to the discipline of party politics, especially on touchy questions like the language issue. As Robert Stanfield and Joe Clark could have told him, and as Mulroney would soon discover for himself, some of them had to be dragged kicking and screaming into the late twentieth century.

But in this regard, the freshman leader would prove to be quite unyielding in his determination to have the unanimous support of his caucus. And the caucus, determined to support its new leader, was inclined to go along with his support of an all-party resolution. That being said, there were a couple of backbenchers who indicated to him that they would find it difficult to go along.

"I'm sorry the caucus can't be unanimous," one recalcitrant MP told Mulroney in a visit to his office the day before the vote.

"My caucus will be unanimous," Mulroney replied. The man went away badly shaken and, in the end, did Mulroney's bidding.

As for finding the high road, the fact that the resolution was to be adopted without debate and without division gave Mulroney an opportunity to make a memorable maiden address on an issue he cared deeply about, with no briefing and no fiddling with a speechwriter's draft. He might be fuzzy on economic questions, unsure of himself on western issues such as the Crowsnest Pass Rate debate, or left searching to find his own ground on the peace and security issue while Trudeau went off on his globe-girdling peace initiative. But the language question was something he knew by heart, in his heart. Even Charley McMillan, who generally worked up policy and texts for important occasions, left his boss alone on this one. "You can't write this speech for him," McMillan was saying on the morning of October 6. "He's got to do it himself, and it has to come from in here."

Indeed, once Mulroney agreed to the resolution and assured himself the previous day that his caucus was onside, he could settle down for the evening at his temporary residence at Kingsmere and go over a final draft of his maiden address.

"When I was very young in Baie Comeau," he began somewhat nervously in French the next afternoon, "we were taught at the local school the very sad story of some of our francophone brothers outside Quebec. Even at that young age we knew that an injustice had been committed in Manitoba. We did not know why or how, but we knew that certain basic rules – which we as Quebecers, anglophones as well as francophones, could benefit from – had been broken."

The Hansard records the words, but it does not capture the moment of the occasion. For the first time in memory, the leaders of the two major parties in the House of Commons agreed on the idea of country, on the bargain of Confederation, on the necessity of righting an historic wrong.

They set about saying so in different ways, Trudeau in an intellectual address on the need "to ensure that the Constitution will be obeyed," Mulroney speaking "in a spirit of conciliation." There was nothing to be gained by comparing the two speeches, for they were as strikingly different in style as cubist and impressionist paintings, one to be admired for its bold lines and the other for its rich array of colours.

Trudeau's performance, on what he referred to, "not without emotion," as possibly "the most important day of my life as a parliamentarian," was simply awesome. He spoke without a note, since the constitutional question was one for which he needed no papers. As he took the House through the sorry history of the Manitoba episode, there were some people in the visitors' gallery who were weeping.

There was still a great clearing of throats when Mulroney rose, with his notes on a stack of green parliamentary briefs. If he was familiar with the minority rights issue, he was equally on the familiar personal territory of trying to win people over. Also, he had an opportunity to remind the wise guys along press row that he had been to law school and was not totally untutored in matters pertaining to the Constitution. Finally, he was able to demonstrate that he had a sense of history, which formed his idea of the country.

"I want to say a word to the people of Manitoba," he said at the mid-point of his twenty-minute address. "I am aware of the problems that have arisen in many of your communities. We do not seek today to make them more difficult." He continued:

The issue before us today is also one of simple justice. There is no painless way to proceed. There is no blame to be apportioned. There are no motives to be impugned. There is only the sanctity of minority rights. There is no obligation more compelling and no duty more irresistible in Canada than to ensure that our minorities, linguistic and otherwise, live at all times in conditions of fairness and justice.

He went on to quote his friend Robert Cliche, quoting Felix-Antoine Savard: " 'Happy are those men and those people who get along together.' "

Mulroney might have remembered that quotation from the back cover of the Cliche report. But he knew from memory the quotation with which he concluded. Gaining a measure of confidence as he came to the end, he referred from memory to American Justice Learned Hand and "the spirit of liberty," which "knows that not even a sparrow falls to the earth unheeded." Sitting across the way, Pierre de Bané recognized the flourish of the orator he had known in law school all those years ago and immediately sent over a note of congratulations.

It was a promising debut for Mulroney's parliamentary career. For the moment, he had defused the dangers to his own caucus and his own Conservative clientele; and he was making a statesmanlike impression on the Liberal constituency of linguistic and ethnic minorities. The trap, if indeed it was a trap, had been neatly sidestepped by the quarry. Or, as his friend Francis Fox put it from the other side of the floor: "Trap? Some fucking trap."

In at least one other respect, Mulroney's parliamentary debut was somewhat less auspicious. It involved a seemingly routine question on Atlantic freight subsidies, and could the minister please assure the House they would be maintained. "I would be very pleased to answer the question of the honourable Leader of the Opposition," Lloyd Axworthy replied in their little exchange of September 21. "However, his question is about seven hours too late because this morning I was in Moncton and met with members of the Atlantic Transportation Commission and told them that the subsidies that are provided to the Maritimes are to be maintained."

Mulroney did his best to recover with thanks "for the smallest of blessings," but he had taken it on the chin, and he knew it. Leaving the office in his limousine at the end of the day, he rolled down the window for a word with CBC correspondent Jason Moscovitz. "I screwed up today, didn't I?" he said. "It won't happen again."

Clearly, he didn't yet know about "this House stuff," as he had called it. His first mistake with Axworthy had been in asking a question of a minister rather than the Prime Minister, when common sense and custom dictate that the Leader of the Opposition asks a question of a minister only if the P.M. is not in the House or dumps it off into a minister's lap. Once this had been pointed out to him, by one of his friends on the other side, Mulroney did not make that mistake again.

In the beginning he also occasionally lapsed from the parliamentary language of addressing his questions in the third person, slipping into second-person salutations in asides across the floor. One controversial instance occurred during Mulroney's second-day exchange with Trudeau on the Manitoba question, when he was on the receiving end of some persistent heckling by Health Minister Monique Bégin, who urged him to get to the point. "Accouchez," she shouted across the floor, literally meaning, "give birth."

"I'm getting there, Monique," he said, interrupting his own question. "And speaking of giving birth, when's it due?"

He later insisted that he was not referring to Mme. Bégin's ample proportions but to her intention to bring in a new Medicare Act, which Mulroney had already decided to support as a means of sidestepping another trap. The Hansard cleared up the controversy by cleaning up his reply. But Mulroney was quickly discovering that the floor of the House of Commons was not a friendly debating society but a place where he could get cut up pretty badly if he wasn't careful.

Until very recently, he had also been a consumer of, rather than a participant in, parliamentary proceedings, and he shared most viewers' low opinion of what went on there, with all the hooting and howling back and forth. Perhaps naively, he thought he could make a modest contribution to improving the quality of debate by raising the level of civility. He specifically instructed his caucus members to stop heckling and gesticulating in the House and so to project a more positive image. In this respect, he meant to lead by example. But he soon found out things don't work that way. "I've had the wrong mindset," he said after a couple of weeks in the House. And he noticed a column that Richard Gwyn had written, pointing out that he was not a man of the House. "Gwyn's right," he said, "I'm not a man of the House. But I'm gonna become one."

If Mulroney was admittedly a parliamentary novice, he was not without political instincts of his own, as the Liberals would discover in the month of November.

Almost gone but not forgotten was a government bill in the Senate to limit provincial agencies to a 10 per cent share of interprovincial transportation and pipeline companies. It was also known as the CPR bill, since its aim was to protect the Montreal-based transportation giant, Canadian Pacific, from the acquisitive designs of Quebec's multi-billion-dollar pension fund, the Caisse de dépôt. The bill had ignited a controversy in Quebec, not only as a federal power play but also in symbolic terms, since the CPR was one of the last bastions of the old English business establishment in Montreal, and the Caisse represented the new muscle of French power on the Rue St. Jacques.

Mulroney decided to oppose S-31 on strategic grounds. First, he would improve his currency in Quebec with the intellectuals without being accused of flirting with the nationalists, a burden Joe Clark had carried on his back in the English-speaking provinces. Then Mulroney could say he was only looking out for the interests of pensioners and defending the principle of an open market. Most of all, he hoped to sow some confusion and consternation among *les rouges*.

First he had to win over his caucus, and then he had to deal with some heavy lobbying from CP executives who were making the rounds of the Hill. Winning over the caucus was easy, even though some of them had natural affinities to the interests of big business. "Brian told them that S-31 and the Caisse had the same cultural and symbolic importance in Quebec as the Crow Rate in the West," said Charley McMillan. The caucus went along willingly enough. As for the CP lobbying effort, Mulroney made his views brutally clear to one top executive who visited him in Ottawa: "Don't get between me and my caucus on this." And caucus members were instructed to inform Mulroney's office if they had been lobbied by CP.

As for the Liberals, Mulroney waited for two things: until Trudeau was out of town on the start of his peace mission, and until a Thursday afternoon, six days before the next Liberal caucus.

For Joe Clark, who had been proud to say that he understood the aspirations of Quebecers, the renewed S-31 uproar proved, as Mulroney had suggested to him, "a way to get back into things."

For Roch LaSalle and Mulroney, it proved to be a field day.

269

Here they were in the absence of the Prime Minister, going after Consumer Affairs Minister Judy Erola with questions as to whether the government intended to revive S-31 and bring it forward to the House. This was the reverse of the Ottawa norm. Tory members were asking questions in French of a minister who could answer only in English. For several nights running, the story played big on Radio-Canada's *Téléjournal* newscast. The Liberals were getting murdered on the issue, and at the next weekly caucus meeting the Quebec backbenchers screamed for relief. Erola and the Quebec leadership made it quite clear to them that the absent Prime Minister's wish was that the bill come forward. For their part, the Quebec backbenchers made it equally clear that on this one they couldn't and wouldn't follow. "If the party of big business doesn't give a damn about the CPR," as Francis Fox later put it, "why the hell should we?"

Before many more days had passed, Erola announced that the bill would die on the order paper at the end of the session. Mulroney had gone into a situation, at no risk to himself, and won big. At his Montreal fund-raising dinner in December, the preliminaries to his speech included a giant-screen video of Mulroney in the House, lambasting the government on S-31. Sitting not far away were a group of CP executives who must have felt like climbing under the table. "We're at table 31," said CP president Bill Stinson, somewhat chagrined, but still making light of the situation.

After the S-31 episode, Mulroney decided to open an unusual front against the government for the manner in which Revenue Canada did business with its clients, the taxpayers of Canada. This was a novel strategy, since Revenue Canada normally generated about as much controversy as a lawn bowling match. Even long-serving inmates of press row would have difficulty naming the revenue ministers in successive Trudeau cabinets, and to the extent that many knew of the incumbent, Pierre Bussières, they often mixed him up with his Quebec colleague, Charles Lapointe.

But in the days on either side of the Christmas recess, Bussières became an overnight celebrity as the methods of his department came under the closest scrutiny. In the Commons on the last day before the 1983 Christmas break, Mulroney went after the Prime Minister for assurances that the Revenue Department would treat taxpayers "fairly and courteously at all times." It was a good issue for the Tories to get onto – after all, you wouldn't want your daughter to marry a tax collector, and the usual targets of revenue audits and reviews were small business people, doctors, lawyers, dentists, and the accountants who did their taxes.

These professional people, clustered in the cities, fit the profile of the upwardly mobile Liberal voter who would never consider voting for the Tories. This was a way of getting their attention. Before long it became the kind of story that fed itself, with anonymous tips and leaks to the Tories and the press. As Mulroney already knew, democracy sometimes came wrapped in a plain brown envelope. The revenue story stayed in the news over the winter and ended with Trudeau finally replacing Deputy Minister Bruce MacDonald. As for Bussières, who was portrayed as a kind of Oilcan Harry, he had more attention in Question Period for weeks than all his colleagues combined. He gave a spirited defence of his department's policies and practices, even if it was evident that, as with most ministers, he wasn't always told everything that was going on.

As the revenue story was playing itself out in February and March of 1984, the Manitoba question was heating up again. With the Pawley government reeling under a Tory filibuster in the Manitoba legislature, Prime Minister Trudeau decided to press for another all-party resolution supporting the Manitoba government's doomed initiative to extend French-language services in the province. This time Trudeau was able to obtain that agreement within a day of negotiations with the Tories and NDP and brought another resolution forward on Friday, February 24, the last day of the session before a scheduled mid-winter break. Mulroney had been in Toronto on party business and was slated to fly to West Palm Beach on Thursday night. Instead, he found himself on the last plane back to Ottawa. As soon as the wheels were up, he had a pen and paper out and began writing the speech he would deliver the next morning. He finished it back in Ottawa and got to bed in the middle of the night.

In his speech, which *Globe and Mail* columnist Jeffrey Simpson called "superb," Mulroney again tried to reconcile the different ideas of the country, the bargain of the two founding peoples at Confederation versus the melting pot of western settlement. "That precious and fragile dimension of linguistic duality which Macdonald and Cartier saw as an indispensable characteristic of nationhood," he observed, "was submerged by growing demographic realities of the new West. The country grew; the English language became more dominant and ultimately more pervasive. This was the silent and inexorable toll of history. In my judgement, it emerged less through contrivance than through the irresistible effect of overwhelming numbers."

271

With that said, he finally flew off to Florida for what he imagined would be a good ten-day rest. He hoped to spend some time with his younger son Mark, to take him over to the Montreal Expos spring training camp at West Palm Beach. It was to be a short-lived holiday. The following Wednesday, February 29, Pierre Trudeau announced his retirement in the way everyone knew he would, when it was least expected, with Parliament shut down, with the press and caucus out of town, and, as it happened, with Brian Mulroney on one beach in Florida and John Turner on another in Jamaica.

Mulroney's private view of the Trudeau retirement question had been much the same as the one he expressed publicly, that the four-term Prime Minister was the best man to lead the Liberals into the election and, needless to say, the best man for him to run against. As far back as the leadership campaign, Mulroney's private guess was that Trudeau might stay to "take the defeat" for the Liberals, but he also knew that it was not Trudeau's style to go out a loser. Among his prospective successors, Mulroney knew there were only two in the game – Turner and Jean Chrétien. Turner clearly represented more of a threat to the Mulroney Conservatives in Ontario and the West, but in a different sense it was Chrétien who worried them more.

Mulroney had staked his political life on winning seats in Quebec, and against Chrétien that would have been very tough indeed. There were other attributes about Chrétien that Mulroney would just as soon not have to worry about in a campaign. He was a fighter with a big heart, and the voters liked him. Moreover, he was a professional politician capable of running a campaign at once all-out and error-free, as the three-month Liberal leadership demonstrated in the spring of 1984. Though the Chrétien candidacy remained an odds-against proposition, he had grown significantly from March to June while Turner kept making unforced errors.

Turner's early statements on minority language rights in general, and on the Manitoba situation in particular, were sufficient evidence of this. "On the Manitoba question," Turner said at his opening March 16 news conference, "I support the spirit of the parliamentary resolution, but I think we have to recognize that what is at issue here is a provincial initiative, and that a solution will have to be provincial, and I would hope that it would be resolved by the political process and not by the judicial process." In an appearance that same evening on *The Journal*, Turner told the CBC's Barbara Frum that "you exercise what persuasive influence you can. But the jurisdiction remains provincial, just as it does for language in Quebec."

Mulroney was privately appalled that Turner would play semantics, if not politics, with a tinderbox issue. But the Conservative leader also saw it as a political opportunity for himself with the staunch Liberal clienteles of linguistic and ethnic minority groups. As he later said privately: "John Turner's got the Liberal Party on the wrong side of minority rights." And if he could, Mulroney meant to keep him there.

For starters, after months of temporizing over what to do about his own Manitoba situation, Mulroney finally decided to go to Winnipeg on March 29. It was a risk, and not the kind he normally likes to run, since he hates to be embarrassed. Yet the idea of a showdown also appealed to him. He was not unmindful of precedents, such as the time Lester Pearson took his idea for a Canadian flag to a Canadian Legion convention, was unmercifully booed, but won the country over at the same time. When Mulroney turned up at the downtown Holiday Inn in Winnipeg, a large and agitated crowd of Manitobans was waiting for him, some party loyalists, some dissidents, and some rednecks, such as the man Mulroney couldn't have paid enough to call him a frog-lover.

Nervous at the outset, Mulroney tried to strike a conciliatory tone while holding firm to his idea of the country and his moral obligations as a national leader:

> I stand before you tonight where the founder of this party, Sir John A. Macdonald, and his Conservative government, stood in 1870 when the Manitoba Act was passed, ensuring linguistic equality in the new province of Manitoba. It is my fundamental belief that, as it was his, that real national unity will never be achieved until French-speaking Canadians living outside Quebec enjoy no less rights than English-speaking Canadians in my native province. That was Macdonald's message 114 years ago. It is my message tonight. . . . The goal of language guarantees is not to make all Canadians bilingual – to force people to become something they are not.
>
> The purpose of language guarantees is to ensure that English- and French-speaking Canadians can be themselves, that they can live their lives, communicate with their governments and with each other in one or the other of Canada's two official languages.

This notion of the bargain of Confederation was essentially the same as the one Mulroney had put forward in his undergraduate thesis a quarter of a century earlier. What the Liberals may not have realized in opening the Pandora's box of language the previous September was that they were also opening a door of opportunity for Mulroney, furnishing him with a unique opportunity to enunciate his ideas of country, as well as to take firm control of his caucus.

The language issue was one on which Mulroney could deal from sure instinct, and since he never deviated from his line it gave him an opportunity to demonstrate that there was substance to go with the matinée profile and the sonorous voice. Above all, it was one issue on which no one could accuse him of being fuzzy.

As for his caucus, Mulroney had to acknowledge early on that "they've been pretty good to me on this." With only a couple of foot-dragging exceptions, the Tories were remarkably supportive of their new leader, perhaps because he was their new leader, and they were riding high in the polls. It was as if they were determined, for once, not to screw things up. For his part, he was working hard through the fall of 1983 at winning them over. Once he had done that, by exercising his talent for the gentle art of stroking, he began to take them over.

There was a day in the fall of 1983 that Mulroney met with his shadow critics to review their position papers and critiques of government policy. Around the table they went. One after another Mulroney said the reports weren't good enough. He told them as a group that if they expected to be ministers when the Tories took office, they had better start shaping up. One senior MP, a veteran of the Diefenbaker wars, called it "the day Brian took over the caucus."

Slowly he was learning that the parliamentary wing was a real power in the party, something he had tried to go around in his 1976 leadership bid. "You can't lead without the caucus, I know that now," he said in December of 1983. And if he wanted to unite the Tory party, it was also true in this pre-electoral period that the Tory party wanted to be united. "We've been on this leadership thing since Dief's time," he said that same December evening. "It's bankrupted the party and left our people exhausted from fighting one another all the time."

For himself, he was looking to two elections and, presumably, two terms in office to achieve his agenda. "Two terms and out" was the way he put it, long enough to get things done. "You've got to do the job and get out," he said. "Nobody will have to ask me to leave twice, I can tell you that. You'll have the biggest parade of moving vans you've ever seen and, pow, right back to Montreal."

And what if he didn't make it, in the 1984 election, or perhaps the one after that. "If we don't make it, we don't make it," he had told his wife.

In the summer of 1984, he was about to find out.

20

CAMPAIGN '84: ONE BIG ROLL OF THE DICE

B elow his fourth-floor windows on the last Wednesday in June, technicians were rehearsing the Canada Day show. In his own mind, Brian Mulroney was rehearsing another show that could begin as early as the next week, and certainly anytime after that.

Considering the task that lay ahead, whose outcome no one could foretell with any certainty, Mulroney looked uncommonly relaxed. In his shirtsleeves, he sauntered rather than paced back and forth behind his desk in the corner of his office. None of the telltale signs of Mulroney's tenseness were apparent: the fidgeting with his fingernails, the brushing back of a comma of his hair. It was nearly three months since he had quit smoking, and he had just gone for nearly an hour and a half without a single cup of coffee. For more than an hour, he had sunk himself into one of the four cream-coloured chairs arranged in front of his desk, talking about his wife and kids. The two air conditioners in his windows, both going full blast, kept out the kind of special Ottawa humidity that causes people less fastidious than Mulroney to wish they had brought a fresh shirt to the office.

Mulroney was unperturbed and unpersuaded by rumours that the Liberals, riding high in the polls after their leadership convention, were heading into an early election.

In these waning days of June, and the dying days of the Trudeau administration, Mulroney was underwhelmed by what he was seeing of the Prime Minister-designate, John Turner. Mulroney thought Turner had shown bad judgement during the leadership campaign and was showing it again as he prepared to form a government. Why, he wondered with no malice, had Turner decided to hang on to all his corporate directorships until his swearing-in three days from now on June 30? Why was he leaving himself open to allegations that secret government papers were being placed in the hands of a man who still had corporate connections? And why, as Mulroney did not have to point out, was Turner doing nothing to shake the Bay Street image?

Even more to the point, perhaps, why was Turner talking about downsizing his cabinet by as many as ten ministers, shutting out many of his own hopeful supporters as well as holdovers from the Trudeau regime? All this would achieve would be a lot of bitter disappointment, with those who were left out or cut out sitting around Ottawa bars in gin-soaked bitching sessions about what a mistake the Liberal Party had made going with Turner. This wasn't the time to reduce the size of the cabinet, it was a time to expand it, get the limousines rolling, get the JetStars out on the ramp, keep everyone happy, and have everyone working like hell to win the new leader's favour and consideration for cabinet if they won the election. That Turner eventually went with a cabinet of twenty-eight members, plus himself, instead of the twenty-four one of his aides had talked about in the last days of the leadership campaign was one indication of the pressures he came under from the party establishment.

That he brought in only five new faces was at once an indication that he was bowing to the pressures for an early election and an admission that it was not a cabinet of change. This much was clear four days before the new government was sworn in, from a newspaper photograph of Turner's top supporters strolling the day before in the backyard of his Forest Hill home in Toronto.

There were Herb Gray and Marc Lalonde, both veteran holdovers from the Trudeau administration, both inextricably linked with the old regime, as were André Ouellet and Gerald Regan, also present at Turner's little garden party. Mulroney thought this demonstrated an appalling lack of judgement. The picture played right into his argument that Turner represented cosmetic as opposed to real change.

When his streamlined cabinet of twenty-eight ministers was sworn in on June 30, Turner acknowledged that it was a "phase-one reorganization only," but equally maintained that it was "a massive reorganization," with thirteen members of his predecessor's cabinet "not returning," even though the downsized structure permitted him to promote only five backbenchers.

This was indicative of a couple of things, first that the professionals in the party establishment had prevailed on Turner not to tinker too much before the election, and second that the election was imminent. Turner had in hand the results of three polls, one of Quebec and two country-wide. The Quebec numbers, reported in by André Ouellet at the beginning of the week, evidently indicated little change from a Sorecom poll in early

June that showed the Liberals leading the Tories 62-28 in Quebec. The national samples, by Liberal Party pollster Martin Goldfarb and Turner's pollster Angus Reid, showed the Liberals with small but soft leads.

Moreover, their post-convention polling showed that the convention itself had changed little, that the Liberals may have already peaked in the leadership campaign. Their numbers fortified the arguments of the hawks for an early election, since things were unlikely to get better for Turner over the summer, and they could get a whole lot worse. The downward pressure on the Canadian dollar offered the prospect of a new round of inflation with consumers buying imported fruits and vegetables. The free fall of the dollar, to below 76 cents U.S. at the end of June, 1984, had already sparked a new flurry of higher interest rates. The Liberals were terrified of a trickle-down effect on public opinion if Turner waited until the fall.

In addition, there was the prospect of Turner standing on Parliament Hill on July 1 as an unelected Prime Minister, with a mandate from less than 2,000 of his countrymen, presiding over the pomp and ceremony of Canada Day. All this made a lot of important Liberals nervous, establishment Liberals who had supported Turner's bid for the leadership and who now argued for the quick and clean solution of a September election. Whether they were ahead six points or only three, it didn't matter. They had to go now.

In these last days of June, Mulroney thought Turner might still wait until the fall, or even get himself a seat in a by-election and try to govern over the winter, to the very end of the five-year mandate in 1985, to try and establish himself as Prime Minister in the voters' minds.

But in the event of an early call, Mulroney was convinced that the real desire for change would assert itself "the minute they drop the writ." His job, he knew, would be to present himself as the agent of real change in the country, while depicting Turner as yesterday's man, wedded to the government of the men strolling in his Forest Hill garden on that last Monday in June. "It's there," he had said a few weeks earlier. "Just as it was in the leadership campaign, it's there, unless I screw it up somehow."

Much was made in those weeks before the 1984 general election of the policy and personal affinities between the Liberal and Conservative leaders. Did it make any difference, some observers asked, as between Brian Turner and John Mulroney, between a liberal Conservative and conservative Liberal? The Tory high command was not unduly alarmed by this cloning factor since, all other things being equal, the voters might be expected to opt for change after more than twenty years of virtually uninterrupted Liberal rule.

The Tories hoped also to persuade the voters that there were some important differences of personality and outlook, of how each saw the country and from where. Against Turner, the Tories and Mulroney decided to play the card of the Boy from Baie Comeau against the candidate from Bay Street. There were two things to recommend this. No one had ever lost anything in Canada by running against Toronto. Second, Mulroney acknowledged that there was only one place to be from Baie Comeau, and that was on Champlain Street.

Turner, in his efforts to woo and win the West, and perhaps in a search for his own identity, announced on the day of his swearing in as Prime Minister that he would seek a seat in British Columbia. There were risks for both leaders in this approach. In finally deciding to run in Manicouagan, Mulroney was choosing a remote riding with no Conservative history and a reputation for militant trade unionism and strikes. The local MP, André Maltais, was a popular figure. Moreover, the biggest town in the riding was not Baie Comeau with its 8,000 voters, but Sept-Iles, with twice as many; Sept-Iles, the town that had taken the brunt of the Iron Ore layoffs and cutbacks during the 1981-82 downturn in the economy. It would be a difficult enough riding to win, even for a favourite son, more difficult still to defend later on. And every time he set foot on the North Shore during a campaign, he would be accused of trying to save his seat.

"My job is to get the party elected," he explained at the time. "Baie Comeau is famous now. I can't play it safe. I have to go home."

In his mind, Baie Comeau had become twinned with all the small cities and towns on the outskirts of Canada, out there in what he called "a country of small towns and big dreams." To the extent that the Baie Comeau connection helped him win in Timmins or Sault Ste. Marie or Thunder Bay, he was prepared to run the risk. Besides, if the party won nationally, the trend and the urge to go with an apparent winner should be enough to put him over in Manicouagan. If not, and the party won anyway, he could always get himself another seat. If not, and the Tories lost badly, he would be released from the purgatory of being leader of an opposition party with a history of devouring leaders who lost. As Mulroney said, he was putting it all "on one big roll of the dice."

Turner, on the other hand, was running in a province where

the Liberals hadn't won a single seat in the 1980 election. He hoped that his commitment to a Vancouver-area riding would help swing over the city and the province where voter volatility had achieved a state of the art.

For their part, the Tories hoped to portray Turner as a wandering, rootless soul, who came from everywhere and nowhere in the country. It was true that Turner came from all over the map: born in England; moved to British Columbia as a child; educated in Ottawa as his mother became an important public servant in the Mackenzie King era; back to British Columbia for his college years; off to England as a Rhodes Scholar at Oxford; then to Montreal for the practice of corporate law at Stikeman, Elliott; into the House of Commons from a Montreal riding and married to a girl from Winnipeg; then seven years as an Ottawa-area member and senior minister until 1975; the boardroom law years in Toronto until 1984; and, finally, his return as Prime Minister and a would-be westerner. That's a lot of places to come from. Mulroney had been a few places in his life, too, mostly in Montreal. But he never claimed to have come from anywhere else but Baie Comeau. It had shaped his outlook, about the pioneer spirit of Canada, the sacrifice and courage of parents, the need to develop Canada's great resource shelf on the outskirts of its small towns. From his own home town to Williams Lake, B.C., Mulroney had often said that "Canada is a network of Baie Comeaus."

Mulroney may have finally decided to run from Baie Comeau on the weekend of the Liberal leadership convention, as he watched the man from Bay Street win the day with the backing of the Liberal establishment. "You could almost see it in his eyes," said Charley McMillan, who was with Mulroney at Stornoway on the afternoon of June 16, along with Elmer MacKay and Sam Wakim, who had come down from Toronto as Mulroney's house guest for the weekend.

"I'm delighted," Mulroney told a caller after Turner's second-ballot victory over Jean Chrétien.

Mulroney was the first to acknowledge that it would have been easier running against Chrétien in Ontario, but that much more difficult in Quebec, where Mulroney had wagered everything on making some kind of breakthrough. As someone who knew him well observed, he had made his bets at Blue Bonnets Raceway in Montreal, not at Fort Erie in Ontario. Against Turner, he would at least not have to concern himself with the conflicting claims of another Quebec favourite son.

It was Chrétien's populist, politics-of-joy campaign that had added some real interest to the Liberal race, and in Quebec it was primarily Chrétien, in the view of the Mulroney brain trust, who was responsible for the ten-point Liberal surge and the corresponding Tory slide to a 62-28 deficit in a June Sorecom survey of Quebec voters' preferences. In the general election, Mulroney would be coming home with the door open wide enough for himself to walk in and, he hoped, to bring at least a dozen Quebec MPs with him.

"I can't tell you what it's going to be," he said with a glance out his office window that June day. "Except that it's going to be somewhere in the teens."

That would be enough, if it proved out, to deliver on his promises. For the rest, he liked to look at election night unfolding from West to East instead of the other way round. With a virtual sweep of the West's eighty seats and a majority of Ontario's ninety-five, he would hit the Ottawa River coming the other away with a minority government and hoped to do no worse than break even in Atlantic Canada's thirty-two seats. Quebec, then, would make the difference for a majority government, one way or the other.

One way or the other. That might yet prove to be the factor on which the election would turn: the party that was able to persuade the voters it was going to form a national government might emerge as the winner.

Mulroney had been back in the boonies during the three months of the Liberal leadership campaign. It was a good regional strategy, well timed for him. While the national media were obsessively covering the Liberal leadership, looking for a second ballot, looking for a third man, Mulroney would be in southern Ontario one week, northern Ontario the next, and getting big regional coverage. As with the leadership campaign of a year earlier, the second boonies tour allowed him to open his show out of town, before he got to the Broadway of the campaign. It allowed him to cut here, tighten there, try out another number somewhere else along the way.

Just as in the Conservative leadership campaign, hardly anyone was paying attention in the spring of 1984 as he covered 25,000 miles back and forth across the country. He was getting into a lot of places that he wouldn't get back to during the general election, and he was seeing a lot of people. The people were mostly the rank and file, like those who paid $30 a head for dinner and wine in the cavernous airplane hangar of a room at the base of the Husky Tower in Niagara Falls on the first Friday in May. Mulroney performed his usual routine, speaking before dinner and dividing up the hall with Mila during the meal. By the time the evening was over, every one of the nearly 1,000 people in the room had shaken hands, had a word, introduced a relative or business partner, and had their picture taken with the Conservative leader or his wife. It was something he had learned from Daniel Johnson: keep your own workers happy.

Whenever Turner decided to go to Government House for his writ, Mulroney's plan was to go to Central Nova to pay his thanks to his constituents and then head on to Baie Comeau to announce his candidacy in Manicouagan. From then on, as Charley McMillan observed over the July 1st weekend, the tour would be "very much oriented to the big cities."

With his boss, McMillan had worked out a policy agenda that he compared to a triangle, with economic issues at the base, social policy on one side, and federal-provincial relations and foreign policy on the other. The economic base was to support the two sides. On the foreign affairs side, for example, the Tories would produce a trade package meticulously put together by Sinclair Stevens that promised to throw off half a million new jobs. And on what McMillan termed "the social side of job creation," the Conservatives would bid to ease the climate of disorientation and discontent among the country's young people.

During the Canada Day weekend, McMillan was waiting for an analysis of the Tory economic platform from Data Resources, the outfit that had worked up the study of Mulroney's productivity and research planks at the Conservative convention.

The preliminary findings of the 1984 study – never released because they weren't needed – suggested that the Conservative economic package would produce 800,000 new jobs over a full term in office. It was a bit short of what McMillan was looking for. He had been hoping that Mulroney would be able to promise the magic figure of one million new jobs over his first term of office. One million was the kind of number that stuck in people's minds, as did Robert Bourassa's campaign pledge to create 100,000 jobs in Quebec back in 1970. And figures that stuck in people's minds, Mulroney knew, could affect their attitudes. Once when negotiating with his employees at Iron Ore, he had instructed his team to work out a final offer that added up to $5,000 in increased pay and benefits during the term of the proposed contract. He then went on the Sept-Iles radio station to describe the offer, and watched with satisfaction as the women of the town practically drove their husbands back to work.

McMillan was working on something else that long weekend – a draft text for Saskatchewan Premier Grant Devine to close

Mulroney's two-day western caucus July 4-5, which was intended to fortify the Tory claims as the party of the West. The Saskatchewan meeting was meant to be the first of three regional caucuses during the campaign, to be followed by meetings in Quebec and the Atlantic region. They were intended to signify the regional character of the Conservative campaign.

Each caucus was keyed to regional issues: in the West, energy, agriculture, forestry, and western transportation; in the Atlantic region, offshore, the fishery, and the imperative of addressing regional economic disparities; in Quebec, where *les petites et moyennes entreprises* and youth unemployment were special concerns, they would announce a small business program and an incentives package for the country's half-million unemployed youth, fully a third of Canada's unemployed in the summer of 1984, a statistical fact to which Mulroney would refer as a "tragic new dimension" of the country's unemployment problems. All these announcements, though of an admittedly regional character, had a national importance. The idea, as McMillan said, was to obtain immediate play in the national media and wait for a trickle-down effect in the regions.

One thing Mulroney wouldn't do was put a cost on many planks in his platform. It was a game the Canadian media played at every election. First, get the leader to say how much his program is going to cost, and then ask him where he's going to find the money.

Mulroney wouldn't play. He would point out that all these things were subject to economic variables, such as interest and exchange rates, as well as levels of unemployment. In Halifax in early August, he would seize on the Conference Board's revised, gloomy economic forecast for the remainder of the year as supporting evidence for this argument. He would fall back on the argument of his July 9 news conference, as the election was called, that the Tories would cost their programs as best they could, with the limited resources available to an opposition as compared with the sophisticated computer forecasting available to a government. Finally, he would receive an incredible gift from John Turner in their July 24 debate in French, when the Liberal leader said he hoped to cut "milliards et des milliards de dollars" of government waste. As Turner uttered the words, Mulroney made a mental note to check the transcript, to make sure Turner had said what he thought he had said. Sure enough, he had, and Mulroney was able to say he would pay for his program with the "billions and billions" saved from government waste whose existence was acknowledged by his opponent.

But that was three weeks away as he left Prince Albert for Regina on July 5, and there was another bad Gallup on the way that night. Gallup's post-convention poll gave the Liberals a 49-38 lead, enough for a majority. Mulroney had to pick himself up again, but by the next morning, as he went down to face the assembled media hordes in his hotel lobby, he was full of that cockeyed optimism of his.

"Boy, I'll tell you," he announced as he walked into a room where Charley McMillan was talking on a phone, "you're gonna see the biggest goddamn upset in history."

The Gallup probably clinched a summer election. It remained only for Turner to fly off to London to see the Queen and to ask Her Majesty to re-schedule her Canadian visit to the fall, assuming she was still determined to cancel her July 14-27 tour in the face of the election Turner had all but decided to call for September 4. So it was that Turner, arriving back in Ottawa on July 8, met one final time with his top aides and decided to go ahead with an election call the next afternoon.

"This Parliament has run its course," Turner declared the following afternoon. As the Thirty-second Parliament expired, Turner granted deathbed indulgences to seventeen Liberal MPs. In doing so, Turner was keeping a bargain he had made with the devil, in this instance Pierre Trudeau. The retiring Prime Minister made a raft of appointments before leaving office and struck a deal in writing with his successor to make the others so that Turner could keep his parliamentary majority. Turner insisted he had two legal opinions that, without a majority, he might not have been invited by the Governor General to form a government. But it is also just as likely that in the week leading up to his swearing in, Turner was still undecided about a summer election and wanted to retain the option of meeting Parliament in the fall, in which case he would have needed his majority to control the timing of an election call.

"There's not a Grit left in town," Mulroney said at his press conference on the heels of Turner's at the theatre of the National Press Building in Ottawa. "They've all gone to Grit heaven."

He knew a ready-made election issue when he saw one, and his high command was not long in getting back the doorstep reaction from voters who were appalled at nominations such as Bryce Mackasey as Canadian ambassador to Portugal. Altogether, the appointments of hacks and has-beens added up to $84 million in patronage, which Charley McMillan turned into one of his "bullets" for Mulroney, figuring it out to be the equivalent of a

$70-million Christmas bonus for senior citizens on the Guaranteed Income Supplement.

But Mulroney temporarily booted away his advantage on the issue a few days later when he wandered toward the back of his campaign plane and got into a bull session with reporters. Mulroney naively assumed the discussion was off the record, and at some point in the conversation stipulated as much. No reporters took notes and no cassettes were rolling. Mulroney said he felt sorry for Mackasey, that in similar circumstances he might be in there himself at the public trough. And referring to himself, he said: "There's no whore like an old whore," an expression friends had heard him use hundreds of times in private. But when it turned up in the *Ottawa Citizen* on July 16, the reference was clearly to Mackasey.

By then, the issue wasn't whether the *Citizen* reporter had broken the ground rules, or even whether Mulroney should continue to treat the matter as an off-the-record conversation that had never occurred. It became a question of how to cut his losses on an incident that reinforced his trust problems with the voters. Largely at the urging of campaign co-chairman Norm Atkins and tour manager Pat Kinsella, Mulroney decided to make a clean breast of it, take the heat for a couple of days, and hope his apology as well as the issue would eventually rebound to his credit.

So, in Sault Ste. Marie on July 18, an ashen-faced Mulroney, with his wife at his side, said he now regretted his remarks, even though they had not been intended for publication and had been meant in a joshing spirit. It was a good lesson in the remorseless discipline of a national campaign. If Mulroney wished to control the agenda, and he did, he would have to stay at the front of the plane, where he belonged.

"I got sandbagged," he said the day the story appeared in the Ottawa paper. "It won't happen again."

Norm Atkins certainly hoped so. His one concern about Mulroney as a client was that he was sometimes a little too cocky. A little humility, Atkins thought, wouldn't hurt him. The one thing Atkins was used to was having his political clients behave in a thoroughly professional manner, and much of the time that meant doing his bidding.

He and Pat Kinsella were the two principal acquisitions from Ontario's vaunted Big Blue Machine. Atkins was the architect of four Bill Davis victories in Ontario and had run successful branch-plant operations for Dick Hatfield in New Brunswick and Brian Peckford in Newfoundland. Kinsella, who had done Bill Bennett's seamless 1983 re-election campaign in British Columbia, came on board the Mulroney campaign as the tour manager. There was no question that he was in charge. When they had to make an early decision between chartering a DC-9 or a Boeing 727, Kinsella did not hesitate. He went, as Pierre Trudeau used to say, for the Cadillac. Though the 124-seat Boeing had 30 per cent more seating than the Air Canada DC-9, it was also 50 per cent more expensive to operate. But the job was to get the story out, and thus to get as many media representatives as possible on board as demands for places on the tour crowded up toward the end of the campaign.

At the outset of the election, Atkins believed it would be won or lost in the campaign, in a range from a Liberal minority over to a Conservative majority. In a close election, he thought a good organization could make a difference on the ground, especially in Ontario, where the enthusiastic participation of Bill Davis wouldn't hurt, either. "You can't win with an organization, but you can lose without one," Atkins observed as he sat in his office at Conservative campaign headquarters in Ottawa. "Apart from the leader's own performance," he continued, "the only measurement the voters have is the ability of our organization to perform."

If nothing else, the Tories were ready on the ground in all regions of the country, even in Quebec. Bernard Roy, as Quebec chairman, had been careful to observe Mulroney's dictum that since the party had no organization in at least half the Quebec ridings, they should recruit quality local candidates who came with their own network of friends who could serve as a ready-made organization. So they tried to recruit credit union managers, directors of junior colleges, heads of school boards, service club presidents, and the like. It was tough going against a century of Liberal tradition. There was also a chicken-and-egg aspect. They wouldn't expect to attract presentable candidates unless they were doing well in the polls, and they couldn't pick up at the local level without good candidates.

In Ontario, though, in that long stretch of key ridings down the 401 highway from Oshawa to Windsor, even in northern Ontario where they were chronically weak, the federal Tories were ready for the election. Not only had Davis loaned out key operatives to Mulroney, the Ontario Premier had put a whip on his Queen's Park caucus, instructing them that they should be available to campaign, even when up in the cottage country of Lake Huron and Georgian Bay. Finally, he had written the Ontario party's rank and file, urging them to get out and work for the national campaign. All this was a far cry from the 1980 campaign, when it was all Joe Clark could do to get a cup of coffee at Queen's Park when he went hat in hand to the Premier, who had spent the first half of the winter campaign at his condominium in Fort Lauderdale.

But Davis wasn't simply going to be onside, he was going to be on tour.

"The week of August 6," Atkins said with a glance at the tour calendar on his office wall, "he'll be on for four days." Four days through southern Ontario – where the Davis philosophy that bland works could be seen in action, as it was a couple of weeks earlier during an appearance for Mulroney at the Hamilton Chamber of Commerce. At that time he noted that some familiar faces had come from near and far, "some from as far away as Brampton." The groans from the audience indicated that they loved it as much as one of Johnny Carson's bad monologues.

"Billy Davis is going to work his ass off," Atkins said. As Atkins spoke, late in the afternoon of July 25, the leaders' English-language debate was only three hours away.

"Tonight's important," he said, as was the previous night, when Mulroney had obviously outperformed Turner. It wasn't just Mulroney's superior command of French, it was his sense of the sensibilities, what Quebec advertising guru Jacques Bouchard had called "les chords sensibles," of Quebecers. Bouchard had listed thirty-six of these right chords in a best-selling book. Mulroney found a few more in the July 24 French-language debate.

Mulroney had thrown down the challenge for the debates at his July 9 news conference, a cause for some dismay to the New Democratic brain trusters, who had been hoping the call for debates would be seen as Ed Broadbent's initiative when he followed Mulroney to the press theatre. The Liberals, understandably, were in no hurry for any debates, but neither could they duck out altogether. It was not to their advantage to have Turner and Mulroney appear together, especially in a television studio, least of all in French.

Turner's advantage was in appearing prime ministerial and giving the impression of competence. He could do that easily enough in his Langevin Block office or simply by meeting his cabinet. But he needed time for this impression to take hold. As Atkins said, "People don't think of him as Prime Minister yet."

Once he got into a TV studio with Mulroney, he was on his own. In television terms, Turner suffered from the handicap of being hot, with those laser blue eyes that nearly burned a hole in the screen. He also appeared ill at ease on camera, which tended to dissipate the impression that he was more competent than Mulroney. Turner was even badly advised as to what to wear to the studio. He turned up both nights in a baggy blue suit and a dark blue shirt, as if it was still the 1960's and you had to wear a blue shirt to a colour television interview. Mulroney wore a dark blue suit that had been picked out for him by Tom Gould, the long-time television news commentator who was serving as his television adviser. It was on Gould's advice that Mulroney finally went out for the first time in years without a pocket puff, since he had been advised that it might distract some viewers' attention from his message.

And his message in French was delivered straight into the living rooms of French Canada. "As a son of the North Shore," he said in his opening statement, "as the Progressive Conservative candidate in Manicouagan, I am making a direct and sincere appeal to you this evening. Help us, help us build a government that will give us, on a regular basis, the political alternation so indispensable to the life of a democracy."

Mulroney had written the basic elements of his opening statement the previous Saturday during a five-hour flight home from Vancouver. His soul-mate, Lucien Bouchard, had also written up a draft opening and closing in French, and though they weren't what Mulroney wanted, they helped sensitize him, put him in a Québécois mindset.

Raymond Garneau, Turner's star candidate in Quebec, at a Montreal press conference with the Liberal leader the previous Thursday, had raised the question of regaining Quebec's claims of a constitutional veto. When the issue came up in the French debate the following Tuesday night, Turner noted that "Mr. Garneau was the one who brought up the subject in his opening statement as a Liberal candidate, and I said at this press conference that he would be in a very privileged position to discuss this matter with a Quebec government, a future Quebec government which believes in Confederation."

It was not a very perceptive answer, since Turner neglected to mention that the old rule of unanimity would come into force to change the amending formula of seven provinces out of ten and 50 per cent of the population. Mulroney's answer indicated both the difficulty in changing the amending formula and the care with which the matter should be approached to avoid another disappointment for Quebecers.

"We regard that as a vote-grabbing gambit by Mr. Garneau," he replied. "He just threw it out without any preparation. But it is so important that we have Quebec's signature on our constitutional agreement, with honour and enthusiasm, that this must be looked at with great care. It should not be a matter for electioneering, because it raises other questions. Would the veto be granted to Ontario? Are Mr. Turner and Mr. Garneau proposing to grant it to western Canada? This is not something to be discussed during an election period, as Mr. Garneau has proposed, but in the hope of achieving a negotiated settlement."

This was Mulroney's way of saying two things. First, that the constitution and the veto question were not on the agenda in Quebec. And then, that the politicians should assess the chances of success before raising expectations again. It was an answer that indicated an awareness of the sensibilities of Quebecers, who would not want to raise the matter only to be humiliated again. But here Mulroney perceived an opening to the soft nationalist vote, those who voted for the Liberals federally but the Parti Québécois provincially. Turner had said he would not negotiate these questions with René Lévesque, on the perfectly sound assumption that his government did not believe in Canada. This was also Mulroney's privately held view, that it would be pointless to have any kind of constitutional discussion until and unless his friend Robert Bourassa was in office in Quebec.

But that did not prevent him from posturing about Turner's "nerve, that is the right term, to say that henceforth we, the Liberal government, will not deal with the duly elected, legitimate government of Quebec." And he continued: "I say quite simply that we have seen the pain and wounds caused by the last constitutional debate. This must not be undertaken lightly."

So he was trying to have it both ways, and judging by the reviews in the French papers, he succeeded in doing so. While most English-language commentators missed the delicate nuances, he was sending a message in the clear, in unmistakable code.

Part of Mulroney's superior performance in the French debate could be attributed to his bicultural dimension. While Turner was fluently bilingual, at least by the standards of his generation, Mulroney was speaking to Quebecers as one of their own, in their own idiom, though he was aware that Quebecers like a leader to look and sound like a leader and so was careful not to speak street French.

More to the point, Mulroney regarded the French debate as crucial to his hopes of making a breakthrough in Quebec and so had prepared himself accordingly. For three days, from Sunday night to Tuesday afternoon, he hunkered down at Stornoway. First he assimilated the briefing materials prepared for him by

Geoff Norquay and Jon Johnson in the policy analysis group of the Opposition Leader's Office. Then on Monday, four advisers sat around the den and sun room at Stornoway and threw every question they could think of at him.

"There were fifteen questions," Jean Bazin said after the French debate, "and we did not miss one of them."

Along with Bazin and Bouchard, there was Charley McMillan. All three were familiar figures in the Mulroney entourage. But there was one outsider, Hugh Segal, the former adviser to Bill Davis who had helped prepare the Ontario Premier for his campaign debates. Segal had written Claude Wagner's outstanding speech at the 1976 leadership convention, and Mulroney had written him a sharp note after reading Segal's comments during the 1983 leadership campaign that Davis might come into the race only to save the party from a right-wing candidate such as Lougheed or Mulroney. But that was past. Segal had a good grasp of television, and a good grasp of French. He could help, and he did.

Mostly, though, it was Mulroney himself, rising to the occasion. He had always thought a French debate would have a significant impact in Quebec. "Just wait till I get John Turner in a TV studio," he used to say. Then people would see the difference for themselves.

And so they did. An overnight CROP survey in Montreal found that, while only 24 per cent of respondents watched the debate, Mulroney was judged to be the winner by a 39-16 margin. As for voting intention, the Liberals slipped from 45 to 41 per cent, while the Conservatives went up from 15 to 26 per cent. This was not at great variance from the Conservative tracking by Decima Research, which indicated a twelve-point swing in Quebec, with the Tories climbing seven points to the mid-30s and the Liberals dropping five points to the mid-50s. The impact of the debate, the Conservative pollsters advised the leader two days later in Hamilton, was "historically startling."

Mulroney was jubilant. He had begun to establish himself in the minds of Quebec voters as a favourite son and prospective prime minister. In this sense, his problem was not Turner but Trudeau. "I've got a bigger problem than Trudeau," he said. "I not only have to remove the legacy of Trudeau, I have to substitute myself. I have to get the voters thinking that he's on the way out, and I'm on the way in."

There was undoubtedly a word-of-mouth effect out of both debates. English-speaking Canadians who didn't bother with or didn't understand the French debate nevertheless heard and read that Mulroney was considered the clear winner. And his winning performance in the English debate reinforced the attitude in French Canada that his showing in the first debate was not merely a question of linguistic advantage.

Turner entered the July 24-25 debates with two advantages, the prime ministerial posture and the perception that he was more competent than Mulroney to manage the country's affairs. By the end of the second debate, Turner had forfeited one advantage and lost the other.

In the English debate, the Liberal leader was holding his own, running no worse than even with his Conservative opponent. The difficult question of the patronage appointments was behind him, as was the awkward question of his propensity to pat women on their posteriors, one of those stories that had developed a life of its own in the previous two weeks. Turner kept it alive by his perplexing refusal to cut his losses, to say it never occurred to him that the gesture might be offensive to contemporary Canadian women, that he was sorry, and that it wouldn't happen again. That would have been the end of it. But Turner kept insisting that he was a "tactile" politician, the sort who liked to come in contact with people. He did try to cut his losses on the question by accepting a mid-August debate in Toronto on women's issues, a matter on which he forcefully stated his legitimate credentials in the July 25 debate.

With all that behind him, with only twenty minutes remaining in the two-hour ordeal by television, Turner suddenly made the Big Mistake. Without any prompting from the panel of three television journalists, or any taunting by Mulroney, the Prime Minister inexplicably came back on the patronage issue as a means of dramatizing the differences between the Conservative leader and himself.

"I have been saying the same thing to my party on all the issues that I say to the country," Turner began. "We have this patronage issue brought up earlier. Mr. Mulroney has not been dealing with the issue in the same way. He told his party last year that every available job would be made available to every living, breathing Conservative."

"I beg your pardon, sir," Mulroney replied.

"I would say, Mr. Mulroney," Turner said later in the exchange, "that on the basis of what you've talked about – getting your nose in the public trough – that you wouldn't offer any newness in the style of government. The style that you have been preaching to your own party reminds me of the old Union Nationale. It reminds me of patronage of its best."

Suddenly Turner had abandoned the prime ministerial pulpit. He had fallen off the high road, right into the gutter. It was a mean and sleazy thing to say. Worse, it was a mistake. Worst of all, it woke up Mulroney, who had been trying to find the right blend of aggressiveness and statesmanship. Now Turner had not only committed an unforced error, he had tweaked Mulroney's nose. It was an almost unbelievable mistake by Turner, a gift outright to Mulroney, who later acknowledged privately that he could "hardly believe my luck." Turner had just handed the patronage issue back to him.

Mulroney thrust out his chin, pointed an accusatory finger, reached deep down for all the self-righteousness he could muster, and lowered the boom on Turner.

"The only person who has ever appointed around here for the last twenty years has been your party; and 99 per cent have been Liberals, and you ought not to be proud of that," he said. "I have apologized to the Canadian people for kidding about it. The least you should do is apologize for having made these horrible appointments."

"Well," Turner replied, "I have told you and told the Canadian people, Mr. Mulroney, that I had no option."

"You had an option, sir," Mulroney shot back. "You could have said, 'I am not going to do it. This is wrong for Canada. And I am not going to ask Canadians to pay the price.' You had an option, sir, to say no, and you chose to say yes, yes to the old attitudes, and the old stories of the Liberal Party."

"I had no option," Turner repeated lamely. "I . . ."

"That is an avowal of failure," Mulroney interrupted. "That is a confession of non-leadership, and this country needs leadership. You had an option, sir, you could have done better."

The entire exchange lasted only a couple of minutes, but they were two of the most electrifying minutes in the history of televised political debates. It's funny what people remember of debates, Richard Nixon's five-o'clock shadow, Joe Clark's hollow laugh, Ronald Reagan capturing Jimmy Carter's meanness of spirit in a single sentence, "There you go again, Mr. President." The Canadian debates of 1984 would be remembered for that single electric exchange in which Turner's stature was diminished and Mulroney's enhanced. If it was not a knockout punch, it certainly left the Prime Minister on the ropes.

Characteristically, Mulroney went home and started calling his friends around the country to ask how they thought it went. "He's down to 'Others' on his list of phone numbers," said one aide in mock despair after leaving his boss, still high, at 1:30 the next morning.

Mulroney knew perfectly well how it had gone, and in the coming days he would press his advantage for everything it was worth. "Mr. Turner could have said no," he thundered everywhere he went in the next week, in French as in English, in Roberval, Quebec, as in Hamilton, Ontario, Bathurst, New Brunswick, and Sydney, Nova Scotia.

"I had no option," Mulroney would cry, mocking Turner and throwing up his hands. "The devil made me do it." He repeated this over and over, at first to the amusement and then to the increasing dismay of the journalists in his entourage. "Jack Kennedy used to say, 'Never throw away a good line,'" Mulroney joked nine days later as his campaign plane flew into his home town of Baie Comeau.

As he knew, the debates had changed things. The CROP overnights in Toronto for the *Globe and Mail* and *La Presse* indicated that 44 per cent of respondents had watched the English debate, and 47 per cent judged Mulroney the winner, as compared with 29 per cent for Broadbent and only 12 per cent for Turner. And it apparently had a significant effect on voters' intentions. Where the Liberals had led in Toronto by a 39-32 margin, with the NDP at 9 per cent, the post-debate sample found the Tories ahead 38-23 with an NDP resurgence to 18 per cent. Broadbent's sparkling performance, his two moral victories in French and in English, had given the NDP voters a reason to go home. The CROP findings were not greatly at variance with what the Tories were getting back from their pollster.

"People are in a mood to kick ass," said Mulroney press secretary Bill Fox when the post-debate numbers were in. The patronage appointments and the debates had put public opinion back on a course for change. How much things had changed would become apparent to the voters only the following Friday, August 3, when the CTV network put out the results of a Thompson-Lightstone survey taken after the debates. Where the same polling organization had found the Liberals ahead 49-39 after their June convention, they now had the Tories ahead 45-36, ahead everywhere in English-speaking Canada and only nine points down, 47-38, in Quebec.

With the release of the CTV poll just a month before the election, the voters knew what the parties had known for a week, that the Liberals had lost all momentum in the debates. They had been doing it with blue smoke and mirrors. Their disarray was soon apparent from the disorganized high command to the demoralized rank and file.

Three days before the release of the CTV survey, Turner acknowledged his difficulties by bringing back "the Rainmaker," the legendary Keith Davey, who had been Liberal campaign director through most of the Pearson and Trudeau years. Turner had said there would be "no rainmakers" in his entourage and he was hard put to explain the sudden return of the senator. Conservative insiders were intrigued that Davey was returning in a very public way, as co-chairman of the campaign, rather than staying out of sight in the back rooms. Davey's comeback further undermined Turner's argument that he represented renewal and change in the Liberal Party.

Moreover, it was clear that Bill Lee's days were numbered as Turner's campaign director. The following Saturday, exactly a month before the election, Turner summoned Lee to Harrington Lake and as a result of their conversation, Turner said he had accepted Lee's resignation and had put Davey in charge of the campaign. Over an entire week of the campaign, the Liberals suffered the downside publicity consequences of Davey's return and the ousting or resignation of Lee, who took several of his top aides with him. The bleeding continued into the next week, as Turner flew off to Mont Joli on August 6 for appearances at Rimouski and Rivière-du-Loup on the South Shore of Quebec. The big story of the day was the continuing purge in the Liberal high command with the sudden grounding of Turner's press secretary, Dennis Baxter, and the return of Trudeau's last press aide, Ralph Coleman, an out-of-uniform Armed Forces colonel who commanded the respect as well as the affection of the Ottawa press corps.

With the newspapers full of negative stories about the disarray of the Liberal campaign, Turner appeared to lose whatever advantage he might have retained on perceived competence to manage the country's affairs. "The question beginning to take shape in the minds of many voters," suggested columnist Richard Gwyn of *The Toronto Star* on August 4, the day Lee would bite the dust, "has to be whether someone who can't run a campaign could in fact actually run the country."

While Gwyn was not known for his high regard of Mulroney's abilities, he had been out on the campaign enough to see a bit of both tours, and the contrast was startling. While the Liberals scrambled to get organized – Turner was travelling commercial until the day after the debates and the party was thoroughly disorganized on the ground – the Mulroney tour was moving with all the precision of a well-oiled machine. Or more precisely, a well-oiled Big Blue Machine.

In the last week of July and the first week of August, the Mulroney tour marched through Ontario, New Brunswick, Nova Scotia, and Quebec without missing a single beat. A convoy of three buses, two for the working wretches of the press and one for the candidate, greeted Mulroney at every stop. Through five and six campaign stops a day, the media might complain that they lacked access to the candidate or figures for policy pronouncements, but they could not complain to wagonmaster Ross Reid about lost luggage, lack of filing time, or even of lack of beer on the bus. If they were going to trash the Mulroney campaign, and any self-respecting pack of press hounds could be counted on to do so at least once a week as a matter of principle, then they would have to find other pretexts than the near flawless organization of the tour in the air or the meetings on the ground.

Mulroney was even able to get some extra mileage out of his campaign jet, christening it *Manicouagan I* on its maiden flight out of Ottawa the day after the English-language debate. In so doing, he was keeping at least one campaign promise, to "put the North Shore on the map." Voters at home in Baie Comeau and in the streets of Sept-Iles would see the television footage and newspaper clippings of Mulroney shamelessly hamming it up before the flight, sticking his head out of the cockpit window, pointing to the bold legend *Manicouagan I*.

But on the first Friday of August he was on the ground in Quebec, in Chicoutimi, Jonquière, Roberval, and Quebec City. All day long he stressed the theme that "democracy requires alternation," that Quebecers were not prisoners of a single party. Quebecers, he said, were not "the hostages of André Ouellet." It was a guaranteed applause line in Roberval, in the Parti Québécois heartland of Lac St-Jean, as it was everywhere else. It was no mystery, as Mulroney himself explained over the weekend in his riding. The Tories had polled Quebecers as to the popularity of their federal and provincial politicians and Ouellet, on nearly every attribute, was the least popular of them all.

As his bus rolled into Quebec City, Mulroney was already aware of the CTV poll that indicated the Tories surging ahead by nine points. The timing could not have been more propitious. He was going home that evening for four days of rest and campaigning in his riding, and he intended to play the card of prime minister.

As he came out of the Concorde Hotel for a brief bit of mainstreeting, Mulroney made a triumphant walk past the sidewalk cafés of the Grande Allée. At the door of his bus he ran into Bob McKenzie, senior Quebec correspondent of *The Toronto Star* and his oldest friend in the newspaper business. A quarter of a century before, Mulroney later recalled, they had sat around the Aux Delices restaurant, with the young law student promising that "some day we're going to shake this place up."

Now he spotted McKenzie in the crowd around his bus and grabbed him by the shoulders. "I told you, Robert," he shouted, "I told you we'd do it."

He hadn't quite done it yet. But as he liked to say himself, he was getting there, a good deal faster than many people would have thought.

21

SEPTEMBER 4, 1984

A light mist was falling as Brian and Mila Mulroney walked down the secluded pathway of Le Manoir de Baie Comeau. It was a few minutes past nine-thirty in the morning of September 4, 1984, and the Conservative leader was going to the Academie Ste. Amélie, where he had attended primary school, to vote for himself in the election that would make him Canada's eighteenth Prime Minister.

He had every reason to hope and believe that the country's thirty-third general election since Confederation would prove to be a watershed. He knew that only two lasting electoral coalitions had been forged in the country's history, by Sir John A. Macdonald in 1867 and Sir Wilfrid Laurier in 1896. Mulroney hoped this day would mark the beginning of a second Conservative and third Canadian electoral dynasty.

He had often referred to Macdonald's "Grand Alliance of English and French, East and West." But he also knew the hallmark of the Laurier era was a fundamental realignment of Canadian voters. With its axis of French Canada and progressive Ontario, the Liberal dynasty had proved to be more enduring. There was no mystery to it. The Liberal Party had given itself three Quebecers as leaders in Laurier, Louis St. Laurent, and Pierre Trudeau. Altogether they governed the country for some forty of its 116 years. And in the Trudeau era, the Liberals had not only maintained their grip on French Canada, but had consolidated their hold on the ethnic voters in Metropolitan Toronto. It was this Liberal clientele of linguistic and ethnic minorities that Mulroney hoped to win over to the Conservative camp in 1984 and, unlike John Diefenbaker after 1958, to keep it there.

The Liberal coalition had kept the Grits in office for most of the twentieth century. Mulroney hoped his "new majority" would keep the Conservatives in power, or within reach of it, into the next century. But his designs were not wholly electoralist. He also came to the job of Prime Minister with an idea of the country and where he wanted to take it.

He had not set a doctrinaire Tory agenda, nor even an anti-Liberal agenda. As Charley McMillan had once observed over a room-service breakfast: "You know Brian, he's about as ideological as that coffee pot." Mulroney's agenda was simply different and, he hoped, right for the times.

In the long lull of election day, McMillan could summarize the Mulroney agenda on a single sheet of Manoir notepaper. He jotted down three bullets – Social, Economic, and Global, and divided the page into two columns – Old and New. A Social hallmark of the Trudeau era, for example, was Medicare. That was under Old. Under New, McMillan noted Aging/Pensions, Women in Work Place, and Native rights. "There's the whole question of an aging society," McMillan explained, "and these pension funds with their actuarial problems. Under Economic, he noted that the former regime had established policies of grants to industry, regional development, the flourishing of Crown corporations, and the establishment of the Foreign Investment Review Agency. Mulroney was more concerned with research and development, manpower and training, management-labour relations, all of which could enhance Canada's competitive position. And under Global, where Trudeau had pursued his third-option policies, Mulroney was more concerned with Canada's role in major international institutions. "He's interested," McMillan said, "in educating Americans to the fact that there are middle-power roles."

At Stornoway one January day in 1984, Mulroney had confided to his top policy adviser that he would like to be remembered in history for four points: first, for eventually achieving a constitutional settlement that included Quebec; then, for a restructuring of the Canadian economy; third, for consolidating a distinctive role for middle powers in the world; and finally, as an extension of his interest in the minority rights question, an improved economic and social situation for the country's native peoples. His interest in the native rights question seemed as surprising as his late-developing interest in women's economic issues. But then, he had always been underestimated, and he had always been capable of growth. There were thousands of native people in his own riding, and he hoped to hasten their economic emancipation. As for women's issues, his significant contribution to the August 15 debate was the observation that women had more trouble than men getting capital from the banks, and he hoped to change that by a policy of moral suasion. As for public policy, the country would be surprised by the number of women he would put in his cabinet and appoint to government office.

"Brian just doesn't want to be Prime Minister," his friend Lucien Bouchard once observed. "He wants to live in history." Still, his first claim on posterity would be as the man who united the Conservative Party and carried it to a resounding national majority.

In Quebec, two weeks before the election, you could almost see the Blue wave coming. Mulroney's Liberal friend Francis Fox could sense it in his suburban Montreal riding of Blainville-Deux-Montagnes, which he had won by a majority of 30,000 votes in 1980. "This election's over," Fox confided to a friend thirteen days before the vote. "Right now it's a question of trying to save the furniture." Fox had looked after the interests of his riding, even to the extent of getting a billion-dollar Bell helicopter plant to locate there. "In a wave," he said dejectedly, "that doesn't mean anything at the riding level." He would be engulfed by it.

The collapse of the Turner campaign, and the subsequent growth of the Tories in Quebec, surpassed Mulroney's fondest hopes. "Can you get to 40 per cent in Quebec?" he was asked at the outset of the campaign. Notorious optimist that he was, even he didn't think so. But if he could get to 37 or 38 per cent, he knew he could win some seats in Quebec, enough for a breakthrough.

Two weeks before the election, Pierre Bibeau sat at a window table at Chez Bernard, a fashionable Old Montreal restaurant, and recited a list of ridings where the Tories were certain of victory or had reasonable prospects. He stopped counting at thirty. Some of the ridings on his list of possibilities were shocking. But Bibeau was not someone to be taken lightly. He was the chief organizer of Robert Bourassa's Quebec Liberal Party, and he knew every riding in the province, federally and provincially, inside out.

Though nominally and insistently neutral in the federal election, the Quebec Liberals were divided in their allegiance. About 80 per cent of the riding executives were still supporting the federal Liberal cousins, by Bibeau's estimate, while at the rank-and-file level they were split "about 50-50" between *les rouges* and *les bleus*.

As for Bourassa and the Quebec high command, notwithstanding their claims of neutrality, it was no secret where their real sympathies lay. It wasn't just a question of settling accounts with the feds for some of their contemptuous and condescending gestures of the Trudeau years, though heaven knows there were enough scores they could have settled. It went back to 1976, to Trudeau's snide treatment of Bourassa as a *mangeur de hot dog*, to the disastrous federal dairy policies and the *Gens de l'Air* bilingual air traffic control crisis, all of which were factors in Bourassa's defeat that year. There was also the matter of the Trudeau patriation package in the fall of 1980, which gave René Lévesque the pretext he needed to postpone an election in the fall of 1980, when he would have lost, and recover to win handily in the spring of the following year.

Nor was Bourassa concerned to get even with the federal Liberals for the lengths to which they had gone to thwart his comeback in 1983, when Trudeau went so far as to invite Raymond and Pauline Garneau to 24 Sussex to urge him to consider entering the Quebec leadership race, and when André Ouellet suggested that Bourassa had had his chance and blown it.

Bourassa wasn't very good at holding grudges, though in Ouellet's case he may have been prepared to make an exception. But the election of any Conservative leader in Ottawa would automatically strengthen the position of any Quebec Liberal leader. The election of Mulroney, his close personal friend, did not mean they wouldn't have their differences if Bourassa became Quebec Premier again. But they would agree on what to disagree on and begin from a basis of mutual esteem. More fundamentally, as Pierre Bibeau acknowledged privately near the end of August, Mulroney represented the beginning of change, and that couldn't hurt the Quebec Liberals to reinforce the attitude of Quebec voters on the imperative of dumping the PQ administration.

Provincial Liberal activists and organizers were not the only ones working for the election of Conservative candidates. In many ridings, the PQ organization had also moved onside. Mulroney had once accused Joe Clark of "playing footsie" with the PQ in offering to revert to the original Vancouver amending formula, which would have granted full compensation to provinces opting out of future federal-provincial programs, rather than limiting it to the educational and cultural domains of the provinces, one of the reasons Quebec didn't sign the 1982 Constitution Act. But in a rather remarkable speech at his nomination in Sept-Iles on August 6, Mulroney offered to reopen the question of the amending formula and, by inference, the matter of the veto for Quebec and other regions of the country. However, he stressed the importance of "ground rules to meet the minimal conditions of success." In other words, he was not prepared to risk another constitutional debacle for Quebec. "We are on the threshold of a true national renewal," he continued. "Let us end the bias of confrontation with the bias of agreement. Let us open avenues to solutions instead of putting up obstacles. Let us listen in order to understand, rather than condemn without hearing."

Again, he was talking, in code but in the clear, to the soft nationalist voters in Quebec, in the thousands upon thousands. Two-thirds of the Quebec electorate supported Trudeau in the 1980 federal election, but half of the same voters turned around and supported Lévesque in the spring of 1981. It is not an apples-and-oranges comparison to suggest there was a certain crossover vote from one election to the next.

Mulroney had certainly placed himself in an anomalous position with respect to his statements in the 1983 leadership campaign about Clark and about not giving "a plugged nickel" from the federal treasury to René Lévesque until he found out what he would do for Canada. The best explanation was also the least elegant: that was last year; this was this year.

Mulroney was trying to build an electoral base in Quebec. Much of this depended on his television appeal in French. But much also depended on the performance of his candidates and their organizations in a province where the party hadn't existed at the riding level. In most cases, his candidates came with their own networks, but that wasn't enough. It took some political experience, and this the Quebec Liberals and the PQ regulars had in abundance. They weren't rubbing elbows in very many committee rooms, but they were working for essentially the same cause: anyone but the federal Liberals.

The 1984 campaign was also vindicating Mulroney's opinion that the vaunted federal Liberal machine in Quebec was a myth. "All they had going for them was Trudeau and the provincial Liberals in the ridings," Mulroney said at the mid-point of the campaign. "Now there's no Trudeau and the provincial machine is in neutral."

For the first time in their careers, Liberal MPs who had taken 30,000-vote majorities as a matter of course, or a reflection of their own talents, found themselves fighting for their lives. They found that Trudeau's gifts as a stump performer, and the extent of his hold on Quebec voters, could be appreciated only now that he was gone. Certainly André Ouellet's reputation as chief Quebec organizer was devalued in the summer campaign. The organization in Quebec, as elsewhere in the country, was in chaos. When Turner, accompanied by Jean Chrétien, turned up for a boat regatta near Montreal in the third weekend in August, they were greeted by a meagre crowd of some 300 people, some of whom booed the Prime Minister, while others hailed Chrétien as the man who should have won the Liberal leadership.

Across the St. Lawrence in the South Shore riding of Verchéres, some 1,000 people turned out for a Tory corn roast that same evening. There was no national aspect to the outing; there wasn't even Joe Clark or someone from the Tories' "B" tour. There was only the local candidate, Marcel Danis, the Clark loyalist whose career the Mulroney organization had no interest in advancing. Clearly, something was going on in Quebec. Mulroney's people called it "Le Tonnere Bleu," the Blue Thunder, and they had gone so far as to put it on a flashy lapel pin. "Avec Brian Mulroney ça va changer" went the tagline of the Tory TV ads. In effect, "Time for a change." It was the oldest political campaign slogan in the world, and, at the right time in the right place, the most effective.

On a more profound level of public policy, Mulroney believed it was a time for healing in Quebec, and that he could introduce his conciliatory skills to the process. After the confrontations of the Trudeau-Lévesque era, the voters appeared unusually receptive to this appeal. This is where Turner and his advisers badly misread the mood of Quebec by suggesting that Mulroney was harbouring separatists in permitting three persons who had supported the "Yes" option in the Quebec referendum to stand as Tory candidates. The logic of this assumption was breathtaking, since 1.4 million voters or 40 per cent of the Quebec electorate had endorsed Lévesque's soft question, and not all of them were separatists by any means. Quite apart from the fact that Turner wouldn't know a separatist if he tripped over one in the lobby of the Ritz, he was unconsciously fostering a climate of treason in the election, and Quebecers had experienced quite enough of that in their family and working lives during the referendum era.

Mulroney's reading of the situation was much closer to the mark, even though some of his advisers were concerned when he received the tacit endorsement of Lévesque, who suggested his posture on federal-provincial relations was more open-minded than the Liberal leader's. Mulroney shrugged off these comments, asserting they were no different than what Bill Davis and Brian Peckford had been saying about the sour state of federal-provincial affairs. But even in the predominantly English-speaking, staunchly Liberal ridings of Montreal, where the Tories were growing by leaps and bounds, there was little apparent slippage from Mulroney's overtures to the nationalists. Perhaps there was a sense that there was no longer very much to be feared from the PQ, which after nearly two terms in office was looking like a tired government on the way out, as attested by Bourassa's incredible 3-1 lead in a Sorecom poll in June of 1984.

"There is room in Canada," Mulroney said in his Sept-Iles speech, "for all identities to be affirmed, for all aspirations to be respected, and for all ideals to be pursued." This was an echo of something he had said a month earlier in Baie Comeau, that he wanted Canada to become the kind of country where someone who had voted "Yes" in the referendum could feel at home.

Beyond electoralism, this had something to do with Mulroney's privately held hopes of winning over the intelligentsia – the nationalist intellectuals in Quebec and the Red Tories in English-speaking Canada. "His secret dream," Lucien Bouchard once confided to a friend, "is to have the approval of the intellectuals."

The way to win them over in Quebec would be to "open at an opportune moment," as he said at Sept-Iles, the outstanding constitutional question of the veto. Realistically, that meant Bourassa would have to be in place as Premier, the other provinces would have to be receptive to the idea, and there would have to be a willingness on all sides to make tradeoffs. If Mulroney and Bourassa could achieve that together, they would both have the approval of the Quebec intellectuals, and both, as Bouchard had put it, would live in history.

As for the Red Tories, who had always regarded him with a mingling of suspicion and disdain, he could win them over simply by running a government that was at least as progressive as it was conservative. His problems with the intellectual wing of the Conservative Party, those people from somewhere between Queen's University and the United Church, arose from the fact that he was simply different from them. They were generally Protestant, high-minded, and disapproving about displays of affluence. He was Catholic, upwardly mobile, with no reticence about living at the top of the hill. Where he came from was part of what it was all about. As he often observed about the guest house at Le Manoir in Baie Comeau, it had formerly been the mill manager's house, and 24 Sussex would be nothing after you'd put your feet up on the table in the town manager's house. In company towns all across the country, the audiences smiled and nodded their heads. The Tory intelligentsia, in their gloomy greystones at the bottom of the hill, would simply never understand this and would probably consider it a bit vulgar. By and large, they had backed Flora MacDonald's leadership candidacy in 1976, and when she walked to Joe Clark they went with her, transferring their affections and loyalty to him.

It was Clark, the Wimp, who had the respect of the Red Tories. And it was Clark, the westerner, who had won the grudging respect of Quebec's intellectuals because of his lonely and brave opposition to Trudeau's unilateral initiative on the constitution.

Deep down, Mulroney may have envied Clark his currency with the intellectuals. For himself, there was nothing to be done for it except to hope he might eventually win them over, as he had people from factions he had met along the way.

His problems with the intelligentsia, French- and English-speaking alike, arose from several factors. First, he was an outsider in the academic sense. Also, he had few intellectual airs or aspirations. Finally, he was perceived as somehow being an anti-egghead. In fact, there was nothing anti-intellectual about Mulroney, he was simply as bored by some of their causes as they were suspicious of his boardroom connections and pinstripe suits. And at least until his election as Prime Minister, the country's intellectual establishment had not taken the time or trouble to inform itself seriously about Mulroney. Among the many things they didn't know about him was that he was a sponge for new ideas, a promoter of new talent, and a defender of some intellectual causes. These traits derived from his makeup, first as an outsider who always had to impose himself, then as someone with a strong tolerance for other people's views.

Interestingly, he was not without his own intellectual and academic network, but again, because of his background, they tended to hail from the newer and less celebrated Canadian universities. After all, he had attended St. F.X. rather than Dalhousie, and Laval law school rather than Montréal. There was no Rhodes Scholarship in his curriculum vitae, no semester at the London School of Economics, the Sorbonne or Harvard, or any of the citadels of learning where members of the Canadian elite had gone to round off the academic phases of their careers.

In later life, the universities with which he was associated in a fund-raising sense were often under-endowed, struggling and striving to establish themselves. His university connections were on the second tier: St. F.X. rather than Dal; Concordia, rather than McGill in Montreal; Waterloo rather than Western Ontario in southern Ontario; York rather than the University of Toronto; Simon Fraser rather than the University of British Columbia in Vancouver. And all he knew about Queen's was that it was in Kingston, and in Flora MacDonald's riding.

Charley McMillan, Doctor Charles McMillan as his boss sometimes insisted on referring to him, had the best understanding of Mulroney's attitude toward and appreciation of the academic community. "It's fine to have ideas," McMillan used to say, "but don't waste his time with ideas that have no practical application in the real world." In that empirical sense, Mulroney's idea of the country, and his sense of its place in the world, was formed by his disposition and his experience.

In both senses, he thought that personal relationships between and among leaders could make a real difference between the federal government and the provinces, or between Ottawa and Washington or London or Paris.

The Americans, the British, and the French were peoples that Mulroney instinctively liked and understood from his own education and experience. He had often referred to the U.S. as Canada's best friend and most important trading partner. There was a key to his thoughts in that turn of phrase – friends and partners. You give your friends the benefit of the doubt, as he was prepared to do for the Americans in their 1983 occupation of Grenada, an episode of gunboat diplomacy in which Ronald Reagan reasserted the Monroe Doctrine of American interests in the Western Hemisphere without giving Pierre Trudeau so much as the courtesy of a phone call.

Mulroney was appalled by that. Trudeau was then a ranking world statesman, an elder of the British Commonwealth, and the four-term Prime Minister of a country that flattered itself as having some influence in the Caribbean basin. Mulroney might not have any experience on the world stage, but he thought in time he could do better than that with the Americans. He had read Lawrence Martin's book, *The Presidents and the Prime Ministers*, and he had been struck by the history of misunderstandings and missed signals across the border. So he had placed special emphasis and made painstaking preparations for his two-day visit to Washington and the White House in June, 1984. The visit was advanced by his chief of staff, Fred Doucet, and his press secretary, Bill Fox, the former Washington correspondent of *The Toronto Star*. When he drove through the wrought-iron gates of the White House, there wasn't even time for him to think what a big deal this was for a boy from Baie Comeau. He was simply moving up to something bigger and making a good impression, something he had been doing all his life. Within five minutes of meeting one another, he and Ronald Reagan were addressing one another as Brian and Ron.

Yet, as eager as he might have been to make a favourable impression on a Reagan, or a Margaret Thatcher, no one should make the mistake of thinking he was enamoured of their economic, social, or defence policies as programs with which Canada could fall in line. Even as a novice Opposition Leader, Mulroney was aware that Canada's interests were not necessarily as one even with its best friends. He was also acutely aware that Canadian voters didn't like their leaders to be too cosy with the Americans, especially with a Republican president, no matter how charming he might be. Mulroney knew that Canadians liked their Prime Minister to be seen in the Rose Garden, but they didn't want him sleeping upstairs in a bedroom of the White House.

Even as Opposition Leader, it was worth noting that Mulroney travelled to Washington with a limited and achievable agenda, pressing the Ontario issues of acid rain and steel exports on the American president. Reagan, who knew something himself about election-year politics, had been well enough briefed and seemed happy enough to listen. The problems of the Canadian steel industry and of acid rain were in Mulroney's mind neither mutually exclusive nor solely the concern of labour economists and the environmental lobby. They had to do with the quality of lifestyle and the quality of life, and both had engaged his interest. The modernization of the smokestack industries on both sides of the border and the cleaning up of lakes were the kinds of problems to which he was prepared to give some attention.

"He's much more contemplative than he's given credit for," McMillan observed just before the election. He was also much more far-sighted than was generally appreciated before the election. The Ontario agenda of his White House trip was one example. It seemed puzzling and parochial in June, far from the global issues of disarmament or economic recovery. It became self-explanatory in July, when Mulroney visited the smokestack and cottage towns of southern Ontario.

There was also the instance of the Gaspé town of Grande Vallée. Ravaged by massive unemployment, it had been the scene of noisy demonstrations against the Lévesque government in the summer of 1983. In the winter of 1984, when the problems of the town were the furthest thing from anyone's mind in Ottawa, Mulroney stood up in Question Period to ask Pierre Trudeau if he wouldn't take "five minutes" of his time to call the Premier of Quebec and discuss the economic well-being of their fellow citizens. Nobody could figure out Mulroney's sudden interest in the plight of Grande Vallée, and nobody paid any notice until the election campaign, when he went back to Quebec and cited his intervention as proof of the healing he would bring to federal-provincial relations, putting the interests of voters ahead of the territorial interests of the two levels of government. He was also pointing out the evident disinterest of the old regime and the disdain of the retiring Prime Minister for the mundane economic concerns of a small town on the Gaspé peninsula.

Even in the tense atmosphere of the July debates, there was something quite striking about the manner in which Mulroney went out of his way to be courteous and correct with NDP leader Ed Broadbent. There was none of his stump oratory about a vote for the NDP being a vote for the Liberals, a line that drove Broadbent to distraction, although Mulroney did luck out in the photo opportunity before the second debate when Turner draped his arm around Broadbent and invited Mulroney to join them in the picture. "You're the Bobbsey Twins of Bay Street," Mulroney replied, pointing his finger at them and keeping his distance as he mimicked Broadbent's refrain on the similarities between Turner and himself. Again, he couldn't believe his luck. The pictures illustrated his argument about the Liberal-NDP marriage of convenience.

But in the debates themselves, Mulroney was careful to a fault not to antagonize Broadbent. The reason was that Mulroney was thinking ahead to a minority government, then a distinct possibility, in which case he would need the support of the NDP for a year or two until he could position himself to go back to the country and ask for a clear mandate. Mulroney's law classmate and political operative, Peter White, had gone so far as to prepare an eyes-only memorandum for him on the subject.

White had been given, also, the unobtrusive but important task of preparing a political transition. When Mulroney got to Baie Comeau on Labour Day weekend, White would have finalized an inventory of political appointees and potential nominees for Mulroney's consideration after the election. As for the bureaucratic transition, Mulroney had been putting his mind to that for more than a year, familiarizing himself with the problems and routine of the central administration in regular briefings with Gordon Osbaldeston, the Clerk of the Privy Council and the top civil servant in the realm.

Mulroney had always known that he would have to make at least a symbolic shakeup in the public and diplomatic service, firing enough senior officials indelibly identified with the Liberal regime to let people know that there was a new game in town. But it wasn't his style to conduct a massive purge, no matter how bloodthirsty some of his caucus members might be. As always, he would prefer to win the public officials over. Mulroney was not particularly fascinated by the actual machinery of government, but he was interested in how it worked. As he was going away to Florida at Christmas of 1983, McMillan had seen to it that he received a copy of Colin Campbell's *Governments Under*

Stress, a fascinating comparative study of the central political and bureaucratic decision-making process in Ottawa, Washington, and London. It was the sort of book that could hold Mulroney's interest since it was written in readable rather than academic prose, full of personalities and lots of interesting statistical bullets, as in how many people worked in the Langevin Block as compared with the White House. The answer was more, when you included the Federal-Provincial Relations office along with the Privy Council Office and the Prime Minister's Office.

Campbell was a Jesuit who, perhaps significantly, had been a professor at York, one of the newer universities where Mulroney had most of his academic contacts. Charley McMillan was out of York, where he was a professor of business policy on the faculty of administrative studies. For years, between political campaigns, consulting jobs, and teaching, he had been working on a book on Japan's economic miracle, entitled *The Japanese Industrial System*, which he finally published at the beginning of the 1984 campaign. It was never going to be a best seller, but after September 4 it might become required reading in certain government circles.

Tom McPhail of the University of Calgary's communications department was one of those professors on the outer circle of Mulroney's academic acquaintances and was an occasional adviser on communications strategy. McPhail had met him some fifteen years earlier during a faculty crisis at Loyola College in Montreal in 1969, when the administration of the Jesuit college tried to fire twenty-three junior profs who had declared their support for another colleague whose contract had not been renewed.

The victims of the purge needed a lawyer to represent them, and a professor named Terry Copp found them one in Brian Mulroney, then an up-and-coming thirty-year-old lawyer at Ogilvy, Cope. Copp was a popular professor in the history department, and he was also a Red Tory who had supported Alvin Hamilton's bid for the leadership in 1967. Mulroney was no stranger to him.

Don Savage, then one of the activist professors and later executive director of the Canadian Association of University Teachers, recounted in an article for the CAUT *Bulletin* in June of 1984 how Mulroney "outmanoeuvred" the college administration and its advisers. First he persuaded his friends in high places in the Union Nationale administration of Jean-Jacques Bertrand in Quebec to intervene and appoint an independent inquiry. As Savage explained, that was the ballgame: "Mulroney really won the case before it ever started." Subsequently, the college administration and its cohorts in the English-Catholic Montreal community tried to bring "pressure of a kind that is not hard to imagine," as Savage put it, on Ogilvy and the young member of the firm. "Fortunately," Savage recalled, "both the firm and Mr. Mulroney ignored these pressures." At the inquiry, Mulroney made occasional appearances "and a devastating summation at the end." The one-man inquiry of Professor Perry Meyer of McGill ultimately reinstated twenty-one of the twenty-three profs. "The result was stunning," as Savage observed. The Loyola crisis "not only showed Mr. Mulroney to be a skilled negotiator, but also someone willing to defend academic freedom and due process."

"He cleaned them," McPhail recalled of the confrontation with the Loyola administration, although as Savage noted Mulroney was more interested in saving the college from itself than humiliating the administration.

The continuing uneasiness with which enlightened Tories regarded Mulroney was shared by the voters in the summer of 1984. For want of a better term, it became known as "the Glib Factor," after a perceptive piece on the *Globe and Mail*'s op-ed page by Peter Desbarats, who had known Mulroney since the early 1960's and was now dean of the graduate school of journalism at the University of Western Ontario in London. "Coming from a background that was middle class rather than poor," Desbarats suggested, "without the intellectual gifts of men such as Robert Cliche or Mr. Trudeau, Mr. Mulroney has had to use his talents aggressively. It was his ability to synthesize issues, to understand personalities, and know when to unlimber the steel behind the Irish-Canadian charm, that made Mr. Mulroney such an effective negotiator for the businessmen who employed him early in his career to resolve difficult labor situations."

Desbarats noted that both Robert Stanfield and Trudeau "were members of local moneyed aristocracies, privately educated and accustomed to privilege." Joe Clark, he suggested, shared Mulroney's "middle class background, but little of his charm, toughness and humor." In any event, he concluded, if the voters wanted something new, "they were going to have to swallow glib in the process."

Mulroney's problems with the Red Tories may have been dispelled somewhat after he received a ringing endorsement from Stanfield at an Atlantic caucus in Halifax on August 2. Stanfield, the party's elder statesman and chairman of the prestigious Ottawa think-tank, the Institute for Research on Public Policy, was the conscience of the intellectual wing of the party. He had

309

always given the impression of being terribly fond of Mulroney without being overwhelmed by his ability. But even by the inflated rhetorical standards of a campaign, the normally restrained Stanfield was effusive in his praise of Mulroney's position on the Manitoba language question, which he knew from his own difficult experience had not been an easy test. He said he was "proud of my leader, proud of my party, hopeful for my country."

Mulroney, sitting a few feet away, nearly fell off his chair. He was deeply touched by Stanfield's unsolicited endorsement and, for once in his life, nearly speechless. "Well, I think for Bob, the language issue is the fundamental test of moral leadership," Mulroney managed to say on the way out of the room, adding that Stanfield found Turner's ambiguous position rather disappointing. Stanfield was rather more plain-spoken than that. He said Turner's statements "almost made me throw up."

In a way, Stanfield was sending a message to the Red Tories, who had always sneered at Mulroney, that maybe they should have another look at him, as Quebec's public opinion leaders were doing in the aftermath of the July debates.

One old friend suggested that Mulroney's long-standing problems with Canadian intellectuals could be compared with those of John Kennedy in the U.S. – before his election as President in 1960. Until then, Adlai Stevenson remained the darling of American intellectuals, who regarded Kennedy with suspicion. Once he was in the White House, there was practically a shuttle service running from the Ivy League to the White House.

After the polls of mid-August, there was not much doubt that Mulroney was going to get himself elected. The Southam, Gallup, CBC, and CROP polls all agreed on one thing: the Liberals were stuck on 32 per cent and the Tories were in a range from 46 to 51 per cent. However you cut it, even subtracting the usual margins of error from the Tories and adding them on the Liberal scores, you still came up with a Conservative majority. In the closing weeks of the campaign, it was only a question of how big.

Sitting by a pool at the Auberge des Gouverneurs in Sept-Iles on the first Sunday in August, Mulroney reminisced with his old friend Bob McKenzie, and recalled what his mentor, Daniel Johnson, would have said in similar circumstances. "Ça sens bon," he said. It smells good. In English, it feels good. As he flew into Toronto on August 28 to unveil the cost and projected benefits of his economic program, there was one irreducible statistic over which no one would quarrel. There was only one week, seven days, to go.

The Toronto speech was important for two reasons that were

not widely perceived at the time. First, it was indicative of how successful Mulroney had been in setting his own agenda rather than having it dictated to him by the news media. And then, by insisting on a cost-benefit approach rather than a simplistic expenditure one, he was changing the rules of the election game in Canada. On the first point, Mulroney had some help from the voters, and on the second from Charley McMillan.

Ever since the outset of the campaign, when Tory finance critic John Crosbie let slip the potential cost of the party program at $20 billion over a full mandate, the press had been yapping away at Mulroney's heels. But his polling showed that the cost of his program simply wasn't an issue with the voters. If it had been, he would not have waited until the last week of the campaign to put out his figures. The Liberals tried desperately to make it an issue in the second half of the campaign, just as they tried to revive the Trudeau peace initiative. It was the politics of desperation, the strategy of Keith Davey, and it was too little, too late.

As for the manner in which Canadian campaigns were waged, Mulroney successfully stuck to a battle plan that would be a model for future elections. He insisted that the news media use a balance sheet rather than an adding machine. As for himself, rather than merely building planks in a platform, he maintained it was possible to construct an economic model, with a cost-benefit analysis, with multiplier effects from his economic program, and with a simple renewal of investor confidence and an injection of foreign capital that, he asserted, would result from the election of a Conservative majority.

But to satisfy the unrelenting demand for a short-term accounting of his program, he told the joint meeting of the Empire and Canadian Clubs that his government would spend $4.3 billion to implement its platform over the first two-and-one-half years of its mandate, offset by $2.2 billion in unspecified cuts, for a net cost of $2.1 billion. The blue suits in the audience, and the media along press row, seemed to think it was a credible performance. "Promises to cost $4.3 billion in 2½ years, Mulroney says," headlined the *Globe and Mail* in its afternoon edition. "Well," someone teased Charley McMillan, "they went for it."

The main thing about the Toronto speech was not the content but the tone, and how it played on television. The campaign high command wanted the voters to start thinking of Mulroney as Prime Minister, and they wanted him to look laid back and prime ministerial. He gave them exactly what they wanted. For weeks, they had been imploring him to lower his voice and let the microphones do the work for him. At evening meetings of party rank and file, he had been doing a lot of shouting and sweating, leaving a much different impression from the laid-back style of his television commercials. In a close election, these contradictory images emanating from the Mulroney camp might have accentuated his perceived problems of trust with the voters.

Mulroney would point out that his days had generally been planned around three types of events: a "process event" in the morning, where he might talk to unemployed youth; a serious public-policy pronouncement at a midday rubber-chicken event; and a barn-burner to keep the troops happy in the evening. By the last week of the campaign, he had ditched the process, had no further need of policy forums, and decided to go on the stump all day long.

From Toronto, Mulroney flew to Mont Joli and Rimouski, where he hoped to begin nailing down his gains in Quebec. For two days, the Mulroney caravan rolled 350 miles along the South Shore from the gateway of the Gaspé all the way into Montreal. Judging by the crowds and their enthusiasm, it was quite clear the Blue wave was still growing. There were more people than the best tour organizers could have bussed in, and more applause than you would hear from the most professional claque.

Since the July debates, Mulroney had achieved the stature of a Prime Minister. He had also become a celebrity, someone the crowds simply came out to see. This was increasingly evident by the second day of the final Quebec swing. In the Eastern Township community of Plessisville, there were 1,000 people at a sweltering community centre to hear him preach his message of renewal and reconciliation. It was ten o'clock in the morning. It was also the home town of Raymond Garneau.

In Drummondville, some people had waited through a torrential late-summer downpour to see him arrive for a midday appearance at an old hotel. On the platform with him were former provincial Liberal and Union Nationale members of the legislature, as well as former leaders of the local "Yes" and "No" committees in the referendum. "John Turner came to Quebec and guess what?" Mulroney cried derisively. "He discovered three separatists." The audience roared its appreciative laughter, as it did again when he heaped his usual scorn on André Ouellet, whose picture Mulroney had noticed in the morning paper at a charity golf tournament in Montreal. After next Tuesday, Mulroney cried, he'll have lots of time to play golf, "he'll become a champion."

In St. Hyacinthe, Claude Wagner's former riding, there were

700 cheering people waiting for him in the parking lot of a shopping centre at four o'clock in the afternoon. "Six weeks ago," explained former Clark Quebec treasurer Pierre Roy, who had come down from Montreal to organize Andrée Champagne's campaign, "we figured we were down by 16,000 votes. Now our canvassing shows us neck and neck, with 30 per cent undecided. What do you think that means?"

It meant something was going on, something big. Just how big was evident in Montreal four hours later, when a crowd of some 1,500 people spilled out of the soggy turf under a tent that had been hastily thrown up as a summer storm raged over a park in suburban St. Laurent.

"Ah, let it rain. Every drop from heaven is another Conservative vote," Mulroney shouted, shamelessly laying on the blarney.

The meeting was for candidates from the West Island of Montreal, considered the last unbreachable stronghold of the Liberal Party. The predominantly English-speaking voters here had worshipped the ground Pierre Trudeau walked on, as indeed they had that very afternoon when he toured two shopping centres in his former riding of Mount Royal. English-speaking Quebecers would have stayed home in the Liberal Party for Jean Chrétien, whom they remembered for his fighting role in the referendum and admired for his strong geographic sense of the country. It was to Chrétien's strong leadership campaign that Mulroney's Quebec organizer Bernard Roy attributed the strong resurgence of the Liberals with their traditional bloc of English-speaking Quebec voters at the onset of the campaign. But in the July debates, it sunk in that Turner wasn't Trudeau, that he wasn't even Chrétien, while Mulroney was bidding to succeed the former Prime Minister as a favourite son. Thus, he was able to force the issue of change. In the August heat, the 30,000-vote Liberal majorities in the West Island Montreal ridings were melting like ice cream cones.

Mulroney's friend Nick Auf der Maur, who had accepted an odds-against proposition to run in Notre Dame-de-Grace-Lachine East, couldn't believe the optimistic reports he was getting from his canvassers. "They're coming in and in some polls it's 3-1 in our favour, so we send them out to do it again and it comes back the same," he said as he leaned down from the stage where the crowd was being warmed up for Mulroney's tumultuous arrival. His opponent, Warren Allmand, was a popular six-term incumbent who hadn't broken a sweat in winning the seat by 22,000 votes in 1980. "If they win this riding," Allmand had said of the surging Tory challenge a couple of weeks earlier, "they're going to win 200 seats." At the last weekend of the campaign, that possibility could not be excluded.

On August 31, Mulroney made one final pass over Ontario, flying to five cities in a single wild day of campaigning, from London in the southwestern end of the province where he hoped to pick up two seats from the Liberals, as far west as Kenora, with stops at Thunder Bay, North Bay, and Gatineau, Quebec, on the way back to Montreal. On September 1, it would be out by bus to Magog at the far end of the Eastern Townships Autoroute, then back to Monteal for an outdoor rally in the ethnic northeast end of the city, and on to Trois-Rivières before flying to Quebec. From this whirlwind of activity, you would never know that the Gallup and CTV polls on the final weekend of the campaign put him ahead by 50-28 and 51-26.

The next day, it was on to Manicouagan and the remote northern mining town of Fermont, and back down to Sept-Iles.

Finally, on September 3, it was home to Baie Comeau. Though he had not lived there since the summers of his college years, it remained his point of reference, and his risky decision to run there had been vindicated by the events of the campaign. Almost alone among his advisers, Jean Bazin had implored him to run in Manicouagan. "When in doubt, go home," Bazin had said. It turned out to be good advice, while poor John Turner appeared doomed in his effort to put down riding roots in the Vancouver riding of Quadra.

As Mulroney put his feet up in the Manoir guest house, his future was closing in on him. There were four points he had to consider in forming a government: cabinet, his own office, the deputy-minister rank of the civil service, and the Tory caucus. The prospective size of the Conservative deputation, ranged around both sides of the Speaker, was a cause for some concern. There seemed to be the possibilities of winning too big and of having too many people to keep happy.

"What are you going to do with 200 members?" Mulroney was asked two weekends before the election as he rested between appearances in Vancouver.

"We will," he said, "worry about that when we get there." He thought they might do even "a bit better" than that, he said on the eve of the election, but he would still settle for "one more" seat "than the other guy."

As he had at the 1983 leadership convention, Mulroney drew his closest friends around him as the moment of victory approached. From his St. F.X. crowd, there were Pembroke lawyer

Terry McCann and aides Pat MacAdam and Fred Doucet. And there was Sam Wakim, sitting beside him as Air Canada's charter 31 dropped out of the clouds and into Baie Comeau on the day before the election. In just a few hours, Mulroney told a cheering crowd of 500 townspeople, the electrician's son would be elected Prime Minister.

From the Laval gang, there were Jean Bazin and Michel Cogger, as well as Lucien Bouchard and his wife, Jocelyne. Bazin would be Mulroney's designated spokesman on television after leaving the guest house on election night. Bouchard had worked on the French part of his victory speech, as Charley McMillan had worked on the English draft. "That's a good text, Lucien," Mulroney said as he came into the guest house living room fifteen minutes before the polls closed in the East. Already, the trend was emerging in the thirty-two ridings of Atlantic Canada, and Mulroney's aides were working the phones to get the numbers. "It's 25-7," Bill Pristanski called across the room to his boss.

"Well," Mulroney said as he sat at the end of a sofa, "that's just about the proportion we want."

The sweep was on everywhere in the Maritimes, nine out of eleven in Nova Scotia, three out of four in Prince Edward Island, eight and eventually nine out of ten in New Brunswick, as even the Acadians of northern New Brunswick deserted the Liberal Party. "Well, Bones, there's the history," said Wakim, the Saint John native who spoke no French but understood the significance of the crossover and how much it meant to his former roommate.

"So that means we must have won three seats up north in New Brunswick," Mulroney said. "Well, that's great. A lot of work went into that." He remembered his forays into Acadia, and how he had been received for his positions on minority rights. On the boony tour during the Liberal leadership campaign he had drawn over 1,000 people in Shediac. "Somebody said to me, well why would you want to spend a Saturday night in Shediac?" he said, "There's the answer."

In his former riding in Nova Scotia, Elmer MacKay resumed his old seat with a majority that surpassed Mulroney's 11,000-vote margin of victory in the 1983 by-election. "I see," Mulroney said, "that the good people of Central Nova sustained my departure. If Elmer gets more than an 11,000-vote majority he's in deep trouble with the leader."

When Pristanski later passed on the message, MacKay had the presence of mind to reply that there had been a smaller turnout in the by-election, that in percentage terms Mulroney's win there had been bigger.

"Doctor McMillan," Mulroney called across the room to his top policy aide. "What's the score in P.E.I.? I went down there three times at *your* request." McMillan's twin brother Tom would win in Hillsborough, and they would get a third Island seat, but not the fourth. "I told you," McMillan replied, "that even a causeway wouldn't have done it."

By the time the television networks came on the air in the East at eight o'clock they were ready to make the call. There were three television sets going in the room, but it was the one in the corner that caught the attention of Mulroney and the people around him. On the CBC, Peter Mansbridge was announcing a majority Conservative government, as he had some minutes earlier for viewers in Atlantic Canada. But in the living room of the guest house, this was the moment of victory.

"I have alway said that the CBC was an intelligent network," Mulroney said with a chuckle.

The first person to shake his hand was his long-time Quebec organizer Rodrigue Pageau, now desperately ill with cancer but terribly brave and so determined to be there that Roger Nantel flew him in on a small plane equipped with a bed.

It was the moment he had been hanging on for. Ravaged and wasted as he was, he was still able to stand on his feet and shake Mulroney's hand. The people in the room knew that Mulroney would not have been elected Prime Minister had he not won the Battle of Quebec at the convention, and he would not have won that without Pageau's fighting in the trenches. "Absolutely right," Mulroney said later. As he took a congratulatory call from Ronald Reagan the next morning, Pageau was with him. "If I got that telephone call," Mulroney told him, "it was because of you."

All night long, the Tory tide rolled in every region of the land, to fifty-eight seats in Quebec. Goodnight, John Diefenbaker. When the final score was in, Mulroney had won 211 seats to Turner's 40, with the NDP at 30 and one independent. In his concession speech, Turner finally found his voice. He had won a courageous personal victory in Quadra. Perhaps he had finally found a home. In another sense, he was finally free of Pierre Trudeau, free to start over again, as his idol Lester Pearson had done. There wasn't much left of the Liberal Party, but it was his to lead, and his to rebuild.

It was after one o'clock in the morning by the time Mulroney reached the podium in the Baie Comeau recreation centre, and such was the applause that it was another seven minutes before he could speak. "Dear friends," he began over and over again, only to be engulfed in another ovation. Finally, he stepped away from the microphone, overcome by the moment, and not sure he could steady his voice. "You have to understand the symbolism of it for them," he said later.

"I will never forget the extraordinary welcome home you gave me," he finally began in French, "at a time when everything depended on your support." He had done it in Manicouagan, defeating André Maltais by 21,000 votes. "So sweeping is the expression of confidence," he told the country a few minutes later, "that I am genuinely torn between two feelings. Firstly, a deep sense of gratitude to the Canadian electorate who have given us an historic opportunity to serve. And secondly, the recognition of the enormous responsibility with which we have been entrusted."

He went on to outline a bit of the agenda that McMillan had talked about earlier in the day. "We must infuse our federalism with a spirit of fraternity and creativity which gave it birth," he said, reading Bouchard's words into history.

In a sense, he was talking about a kind of country where Terry McCann, a lawyer from Pembroke, could meet Lucien Bouchard, a lawyer from Chicoutimi. "I'm just a country lawyer," Bouchard had said earlier in the evening, as they shook hands in the living room of the guest house, and the room erupted in laughter.

Peter and Eva Pocklington, who had just flown in, were about the last to arrive. Mulroney had been reserved and restrained throughout. He had seldom looked so relaxed as he did lounging around in a pair of slacks and a green pullover.

For all the times when he struck people as grasping, and a bit of a braggart, he was always serene when he finally achieved something he had set his sights on.

"How do you feel?" he was asked as the Tory wave swept through the East.

"I feel fine," he said in a low voice. He also felt genuinely humbled.

He was at the end of one road, and the beginning of another. But something he had said before the 1983 leadership campaign came back now. "One thing I've learned," he said then, "and that's how to keep my eye on the ball. It's going to take me all the way to 24 Sussex Drive."

So he had. And so it did. The electrician's son had long sought, and finally won, the highest office in the land. He was home, at last.

ACKNOWLEDGEMENTS

Most of the more than 100 persons interviewed for this book had no trouble remembering when, where, and under what circumstances they first met Brian Mulroney. In my own case, it was in the Carrefour bar of Montreal's Place Ville Marie complex in the early months of 1972. I was sitting with a colleague, seriously contemplating the possibilities of a Friday afternoon drink, when a man who was introduced as Brian Mulroney sat down at our table. It was explained that he was an organizer for the Conservative Party in Quebec, a lonely and curious calling in those days. Never mind, he insisted, the Tories would be coming on in the election that year, and he had the numbers to prove it. "What if I told you," he said, "that we had a poll that showed Claude Wagner was more popular in Quebec than Pierre Trudeau?" It later turned out that the Tory pollster had neglected to ask respondents if they would vote for Wagner as a Conservative in preference to the Liberal leader.

The impression of Mulroney then was that he was a bit of an operator, but a gregarious personality and a congenial companion. It was impossible to dislike him, even when you realized he was trying to sell you a line. In the small village of the Montreal political milieu, he became someone one met along the way. We met quite often after that.

This is in no sense an authorized biography of Brian Mulroney, though it is very much a first biography. Nor is it meant to serve as a critical biography, since there is no record of achievement or disappointment in office. It will take at least one term of Mulroney as Prime Minister, if not two, before that kind of appraisal can be written. Still, it is not too early to place the man in the context of places and events that have shaped his life and brought him from Champlain Street in Baie Comeau to 24 Sussex Drive in Ottawa.

318

Mulroney was a willing and co-operative subject. Though he must have been a bit twitchy and apprehensive at times, he never once asked why he was being asked a question. He made himself available for six formal taped interviews between December, 1983, and July, 1984. One interview was conducted in his study at Stornoway, the Opposition Leader's residence, one in a motel room in Niagara Falls, and the remainder in his Centre Block office. In addition to these ninety-minute sessions, there were two other long conversations that yielded material for this book, the first aboard a three-hour flight from Canso, Nova Scotia, to Montreal in December of 1983, and the second in his hotel suite in Hamilton in July of 1984, two days after the debates that had such an impact on the campaign. In the nearly year-long period of researching and writing the manuscript, Mulroney answered dozens more questions on the phone.

In short, he was available himself and granted access to his aides and to some confidential material from the 1983 leadership campaign. Before publication, Mulroney had not seen a word of the manuscript, nor had he asked to.

I'm indebted to certain people, and they know who they are, who agreed to read part of the manuscript for accuracy, always on the understanding they wouldn't discuss it with Mulroney. I must acknowledge the encouragement of one close friend, Robert McKenzie, the distinguished Quebec correspondent of *The Toronto Star*.

There are many others to be thanked. In Toronto, my friend and attorney, Sam Wakim, found a publisher for this project and never wavered in his support for it. At McClelland and Stewart, I have to thank the chairman, Jack McClelland, and the president, Linda McKnight, as well as Dick Tallman, who edited the manuscript. Also thanks to Valerie Thompson and to Jan Walter.

In Ottawa, I'm indebted to Charley McMillan, Mulroney's senior policy adviser, and Fred Doucet, who was also the source of instant and generous access at St. Francis Xavier University in Nova Scotia, where his former secretary, Mina Long, was of enormous assistance, loading me up with yearbooks and photocopies of every Mulroney clipping from the student newspaper, the *Xaverian Weekly*, during his four-year stay there.

In Mulroney's office, I have to thank press secretary Bill Fox for putting up with my many demands for information and access. I'm equally grateful to Mulroney's special assistant, Pat MacAdam, executive assistant, Bill Pristanski, and executive secretary, Ginette Pilotte, for getting me in the door and making sure it stayed shut long enough to get the job done.

In Montreal, Bernard Roy, Jean Bazin, and Michel Cogger were particularly helpful, as was Mulroney's former law partner, Tommy Montgomery, who happened to dig up the only copy of Mulroney's undergraduate thesis. I must also thank Mulroney's mother, Irene, for lending some of the family photos that appear in this book, as well as his brother Gary and sister Olive for their openness and generosity. I am equally indebted to Mulroney's uncle, Jimmy O'Shea, of Shannon, Quebec, who rooted around in the church and family records for weeks until he traced the Mulroney family roots all the way back to County Cavan in Ireland. Special thanks to Lucien Bouchard of Chicoutimi, Quebec, for his unique insights into his friend of all the years since Laval law school.

I must also thank my colleagues at the *Montreal Gazette*, first and foremost, the incomparable Milly Thompson, chief switchboard operator to whom no one is "out" or "in a meeting." Then Agnes McFarlane, the head of the paper's marvellous library, whose staff also answered dozens of queries without ever asking why. I'm grateful as always to Joan Fraser, editorial page editor, Mark Harrison, editor, and Clark Davey, publisher, for their support and encouragement. In this context, I also wish to thank four editors who helped me along at earlier stops along the way: Denis Harvey, Dave Billington, George Brimmell, and Lindsay Crysler.

At Perspectra Inc. in Montreal, I'm most grateful to Robert Roll, Johanne Semintin, Catherine Deziel, and Kim Mullin for giving my work priority on their word-processing system.

Finally, as always, I must thank the former Andrée Dontigny, whose forbearance and encouragement have contributed more to this book than even she will ever know. As she knows, one doesn't do this for fun, or for profit. But if pressed to give a reason, I would have to say that Mulroney is a man from my time and my place, and as Mordecai Richler once said in another context, I've elected myself to try and get it right.

Any errors, of fact or fancy, are entirely my own.

L. Ian MacDonald
Montreal
September, 1984

INDEX

328

329

331

Printed in Canada

g